MIDI for the Professional

by Paul D. Lehrman and Tim Tully
Foreword by Robert Moog

Amsco Publications
New York • London • Sydney

Cover photography by Comstock Inc.
Cover design and illustration by Dan Earley
Interior design and layout by Len Vogler

Copyright © 1993 by Amsco Publications,
A Division of Music Sales Corporation, New York

Order No. AM 91049
US International Standard Book Number: 0.8256.1374.4
UK International Standard Book Number: 0.7119.2327.2

Exclusive Distributors:
Music Sales Corporation
257 Park Avenue South, New York, NY 10010 USA
Music Sales Limited
8/9 Frith Street, London W1V 5TZ England
Music Sales Pty. Limited
120 Rothschild Street, Rosebery, Sydney, NSW 2018, Australia

Printed in the United States of America by
Vicks Lithograph and Printing Corporation

Contents

Acknowledgements

The authors wish to thank the following individuals for their invaluable contributions towards the creation of this book:

Craig Anderton for paving the way with *Midi for Musicians,* the first and still the best of the early books on MIDI.

Peter Pickow at Music Sales, for patience far beyond the call of sanity, not to mention duty.

All of the major forces, past and present, behind the development of the MIDI specification, including (forgive us for we are surely leaving many deserving people out) Evan Brooks, Shoji Fujiwara, Stanley Junglieb, Gerry Lester, Charlie Richmond, Jeff Rona, and Dave Smith.

Chris Meyer, who has done the most of any one human being to advance the development of MIDI in the last half-decade, and who served as fact-checker for most of the technical information in this book.

Denis LaBrecque and Scott Peer at Passport, Paul DeBenedictis at Opcode Systems, Suz Howells and Brent Hurtig at Digidesign, Daniel Rose at Mark of the Unicorn, Bill Black at Steinberg Jones, and all the other MIDI manufacturers for their generous supply of time and information.

Michael Starobin, David Roach, David Silver, Emile Tobenfeld, Dave Miller, and Nigel Redmon, for their contributions and guidance.

Paul Burdick, of the New England Conservatory of Music, who is largely responsible for Chapter 11.

Paul additionally wishes to thank:

Clif Garboden, Richard Elen, Mel Lambert, Hector La Torre, Ian Gilby, Paul Ireson, Dominic Milano, Louise Kohl, Jon Zilber, Craig Anderton, and all of the other editors (including Tim) who over the years helped me learn the craft of writing and explaining technology in words and pictures.

AKG Digital, Roland, Passport Designs, Tascam, and all of the other companies who have hired me to write manuals and instructional books which ended up teaching me as much as they did their intended audience.

Ellen Lapham and the visionary crew at Syntauri Corporation who were so important when all this desktop-computer-music stuff began, and regrettably couldn't stick around long enough to see their work blossom so magnificently.

My colleagues, past and present, on the Executive Board of the MIDI Manufacturers Association, who constantly strive to maintain order in the face of chaos.

My music teachers, especially Vladimir Ussachevsky, Charles Dodge, Mario Davidovsky, Ralph Wilkinson, Anthony Taglino, William Polisi, and Donald MacCourt.

My friends and electronic-musical inspirations Laurie Spiegel, Wendy Carlos, Mark Isham, David Torn, and Tod Machover.

My wife, Sharon Kennedy, the inspiration behind my first (and the world's first) all-MIDI album, *The Celtic Macintosh,* and so much more.

And finally, I'd like to dedicate my contribution to this book to the students in the Sound Recording Technology program at the University of Massachusetts at Lowell, who continue to inspire me with their enthusiasm, inquisitiveness, inventiveness, and talent. Very special thanks are extended to those who miraculously keep the program running at the highest standard I can imagine, Dr. William Moylan and Bill Carman.

Tim wishes to thank the following people, without whom the cookie would have crumbled:

My Mom, who gave me music in the first place.

My wife, Kathy Marty, who provided the reasons for me to work this hard, and found the patience to put up with me doing it.

Clyde Stubblefield, the great drummer, who showed me so much about music in such a very short time.

Joe Viola of the Berklee School of Music, for the magic mouthpiece.

Craig Anderton, before, during, and after the Extreme Moments.

Phil Cochlin, George Petersen, Hector LaTorre, Jeff Rona, Bob Lindstrom, Lucky Westfall, Greg Alper, and many others who kept it going with a faithful supply of technical, musical, and editorial skinny.

My friend Paul, for the whole rest of the enchilada.

Foreword

When I began designing synthesis equipment some thirty years ago, musicians were just getting used to the notion that they could use electronics to shape sounds. The early modular analog synthesizers enabled creative and adventurous musicians to push the limits of musical sound far beyond the boundaries of traditional acoustic instruments, and to produce music that contributed to the explosion of musical creativity of the sixties.

But being creative with musical electronics back then was hard work! Most instruments had no provision for user-defined presets. You would spend hours getting the sound you wanted, but you had no way of saving it. You had to do all your recording with that sound right then and there, because once you changed your setup to get a different sound, you would probably never get back to that first sound. And in addition, once you recorded a track on multi-track tape, it was difficult if not impossible to edit it.

Relief came in small but much-appreciated steps. The late seventies saw the introduction of the Sequential Prophet 5, an instrument that sounded like many other analog axes of the time but enabled the player to store and edit complex presets in digital memory. Similar instruments were soon designed by other synth builders. Some, like Oberheim, even provided the ability to interconnect two or three of their instruments to form an integrated system. And around that same time a couple of computer makers designed peripherals that were able to store and play back digital recordings of short musical sounds, thereby introducing the technologies of digital sampling and sequencing.

By the early eighties, engineers and technically hip musicians knew it was feasible for instruments to be connected into a digital network so they could work together as a system. But how to standardize these connections so that different manufacturers' instruments could "talk" together? It had not been possible to get instrument manufacturers to agree on any standards up until then. Indeed, manufacturers, especially domestic manufacturers, prided themselves on the uniqueness of their designs, and bragged in their advertisements about how *different* their instruments were from those of their competitors. Get manufacturers to *agree* to the same communications protocol? For most of us, that was unthinkable!

But not for Dave Smith and Chet Wood of Sequential Circuits. In 1981 they proposed a *Universal Synthesizer Interface*. Then, after many conferences with other synth builders, they changed the name of their proposed interface to MIDI (Musical Instrument Digital Interface) and published a short document entitled "The Complete SCI MIDI." This document provided the basic specifications for MIDI, and has served as the foundation for all of MIDI's developments since then.

The first time that two MIDI-equipped instruments built by different companies were hooked up and played together was at the January 1983 National Association of Music Merchants (NAMM) show. A few months after that NAMM show I found myself writing a feature-length article on MIDI for *Keyboard* magazine. After describing MIDI's basic features, I reported that Sequential, Roland, and Yamaha were planning MIDI equipped-instruments for release later that year, but many other instrument manufacturers had adopted a wait-and-see position. I ended the article with some blue-sky predictions: that the MIDI spec would be expanded and refined, that keyboard stacks would give way to rack-mounted sound modules which would be played from a touch-sensitive keyboard controller, and that the studio of the future would include a personal computer with hard disk storage and interactive graphic display.

Thinking back to those days—before musicians embraced the computer and MIDI became a universally accepted means of interfacing electronic music gear—I'm inclined to give myself a pat on the back for seeing some of the coming importance of MIDI. For sure, I was a lot more upbeat about the future of MIDI than a lot of then-active synth builders. But no way did I foresee all the directions in which MIDI would grow, or the amazing variety of music software that it would spawn! And it *still* blows my mind that hundreds of manufacturers around the world conform (or almost conform) *voluntarily* to the MIDI specification.

Today, so much has been built on the foundation of Dave Smith's original MIDI specifications that no matter where in the electronic entertainment media you choose to put your professional playpen, MIDI will be a significant factor in your life. For sure, you will do well to learn MIDI's capabilities, its limitations, and tricks for getting the most out of your MIDI system.

MIDI for the Professional guides you around all the bases, from live performance, studio composition, and sound editing, to synchronization, post production, and multimedia. The authors are two experienced, skilled MIDI musicians and teachers. Their writing is clear and easy to understand. The information that they supply is accurate, complete, and easy to find. This book is exactly what a professional's text should be: an omnipresent partner, always ready to help you do your best work and get the most out of your resources.

Robert Moog

Introduction

MIDI—the Musical Instrument Digital Interface—has changed the way we produce music more than any other single technology since magnetic tape. It has revolutionized the way people work in every aspect of music and sound production from the bedroom studio to the multimillion-dollar production suite.

Children learn elementary keyboard skills with MIDI. It shows up in computer games—and it's used to produce music and sound effects for movies, TV, and music videos. Composers use MIDI to expand their musical vocabulary and to get closer to their music than they ever could using staff paper. Multimedia artists use MIDI to integrate the visual and aural aspects of their performances and installations. Teachers improve the quality of music education with MIDI, and use it to show students, firsthand, the potential of music technology.

The year 1993 marks the tenth anniversary of the creation of MIDI. In ten years, many books have been written on the subject. Most of these provide an introduction to basic MIDI setups, synthesis, audio, and electronics. While beginners and amateurs can certainly benefit from this book, it's aimed in a different direction.

MIDI for the Professional is intended to serve the needs of professional musicians, engineers, producers, and other artists and technicians already active in their fields. Professionals responsible for getting the most out of their equipment need a resource that will dig all the way to the bottom of a topic—or throw the doors to a new topic wide open. This book is designed to do both. *MIDI for the Professional* will not tell you how to connect your synth to your computer, but it will explain (down to the byte) what they say to one another and how to control them. This book does not review sequencers, but it will tell you what you can expect a good sequencer to do—and how a sequencer differs from a multimedia authoring application.

MIDI for the Professional is also designed for students who are serious about MIDI technology. In fact, one of the principal motivations for writing this book was to create a text for the courses in MIDI that Paul Lehrman teaches at the University of Massachusetts at Lowell. After five years of teaching from various magazine articles and his own scribbled notes, he figured it's time his students received a real textbook.

Here are a few of the types of professionals who will benefit from this book:

- Composers and arrangers who want to expand their horizons beyond traditional techniques and instruments. (Using MIDI instruments and computers makes it easier to try out ideas in composition and orchestration—and to generate sheet music quickly.)

- Composers of video and film soundtracks who want to throw away their click books and digital metronomes and compose in an immediate, interactive environment of synchronized sound and picture.

- Post-production professionals who want to use the new tools and techniques MIDI offers for creating, editing, and placing music, sound effects, and dialog in video and film.

- Audio engineers and producers who want to automate and simplify sound control, lighting, and other production elements during live performances.

- Educators who teach composition, arranging, theory, ear-training, acoustics, principles of synthesis, experimental music, programming, or software and hardware interface design.

Experimental musicians and other artists who want to use technology to advance their own art.

Programmers and software designers who want to create new tools for MIDI users.

Other people in diverse fields can benefit from this book. MIDI has become such a useful and universally accepted language that its applications continue to grow by leaps and bounds. We hope that, by explaining the language and technology of MIDI in a thorough yet understandable way, *MIDI for the Professional* can stimulate even more growth—and can help to inspire the next generation of MIDI users and designers.

Chapter 1
An Overview of MIDI

MIDI is a *specification* for a communications protocol principally used to control electronic musical instruments. It consists of two parts.

- a set of commands, or the MIDI "language," and

- the details for the electrical way those commands are transmitted and received

The MIDI specification is presented in a document entitled *MIDI 1.0 Detailed Specification* (affectionately known as "the spec") which is published and distributed by the International MIDI Association.

MIDI's original, and still primary, use is in music performance and composition. In recent years it has moved into related areas, such as audio editing and production, stage lighting, and other aspects of live performance. Its command set describes a language that is designed specifically for conveying information about musical performances. It is not "music," in that a set of MIDI commands is not the same as a recording of, say, a tune played on a French horn. However, MIDI commands can describe the horn player's performance in such a way that a synthesizer receiving them can reconstruct the performance with great accuracy.

Although MIDI is often referred to as a "standard," that term can be misleading because it implies a certain legal standing. Unlike standards set by the American National Standards Institute (ANSI), MIDI has no basis in law at all. In fact, compliance with the specification on the part of a manufacturer is strictly voluntary. Fortunately, most manufacturers making MIDI-compatible equipment follow the specification closely, so that there is a very high degree of compatibility among all MIDI-capable devices.

A Brief History of Electronic Music

Electronic music has been around since the 1940s—and some would argue that it's even older than that. The pioneers of electronic music built their studios with discrete components—like oscillators, filters, mixers, and frequency shifters—that were originally designed for use in decidedly non-musical contexts, such as radio testing benches, audiology labs, and telephone networks. From these tools (which made up the "classical" electronic-music studio), composers could create a wide variety of interesting and musical sounds. A few inventors in those early days designed electronic instruments that had their own distinct sounds, like the Theremin and the Ondes Martenot. Others created imitative instruments, such as the Hammond organ and the Cordovox accordion, which mimicked the feel and sound of conventional instruments.

By the 1960s, the first dedicated electronic-music systems, known as *synthesizers,* appeared. Early synthesizers consisted of modules that took over the functions of the discrete components of the classical studio. These synthesizers also made use of new types of modules specially designed for music manipulation. These included *envelope generators,* which change a sound's *amplitude* (volume) over time; *envelope followers,* which impose the amplitude envelope of one sound onto another; *modulators,* which combine two or more sounds in ways that create more complex sounds; and *sequencers,* in which discrete events or parameter values can be stored and played back over time, with the tempo determined by a timer, or *clock,* which itself was often a module.

Because the modules in a synthesizer were designed to work together, interfacing them in unusual and creative ways was relatively easy. For example, an envelope generator could be used to open and close a filter so that a sound's tone or timbre (as well as, or instead of, its volume) could evolve over time. A sequencer could be used not only to play a series of pitches, but to change—in discrete steps—the volume or tonal characteristics of a sound over time.

Patch Cords and Voltage Control

Early synthesizer modules were connected with short cables known as *patch cords*. The connection of many cables to create a particular sound or sequence of sounds became known as a *patch*. This term survives today to describe a particular synthesizer sound or *voice*. The patch cable carried voltages. The modules communicated with each other using *voltage control,* by which a module receiving a varying voltage behaved as if one of its knobs was being turned.

Here's an example: A conventional oscillator has a knob for setting its output frequency. Instead of a knob, a voltage-controlled oscillator has a control input that accepts varying voltages and changes the output frequency based on that voltage. In this way, a 1-volt signal may produce a tone at 100Hz, a 2-volt signal produces a 200Hz tone, a 3-volt signal a 400Hz tone, and so on. With each 1-volt increase in the control voltage, the pitch of the oscillator rises by one octave; that is, its frequency doubles. This is known as *1-volt-per-octave* voltage control. Voltage control can also be applied to a filter, in which it can vary the cutoff frequency or bandwidth; to a mixer, in which it can change the level of one or more inputs; or to a sequencer's clock, in which it can control the tempo.

Voltage control became very popular among synthesizer manufacturers, but it had its problems. Since there was no standardization of voltage-control schemes, synthesizers from different manufacturers were often incompatible. Some used one volt per octave, while others used different ratios or curves. This meant that a control change that raised the pitch an octave on one synthesizer might only raise the pitch a minor third on another. Also, because the signals were analog in nature, absolute accuracy was hard to achieve. Two sounds in a patch might be in tune one moment and out of tune a few minutes later; for as the components heated up, the voltages drifted.

A different type of signal was necessary for synchronizing audio events produced by different modules. Instead of voltages, which change smoothly, what was needed was a more immediate, binary, on/off signal. These signals, generally pulses of a certain length, were known as *triggers*. A sequencer could fire off triggers to initiate sounds as easily as it sent voltages that controlled timbres. Unfortunately, the variations in triggering schemes among different synthesizer manufacturers were even greater than those in voltage control.

Digital Communications

In the late 1970s, synthesizers began using *digital electronics*, which largely solved the problems of repeatability and drifting. Digital synthesizers use mathematical algorithms to produce digital "models" of *waveforms* and to convert them into audio signals using a digital-to-analog converter, or *DAC.* "Modules" were now all software—and mixing and routing circuitry could also be completely internal. "Patches", now also known as *programs,* became sets of digital parameters describing module settings and signal routings. Programs could be stored in a synthesizer's internal digital memory—and recalling one became a simple matter of pushing a button.

The next challenge was to figure out a way to use digital electronics to connect synthesizers to each other. As synthesizer-based rock bands became more popular, performers found themselves trucking around huge arsenals of electronic keyboards. The common plea was for a system that would let them control and operate all these instruments from a single, common keyboard.

Roland, Oberheim, Sequential Circuits, and Fender Rhodes were among the manufacturers who developed digital control schemes that allowed keyboard synthesizers to be slaved to each other, and external sequencers to be integrated with them. For example, a musician using a Roland synthesizer would play a piece of music on the keyboard—and data representing all the keystrokes would be sent out of the synthesizer on a special digital control cable, connected to a Roland sequencer in its own box. The sequencer recorded the keystroke data in real time, and could play it back later with great accuracy. The sequencer could be connected—again with a digital cable—either to the instrument from which the performance originated, or to another Roland synthesizer capable of reading the digital information.

Although some of these digital control schemes were highly evolved, the problem of incompatibility remained. Each manufacturer had its own ideas for implementing digital control, so instruments from different manufacturers still couldn't communicate with each other. Sequential Circuits, a California synthesizer maker (since taken over by Yamaha and Korg), became the first company to propose a common digital interface for synthesizers from different manufacturers. They introduced the Universal Synthesizer Interface (USI) in October, 1981, in a technical paper delivered at a convention of the Audio Engineering Society (AES). Meetings followed over the next year among representatives of several American and Japanese electronic instrument makers. The first MIDI synthesizer, Sequential's Prophet 600, shipped in December, 1982. The first two MIDI synthesizers from different companies were publicly hooked together a month later (a Prophet 600 and a Roland Jupiter 6) to an astonished crowd at a meeting of the National Association of Music Merchandisers (NAMM).

MIDI synthesizers immediately hit the market from a number of manufacturers, and the official *MIDI 1.0 Detailed Specification* was published in October of 1983. Some manufacturers held onto their own control schemes for a little while, thinking theirs was still a better way to do things—but it quickly became obvious that MIDI was going to become the undisputed industry standard. Soon, just about every serious electronic instrument under development included MIDI capability.

The Goals of MIDI

MIDI is based on two major principles: universality and expandability. Every manufacturer of MIDI equipment that uses the term "MIDI" anywhere on the case or in the documentation is expected to implement the specification correctly. This means that the unit can accept and correctly act upon data generated from any other MIDI device—and that any MIDI data it generates must be understood by any other MIDI device. It also means that every MIDI command has the same meaning to the receiver as it does to the transmitter (although the interpretation may vary, as discussed later).

A MIDI device must not only know what to do when it receives a MIDI command, it must also know what not to do. The MIDI specification is a very comprehensive set of commands—and no device on the market can respond to every one of them. That's why it's important that a MIDI device know enough to ignore the commands it doesn't understand rather than trying to interpret them. This feature is a key aspect of MIDI's universality.

The MIDI specification was deliberately designed with "holes" in it for commands that are not yet defined. This was done so that as new uses for MIDI are developed, the command set can be expanded to accommodate them. For example, MIDI *Time Code Quarter Frame* messages were not in the original specification. MIDI *Time Code* was added in 1987, and the command it uses was "Undefined" in the original spec. Since devices built before 1987 were designed to ignore commands that were undefined at the time, MIDI Time Code messages should not pose any problems.

Other new functions are possible using new combinations of commands. The MIDI *Sample Dump Standard*, added in 1986, uses a previously unused form of System Exclusive messages known as *Universal System Exclusive*. Devices, new or old, that don't understand these messages will ignore them. Other MIDI commands have been redefined or clarified through periodic published supplements and revisions of the MIDI specification. However, these commands remain basically unchanged—and their compatibility with existing MIDI devices is never compromised.

Today, the MIDI Specification is still referred to as "1.0," even though it has expanded a lot. That is because the original command set is still contained in the specification. There will almost certainly never be a "MIDI 2.0," because that would imply changes that would make existing MIDI devices obsolete. Every MIDI device ever made will always be compatible with every other MIDI device ever made—even though some devices will certainly do a lot more than others.

Compared to some other data-exchange protocols, such as PostScript, the MIDI specification is relatively simple. PostScript is a page-description language used by computers and printers in desktop and professional publishing systems. It is a highly complex language that requires that the controlling computer tell the printer everything about the page it is going to print: the description of every letter in every font; every bit, line, and curve in a graphic; the text itself; and the position of all of these elements. The comprehensive nature of PostScript is one of the reasons that laser printers (and other high-quality printers) take a long time to output a complex page. MIDI, on the other hand, takes advantage of a principle called "distributed intelligence." Instead of a central controller doing all the work, and the peripherals being merely dumb producers of sound, the peripherals themselves have computer processors and memory. MIDI assumes that the receiving device can take care of defining and producing a sound when it receives a simple command. This means that the structure of the language can be kept small and simple.

Another goal of the designers of MIDI was to keep costs down. This was done in the interest of universality, so that as many manufacturers as possible would adopt the protocol. When it was first introduced, it was estimated that adding MIDI to a digital synthesizer would cost between $5 and $10 at the manufacturing level. It was felt that anything more than that would give manufacturers an excuse to balk at incorporating it into their products. Certain trade-offs had to be made to keep down the cost of MIDI—and many people thought that these would severely limit its capabilities. As it turns out, these critics were not entirely wrong. There are a number of issues involving the speed and data capacity of MIDI, which are limited by the specification itself, that are now being confronted by those who are dealing with the future of the spec.

How MIDI Works

MIDI is a *serial* data protocol, which means that it sends one bit at a time over a piece of wire. (The other major type of protocol, *parallel,* can be much faster, but is also much more expensive to implement on a hardware level.) A *bit* is a single binary digit—on or off, 0 or 1. These bits are grouped into *bytes* of eight or ten bits (depending on how you count them), and bytes are combined into *commands,* or *messages.* A MIDI command may consist of one or more bytes. What the MIDI specification does, in a nutshell, is to delineate how the commands are structured and deciphered—and to stipulate the electrical characteristics of the circuitry that creates and interprets the data.

Bits and Bytes

The MIDI signal is a pulse, like a square wave, transmitted 31,250 times per second on a 5-volt line. The MIDI spec allows a ±1% tolerance in the speed; anything slower or faster than that will not work. This speed was chosen because 31,250 is a power-of-two factor (1/32) of 1,000,000. One million cycles-per-second (1MHz) or half of that rate (500kHz) were common clock

speeds for the integrated circuits (or *CPUs,* for *Central Processing Units*) at the heart of personal computers, synthesizers, and other digital devices. Dividing that clock rate by a power of two to generate a MIDI stream is a simple thing for software and circuit designers to accomplish. Today's personal computers operate at multiples of 1MHz, so that initial choice remains a good one. The MIDI signal is *asynchronous,* which means there is no universal clock pulse going all the time (as is the case with digital audio and SMPTE timecode). A transmitter can start sending MIDI data at any moment—and the receiver is expected to understand it as soon as it arrives.

Since MIDI is based on a digital signal, the pulse has two states: Logical 0 and Logical 1. (These are actually "backwards" electrically: a Logical 0 is the current-on pulse, and Logical 1 is current-off.) Since an idle MIDI line is a line with no current flowing, the first bit in any MIDI byte is always 0 (on), and is known as the *start bit.* Following the start bit are eight *data bits,* which can either be 1s or 0s. These are followed by the *stop bit,* which is always 1 (off). Therefore, a MIDI byte has ten bits, but only eight of them actually carry information. The fact that the last bit is off simply means that there has to be a minimum amount of off time between one MIDI byte and the next: a resting interval of 1/31,250 second. If that tiny rest is not there, and the next start bit (on) comes too early, the result is called a *framing error,* which causes data to be received incorrectly.

a MIDI *byte*

Since the MIDI bit rate is 31,250 per second, and there are ten bits in a byte, the MIDI byte rate is 3,125 per second. Most complete MIDI messages require two or three bytes, so the transmission rate of musical data is considered to be approximately 1,000 to 1,500 events per second. This is pretty fast, but not infinitely so. It means, for example, that there is no such thing as two absolutely simultaneous events in MIDI: Any two events must be at least 0.6 milliseconds apart. For the most part this is an acceptable situation, but under some circumstances it can be a limiting factor in the performance of a MIDI system.

Jacks and Cables

MIDI data created on a transmitting device is sent from a *MIDI Out* jack on the device through a MIDI cable, which is a shielded two-conductor twisted pair, the same as balanced-line audio cable. The MIDI Out jack is a 5-pin circular DIN *connector.* DIN connectors used to be common in European hi-fi equipment, which is where the name comes from: it's an acronym for *"Deutsche Industrie Norm,"* which means nothing more exotic than "German Industrial Standard." The MIDI signal is on Pin 5 of the connector, and a +5 bias voltage is on Pin 4. Pin 2 is connected to the cable shield, and Pins 1 and 3 are normally not connected.

The cable is then plugged into a *MIDI In* jack on the receiving device, which uses the same pin configurations except that Pin 2 of the jack, the shield, is not connected. This is done to avoid the possibility of ground loops, in which the different ground potentials of various connected devices cause hum. In a studio containing dozens of discrete components, ground loops from audio and power cables are always a danger—and the designers of MIDI didn't want their cables to contribute to the problem. In addition, the MIDI specification states that the actual shield connections on the MIDI jacks should never be connected to any chassis or electrical grounds.

To prevent other possible electrical problems, MIDI In jacks are not hard-wired to the device on which they're mounted. Instead, all MIDI In jacks contain an *optoisolator,* which is an electronic device consisting of a tiny light-emitting diode (*LED*) and a photocell. When the jack receives a bit, the LED lights up, and the photocell responds by sending current into the rest of the receiving device. In this way, there is never any direct electrical connection between the MIDI encoding/decoding circuitry of two different pieces of equipment.

The optoisolator is connected to a chip known as a UART (for "Universal Asynchronous Receiver/Transmitter"). The UART translates the MIDI pulses into a form that the receiving device can understand (or vice versa, in the case of a transmitter).

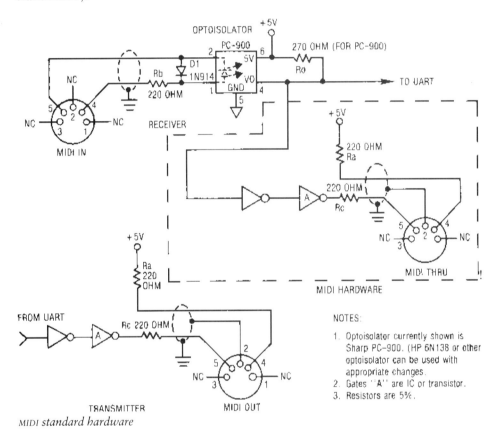

MIDI *standard hardware*

Thru Jacks, Boxes, and Mergers

Many MIDI devices have a third MIDI jack, labeled *MIDI Thru.* Thru jacks are needed because, unlike an audio signal, a MIDI signal cannot be sent to two different destinations merely by running it through a Y-connector. The optoisolator of the receiving device is designed to detect only signals above a certain voltage level. This enables it to screen out unwanted noise. Dividing the MIDI signal would cause its bias voltage to drop to 2.5—and this would cause the optoisolator not to fire when a bit came in. Thru jacks are provided to echo the MIDI data coming into the MIDI In jack of a device, so that it can be passed on to another device. The MIDI spec says that this echo must be instantaneous with no data changed or filtered. The output of the optoisolator at the In jack must be directly connected to the Thru jack. In addition, the Thru jack normally does not pass MIDI data created by the device on which it is mounted. So, to get the data from one MIDI transmitter to two different receivers, you must run a cable from the MIDI Out jack of the transmitter to the MIDI In jack of one receiver—and then run another cable from the Thru jack of that receiver to the MIDI In jack of the second receiver. In most cases, the order of cabling doesn't matter—that is, it makes no difference which one of the receivers gets the direct line from the transmitter and which receiver gets input from the Thru jack of the other. This common cabling technique is called *daisy-chaining*. The number of receivers that can be in a daisy-chain is theoretically unlimited—although there are some practical limitations.

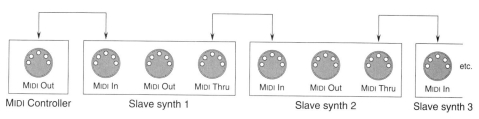

a daisy chain

Sometimes a MIDI transmitter, such as a sequencer, needs many MIDI Outs. This makes daisy-chaining impractical. In these situations, it makes sense to use a MIDI *thru box*, which contains a single MIDI In jack, and four, eight, or even more MIDI Thru jacks.

Some devices offer a *Thru/Merge* option, which is a variation on the Thru jack. With this option, MIDI data entering the MIDI In jack is merged with data being generated by the device and both are sent to the Thru jack—so that the Thru jack serves as both an Out and a Thru. (Often it serves as a conventional Thru jack unless a special software switch is set.)

Just as a MIDI output line cannot be electrically split, two MIDI input lines cannot be combined with a Y-connector. Besides creating voltage problems, this could cause two MIDI commands to interfere with one another. This problem can be solved by using a MIDI *merger box*, which has two or more MIDI Ins and a single MIDI Out, as well as internal electronics with sufficient intelligence to keep commands from colliding.

MIDI Commands

When someone plays a MIDI transmitter, or *controller*, it generates one or more MIDI commands, or *messages*. For example, playing a note on a keyboard sends a message corresponding to that action to the keyboard's MIDI Out jack. The same thing happens when you hit a drum pad, press a pedal, move a pitch bend lever, or blow into a wind controller. A MIDI message contains the information for a complete musical action. When you press a key on a keyboard, it generates a message that consists of three bytes. The first byte describes the kind of action: a key has been pressed. The second byte is the number of the key that's been pressed; that is, which note you've played. The third is the velocity with which the key has been pressed: the amount of time that has elapsed between the start and end of the key's travel. (A higher velocity number means the travel time was less, which generally means the key was struck harder.)

The first byte is known as a *command byte* or *status byte*. (In this example the command byte is a *Note On* message.) The second and third bytes are the *data bytes*. The MIDI specification dictates the exact meaning of all of the status bytes (except the few that remain undefined). It also prescribes the number of data bytes that must follow each status byte, their permissible values, and their meaning. Some MIDI commands have one data byte, some have two, and some have none. *System Exclusive* commands are followed by an undefined, and often very large, number of data bytes.

Binary, Decimal, and Hexadecimal Notation

MIDI commands can be written in *binary notation* (or base-2), with the digits 0 or 1 corresponding to each of the eight bits in each byte. However, most human beings do not read binary notation easily: Try calculating 10011101 minus 01110101. We are used to reading numbers in *decimal notation* (or base-10). Now the problem becomes 157 minus 117, which is much easier to solve. So, when we talk about MIDI bytes, we often use decimal notation. However, there is another form of notation that works even better, although it takes some getting used to. This is base-16, or *hexadecimal notation*, often called simply "hex." In hexadecimal notation, the column on the right is the ones column and the second-from-the-right column is the sixteens column (instead of being the tens column as it is in decimal). So, the number 14 in hex is equal to the number 20 in decimal: $(1 \times 16)+(4 \times 1)$. The number 38 in hex is 56 in decimal: $(3 \times 16)+(8 \times 1)$. In this book, numbers in hexadecimal notation will always be followed by the letter *H*. (In some technical documents, you may see hex numbers preceded by a dollar sign. Thus $40 equals 64 in decimal.)

Hexadecimal notation is a very convenient way to express MIDI commands. Every eight-bit MIDI value can be expressed as a two-digit hex number, which makes things very tidy. For example, the MIDI command 10010011 can be broken up into two parts: 1001 and 0011. Each of these parts may then be assigned a hex value: in this case, 9 and 3, respectively. So, the MIDI byte 10010011 is 147 in decimal or 93 in hex. The byte isn't really broken up when it is sent—this is just a convenience to let us look at and understand a MIDI data stream quickly.

Here is an example of how a MIDI byte looks in binary, decimal, and hexadecimal. Remember, since the start and stop bits are always the same, they are not considered part of the byte (and 0 is "on" while 1 is "off").

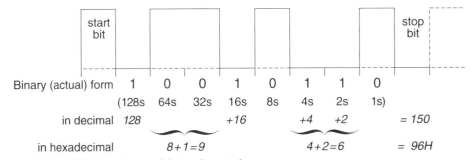

a MIDI byte with binary, hex, and decimal equivalents

One problem with hex notation is what to do with numbers above nine. The answer is to use letters.

Decimal Value		Hexadecimal
10	=	A
11	=	B
12	=	C
13	=	D
14	=	E
15	=	F

The number 47 in decimal is thus expressed in hex as 2F: $(2 \times 16) + (1 \times 15)$. The possible values of a MIDI byte are 0 through 2^8-1, which is 0 through 255 in decimal or 00 through FF in hex.

The Anatomy of a MIDI Command

Here's a typical MIDI command in binary notation: 10010000 01000101 01100101. In hex, this command is noted as: 90H 45H 65H. The first byte is the command or status byte. The MIDI specification states that any status byte that starts with a 9 (in hex) is defined as a *Note On*. The second byte is the note number. The lowest MIDI note (00H) is C, five octaves below Middle C. The number 45H in the example translates to 69 in decimal—and the sixty-ninth note above the bottom C is F above Middle C. The third byte, 65H, according to the specification, is the velocity. In decimal, this number is 101.

Status bytes always have a value of at least 80H (128 in decimal). Data bytes always have a value of between 00H and 7FH (0 and 127 in decimal). In binary terms, this means that the *most significant bit* or *high bit,* in a status byte is always 1, while the high bit in a data byte is always 0. This makes a receiver's initial task when it analyzes a received MIDI byte very simple: If it sees that the high bit is 1, it knows the byte is a status byte; if it sees that the high bit is 0, it knows the byte is a data byte and it knows to relate the data byte to the last-received status byte.

For a MIDI message to be interpreted properly, it must consist of the correct number of bytes, as dictated by the MIDI specification. The message may not be interrupted, except in a few very special cases. If an insufficient number of data bytes follow a status byte before the next status byte is received, the receiving device will assume the information is erroneous. In the best of circumstances, this kind of error is simply ignored, but in some devices it can cause strange behavior or even hang them up completely. For this reason, it is important to maintain a clean MIDI data stream. A special case occurs when the number of data bytes following a status byte is too high. This creates a condition called *running status,* which we'll discuss a little later.

MIDI Channels

The MIDI specification allows for <u>sixteen data channels</u>. This allows multiple MIDI devices to each receive distinct information with only a single MIDI line connecting them. Like the tuner in a television set, each receiving device can be set to recognize data on one specific MIDI channel, and to ignore data on all the other channels. Here's an example: A sequencer sends data to three synthesizers—one playing drum sounds, one playing bass sounds, and one playing piano sounds. The sequencer can put each musical part on its own MIDI channel and send all three through the same cable. Since each synthesizer is tuned to the appropriate channel, it plays only the notes intended for it, and ignores the rest.

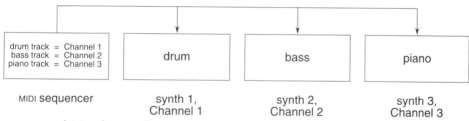

a sequencer driving three synths

The channel identity of a MIDI command is located in the second half of the status byte—the second four bits, which (so conveniently!) make up the second hex digit. That digit can be 0 to F in hex, or 0 to 15 in decimal, resulting in sixteen MIDI channels. By convention, we don't speak of "Channel 0," so MIDI channels are normally referred to as Channels 1 through 16. Therefore, the MIDI channel of a status byte whose second digit is *n* is actually *n*+1. The status byte for a Note On command on MIDI Channel 8 will be 97H. A Note On command on Channel 12 will begin with the Status byte 9BH.

The Command Set

The first half (four bits, or first hex digit) of the status byte determines the nature of the command. Because the high bit will always be a 1, the first hex digit of a status byte must be between 8 and F (representing 1000 to 1111 in binary).

Command Set Summary

Name	Hex Values	Decimal Values	Data Bytes
Note Off	80–8F	128–143	2 (note number, velocity)
Note On	90–9F	144–159	2 (note number, velocity)
Key Pressure	A0–AF	160–175	2 (note number, pressure)
Control Change	B0–BF	176–191	2 (controller number, value)
Program Change	C0–CF	192–207	1 (program number)
Channel Pressure	D0–DF	208–223	1 (pressure)
Pitch Bend	E0–EF	224–239	2 (LSB, MSB)
System Exclusive	F0	240	variable
System Common	F1–F6	241–246	0, 1, or 2
End of System Exclusive	F7	247	0
System Real Time	F8–FF	248–255	0

Notes and Programs

9nH is a Note On command. (Remember, n+1 indicates the channel number.) When this message is received, a note starts playing. As we saw earlier, this command has two data bytes: note number and velocity. Since the high bit of a MIDI data byte is always zero, this gives us a range of 00000000 to 01111111 in binary, or 00H to 7FH, or 0 to 127 in decimal, for both note numbers and velocities. Where note number is concerned, each increment in value is usually equal to a half step in pitch, so this numerical range gives us a musical range of 127 half-steps, or more than 10 1/2 octaves. That's a lot bigger than your average piano (which has eighty-eight keys, or 7 1/4 octaves), and in fact is greater than the range of human hearing, which, at its best (about 20Hz to 20kHz), is just under ten octaves. As far as velocities are concerned, this gives us 128 values from *pppp* to *ffff* (inclusive), which is plenty. (For reasons we'll explain a little later, a velocity value of zero gives this command a different meaning, so there are actually only 127 values.)

Even "primitive" keyboards that are not velocity sensitive need to send a velocity byte with their Note On messages. The spec requires these keyboards to send a velocity byte of 40H.

8nH is a Note Off command. When this message is received, the note stops playing—or its envelope goes into the *release* stage, if appropriate. Like Note On, Note Off needs two data bytes: note number and velocity. You can't stop a given note by sending just any Note Off command—you must send a Note Off with the same note number as that used in the Note On command.

The ability to respond to Note Off velocity has not been a common feature of MIDI synthesizers in the past, but it is becoming more prevalent. Note Off velocity can be used to affect the speed of a release stage. It can also affect the volume of an *aftersound*, such as in a harpsichord sound where the quill is heard to briefly touch the string when a key is released. By convention, a Note On followed by a velocity of 00 is considered equivalent to a Note Off. Some devices transmit only Note Ons, and use velocity-zero Note Ons to turn notes off. The spec says that either method is just fine.

CnH is a *Program Change* command (sometimes called *patch change*). The Program Change message has only one data byte: the program number. A digital synthesizer "program" is a memory location containing all the values of the parameters that determine an instrument's timbre. One set of values—for waveforms, frequencies, envelopes, signal routings, and so on—might define a brass sound, while another defines a flute sound, and still another, a funky bass. You can change programs by pressing a button on a synthesizer's front panel, but the MIDI Program Change message lets you do this remotely. In live performance, this means you can press one button on a keyboard and every synth in your stack will change its sound. When playing a sequenced song, this means that a single synthesizer can assume a different instrumental identity whenever the sequence sends out the appropriate Program Change command. Program Changes can also be used to change presets on effects devices. For example, one program in a device may be for flanging, while another may be for hall-type reverb. A well-timed Program Change message transmitted from a keyboard or a sequencer will cause the device to change from one effect to the other at precisely the right moment.

If a Program Change message is received while a synthesizer is in the middle of a note, a number of things can happen (depending on how the synthesizer is designed). Some synthesizers immediately cause the note to fade out. Some try to execute the Program Change and impose the new program's parameters on the current program (often with unpleasant results). More recent devices (usually ones that have a feature called *dynamic voice allocation*) will let the current note finish unaltered, and change the sound only for notes that start after the Program Change message was received.

Controllers

B*n*H is a *Control Change* command (often called a *Continuous Controller*, or just *Controller*—not to be confused with a controller device, like a keyboard). This command generally refers to a musical gesture that is not a note. Often it is something that can change the character of a sound after the note has started. Common examples of Controllers include *modulation wheel,* which normally adds vibrato; *sustain pedal* (usually a switch), which keeps the sustain portion of the envelope going; and *volume pedal,* which allows level changes or fade-ins and fade-outs. Note that MIDI volume is a very different concept from MIDI velocity. The former is a continuous parameter that can change while the note continues to sound, while the latter only affects the note when it starts (or stops, in the case of Note Off velocity).

A Control Change message has two data bytes: the Controller number, and the value of the Controller at that moment. Control Change messages often occur in streams, representing the continuous movement of a wheel, pedal, or slider. Since the Controller number (the first Data byte) can be from 00H to 7FH, there can potentially be up to 128 different Controllers active on any MIDI channel. Many controllers have designated functions in the MIDI specification: Modulation wheel is Controller 01, volume pedal (knob or slider) is Controller 07, and sustain pedal is Controller 40H (64 decimal). These designations are not absolutely required in a piece of MIDI gear, but they are provided to minimize confusion and make communications as smooth as possible.

Controllers 00 through 19H (0 through 31 decimal) were designated in the original MIDI specification as *double-precision controllers* or *14-bit controllers,* meaning that each of these controllers had a second controller, in the range of 20H to 39H (32 to 63 decimal) that addressed the same function. The reasoning behind this idea was that some musicians might want more resolution than the 128 values available with a single controller, and by using a pair of controllers, could achieve a resolution of 16,384 values. The lower-numbered controllers are the *Most Significant Bytes (MSB),* while the higher-numbered ones are the *Least Significant Bytes (LSB).* Very few manufacturers have implemented 14-bit controllers, sticking with just the lower-numbered (MSB) controllers—so the practice of pairing controllers is now considered essentially theoretical. (One exception is *Bank Select,* Controller 00/20H, a recently defined controller which is discussed later in the book.)

Channel Mode Messages

Controller numbers 78H (120 decimal) and above are called *Channel Mode* messages, because they have very specific functions.

Controller 78H is *All Sound Off* command. Any device that receives this message is supposed to immediately turn off all notes, and set the volume of all voices to zero (without fading). In an effects device, this message cuts off the tail of a delay or a reverb, but it doesn't turn off the effect: new signals coming into the audio input are processed normally. The second data byte, following the controller number, is 00. This is a fairly new addition to the MIDI spec, and is not implemented in very many devices as of yet.

Controller 79H means *Reset All Controllers* (on the designated channel). In other words, set all controller values to zero or to their normal settings (for example, volume might be set to 7FH). The second data byte is irrelevant. Not every MIDI device responds to this message.

Controller 7AH is a *Local Control* command. This determines whether the keyboard on a synthesizer and the sound-generating circuitry are linked—in other words, when you press a key, does it make a sound? It will when Local Control is On (that is, when the data byte following the controller number is 7FH). It won't if Local Control is Off (if the data byte is 00). Any other values for the last data byte should be ignored (although some devices interpret any non-zero value as On). The purpose of it may not be obvious, but Local Control is a very important function. The ability to "decouple" a synthesizer from its keyboard (which occurs when Local Control is Off) is crucial in a multisynth setup.

Controller 7BH means *All Notes Off* (on the designated channel). This command is useful in emergencies when notes are stuck on and you don't know why. It lets you silence the sound quickly. Sending specific Note Off messages is always the best way to silence a synthesizer, but this command lets you accomplish the same thing in a hurry, without your having to figure out which notes are sounding. Again, the second data byte is ignored (and not every MIDI device responds to this message). All Notes Off is not quite the same as All Sounds Off, because notes are allowed to decay naturally (and it doesn't necessarily have any effect on effects units). Some MIDI transmitters send this message any time all physical stimuli are stopped—for example, when you take all of your fingers off of the keyboard. However, this feature can cause undesirable effects.

Controllers 7CH through 7FH are discussed under "Modes" later in this chapter. Two other special types of Control Change messages are *Registered Parameters* and *Nonregistered Parameters* (62H through 65H), which are discussed in the chapter "Composing Techniques."

Pressure and Pitch Bend

D*n*H is a *Channel Pressure* command, sometimes known as *Mono Aftertouch,* or just *Aftertouch.* Channel Pressure is a measure of how hard a key is pressed after it is struck. A Channel Pressure command has one data byte: the pressure value. Special sensors below the keyboard are used to detect this pressure, which is often used to add vibrato to a voice, or to change its timbre, volume, or pitch. It works on all notes on a channel—that is, if pressure is applied to one key, all the notes are affected.

A*n*H is a *Polyphonic Key Pressure* command, sometimes known as *Polyphonic Aftertouch,* or just *Poly Aftertouch.* It is similar to Channel Pressure, except that each note has an independent sensor, and can be addressed individually. It allows, for example, a change in vibrato depth or timbre to be applied to one note in a chord without affecting the others. A Polyphonic Key Pressure command has two data bytes that represent the note number and the amount of pressure. Polyphonic Key Pressure is somewhat rare in the world of MIDI, because it is difficult and expensive to implement in hardware—and it is highly data intensive. Like Note Off velocity, however, it is becoming more common—and when used well, it can be very cool.

E*n*H is a *Pitch Bend* command. Pitch Bend is usually generated by a wheel, lever, or joystick, with a spring-loaded center return. This command allows for both upward and downward bends. However, since there is no real way to send negative numbers over MIDI, a data value of zero is considered to be the maximum downward bend, while "no bend" is a value in the middle of the range (40H, or 64 decimal). Obviously, no command at all is also interpreted as "no bend." The Reset All Controllers message described above also resets Pitch Bend to the middle of its range (not to zero).

The amount that a sound's pitch will change in response to a Pitch Bend command is determined by the receiving synthesizer. There will usually be a parameter in that device called "pitch bend range" or some equivalent, which determines the pitch change, in half steps, that will occur when a Pitch Bend command of maximum value (or zero) is received. In some devices this parameter can be remotely controlled using a Registered Parameter called *Pitch Bend Sensitivity.*

Pitch Bend can sometimes be *quantized,* so that instead of bending as a smooth glissando, the pitch can jump in half steps, whole steps, or even larger intervals. Again, this is a feature of the receiving device. Some devices can apply incoming Pitch Bend commands only to those keys being held down on the keyboard—and not to those being sustained through use of a pedal. In this way, if you play a chord and hold it with a sustain pedal, and then play a key and hold it while you send a Pitch Bend command, the notes of the sustained chord will remain constant, but the pitch of the single note you're holding will bend.

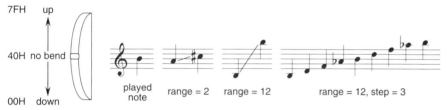

different pitchbend ranges, quantized pitchbend

Pitch Bend takes two data bytes, the first one being the Least Significant Byte (LSB) and the second being the Most Significant Byte (MSB). This means that the possible range of Pitch Bend values is not 00H to 7FH, but 00H to 7FH times 00H to 7FH, or 0 through 16,383 decimal ([128×128]−1). This was set up so that even at the highest Pitch Bend ranges, smooth-sounding sweeps could still be created. Practically speaking, however, the LSB is almost never used—and it is normally set either to zero, or to some arbitrary constant (or to the same value as the MSB). The MSB handles the entire range: 00 is maximum downward bend, 7FH is maximum upward bend, and 40H is no bend. In decimal these parameters are 0, 127, and 64, respectively.

Running Status

Normally, a MIDI message consists of a status byte and its appropriate data bytes. These are followed by the next message's status byte, and so on. However, the MIDI specification allows for a special condition in which a single status byte can be followed by a long string of data bytes. Imagine you are playing a key, and while you hold it down, you vary the pressure to create vibrato. You start with no pressure, increase it to maximum, and then slowly release it. This action could produce a total of 254 different Channel Pressure messages: 127 up and 127 down. Since the status byte is always the same, and only the data byte changes, if it were possible to send just the changing data bytes, it would reduce the amount of data by fifty percent. *Running Status* allows you to do exactly this. It can be used with any of the messages described so far, whether they take one data byte or two. Running Status is a "condition" of the MIDI data stream. It is invoked if a status byte is received which is followed by a number of data bytes higher than the normal number associated with that status byte. The extra data bytes are assumed to be associated with the last status byte received—and they are processed just as if the status byte had been repeated.

Here is an example of how the Channel Pressure messages described above would be sent using Running Status. (The messages are on Channel 1, and all numbers are shown in hex.)

D0 01 02 03 04 . . . 7D 7E 7F 7E 7D . . . 03 02 01 00

If not for Running Status, the transmitter would have to send this longer version of the same message.

D0 01 D0 02 D0 03 D0 04 . . . D0 7D D0 7E D0 7F D0 7E D0 7D . . . D0 03 D0 02 D0 01 D0 00

Here is another example. Under Running Status, sending the values 40H, 32H, 26H, 14H, and 00 to Controller 1 on Channel 3 could be accomplished by the following data stream.

B2 01 40 01 32 01 26 01 14 01 00

This will be interpreted as if it were sent as follows.

B2 01 40 B2 01 32 B2 01 26 B2 01 14 B2 01 00

Running Status can also be used in sending a long string of notes—but only if the Note Off commands are sent as Note Ons with zero velocity. Here is an example of a string of two notes as they would be sent without using Running Status.

90 45 31 80 45 40 90 62 7A 80 62 40

This series of commands contains the following information: Note 45H on with velocity 31H, same note off with velocity 40H, Note 62H on with velocity 7AH, same note off with velocity 40H. Thanks to Running Status, this string can be streamlined to the following.

90 45 31 45 00 62 7A 62 00.

Using Running Status with messages that require one data byte (such as Channel Pressure) improves the efficiency of the MIDI data stream by fifty percent. Using it with messages that require two data bytes improves the efficiency by thirty-three percent.

Running Status remains in effect until a new status byte is received. *System Real Time* messages (single-byte messages F8H through FFH) can be inside a Running Status group of messages without interfering. Here's an example of such a string.

90 45 31 45 00 F8 62 9A 62 00

The F8H is a *Timing Clock* command, after which Running Status continues as if nothing had happened.

System Messages

The commands discussed so far are collectively known as *Channel Voice* messages, because they contain channel numbers and they address one voice at a time. The remaining commands in the MIDI specification are called *System* messages. A System message does not contain a channel number, and its first digit will always be F.

System Exclusive

A message that starts with F0H is called a *System Exclusive* or *SysEx* message. This type of message allows a specific make or model MIDI device to receive information that other devices on the line will ignore (even those tuned to the same MIDI channel).

Here's a simple application of System Exclusive commands: A set of parameters describes a program, say a piano sound, on a certain model of synthesizer. You have another synthesizer that's the same model, and you want that piano sound to be available in the second synthesizer as well. You could look at all of the parameters on the first synthesizer, write them down, and then enter them one at a time into the second synthesizer. Or, you can instruct the first synthesizer to arrange all of the parameters in a System Exclusive message and send the message by MIDI cable to the second synthesizer. If the second synthesizer is set up to accept System Exclusive messages, it will receive and store the parameters in one of its program registers. When you call up that register on the second synth, it will play the same piano sound. Because the messages describe a sound for a certain type of synthesizer, other models on the line will ignore the message completely. This type of parameter-list exchange is called a *System Exclusive dump* or *Parameter dump*. A dump can contain the parameters of a single voice or the parameters of all of the voices in a synth's memory (in which case it's often called a *bulk dump*). Thus a System Exclusive message can contain hundreds or even thousands of bytes.

A System Exclusive message has a special identification number called a *manufacturer's ID* in the byte immediately following the F0H *header*. Every manufacturer of MIDI equipment is issued a unique ID number by the governing bodies of MIDI: the MIDI Manufacturers Association (MMA) and the Japan MIDI Standards Committee (JMSC). For example, Yamaha's ID number is 43H, and therefore, any System Exclusive message designed for Yamaha equipment will start out with F0 43H. Casio's ID is 44H, Lexicon's is 06H, and so on. With the explosive growth of MIDI after its inception, it was soon apparent that these single-byte numbers might well run out. Thus a new set of manufacturer IDs with three bytes—the first one of which is always 00H—was issued. The IDs are divided up geographically as follows (all values are hex).

American companies get the numbers 00 00 01 to 00 1F 7F;
European and Australian companies get 00 20 00 to 00 3F 7F;
Japanese companies get 00 40 00 to 00 5F 7F;
and companies in other areas get 00 60 00 to 00 7F 7F.

What comes after the manufacturer's ID is entirely up to the manufacturer. The only restriction is that no bytes have values higher than 7F, so the receiving device never confuses any part of the message with a new Status byte. There's no such thing as Running Status when it comes to SysEx messages—and they cannot be interrupted by any other messages. If a high-value status byte is sent during a SysEx message, the message is terminated.

Many manufacturers use *sub-IDs* to identify different models, and/or *device IDs* to address devices tuned to different MIDI channels. For example, you might have a system with eight identical synths—but if you want to send a new sound to only one of them, you can distinguish it by its device ID. Device IDs don't necessarily have to correspond with MIDI channels; since you can use a full byte for a device ID, you can address 128 different devices, not just sixteen. This is particularly helpful when you are working with multitimbral synths (which receive on multiple MIDI channels)—or when you have a very large system using multiple MIDI cables.

At the end of any System Exclusive message is an F7H byte. This byte is called *End of System Exclusive*, and is sometimes abbreviated in documentation as *EOX*. When an F7H is received, all the devices on the system that had been ignoring the System Exclusive message "wake up" and pay attention to whatever comes next. Until the F7H is received, a System Exclusive message is not supposed to be interrupted.

System Exclusive messages can be used to change a single program parameter in certain devices. In this case, the entire list of parameters is not sent, but merely a message (the nature of which is up to the manufacturer) saying "I want to change a single parameter," followed by the parameter number and then the new value. In this way, System Exclusive commands can be used like Continuous Controller commands, but with more flexibility, since any parameter can be changed, not just those assigned to Controllers. (Be aware that this capability is far from universal. Some synths will not like it—and they may audibly glitch if you send them a SysEx parameter change while a note is sounding.)

Short SysEx messages can generally be sent in "real time" as part of a sequence—while bulk dumps are usually sent "off-line," due to their length. Sometimes a bulk dump is sent as part of a sequence at a time when no notes are playing (such as during count-off bars) so that it doesn't disrupt the timing of the music.

System Exclusive messages have a wide variety of uses. They are commonly used to allow synthesizers to be programmed from computers, using "patch editor" programs. This capability has brought about the introduction of synthesizers with very few front-panel controls, or even none at all. These synths can be programmed only from an external MIDI source, such as a computer or another synth.

The manufacturer whose ID goes into a System Exclusive message has the exclusive right to decide how its messages are going to be sent and interpreted, but it does not own them. Anyone can use the messages without the manufacturer's permission, as long as the way they use them doesn't conflict with the way the manufacturer uses them. In fact, the manufacturer is required to publish the complete SysEx format for every new device it introduces (although some manufacturers are a little slow in this regard). This means that anyone can write a computer program, or invent a new type of controller, that directly addresses the SysEx parameters of any MIDI synthesizer or other device.

Most synthesizers can initiate a System Exclusive dump from their own controls. This makes it easy to send out banks of voices and retrieve them. Other synths require the dump to be initiated by another device, which must send a short "request for dump" message before the synthesizer will start to send data. Sometimes several short SysEx messages and acknowledgements must be sent between the receiver and the transmitter before a dump can be accomplished. This interchange is called *handshaking*.

Often a device will not accept a SysEx message, short or long, unless it includes a *checksum*, which is a byte at the end of the message, just before the EOX. The checksum value is calculated by summing all of the previous bytes in the message, and then processing that sum in such a way that it fits into a single byte. Different manufacturers have their own way of calculating checksums—and if you want to send a SysEx message of your own creation to a device, you have to know how to calculate the checksum that the device expects. Some methods are relatively straightforward, such as removing all but the last two digits of the sum. Others involve complex arithmetic operations that can be a real pain to deal with.

Universal System Exclusive messages form a sub-class of System Exclusive messages. Most extensions to the MIDI specification in recent years have fallen into this category, because it remains the most "open" part of the spec. These extensions include:

- **Experimental or "Non-Commercial":** for internal use by research and educational institutions, and not for use in any products that are released to the public.

- **Sample Dump Standard:** allows different MIDI-based sampling synthesizers and computers to exchange data.

- **Tuning Standard:** allows alternative tunings to be used in different devices.

- **Some MIDI Time Code messages:** allow synchronization and control of MIDI devices.

- **MIDI Machine Control** and **MIDI Show Control:** expand MIDI into the worlds of transport automation and live presentations.

Noncommercial SysEx messages have an ID of 7DH, so such messages will always start with F0 7DH. Sample Dump Standard and Tuning Standard messages fall under the classification of *Non-Real Time* Universal System Exclusive, which have an ID of 7EH. MIDI Time Code, MIDI Machine Control, and MIDI Show Control messages are classed as *Real Time,* and have an ID of 7FH. Like all SysEx messages, Universal System Exclusive messages must feature an EOX byte (F7H) at the end.

System Common

Messages **F1H** through **F7H** are known as *System Common* messages because they have no channel numbers, and are common to all receiving devices. Here are the defined values. (At the present time, F4H and F5H are undefined.)

System Common Messages

Name	Hex Value	Decimal Value	Data Bytes
MIDI Time Code 1/4 Frame	F1	241	1 (timecode nibble)
Song Position Pointer	F2	242	2 (MSB, LSB)
Song Select	F3	243	1 (song number)
Tune Request	F6	246	0

F1H is a MIDI *Time Code Quarter Frame* message. MIDI *Time Code* (abbreviated *MTC*) is used to synchronize various types of MIDI equipment to one another or to synchronize these devices to tape or other time-related media. It allows timing information to be conveyed by the MIDI data stream in a format that parallels *SMPTE timecode,* which is ubiquitous in the world of film, video, and professional audio.

The Quarter Frame message is used when timing data is being generated continuously, such as when a tape is rolling. It conveys timing information in hours, minutes, seconds, and frames (fractions of a second). Each message has a single data byte and conveys part of the location information. Eight messages communicate an entire location number. The speed of the incoming Quarter Frame messages tells the receiver how fast the tape is going.

F2H is a *Song Position Pointer* message, sometimes called simply *Song Pointer.* Like MIDI Time Code, Song Position Pointer is used in synchronizing MIDI equipment to both MIDI and non-MIDI time-based equipment. A Song Position Pointer message tells a receiving device, such as a sequencer, what measure, bar, and beat to set itself to. This message has two data bytes—a Most Significant Byte and a Least Significant Byte—which together comprise a number from 0 to 16,383 decimal. This number reflects the number of sixteenth notes since the beginning of the sequence.

F3H is a *Song Select* message, which is, unfortunately, also sometimes called "Song Pointer." Song Select allows a particular song or sequence to be called up from a device that can contain multiple songs, like a sequencer or drum machine. The process is not unlike the way the buttons on a jukebox call up a particular record. A Song Select command has one data byte, so the number of songs that can be called by it is 128 (00H through 7FH).

F6H is a *Tune Request* message. This is used with digitally controlled analog synthesizers to tell them to execute whatever self-tuning procedures they have on board. Although there are still plenty of this type of synth around, very few respond to this command. This is largely because these synths are stable enough that they don't need to be retuned after they are turned on. This message requires no data bytes.

As discussed earlier, **F7H** is the End of System Exclusive message. This message requires no data bytes.

System Real Time

System Real Time messages are used to synchronize equipment as it is running. System Real Time messages have no channel numbers and require no data bytes. They can be inserted into the MIDI data stream at any time, even in the middle of another message. As mentioned earlier, they can even pop up in the middle of Running Status without interrupting it (that is, they are not interpreted as new Status bytes).

Here are the defined System Real Time values. (F9H and FDH are undefined at present.)

System Real Time Messages

Name	Hex Value	Decimal Value
Timing Clock	F8	248
Start	FA	250
Continue	FB	251
Stop	FC	252
Active Sensing	FE	254
System Reset	FF	255

F8H is a *Timing Clock* (or just *Clock*) message. Timing Clocks are used to make two or more MIDI devices lock in to the same tempo. These messages are generated twenty-four times per quarter note so that their frequency varies with tempo (unlike MTC Quarter Frame messages, which change with tape speed, but not tempo). A *master* device sends out Timing Clocks, and *slave* devices follow them.

Timing Clock is also called *MIDI Sync* (although this term doesn't appear in the MIDI specification). The term MIDI Sync is perhaps more appropriate when used in a broader sense, encompassing the Start, Stop, and Continue commands (and sometimes Song Position Pointer as well). In this way, when we speak of a device being "MIDI Sync compatible," it means that the device responds to all of these commands.

FAH is a *Start* message. This tells a device to go to the beginning of its song and start playing at the tempo determined by the incoming Timing Clock messages that immediately follow.

FBH is a *Continue* message, which is similar to Start, except that the receiving device will play from its current location, not necessarily from the beginning. A Song Position Pointer message with a data value of 00 00, followed by a Continue message, is equivalent to a Start message. In fact, to avoid ambiguity, some MIDI devices use this combination instead of a Start message.

FCH is a *Stop* message. This tells a device to stop playing and wait for a Start or Continue (not just a Timing Clock).

FEH is an *Active Sensing* message. Active Sensing is an optional feature of MIDI transmitters. When this feature is used, a message is sent every 300 milliseconds or less which serves to tell a receiving device that the cable plugged in to its MIDI In jack is still there. If Active Sensing should stop, the receiving device is required to turn off all of its notes. This command was designed to prevent situations in which a synthesizer receives a Note On message, and then somehow loses its input before the corresponding Note Off is received. This situation results in a note that never stops (known as a "stuck note"). If a device never receives an Active Sensing message, it will behave as if the idea never existed. However, once a device receives its first FE, it expects one every 300msec—if it misses one, it stops all sound. Active Sensing is actually used quite rarely because it adds a small amount of extra overhead to the MIDI data stream. The Active Sensing data can also confuse some devices when they are receiving large blocks of data, such as Sample Dumps.

FFH is a *System Reset* message. This instructs all devices to return to their initial power-up condition; that is, to turn off all notes, stop sending out clocks, reset all controllers, and so on. This message is also rarely used.

Modes

In the early days of MIDI, *modes* were a very big deal, and a description of them was found at the beginning of every discussion of the MIDI specification. The advent of polyphonic, multitimbral synthesizers and samplers has made modes far less important than they were. There are however, situations in which they can be useful. There are four MIDI modes. These are usually set from a synth's front panel, or by using two Continuous Controller switches: *Omni On/Off* (Controllers 7DH and 7CH) and *Poly On/Mono On* (Controllers 7FH and 7EH). The data bytes of all of these commands (except sometimes Mono On) are supposed to be irrelevant—but some synths require non-zero values (or even 7FH) in order to act on them.

In *Omni On* mode, a receiving device will respond to data on all MIDI channels. In *Omni Off* mode, it will respond on just one channel—or in the case of multitimbral synthesizers, multiple, but specific, channels. In *Poly* mode, a device will respond to multiple incoming notes polyphonically. In *Mono* mode, it will respond monophonically; that is, only one note at a time will sound no matter how many you try to play. These four mode messages also imply an All Notes Off message—whenever any one of them is received by a synthesizer, it must turn off all of its voices before switching modes. However, a mode message is not supposed to be used instead of a true All Notes Off message (B*n* 7BH).

Here's how the four modes correspond to the four possible states of the controller switches.

- **Omni On/Poly:** also known as *Mode 1,* is useful in situations with one MIDI transmitter and a small number of receivers—all of which are to be played simultaneously without any distinction by channel number.

- **Omni On/Mono:** or *Mode 2* is very rarely used.

- **Omni Off/Poly:** or *Mode 3,* is by far the most common mode.

- **Omni Off/Mono:** or *Mode 4,* is discussed below.

Mono Mode

Omni Off/Mono mode has some interesting peculiarities. First of all, a synth in Mono mode will assign priorities to incoming MIDI notes to determine which note will actually sound. The priority scheme may favor the last note received, the note that has been held the longest, the highest note, or the lowest note. Secondly, in Mono mode, many synths assume a rudimentary kind of multitimbral identity. In some early polyphonic MIDI synthesizers, such as the Six-Trak by Sequential Circuits and Casio's CZ-101, the user had a choice in this regard. One option was to have all of the available voices (that is, the number of simultaneous notes the device was capable of playing) respond to one MIDI channel with a single sound or timbre (Poly mode). Alternatively, the user could assign each voice to its own MIDI channel, with its own timbre (Mono mode). The number of channels it could play was equal to the number of voices: six in the case of the Six-Trak, four in the CZ-101. This meant that one synthesizer could function as the equivalent of four or six individual instruments—each capable of playing only one note at a time.

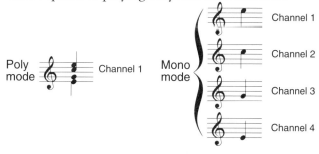

Mono-mode synthesizers have a *Basic Channel*. Notes are received on this channel, as well as on the next $n1$ channels (with n being the number of voices in the synthesizer). For example, if a four-voice mono synthesizer has its Basic Channel set to 11, it will receive notes on Channels 11, 12, 13, and 14. If a four-voice Mono synth has its Basic Channel set higher than 13, either it will run out of voice/channel assignments, or it will "wrap" the upper voices around to Channels 1, 2, etc. Normally, Control Change, Program Change, and other voice messages can be sent on any of a mono synth's active channels, and they will only affect that channel. System Exclusive messages intended for a mono synth are normally sent with the message's device ID byte corresponding to the synth's Basic Channel.

When a Mono On message is sent, the data byte following it specifies how many MIDI voice/channel assignments will be made. For example, the command B3H 7EH 05H will put the receiving device in Mono mode, and tell it to respond on five channels, beginning with Channel 4 (that is, 4 through 8). If the second Data byte is 0, the device is supposed to respond on the Basic Channel and as many MIDI channels above it as it has voices for. In practice, however, mono synths have a fixed number of voices and channels—and so the second data byte in the Mono On message is usually ignored.

Multi Mode

The term "Multi mode" (coined by Kurzweil Music Systems) describes a new type of synthesizer (or sampler) not originally envisioned by the creators of the MIDI spec. A Multi-mode device that can respond on multiple channels with two or more notes on each channel, thereby acting as multiple polyphonic sound sources. Kurzweil's K250 was the first device to offer this feature, but since it is not part of the MIDI specification, it cannot be enabled or disabled by MIDI Mode messages.

Some Multi-mode synths require you to preassign a certain number of voices to each channel. Others allow voices to be assigned on the fly according to the instantaneous conditions—a feature often called *dynamic voice allocation*. Like the original Mono-mode synths, Multi-mode synths usually have a Basic Channel over which System Exclusive and other non-real-time data is sent. There are, however, no restrictions on which channels (relative to the Basic Channel) can be used for real-time performance.

Modern Uses of Mono Mode

The original Mono mode still has some important functions. A guitar controller connected to a six-voice synthesizer in Mono mode can send information for each string on its own MIDI channel. This is particularly important when bending a string so that the Pitch Bend messages generated will affect only the channel controlled by that string. A special mode is available with some guitars to accommodate "whammy bar" information. Instead of sending out six simultaneous Pitch Bend messages, they send out a single message on an extra channel, usually the Basic Channel minus 1. Other controllers can be sent on this channel as well, which is referred to as the *Global Channel*.

The fact that Mono mode only allows one note to sound on a given channel is even useful in polyphonic synthesizers. In Poly mode, when you play two notes in quick succession, the envelope of the first may ring over into the second. In Mono mode, the envelope of the first note will be cut off when the second note starts. This allows the playing of old-fashioned "synth-style" leads—and makes for more realistic simulation of wind instruments and guitar hammerons.

Many synthesizers use an implementation of Mono mode that allows smooth legatos to be played from a keyboard. When the second note is played, the envelope is not retriggered—instead the first envelope continues at the pitch of the second note. This is particularly useful when using a wind controller, or when emulating a wind instrument or the human voice. *Portamento Control* and *Legato Footswitch* are new additions to the MIDI spec which take this idea even further.

Chapter 2

MIDI Equipment

There are many types of MIDI equipment available—and new ideas and products are coming out all the time. Despite the profusion of gear, most MIDI users start with a basic setup. This chapter describes the basic studio setup. It also provides details about various types of MIDI devices, and their applications in the studio.

The MIDI studio starts with a transmitter—most commonly, a synthesizer. The MIDI data you generate by playing the keyboard is recorded by a sequencer—which can be a stand-alone device or a program running on a personal computer. The sequencer allows you to record and overdub multiple tracks; so individual parts can be recorded one at a time. The MIDI output of the sequencer is connected to the inputs of one or more receivers or sound modules—which can be drum machines, synthesizers, or samplers. Each track in the sequencer is normally assigned to a different MIDI channel. Each sound module is also set to receive MIDI data on a unique channel, so each track controls one instrument and is responsible for one type of sound at a time. (Multitimbral synthesizers may act as several "virtual" instruments, receiving on multiple channels and producing several different sounds.) Every module produces an audio signal, and these signals go to a mixer. The output of the mixer is then recorded on some form of tape or disk as a finished audio track. Signals can be processed through outboard equalizers, delays, compressors, or reverbs.

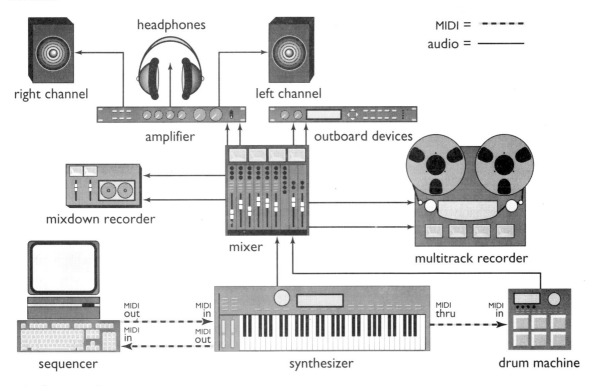

a simple MIDI *studio*

A MIDI studio may consist of nothing but MIDI modules and a master recorder to capture the finished product. MIDI devices may also be used in conjunction with multitrack tape or a hard disk–based audio system to accommodate vocals and acoustic instruments. To make sure the sequencer and multitrack tape are synchronized, one track of the tape is dedicated to some form of timecode signal, which may be FSK or SMPTE. A converter interprets the timecode (which is an audio signal) and changes it into MIDI timing data which the sequencer can follow—either MIDI Clocks and Song Position Pointers or MIDI Time Code. When the studio is being used to produce music for video—an increasingly common function of MIDI studios—the timecode track (usually SMPTE) appears on the videotape. This track is present either on an audio track or on its own special track, depending on the video format. The sequencer uses this timecode to stay in sync with the picture.

MIDI gear generally falls into three broad categories: transmitters, receivers, and processors. Transmitters generate MIDI data in response to physical stimuli—such as being played or being fed a timing signal. Receivers translate the MIDI data they receive into sound or some other kind of performance-related function. Processors alter MIDI data or convert it into other kinds of data (or vice versa). Many, if not most, MIDI devices fit into more than one of these categories.

Transmitters

Transmitters are sometimes known as *controllers* (not to be confused with MIDI Control Change messages, which are also often called "controllers"). Common MIDI transmitters include keyboards, guitar controllers, percussion controllers, and wind controllers.

Keyboards

The most common MIDI transmitter is the keyboard synthesizer. When notes are played on the keyboard, MIDI Note On and Note Off messages are sent from its MIDI Out jack. Any wheels, sliders, buttons, pedals, breath controllers, or switches that are mounted on or connected to the keyboard may also generate and transmit MIDI data in the form of Control Change, Pitch Bend, Program Change, or other messages.

Keyboards are available in a wide variety of sizes and grades, ranging from thirty-six to eighty-eight keys. Various key sizes are also available, ranging from about half the size of a standard piano key to full size. Most require only a light keystroke to sound a note, but other models have weighted actions to make them feel more like an acoustic piano. Portable keyboards, designed to be worn around the neck, let you step out in front of a band like a lead guitar player.

Sensors at the top and bottom of each key's travel measure the time interval between the start and the end of the key press. These sensors interpret that time as the keystroke velocity. Some inexpensive keyboards lack this feature—but since a Note On message must always have a velocity byte, they transmit a default velocity of 40H (64 decimal) for every keystroke. A few, more expensive keyboards generate Note Off velocity, which measures the time a released key takes to move from the bottom of its travel back to the top. Keyboards equipped to send Channel Pressure have a pressure sensor under the keyboard. Those equipped to send Key Pressure have individual sensors under each key.

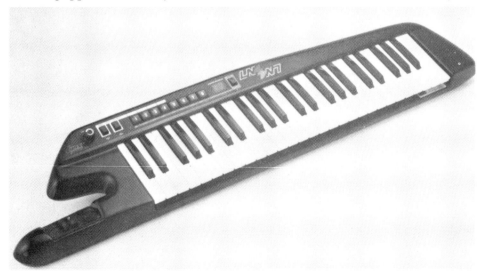

Lync Systems Keyboard Controller

A keyboard synthesizer can both transmit and receive MIDI data. When Local Control is turned on, the keyboard controls the sound the synthesizer produces. When it is turned off, the keyboard and the sound-generating circuitry become completely independent, or "decoupled," from each other, although they both remain fully functional. The synthesizer keyboard can then be used to control another device, while a different transmitter may be used to control the synthesizer's sound-generating circuitry.

Local Control is extremely important in the multisynth, sequencer-based studio—and understanding when to turn it on and off can help the user out of many a confusing situation. Picture this scenario: A keyboard synthesizer transmits and receives on Channel 1 with Local Control turned on. Its MIDI output is sent to a sequencer and recorded. When the sequence is played back, the sequencer sends the data out on Channel 1 into the synthesizer's MIDI In jack, and the music plays. Everyone's happy. Now imagine that you have an additional synth module, which is set to receive on Channel 2—and you want to overdub a second sequencer track using that synth. You set your keyboard synthesizer to transmit on Channel 2 (still receiving on Channel 1), or you tell the sequencer to *channelize* all incoming MIDI data to Channel 2. The sequencer, using its Thru function, will pass the data on to the second synth, which lets you hear what you're playing.

You now can record the second track by playing it on the keyboard as you listen to the first track play back. You'll notice right away, however, that you're hearing too much music: the notes you're playing on the keyboard are not only sounding on the synth set to Channel 2, they're also sounding on the keyboard synthesizer itself. You could turn down the volume on the keyboard synth, but then you won't be able to hear the first track you recorded. This is when you turn the Local Control parameter on the keyboard off. This can usually be done either from the unit's front panel, or by having the sequencer send a Local Control Off message (B0 79 00H) to the synth. Now, the track that you intended to play on Channel 1 (the one being played back by the sequencer) will come out of the keyboard synthesizer, while the notes you play on the keyboard will only be heard on the synth set to Channel 2. With Local Control Off, any keyboard synthesizer can become a master controller for a complex multimodule MIDI studio, with no danger of sounds interfering with each other.

Some synthesizers allow you to choose which functions will be locally controlled. For example, local control of keys can be disabled, so that pressing a key does not produce a sound on the synth—but local control of Program Change buttons can be enabled, so that when you press one, the synthesizer sound changes. (The MIDI Local Control message does not deal with such subtleties—it's either all or nothing.)

Some more elaborate keyboards have the ability to generate data on multiple channels. This is done in a number of ways.

- a "split" or "zone," where different areas of the keyboard—distinct or overlapping—transmit on different channels

- a "layer," where pressing a key transmits data on two or more channels simultaneously

- a program change "map," where pressing a button transmits different user-defined Program Change messages on different MIDI channels

Other features of sophisticated MIDI keyboards include:

- the ability to transmit user-defined System Exclusive messages

- velocity mapping, where the velocity response of the keyboard is changed to suit different playing styles or the velocity-response curves of different receiving synthesizers

- pressure mapping, which does the same thing as velocity mapping except for Channel or Key Pressure

- controller definition, in which the various wheels and sliders can be programmed to send out Controller messages specified by the user

- controller scaling, in which high and low limits can be set for the Continuous Controller data being generated

- breath control, which uses a harmonica-like object that plugs into the keyboard, allowing you to use your breathing and tongue articulation to control various sound parameters

- automatic transposition of outgoing note data

Some MIDI keyboards produce no sound at all. These are sometimes called *master keyboards, mother keyboards,* or even *dumb keyboards*—although the latter is a bit of a misnomer because many of them contain extremely sophisticated control features, and are of very high quality. Non-sounding keyboards are often used as the central controller for large MIDI setups.

Guitar Controllers

Since many modern musicians learned their craft on the guitar, *guitar controllers* have become popular tools for generating MIDI data. Unlike keyboards, however, which lend themselves well to handling the binary nature of MIDI, guitar controllers present a multitude of problems. There is no best solution for designing a guitar that will produce MIDI data, and for this reason, many types of guitar controllers have been developed. Although many have arrived with great promise only to disappear within a few months or years, there have been a few moderately successful models.

Roland GK1

The simplest approach to designing a guitar controller is to take an ordinary guitar, electric or acoustic, and put a *pitch-to-MIDI converter* on it. This detects the presence of a string vibrating and analyzes its pitch. It then generates a MIDI Note On command, whose number is based on the detected pitch and whose velocity is based on the peak level of the attack. If the pitch changes a small amount, either from bending a string or using finger vibrato, a Pitch

Bend message is sent. If it changes a large amount, as when the guitarist moves a finger to a different fret, a new Note On is sent. When the string amplitude goes below a certain level—either because it is damped or because it dies out naturally—a Note Off message (or a Note On with a velocity of zero) is sent.

This approach is not without its problems. The response to a played guitar note (known as *tracking response*) is not instantaneous. It normally takes the pitch detector at least a couple of cycles of string vibration before it can accurately determine the pitch. At low frequencies this can take a while: a low E string vibrates at about 73Hz, so two cycles at that pitch require over 27 milliseconds. This is a long time to wait to hear a sound after you've plucked a string. In addition, strings naturally change their pitch over the course of a note. The change is most rapid at the beginning, so a pitch detector has to have some kind of "intelligent damping" to filter this information and not pass it on to the receiving device. The pitch can also change when a string's vibration is dying out, or when the vibration is stopped by the guitar player's damping the string. If the cutoff threshold of the converter is not set to ignore this, it will create *false triggers* (brief notes at low velocities), which can be very annoying.

These problems have led to many alternative methods of translating guitar information into MIDI data. Some guitar controllers do not use standard guitar strings or tuning, but instead make all of the strings the same thickness (as thin as possible). Electrical circuits run through the frets themselves, so that fingering a string completes a conductive path from the fret to the bridge. The note number is determined by sensors in the frets—and the action of plucking the string creates the Note On command and the velocity byte. Tracking response is enhanced by the higher pitch of the strings—and pitch ambiguity is minimized. However, this instrument cannot be played as a normal guitar, and many players need time to get used to a low E string that is only .009.

Optical, infrared, and sonar sensors have been employed in some models to speed up tracking response even further—and there continues to be development on pitch-analysis designs that can work with less than a full cycle of audio. Taking this one step further, some guitar controllers feature two sets of strings: one for plucking and one for fretting. These devices sometimes appear to be broken, because the neck is attached to the body at an angle.

Guitar controllers often send MIDI data in Mono mode, with each string transmitting on a different MIDI channel. This is so that Pitch Bend information generated by executing a bend on one string does not affect the pitch of all the other strings. Some controllers, when in Mono mode, also have a special provision for transmitting "whammy bar" information. Rather than send Pitch Bend messages on all six channels simultaneously (which would create a flood of MIDI data) the whammy bar generates Pitch Bend on only one channel. This is usually the channel immediately below the Basic Channel of the device, known as the Global Channel. In other words, if the Basic Channel is 8, the strings are transmitting data on Channels 8 through 13, and the whammy bar information is on Channel 7. The receiving device, of course, has to know that this is happening, and apply the Pitch Bend data coming in on Channel 7 to the sounds on Channels 8 through 13. Other types of global information, such as Program Changes and MIDI Volume, may also be transmitted on the Global Channel. The ability to recognize Global Channel commands is certainly not universal among receiving synthesizers, and so it is important to consider this feature when purchasing a MIDI guitar system.

Even for a good keyboard player, guitar controllers can be very useful. Although many synths and samplers now offer excellent guitar sounds, both acoustic and electric, getting a keyboard to sound as if it is strummed can be very difficult. (Some hardware and software products have been made to overcome this problem. These products analyze existing MIDI chords in sequences or from live instruments and create guitaristic strums or arpeggios for them.) In addition, certain types of chord voicings and voice-leadings lend themselves much more to a guitar than a keyboard. Therefore, even a simple guitar controller played by a musician with limited guitar chops can add welcome variety to a sequence that is otherwise created from a keyboard.

The same technology used for guitar controllers (and the same problems) can be found in MIDI basses, MIDI violins, and the MIDI version of the Chapman Stick (a fretted string instrument played by tapping on the strings with both hands). Most of these use pitch-to-MIDI conversion.

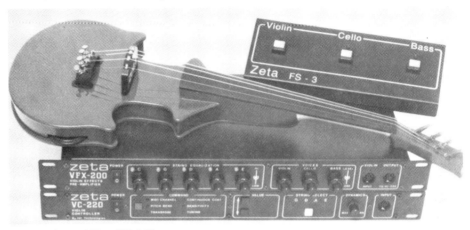

Zeta Violin and Zeta VC-220

Percussion Controllers

A *percussion controller*, or MIDI drum pad, is a device that produces a MIDI Note On when hit with a stick, hand, or beater pedal. A simple percussion controller produces the same note number every time it is hit, with the velocity determined by the force of the blow. Since there is usually no release to a drum's sound, a percussion controller generates a corresponding Note Off message soon after each Note On. Since these controllers are primarily used to trigger drum sounds (which have no sustain portion to their envelopes), the time between Note On and Note Off is usually not critical. However, some advanced percussion controllers do have a "choke" function—which sends Note Off messages for use with cymbal or hi-hat sounds.

Many drum pads are programmable with respect to note number, MIDI transmission channel, note duration, and sensitivity (that is, how hard you have to hit them to produce a given velocity value). Some offer *velocity switching*, in which different amounts of force will cause different note numbers to be generated. For example, a soft blow will play an ordinary snare drum hit, while a harder blow on the same pad will trigger a rim shot. Some drum pads have positional sensing that will switch or crossfade sounds based on the position of the hit. A few offer Channel Pressure, for bending or otherwise changing notes after they are hit.

Pads are available as single devices for triggering one drum, or in groups or arrays, for emulating a whole drum set. Pad arrays sometimes can store multiple programs, so that several different note/channel/sensitivity/switching layouts can be quickly memorized and recalled. In addition, sometimes the pads themselves can be used to program the device, much as the knobs and buttons on a synthesizer have multiple uses. For example, pressing a footswitch and hitting a certain pad will call up a memory location and reconfigure the entire instrument.

One type of multiple pad is the MIDI *marimba*, a percussion controller with one or more octaves of bars (called "keys") which are laid out like a marimba or vibraphone. Other controllers feature a single pad that is marked off to delineate different areas that produce different sounds, something like a Caribbean steel drum.

A very different type of touch controller is Thunder, from electronic-music pioneer Donald Buchla. This device uses some two dozen sensitive plates, arranged on a flat surface more or less in the form of two hands. Each plate can be sensitive to contact, pressure, and finger location, and can use any of these parameters to generate MIDI notes, controllers, clocks, and/or riffs. The plates can also control effects that alter the output of other plates, such as transposition, delay, velocity fading, and looping.

Airdrums, by Palmtree Instruments, is another type of percussion controller which has earned the nickname "MIDI maracas." This instrument consists of a pair of hand-held cylinders with wires coming out the back, which respond to physical movement in six directions: up, down, left, right, rotate clockwise, and rotate counter-clockwise. A movement creates a MIDI Note On or Note Off. The hand used and the direction of the movement determine the MIDI note number, resulting in twelve distinct possibilities. The speed of the movement controls the velocity. A control panel lets the user program the effect of each movement—and many different setups can be quickly stored and recalled.

Percussionists who prefer to play real drums can use *trigger-to-MIDI converters*. These are contact-microphonelike devices that attach to a drum and send a pulse whenever the drum is hit. The pulse is then translated to a MIDI Note On message, with a preset note number. The velocity value of the Note On message is determined by the strength of the hit. These devices are often used in studio situations when a drummer wants to play a real set of drums, but the producer wants to use sampled drum sounds on the recording.

Trigger-to-MIDI converters can be attached to other objects, or even to clothing, so that performance artists can wear body suits or tap shoes that generate MIDI data. The Flying Karamazov Brothers, a technologically hip comedy/juggling troupe, attach triggers to helmets, then play Beethoven's "Ode to Joy" by bonking themselves on the head with clubs.

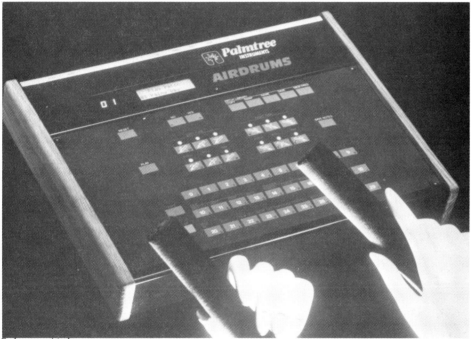
Palmtree Airdrums

Wind Controllers
Wind controllers are saxophone- or trumpet-like instruments that generate MIDI data in response to physical gestures similar to those used to play a wind instrument. Some wind controllers are actual acoustic wind instruments fitted with custom mouthpieces and other mechanical and electronic parts that convert gestures like blowing and fingering into MIDI messages. Other wind controllers are dedicated units that don't much resemble their acoustic counterparts. Wind players also have the option of using pitch to MIDI converters, as described in the following section.

Wind controllers generate a combination of data from different gestures.

- Note On messages, from pressing keys and/or blowing into a mouthpiece

- note numbers, from combinations of key presses

- Velocity, Volume, and/or Channel Pressure, from breath pressure

- Pitch Bend and/or Modulation, from lip pressure or special keys

- Program Change and Sustain Pedal, from special keys or specially designed pedals

MIDI wind controllers are markedly different from MIDI keyboards. Most keyboardists play a note and then let the patch's envelope generators and LFOs determine what happens from there. Although Continuous Controllers and Pressure are available, a surprisingly small number of keyboard players actually use them creatively. Wind instruments give the player wide, subtle, and continuous control over the pitch, dynamics, and timbre of each note, from the moment it's attacked until it dies. However, the number of discrete ways to control the elements of a note with a wind controller can be seen as being out of balance: too many timbral elements are being controlled with too few aspects of the interface. A player might find Velocity and Pressure data, for example, conflicting over the dynamic control of a note. This is not only a limitation of most wind controllers; it is a problem reflected in the sound architecture of many instruments. In fact, only a handful of MIDI instruments have the type of structure that is friendly to wind controllers.

Wind controllers generate a lot of MIDI data. While a note from a MIDI keyboard may be described by a Note On, a Note Off, and maybe a few Modulation Wheel bytes in between, a MIDI wind controller spews out continuous MIDI data all the time. Because of the finite nature of the speed of MIDI, this data must often be filtered or reduced somehow. This can occur either on the way into the sequencer or synthesizer (using some sort of input filter), or after the fact, by using a sequencer's thinning feature. Some wind controllers generate so much data that their designers use non-MIDI protocols between the controllers and specially designed dedicated synthesizers. This works well in live performance, but in a sequencing situation, not all of the data gets recorded. A synthesizer connected to the sequencer will play back a somewhat reduced version of the performance.

Pitch-to-MIDI Converters

Pitch-to-MIDI converters can be used with anything that produces sound, including the human voice. In fact, there are a variety of MIDI microphones available that convert singing into MIDI data. One of the major issues in designing a pitch-to-MIDI converter is determining how it responds to a continuous sound that changes in pitch and/or volume. Should it generate a single Note On at the beginning of the sound and then track the changes by generating Pitch Bend messages? Or, should it generate a new Note On with a different number when the pitch crosses a certain threshold? Will a change in volume generate MIDI Volume (Controller 07) messages? Or, will new Note Ons be issued that have different velocities? At what point in the decay of a sound will a Note Off be sent? The more versatile of these devices allow the user to make some of these decisions—and thus adapt the unit to differing conditions, instruments, and performance styles.

The filtering capability of a pitch-to-MIDI converter is another important issue. Sounds that are rich in harmonics may make the converter interpret the pitch as being higher than it actually is, and MIDI note numbers an octave, a twelfth, or some random interval higher than the fundamental may be generated.

Auxiliary Controllers

Because MIDI is such a rich language, designing a controller that can take advantage of the entire command set is almost impossible. To keep costs down, manufacturers usually don't include more than a couple of sliders, pedals, or other physical controllers on the typical keyboard. But since musicians can take advantage of a large number of control surfaces—especially in live performance—some manufacturers have created add-on devices that expand the musician's control over the synthesizer. These are usually boxes mounted with sliders, pedals, buttons, or other mechanical controls. The simpler of these devices generate Controller or Pitch Bend data, while the more sophisticated can send program changes and complex command strings on multiple channels. An *auxiliary controller* may even have internal memory for a number of setups that assign different functions to the various physical controllers. In live performance, these setups can correspond to different songs—causing the auxiliary controller to assume a totally new identity with each song.

Experimental Controllers

Coming up with unusual ways of generating MIDI data is a favorite occupation of engineers and musicians. Unfortunately, most large electronic musical instrument companies avoid manufacturing unusual controllers because they feel that potential sales will not support the research and development necessary to bring such a device to the marketplace. However, small companies and individuals have designed some novel, and potentially useful, devices. Here are a few interesting examples of *experimental controllers*.

The Hands is a custom controller (which is not commercially available) designed by Dutch composer Michel Waisvisz. The device consists of two strap-on aluminum units which are worn on the performer's hands. Each unit contains twelve finger-controlled buttons, which send Note Ons and Note Offs for the twelve tones of the chromatic scale. Four mercury switches, which detect tilting motions, change octaves. A button for one thumb changes MIDI channels, while a button for the other thumb sends Program Change commands. Another button sends Sustain On and Sustain Off (Controller 40H), and a thumb-controlled potentiometer sends Pitch Bend. Most interestingly, a sonar detector is built into the system, which constantly measures the distance between the two units and translates it into note velocities. When a "scratch" button is held down, and the hands are moved towards or away from each other, the system generates a new Note On every time it detects a change in the distance between the hands. This creates a "scratching" or "ripping" effect.

The Video Harp is the invention of Paul McAvinney of Carnegie-Mellon University. It contains a light source and an array of mirrors that sense the changing positions of the user's fingers. The device is worn on the player's shoulders and chest, something like a large accordion. Finger position is used to determine pitches; the distance from the surface translates to velocity; and the speed of motion controls MIDI Volume (Controller 07), which allows for a bowing effect. The distance between two fingers can be interpreted as Pitch Bend. Like the Thunder, the Video Harp can be used to modify preprogrammed MIDI events in real time, thereby acting as a "conductor."

Other new devices are coming out of inventors' workshops all the time. One engineer has created a device that translates motion from a Nintendo Power Glove (normally used for sophisticated computer games) into MIDI data, so that simply moving the hand and fingers in space can control MIDI-based sound. Engineers at the Media Lab at the Massachusetts Institute of Technology (under the direction of composer Tod Machover) have developed *Hyperinstruments,* such as the Hypercello, which translates finger position; cello bowing position, speed, and angle; and other physical parameters into computer data, including MIDI. This information can directly control synthesizers or feed data to complex performance algorithms. In this way, artists can create entire pieces out of a few physical gestures.

There are even direct human-to-MIDI interfaces, which read changes in the minute electrical currents that flow through the body and translate them into MIDI commands. The Biomuse (developed at Stanford University and now distributed by BioControl Systems) uses sensors attached to the brain, the eyes, and various muscles to produce up to eight channels of data. This physical data can be translated into any MIDI data: muscle tension into note numbers and velocities, eye movements into Pan Control (Controller 0AH), brain waves into Program Changes, and so on. It lets a person perform complete musical compositions without using any controller hardware at all. The machine can be taught to respond to certain combinations of muscle gestures. For example, different right-hand finger movements might have different meanings depending on the position of the left arm. The inventors claim that future versions of the brain-wave sensor may be two-way interactive. This would allow the performer and the system to actually learn from each other—thus pointing the way to some of the favorite scenarios of science fiction writers.

Such radically different controllers are difficult to market largely because musicians, especially successful and busy ones, are reluctant to take the time to learn a totally new way of playing music. However, experimental controllers are an important vanguard in expanding the parameters of music performance.

Studio Control with MIDI Hardware Controllers

MIDI has many nonmusical uses. MIDI can run mixers, effects, tape decks, and other studio gear—as well as lighting rigs, museum exhibits, and almost anything else that can benefit from real-time digital control. Keyboards and other music-oriented input devices are not necessarily the most efficient way to generate the kind of control data needed to run nonmusical gear. For this reason, several manufacturers have developed programmable control surfaces for nonmusical applications. Some are simply a bank of faders designed for MIDI-based level control in a mixer or sequencer. Some are switch or relay boxes that provide contact closures to create audio mutes—or to trigger other electrical devices via specific MIDI commands. Others, designed for more elaborate types of control, combine sliders, buttons, and jacks for footswitches or pedals that are similar to the auxiliary controllers described earlier. Some devices are designed for transport control, and may combine some of these features with large tape recorder–style buttons and "scrub" wheels. More sophisticated hardware controllers may be programmed to allow any physical control to generate almost any kind of MIDI data as single events or in programmable strings of data. These can be notes, Controllers, Program Changes, Start/Stop commands, Clocks, Song Position Pointers, and even System Exclusive messages.

Synthesizers

Most synthesizers, both with and without keyboards, are polyphonic. Monophonic (Mode 4) synthesizers are those that can simultaneously play different programs on different MIDI channels, where each channel has exactly one voice. Although very few truly monophonic synthesizers are available today, most synthesizers can be programmed to behave as if they can only play one note at a time. Multitimbral synthesizers will respond to multiple MIDI channels simultaneously with different programs on each channel, and will play more than one note on each of those channels, thereby simulating the function of several polyphonic synthesizers in one unit. Many multitimbral synthesizers have built-in multitrack sequencers that take advantage of the multitimbral capabilities.

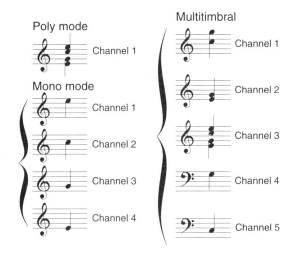

Drum Machines

Drum machines are synthesizers that produce percussion sounds in response to physical stimuli or MIDI data. The sounds themselves can be sampled (digitally recorded) or synthesized and stored in internal Read-Only Memory (ROM), or on external cards or cartridges. Drum machines contain built-in sequencers, which allow you to program short sequences (called *patterns*) a measure or two long. These patterns (which are sometimes also called *programs*) can be combined to form *chains* (or *songs*). More sophisticated drum machine features include:

- velocity-sensitive pads, which give each drum sound a range of volumes

- pressure-sensitive and/or position-sensitive pads

- switching among sound banks via MIDI Program Change messages

- ability to sample live or recorded sounds

- programmable and storable envelope, pitch, or direction (forward or backward) of their ROM sounds

When used in a MIDI setup, a drum machine usually operates in one of four ways.

1. It plays its internal sequences, using its internal clock, and sends MIDI Timing Clocks from its MIDI Out jack to control the tempo of a sequencer.
2. It plays its internal sequences, not locked to its internal clock, but rather to MIDI Timing Clocks coming from an external source (such as another sequencer or a tape recorder with a SMPTE timecode or FSK track). Some machines can even play from SMPTE or MIDI Time Code directly.
3. It generates MIDI notes based on its internal sequencer, and uses either its own clock or an external one. This technique allows a very limited set of notes and dynamics, and so is favored by minimalist composers.
4. It ignores its internal sequencer entirely, and simply receives MIDI notes like any other MIDI instrument.

In most professional setups, the fourth mode is the preferred one, because it centralizes control in the main sequencer. Some newer drum machines dispense with internal sequencing capabilities entirely, and are designed to be used this way exclusively. (These are known as *drum synths* or *percussion modules*.) Each sound in a drum machine responds to a particular MIDI Note On message (for example, the kick drum might be note number 24H, crash cymbal 31H, and so on). So, you can play percussion parts in to the sequencer in the same way that you play any other part, using the controller of your choice. Drum machines played this way respond to MIDI velocity, and usually offer many more gradations in volume than when playing back their internal sequences, even if they have velocity-sensitive pads.

Note	Instrument	
27	High Q	
28	Slap	
29	Scratch Push	
30	Scratch Pull	
31	Sticks	
32	Square Click	
33	Metronome Click	
34	Metronome Bell	
35	Kick Drum 2	
36	Kick Drum 1	
37	Side Stick	
38	Snare Drum 1	
39	Hand Clap	
40	Snare Drum 2	
41	Low Tom 2	
42	Closed Hi – hat	[EXC1]
43	Low Tom 1	
44	Pedal Hi – hat	[EXC1]
45	Mid Tom 2	
46	Open Hi – hat	[EXC1]
47	Mid Tom 1	
48	High Tom 2	
49	Crash Cymbal 1	
50	High Tom 1	
51	Ride Cymbal 1	
52	Chinese Cymbal	
53	Ride Bell	
54	Tambourine	
55	Splash Cymbal	
56	Cowbell	
57	Crash Cymbal 2	
58	Vibra – slap	
59	Ride Cymbal 2	
60	High Bongo	
61	Low Bongo	
62	Mute High Conga	
63	Open High Conga	
64	Low Conga	
65	High Timbale	
66	Low Timbale	
67	High Agogo	
68	Low Agogo	
69	Cabasa	
70	Maracas	
71	Short Hi Whistle	[EXC2]
72	Long Low Whistle	[EXC2]
73	Short Guiro	[EXC3]
74	Long Guiro	[EXC3]
75	Claves	
76	High Wood Block	
77	Low Wood Block	
78	Mute Cuica	[EXC4]
79	Open Cuica	[EXC4]
80	Mute Triangle	[EXC5]
81	Open Triangle	[EXC5]
82	Shaker	
83	Jingle Bell	
84	Bell Tree	
85	Castanets	
86	Mute Surdo	[EXC6]
87	Open Surdo	[EXC6]
88		

Midi notes on a keyboard correspond to percussion instruments

When drum machines are played via MIDI, usually all the sounds respond to data on a single MIDI channel. Many machines offer separate audio outputs for different drum sounds. In this way, individual sounds can be isolated in a mix for processing, just as you'd put individual drums on their own tracks in a multitrack tape session. The sounds in drum machines are usually "one-shot" samples, with no real-time control over duration. This means that the machine can get a Note Off message almost immediately after the Note On with no effect on the sound. Some machines will let you cut off a drum sound before its natural envelope plays out (such as damping a crash cymbal), if you follow the initial Note On with an identical Note On that has a very low (but not zero) velocity value.

Samplers

Samplers are devices that play back digital recordings of actual sounds rather than using digital mathematical processes or analog oscillators and filters to generate sound as do conventional synthesizers. A sampler's sounds are loaded in to RAM while the sampler is in use, and stored on disks (floppy, hard, or optical) before the power is turned off. Most samplers include a record function, with line-level inputs and often microphone preamps as well. Some samplers have a fixed amount of RAM, while others can be expanded by using SIMM chips (*Single In-line Memory Module*), which are commonly used in personal computers.

Samplers can produce more realistic sounds than synthesizers can, but they also require significantly more memory for playing and storing sounds. Besides playing music, samplers can record and play back sound effects, ambient background tracks for films and other visual media, sung vocals, and even dialogue.

Samplers usually have onboard editing facilities for recorded sounds. They can also transfer sounds to a computer for editing, using System Exclusive, Sample Dump Standard, serial protocols other than MIDI, or a SCSI-based protocol called SMDI.

Like synths, samplers come in two flavors: with keyboards and without. As far as MIDI is concerned, they behave essentially the same as synthesizers—both transmitting and receiving. Models are available that play multitimbrally, and a number of these have multiple output jacks so that individual sounds can be isolated in a mix. Some drum machines allow the user to record his or her own sounds, although this type of device is disappearing in favor of general-purpose samplers.

A special class of samplers can only play back sampled sounds, and not record them. These are known as *sample players* or ROM *samplers*. The sounds are burned into ROM, either internally or on cards. (You might consider nonsampling drum machines to be in this class.) Some sample players produce only a few sounds (such as an assortment of different piano sounds) while others have a very wide range of choices.

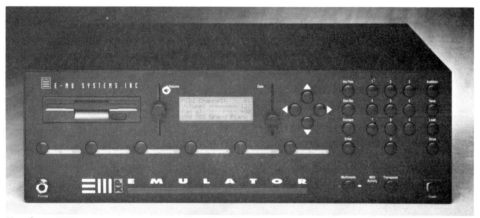

Emulator EIIIXP

As with synthesizers, some samplers exist as add-on circuit boards designed to fit inside a computer. These are available in several forms, including:

- ROM-based, playback-only units

- playback only units with RAM that load samples over a SCSI bus from a hard disk, CD-ROM, or sample-editing program

- full-function recording and playback samplers

Sampler cards are useful in sound research, multimedia production, audio post-production, and conventional music composition.

The distinction between synthesizers, samplers, and sample players is becoming fuzzier as the cost of the technology comes down. Some samplers include a basic library of sounds in ROM, as well as user-recordable RAM. Many sample players without sampling capabilities of their own can load new samples from cartridges, floppy disks, or from other samplers or computers using MIDI Sample Dump Standard messages, or a new non-MIDI protocol called SMDI. Most newer synthesizers use ROM samples as part of their sound-making machinery (along with more conventional digital synthesis and processing methods). Some can even replace their internal samples using external media, MIDI, or SMDI. The term MIDI *workstation* usually refers to an instrument that combines multitimbral synthesis, sampling, and sequencing into one package.

Receivers

Some devices are designed only to receive the MIDI data generated by transmitters. These include synthesizers and samplers without keyboards, computer add-on cards, signal processors, and other devices discussed in this section.

Synthesizer Modules

A major new category of products which appeared soon after the adoption of MIDI was the keyboard-less synthesizer (called a *synth module, sound module, expander module,* or *slave*. The MIDI In jack allows a synth module to be controlled from any MIDI transmitter, and operate just as if it had its own keyboard. When developing a new synthesizer, many manufacturers release versions both with and without keyboards. The advantages of a keyboard-less synth module are in its size, weight, portability, mechanical simplicity, reliability, and cost. Some of these modules are exact duplicates of their keyboard brethren—and include the identical programming controls. Others have almost no controls, and are designed simply for playing sounds, not programming them. You can edit the sounds in most synth modules, however, using MIDI System Exclusive messages—either from a compatible synthesizer or from a computer patch-editing program.

Proteus/1 sound module

Computer Add-ons

Some synthesizers fit on a card that goes inside a computer. The simplest of these are fairly crude limited-polyphony boards primarily for use with computer games. Sophisticated synth cards are multichannel, multitimbral, high-quality devices designed for professional music production. Since they are inside the computer, they are not accessed with standard MIDI cables, but directly through the computer bus to which they're connected. Because of this, they need special *software drivers* installed in the computer's system software that make them accessible to sequencer software, keyboard controllers, and other MIDI transmitters. Apple's MIDI Manager is one such system. Synth cards (also called *sound cards*) form an integral part of most *multimedia* computer systems.

Pre-MIDI Synths

Many musicians have a favorite, pre-MIDI synthesizer, and feel that its sound can't be duplicated by newer MIDI instruments. Some pre-MIDI synthesizers can be fitted with MIDI, but these *retrofits* are usually not simple, and often involve heavy modification to the original instrument's electronics. Some require translation circuits, to convert MIDI data into digital or control-voltage signals that a pre-MIDI synth will understand. This isn't a project most musicians would want to take on alone—but there are commercially available retrofits for many popular pre-MIDI synths. There are also general-purpose MIDI-to-control-voltage and MIDI-to-trigger converters available that can be useful with some older instruments. The latter are particularly popular with dance music artists who value the sounds of pre-MIDI drum machines.

Signal Processors

MIDI control has become an important feature of audio processing gear. Any processing device that uses digital electronics—whether in the signal path itself, or merely to control analog signals—has the potential to be a MIDI receiver. The first such devices to appear were digital reverbs. These used MIDI Program Change messages to allow them to switch programs on cue in the middle of a mix—for example, from a short slapback echo to a long, stadium-sized reverb.

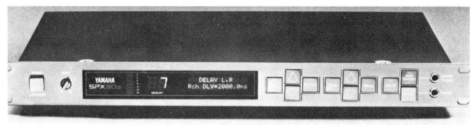

Yamaha SPX90II

More elaborate devices allow individual processing parameters to be altered in real time using MIDI notes, Controllers, and even Clocks. Here are a few examples of how MIDI messages can control the functions of signal processors.

Midi-Controlled Effects

Processor	Function	Midi message
Reverb	Decay time	Controller, note number
	Predelay	Controller, tempo (Clock)
	Wet/dry mix	Controller
	Early reflection level	Controller, note velocity
	Gate time and level	note duration (Note On/Off) and/or Note Velocity
Digital Delay	Delay time	Controller, tempo
	Feedback	Controller, Note Velocity
	Change in delay (chorus or flanging)	Controller, note number, or Channel Pressure
	Mix	Controller
	Pan position	Controller, note number
Pitch Shifter (Harmonizer)	Pitch change	note number, Pitch bend
Equalizer	Center frequency	Controller, note number
	Bandwidth (Q)	Controller, Note Velocity
	Level	Controller, Note Velocity, Channel Pressure
Compressor/Limiter	Attack/decay time	Controller, Note Velocity
	Thresholds	Controller
	Gate time and level	Controller, note duration, Note Velocity
Guitar Preamp	Distortion level or mix	Controller
	Harmonic structure	Channel Pressure
	Filter resonance	Note number, Note Velocity

Patch Bays

A valuable adjunct to any mixing console is a MIDI-switchable patch bay. This serves the same purpose as a conventional audio patch bay—but instead of using removable cables to change signal routings, the routings are all done internally using relays and/or logic circuitry. Every routing can be stored as a "snapshot" in an internal memory register, and the memories are then accessed by MIDI Program Changes. For large studios with many sound sources and processors, being able to recall instantly a complex set of signal routings can be a major time-saver, especially when many different projects are in the works. A MIDI-controlled patch bay can also be extremely helpful in live performance, when a guitarist has a large number of "stomp boxes," and needs to change effects configurations with a single stomp. (MIDI-controlled audio patch bays are not to be confused with patch bays that switch MIDI signals themselves, which we'll discuss a little later.)

Mixers and Level Controllers

MIDI-controlled mixers and level controllers fall into three general categories. The simplest is the multichannel MIDI-controlled *VCA (voltage-controlled amplifier)*. This device contains a number of discrete amplifiers (eight channels is common). Each of these channels has its own input and output—and each channel's level can be controlled in real time using MIDI note or Controller messages. These devices are used in conjunction with a conventional mixer (although some of them have stereo mix outputs as well). The second type of MIDI mixer may be characterized as a true mixer. This device stores control settings in an internal memory register. These settings can then be recalled with a Program Change message. These "snapshot" mixers can normally have up to 128 memories, corresponding to the 128 available Program Change messages. Some mixers can have even more, using auxiliary messages—including Bank Select (Controllers 00 and 20H)—to switch banks of programs. The third type of MIDI mixer is a real-time device, in which specific mixing controls can be moved in real time with Note On or Controller messages.

The amount of MIDI control available from mixer to mixer varies widely. Most of the mixers used in large multitrack tape studios use MIDI simply to set channel mutes and routings. Other mixers provide complete control over fader levels, send and return levels, eq frequency and gain, pans, and even internal effects. In addition to providing onboard storage, many mixers allow their internal memories to be dumped over SysEx to an external medium—so many sessions can be stored off-line and recalled quickly.

Lighting Controllers and Theatrical Devices

Since lighting and special effects are such an important part of music performance today, it only makes sense that devices for controlling visuals should be able to respond to the same types of commands that are creating the music. Simple *lighting controllers* execute individual contact closures from MIDI note, Controller, or Program Change commands. In addition to lights, this type of device can be used to control slide projectors, flash pots, or even household appliances (yes, there could yet be a MIDI toaster!). More sophisticated controllers can execute preset commands or scenes from Program Changes or Song Select messages. They also permit real-time control over individual or groups of lighting instruments using note or Controller commands, much like audio mixers. In addition, some controllers can manipulate chaser lights, lightning effects, and other types of rapid visual movements with MIDI Clocks. The new MIDI Show Control addendum to the MIDI spec expands this concept by an enormous amount—extending it to all possible functions of any kind of live show.

MIDI Processors

This class of equipment differs from MIDI-controlled audio processors, in that a *MIDI processor* allows for MIDI data itself to be changed as it passes through the device. Though they're discussed here as individual devices, many products combine several of these functions.

Splitters and Mergers

As we mentioned earlier, MIDI signal lines can't be split or combined electrically as easily as audio signals. *Splitters* (also known as *thru boxes*) and *mergers* are required for those tasks. Mergers are the more complex of the two, because they have to be able to tell when a message is complete, so as not to interrupt it.

Channel Filters

In the early days of MIDI, a number of synthesizers were produced that could only receive in Omni mode. These instruments were useless in a sequencer/multisynthesizer setup, because there was no way to get them to play individual sequencer tracks. They would play everything the sequencer sent out, on every channel. *MIDI channel filters* were introduced in response to this problem. These remove the data on all but one particular channel and feed the result to the synth. Although this particular problem is largely a thing of the past, channel filters are still useful, and can improve the MIDI response of some devices. In many setups—especially those that use daisy-chains—all MIDI data goes through every device on line. If the data is particularly dense, some devices will respond more slowly as their microprocessors sort out which data to respond to and which to ignore. (Note that the speed of the MIDI data passing through is unaffected.) A channel filter placed before the device's input can thin the data stream enough to eliminate such delays. (Of course, that instrument can no longer pass on the complete stream of information to the rest of the devices in the daisy-chain, so a splitter will sometimes be required as well.)

Other Filters

There are other devices designed to filter out specific types of MIDI data—either that coming from a transmitter or going to a receiver. For instance, some keyboards constantly send Channel Pressure messages, to which many other synthesizers do not respond (or which result in undesired types of responses). This can result in excess data on the MIDI line. And if the keyboard's output is being recorded by a sequencer, much of the sequencer's capacity will be wasted on these superfluous Channel Pressure commands. Inserting a filter at the keyboard's output can solve this problem. A filter can also be helpful when used with a transmitter that sends All Notes Off messages too often. Filters can also be used to eliminate unwanted Program Changes, Controllers, and/or Clocks in a variety of situations.

Time Shifters

A *time shifter* allows several tracks of MIDI data to be delayed or advanced in relation to one another while they are playing. The best example of this type of device is the Feel Factory, which, sadly, is no longer available. This remarkable device was used primarily to establish rhythmic grooves in which tiny adjustments of different beats could create significant changes in the "feel" of the track. The concept was born in an article written by Michael Stewart, a composer and programmer, which appeared in *Electronic Musician* magazine in 1987 (and was subsequently reprinted in Craig Anderton's book *Power Sequencing for Master Tracks Pro* [Amsco Publications]). While some other companies have made tentative attempts to create real-time delay controllers, none have been as comprehensive as Stewart's device.

Midi Patch Bays

Not to be confused with MIDI-controlled audio patch bays, MIDI *patch bays* serve a parallel function: they are switchers for MIDI lines. In a studio with many transmitters and receivers, a MIDI patch bay can be enormously helpful in organizing and storing MIDI cable routings. In a studio with multiple devices, MIDI patch bays facilitate System Exclusive bulk dumps from the devices to a computer. This is particularly important when each device demands two-way communication with the computer (for handshaking) but only a limited number of MIDI Ins to the computer are available. A patch bay can quickly change which devices are connected to which inputs, allowing the dumps to occur.

Some patch bays consist simply of switches, which allow changing of MIDI cable routings from the front panel. More elaborate patch bays may contain filtering, processing, and merging functions. Another useful feature found on more sophisticated devices is the ability to store "snapshots" of routings to internal memory locations, from which they can be recalled with Program Change messages. There is one important thing to watch out for in such a setup: it is possible to send a Program Change that will call up a new routing that disconnects the input cable that carried the Program Change to the MIDI patch bay. If that happens, you won't have any further control over the patch bay.

Mappers and Event Processors

Mappers and *event processors* are devices that change one kind of MIDI data into another in real time. They are most useful in live performance situations, but can be found in studios as well. These devices can move data from one MIDI channel to a different channel or transpose note numbers by a fixed amount. They may also be able to store Program Change maps, through which the reception of a specific Program Change number triggers the transmission of a different Program Change number. This is useful for controlling a synth that has fixed (or limited) program registers from another synth with a higher capacity. Processors can also be used to alter velocity curves so that a keyboard that doesn't send extreme high or low velocity values can control a synthesizer that expects the whole range of values. Processors can change the *taper* of a keyboard (that is, how it responds to physical velocity), giving the illusion of a "harder" or "softer" keyboard. Similar features are available that alter Channel Pressure.

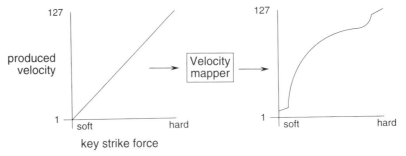

velocity mapping

Other event processors perform more elaborate functions, including: repeating or arpeggiating notes by varying either note numbers or channels, turning chords played on a keyboard into guitarlike strums, sending Start or Stop messages in response to certain note or Controller messages, translating one Controller to a different one (or to Channel Pressure), inverting Controller or note information, or even serving as one- or two-track minisequencers. Computers make excellent event processors, and programs that carry out these tasks are relatively easy to write. Many processing functions are also included in larger programs like sequencers. Several high-level dedicated programming languages have been developed that can serve as extremely sophisticated event processors.

Some processors can assign incoming data from individual channels to specific outgoing MIDI cables—thus filtering and channelizing in one operation. Some of these devices are designed to work with conventional MIDI inputs, while others work with special high-speed protocols that communicate directly with a computer. These processors can also enable a system to have more than sixteen MIDI channels.

Sequencers and Computers

Sequencers are devices that record MIDI data, store it in memory along with timing information, and play it back on command. A sequencer can be a stand-alone box, software in a computer, or a component of a synthesizer.

Simple sequencers record on a single track and store all recorded MIDI data together. These sequencers may mix data from several MIDI channels and allow overdubs, but they don't allow different overdubs to be edited separately. More sophisticated sequencers have multitrack capabilities and allow for separate recording, editing, and playback of four, sixteen, sixty-four, or up to several hundred tracks.

A sequencer built in to a synthesizer is usually designed primarily to play that synthesizer's internal sounds. Usually the synth can be put in multitimbral mode so that different timbres may be played on different tracks. Many of these sequencers can also output MIDI event data and control other synthesizers as well.

Computers make excellent platforms for sequencers because they usually have plenty of internal memory, disk storage, and large visual displays. Special software is needed to turn a computer into a sequencer. Specialized hardware may also be needed to enable communication between the computer's serial ports and MIDI instruments. This gadget is called a MIDI *interface.*

Aside from acting as a sequencer, a computer may serve in a wide range of other roles in the MIDI studio, including:

- *patch editors,* which use System Exclusive data to store and edit programs in synthesizers and other MIDI devices

- *patch librarians,* which store and organize programs for particular models of synthesizers

- *algorithmic* and *interactive composition tools,* which generate and process musical data in real time according to a set of preset or user-defined rules

- *sample editors,* which import sounds from samplers, edit them, and send them back again

- *notation programs,* which convert real-time playing into readable music notation, and conversely, create MIDI performances from scores entered manually into the computer

- *hard-disk recording systems,* which digitally store audio, often in conjunction with MIDI sequencers and synchronizers

- *educational programs,* which use MIDI for ear-training, dictation, theory, and performance exercises

- *film* and *video programs,* used to create lists of events and tempos for film scoring and sound-effects editing (and automate the process)

- *real-time* MIDI *data processors* (described above)

- *multimedia programs* and *authoring systems,* which use MIDI for producing music and sound effects

Synchronizers and Converters

A MIDI *synchronizer* is a special type of processor that works with timing signals to allow time-based MIDI equipment—drum machines and sequencers—to play in sync with other time-based equipment—such as audio and video tape recorders or pre-MIDI sequencers and drum machines. We'll deal extensively with synchronization in Chapter 7, but here is a brief discussion of some of the devices available.

MIDI to Non-MIDI Drum Machines

These convert MIDI Timing Clock commands to discrete electrical logic (or *TTL*) pulses in order to drive drum machines that sync to such pulses. Like MIDI devices, some of these drum machines use 24 pulses per quarter note (*ppq*). Other machines use 48, 96, 192, or other ppq rates which must be interpolated from the MIDI Timing Clocks. TTL sync is sometimes called DIN *sync* because it can appear at a DIN connector (which, on the outside looks just like a MIDI connector).

MIDI to FSK

FSK stands for *frequency-shift keying,* a technique that imposes binary data onto an audio signal by varying the signal's frequency in step with the timing pulses. The speed of the pulses is controlled by incoming MIDI Timing Clocks. The audio signal can then be used to drive a device that recognizes it (as some drum machines do)—or it can be recorded on tape. When the tape plays back, it is converted back to MIDI Timing Clocks, which can then be used to control a sequencer or MIDI drum machine. Unfortunately, there is no standard FSK configuration, so signals generated by one such converter often will not be understood by a different model.

A variation on FSK, called *Smart FSK,* periodically encodes location information (in the form of a Song Position Pointer) into its signal. When a tape is started at some point other than the beginning of the piece, the Position Pointer is sent out before the Timing Clocks start. Thus, the receiving sequencer or drum machine knows the point in the piece at which to start playing.

SMPTE to MIDI

SMPTE timecode (also called *SMPTE/EBU timecode* to include its European equivalent) is an audio signal that can be recorded on tape. This signal contains timing information in an absolute "time-of-day" format: hours, minutes, seconds, and frames (approximately 1/30 seconds). Unlike FSK or TTL sync, there is no tempo information included. A *SMPTE-to-MIDI converter* must therefore create its own tempos using an internally programmed *tempo map.* The SMPTE timecode numbers are used to determine starting and ending points. These provide an unchanging time reference from which to generate MIDI Timing Clocks (based on the tempo map). As with Smart FSK, a Song Position Pointer message is generated when SMPTE timecode first enters the converter (as tape starts to roll). The Pointer value is then calculated by comparing the incoming SMPTE numbers to the internal tempo map. These converters are sometimes called, for sake of clarity, SMPTE *to* MIDI *Clocks and Pointers.*

SMPTE to MIDI Time Code

MIDI Time Code is a way to get SMPTE information onto a MIDI line. It is used to synchronize sequencers that have their own built-in tempo maps, and can also trigger individual events in a program or device that contains a cue list. The cue list may include sound effects, a processing change, or some other studio function.

Transport Control

When tape and MIDI equipment are used together, the usual scenario is that the MIDI equipment follows the tape. This is changing, however, with the introduction of the MIDI *Machine Control* (MMC) and MIDI-controllable tape decks. These devices have transport controls that respond to MIDI messages (earlier models used System Exclusive messages, but these are being replaced by MMC-compatible devices). So, a Start command from a sequencer can start the tape deck, a Locate command from a sequencer can cause the tape deck to shuttle until it finds a particular SMPTE number, and a record-enable switch in the computer program can put an individual tape track into record mode. However, once the tape starts rolling, it becomes the master again as far as timing synchronization is concerned.

The MIDI Studio

Because MIDI has become so universally accepted, and because the compatibility aspect of it has been so successful, there is a nearly infinite number of combinations of equipment that can make up a MIDI studio. Theoretically, if a MIDI device conforms properly to the MIDI specification, it cannot become obsolete. Thus, a ten-year-old synthesizer can coexist very happily with the very latest samplers and processors. As the MIDI spec grows, new gear will appear with new capabilities—but every piece of MIDI equipment ever made will still be able to function with these new devices in the studio. True, there are some old synths in our studios we don't use very much, but that's because we don't like their sound much anymore—or because we can't control their performance parameters as we would like. It's not because anything has happened to MIDI to make them unusable. (And we still haven't found a whistle patch that can beat the one on the Casio CZ-101, especially in Mono mode.)

A MIDI studio will always have some kind of master controller. That controller is often a keyboard: either a synthesizer or a silent keyboard. Guitarists, wind players, or percussionists may also have auxiliary controllers in the studio. In the MIDI-automated studio, a faderlike control surface may also be used to simulate the action of a mixing console. A computer or sequencer will be used to record tracks of MIDI data. A computer may also function as a patch-editor or sample-editor. The sound-generating modules—synthesizers and samplers—will receive data from the sequencer or computer, which will also often perform the channelizing, filtering, and routing of the data. A MIDI patch bay is a helpful addition to allow easy changeover from one master controller to another. This device also allows the user to edit or load patches or samples into the modules or otherwise route data to and from various transmitters and receivers without going through the sequencer or computer.

Each sound module will be set up to receive on one or more MIDI channels, and will be responsible for a particular sound or set of sounds. Each module will also have one or more audio outputs. A drum machine connected to the sequencer can either play MIDI notes from a sequencer track, or it can play its own internal songs and patterns (which are synchronized to MIDI Timing Clocks generated by the sequencer). All of the audio signals produced by the modules go to a mixer, which in turn can be controlled by MIDI Program Change and Control Change messages. The automation data handling the mix can be part of the same sequence that is playing the notes. Outboard processing—such as reverb, eq, delay, or compression—can also be controlled by MIDI messages, so that different effects can be called up or modified at specific points in the sequence.

Some studios use multitrack tape decks to allow vocals and acoustic instruments to be recorded with MIDI tracks. Multitrack tape has another use, particularly in the smaller MIDI studio. If a studio has a limited number of sound sources, multitrack tape can allow each sound source to be used more than once in a composition. On the first pass the synthesizers and samplers play one set of sequencer tracks using one set of sounds, and these are recorded on one or more tape tracks. Then the synths and samplers are reset to different MIDI channels, and on the next pass they play different sequencer tracks with different sounds. These are recorded on different tape tracks. The process can be repeated until you run out of tape tracks, and of course tape tracks can be bounced down to make room for more tracks (within the limitations of the equipment with regard to distortion and noise generation).

As in other MIDI-with-tape setups, a timecode track is required on the tape for the sequencer to follow—this can be either FSK or SMPTE. A converter is also needed to change the recorded timecode into MIDI Clocks and Pointers or MIDI Time Code. The FSK tape track performs another important service in the smaller, multitrack studio. Instead of recording the output of a drum machine on several tape tracks and overdubbing acoustic instruments and vocals on the remaining tracks, a single track can be used for FSK. This timecode will drive the drum machine in perfect sync, just as if the drums were on the tape, but the tape tracks the drums would normally occupy are free for other instruments. When it comes time to mix, you can take the outputs of the drum machine directly into the board, alongside the tape outputs, and treat them just like extra tape tracks.

When producing music or effects for video, the videotape serves as the synchronization master. The videotape contains a SMPTE timecode stripe on one of its audio tracks, or *Vertical Interval Time Code (VITC)* inserted into its video signal. A sequence is constructed around the timings of images on the videotape. When it is played back, it locks to the videotape so that every audio event corresponds to the appropriate visual event.

Many video formats allow multiple audio tracks or have a dedicated track for SMPTE timecode in addition to the audio tracks. This allows the audio on the videotape (dialogue, ambiance, and sound effects) to be mixed in with the MIDI tracks. A more elaborate setup would slave both a multitrack audio deck and a sequencer to a video master for maximum flexibility. This requires special transport synchronizers (which are much more complex than timecode-to-MIDI converters).

Chapter 3
Composing Tools

MIDI equipment is commonly used to facilitate music composition. A MIDI sequencer allows you to record multiple musical performances on perfectly synchronized, independent, "virtual" tracks. Each of these tracks can play a different MIDI instrument. This gives you the capability of creating fully orchestrated works without the need to hire a lot of other musicians and without the expense of multitrack tape. The MIDI medium allows a great deal of flexibility when editing and manipulating the data. There are also ways to create MIDI data that don't involve any actual performance at all. In this chapter you will get a chance to explore the basic functions and features of compositional MIDI tools. In the following chapter, you will learn how to use many of the music-making techniques made available by MIDI.

Using a Sequencer

As you know, a sequencer records incoming MIDI messages from one or more transmitters or controllers, and records the time of each message. Calculation of the time is usually accomplished by comparing a particular message either to the time of the last message or to the starting time of the sequence. This process is known as *time stamping*. The sequencer then stores the messages with their time stamps in digital memory (usually RAM, although some sequencers write directly to disk). The composer can then tell the sequencer to recall the material at any time—causing a perfect copy of the original MIDI performance to be sent to one or more MIDI receivers.

Most sequencers are multitrack, which means that they allow a number of tracks to be recorded and overdubbed simultaneously. The tracks can then be edited, either individually or globally, and all played back together in sync. The number of tracks in a sequencer is limited by the capabilities of the hardware platform it uses and by the design of the sequencer itself. The simplest multitrack sequencers have 4 tracks, while larger ones have 64, 128, or even more.

Tracks and Channels

Often you'll want to assign each track to a single MIDI channel, so that it plays one instrumental sound. This follows the one-instrument-per-track convention of multitrack tape recording. There is no reason, however, why a track cannot contain data on multiple channels, and thereby address multiple instruments. Many sequencers that have fewer than sixteen tracks allow multiple-channel tracks, so that they can send data to all sixteen MIDI channels at once.

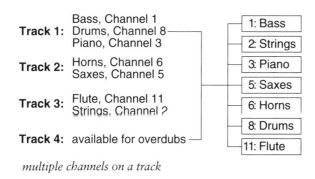

multiple channels on a track

multiple tracks on one channel

In a sequencer that plays multiple channels on each track, you don't normally do overdubs by assigning each instrument to a new track. This would use up the available tracks very quickly. Instead, tracks are *bounced;* that is, recorded tracks are merged to make room for new tracks. This technique is similar to bouncing on a small multitrack tape deck. However, because sequencer data is digital, there is no loss of fidelity over multiple generations. Once tracks are merged, separating them again for editing may be difficult (or, depending on the sequencer, impossible).

Contrastingly, in larger sequencers multiple tracks often play over the same channel. Most sequencers with more than sixteen tracks have this capability. The ability to place same-channel sequencer data on multiple tracks is useful when sending to a drum machine that's being played simply as a MIDI instrument (not using its internal patterns synced to MIDI clocks). A drum machine will typically receive all data on a single channel, but it can be very helpful to separate kick, snare, and tom notes, for example, onto individual tracks for easier editing. A similar technique is effective when simulating a large string section. You can enter the violin, viola, cello, and bass parts on separate tracks, but have them all play from one synthesizer or sampler by assigning each string track to the same channel.

Instruments that are separated on different tracks do not necessarily produce separate audio signals: If five tracks share a common MIDI channel, and if the synthesizer receiving that channel has only one audio output, then all five tracks will appear at that output. On the other hand, some MIDI instruments allow you to send different notes or sounds to different audio outputs—even if they are all triggered from the same MIDI channel. A common example of this is a drum machine that has individual audio outputs for different drum sounds. In this case, each track in the sequencer can correspond to an individual audio output on the drum machine. So, even though only one MIDI channel is used, each sequencer track can have its own audio fader on the mixing console.

multiple tracks sent to a drum machine

Data Manipulation

MIDI data recorded in a sequencer is performance data, not music or sound. It describes certain performance events—such as which key was pressed and how hard, or which pedal was pushed and how far. Since these events are recorded as numbers, they can be manipulated mathematically, and any parameter or group of parameters can be altered without affecting other parameters. This creates many interesting editing possibilities that are not possible in recorded audio. For example, a MIDI sequence can be played back at a speed different from the one at which it was recorded without changing the pitch of the music or its timbre. The events occur closer together or further apart, but they are otherwise unchanged. Conversely, a sequence can be transposed in pitch, by adding or subtracting a constant to each of the note numbers, without changing its speed. A piece of music can be reorchestrated simply by changing the channel number assignment of one or more tracks (so that they are played by different synthesizers) or by changing the programs on the receiving synthesizers. Individual events can be singled out and altered as well by changing a note's timing, pitch, velocity, and/or duration. Entire measures can be removed from a sequence, and the result will always be clean (unlike audio edits, where sustained envelopes, interrupted notes, and reverb tails can cause problems). Measures, beats, or time intervals as small as a tiny fraction of a beat can be removed from individual tracks without affecting the others. This allows a given track to "slide" forward or backward with respect to other tracks.

All sequencers let you edit data while they are not actually playing—but some let you perform edits in real time. This is a very fast way of trying out different editing operations and adjusting them on the fly. Of course, it is only really useful if the sequencer has an *Undo* function (described later).

Cut, Copy, and Paste

A sequencer allows you to move MIDI data around: changing the starting time of segments, juggling their order, repeating them, moving them to different tracks, merging two or more measures or tracks, and so forth. *Cutting, copying,* and *pasting* can involve whole tracks, multiple tracks, parts of tracks, or parts of multiple tracks. By copying a part of a sequence and pasting it immediately after itself, you've created a repeat. By copying from one track and pasting it onto another that plays at the same time, you've created an orchestral doubling. By pasting it slightly later, you've created an echo or a canon; or if you paste it to a track playing the same channel, and make the time differential only a few milliseconds, you can create a flanging effect. Pastes come in two flavors: *destructive* and *nondestructive.* Destructive pasting means that the information being pasted erases any information that already exists on that track during that period of time. Nondestructive pasting merges the data being pasted with the data that's already there.

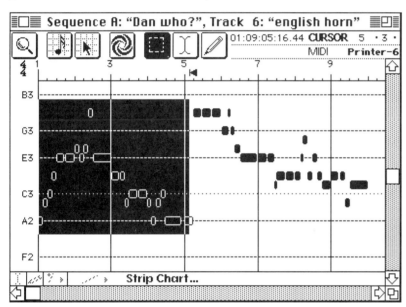

selecting an area to cut

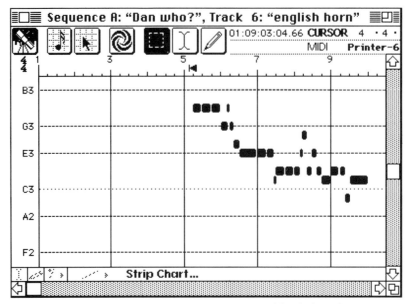

Cutting removes the selection and places it on an invisible Clipboard.

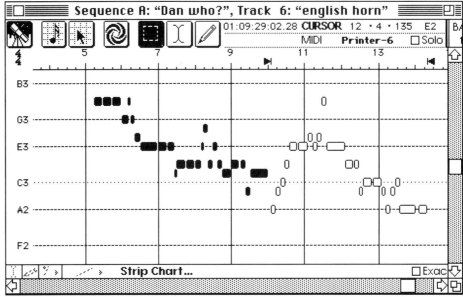

The contents of the Clipboard can then be pasted anywhere.

Step-time Entry

A sequencer's ability to play at different tempos makes it possible to record difficult passages at a slow tempo, then play them back much faster. *Step-time entry* allows even more accurate recording by letting you first specify the duration of notes, and then play them at any speed or rhythm. Most step-time functions allow a wide range of durations, including complex rhythms (like filling two beats with three notes, filling five beats with seven notes, filling three beats with nineteen notes, and so on). A new duration can be selected as you enter each note, so that you can program any conceivable musical line.

Some sequencing programs also include an articulation parameter, so you can specify *staccato* or *legato* playing. For example, if the step-time interval were set to a quarter note and the articulation to 50 percent, the result would be a series of eighth notes with eighth rests in between them. If it were set to 150 percent, the result would be a series of overlapping dotted quarter notes, playing one beat apart. Some sequencers get even fancier and allow you to specify a "swing" or "shuffle" ratio, which alternates lengths of notes. To get a swing pattern of dotted eighth notes followed by sixteenth notes, for example, you would specify a swing ratio of 75 percent.

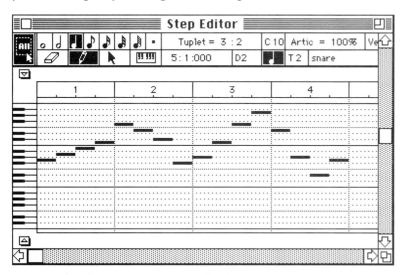

Step-timing with 100% articulation makes legato notes.

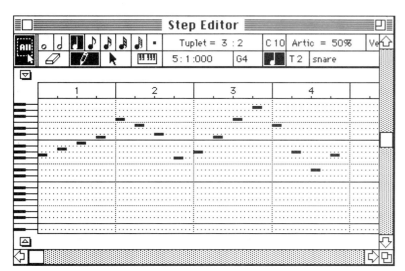

Step-timing with 50% articulation makes detached notes.

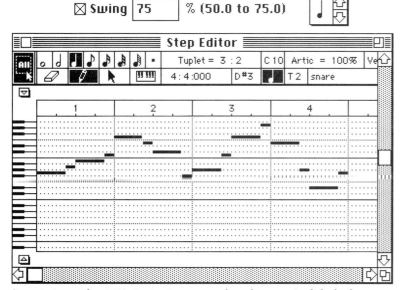

Step-timing with a 75% "swing" creates a dotted-quarter/eighth rhythmic pattern.

Quantizing

Quantizing, also known as *rhythm correction,* is used to correct rhythmic errors and inconsistencies in a recorded performance, such as notes that were played early or late. The degree of correction may be adjusted to the nearest beat or fraction of a beat, according to taste or usage. As with step-time entry, some sequencers allow swing or shuffle ratios to be specified when quantizing. Other sequencers allow you to take a rhythm pattern from one track and quantize the notes on another track in relation to it.

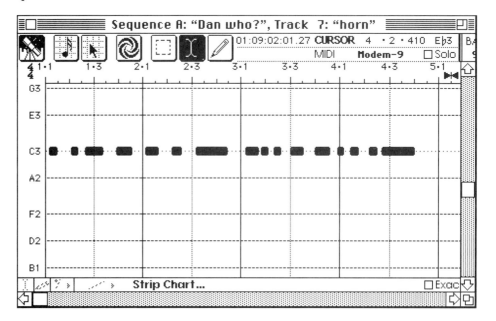

before quantizing

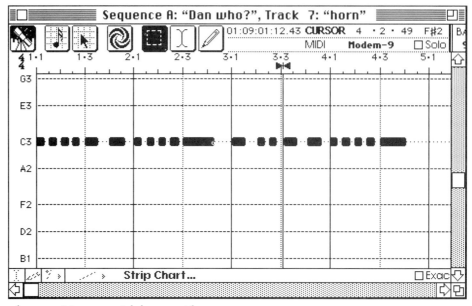

after quantizing to an eighth-note grid

A variation on quantizing is *deflamming,* in which notes that occur very close to each other in time are brought together so that they sound simultaneously, usually coinciding with the beginning of the first note in the group. *Arpeggiation* creates the opposite effect as the notes of a chord are separated out at a specified speed to create rhythmic patterns or guitarlike strums.

Along with step-time programming, quantizing is one of the major culprits responsible for giving MIDI-produced music a robotical or canned sound. Some sequencers have a sensitivity control, which moves early or late notes slightly off the beat to preserve a human quality in the performance. Other sequencers allow selective quantization, so that only notes on certain beats or sub-beats within a bar are quantized. Still others allow you to randomly move notes slightly off the beat to create a natural sound.

Punching

Like a tape recorder, a sequencer may allow replacement recording on a segment of a track. *Punch-in* and *punch-out* points can be predetermined, or they can be set on the fly. A sequencer can be told to punch in or punch out when a certain keystroke is received—or when a pedal is pressed. Setting correct punch points on a sequencer is less critical than on a tape recorder, because you generally don't have to worry about interrupting sustained notes or leaving notes hanging. The sequencer will perform appropriate edits automatically.

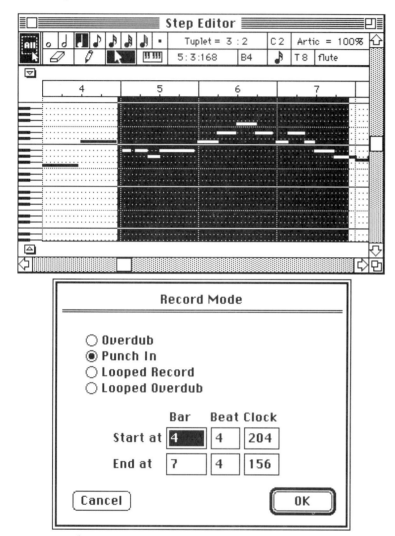

setting punch points

Because there is no "erase head" in a sequencer, it is possible to perform nondestructive punches. These allow new material to be laid over old without disturbing the earlier material. In this way, a drum fill can be put on top of an existing continuous pattern on the same track.

Undo

Most sequencers that run on a computer (and some standalone units) have an *Undo* function. This command tells the sequencer to ignore a take, punch, or edit and restore the sequence to the state it was in prior to the last operation. A *Redo* function lets you change your mind—and compare the "before" and "after" versions. The ability to undo an action is one of the more significant advantages of composing with a sequencer versus composing with tape.

Transposition and Scales

Transposing one or more events on one or more tracks is easy. Some sequencers offer a more sophisticated function called *scale mapping*. This function permits transposition according to a predetermined scale to maintain tonality. In this way, you could transpose the notes A-B-C up a third, yet remain in the key of C major. Without a predetermined scale, the passage would become C-D-Eb. However, by specifying a C major scale, the passage becomes C-D-E. This feature is useful when creating tonal harmonies. A variation on this feature is the ability to bring a passage into a certain key or mode without transposing it.

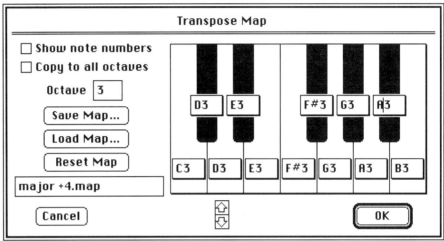

scale mapping

Parameter Translation

As mentioned earlier, hardware mappers are often used to change one type of MIDI message into another. Sequencers can do this too—and because they have the luxury of working with existing data, their functions can be even more elaborate. Using *parameter translation,* velocities can be changed into Controller values, note numbers, or pressure values—and vice versa. Modulation wheel positions can be recalculated as tempos. Note numbers can become Program Change messages. A set of pitches from one passage can be combined with a set of durations from another. Among other things, this capability allows MIDI transmitters with a limited range of data sources (for example, only a sustain pedal and a modulation wheel) to control a great many more performance parameters in a sequence than they could in a live performance.

Parameter Scaling

Scaling is another form of parameter manipulation offered by many sequencers. For example, you might use scaling to add thirty percent to all Channel Pressure messages to increase a track's brightness; or subtract 22H from all velocity bytes. A violin line might sound great with lots of vibrato, but when you double that line on a trumpet, the same amount of vibrato sounds totally wrong—by dividing the value of all Modulation Wheel messages on the trumpet track by three, you can solve the problem.

A very useful variation on this is changing and scaling over time. You can create a powerful crescendo, for instance, with a single command by having the sequencer set the velocities at the beginning of a passage to 64 (40H) and change them gradually to 122 (FBH) by the end of the passage.

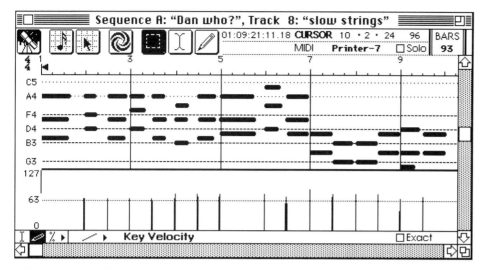

before velocity scaling

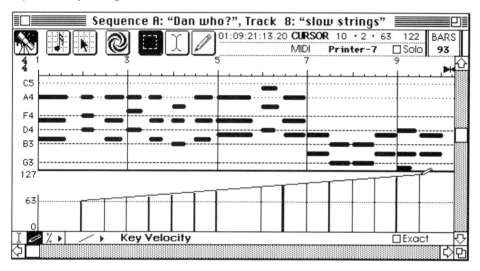

velocity scaling over time

Some sequencers also let you effect a percentage change over time. Using this feature, you could add a crescendo to an existing passage, yet preserve any velocity variations between notes. Specifying a starting velocity percentage of 60 percent and an ending percentage of 140 percent will produce a gradual increase in intensity—but it won't ruin the subtle note-to-note variations by replacing them with a strictly linear crescendo.

Logical Editing

Also known as *constrained editing,* or *editing by rule, logical editing* allows you to specify certain events within a group for editing. Specifications can often be combined with *Boolean logic* functions (such as *And, Or,* and *Except*). Here are some examples of logical editing specifications.

- Quantize all of the downbeats of a bass track, but not the notes in the middle of the measure.

- Take the pitchbend pattern from one track and apply it to a different track with different notes.

- Copy the notes from one track to another, but don't copy the sustain pedal movements.

- Remove all the Channel Pressure from a track. (You'd be surprised how useful this one can be.)

- Cut all of the notes that have a velocity value under 20H and are shorter than a sixteenth note (to correct errors in a part).

- Double a string part onto a clarinet track, but leave the bass notes and sustained treble notes out (by specifying that only notes whose numbers are above middle C [40H] and are shorter than a quarter note get copied to the clarinet track).

- Change a passage from C minor to C major (by transposing all E♭s, A♭s, and B♭s up one half-step).

Thinning

In the heat of performance, when using a good MIDI controller, it's easy to load up tracks with Pitch Bend, Modulation Wheel, Foot Pedal, Channel Pressure, and other continuous data. Excess data on a MIDI cable can cause problems, so it can be advantageous to remove unnecessary or redundant data. Many sequencers have a *thinning* function that allows this.

Graphic, Numerical, and Notation Editing

Especially on computer-based sequencers, a number of options are available for displaying MIDI data. Each has its advantages and disadvantages—and more sophisticated sequencers offer a choice of display modes. One of the most popular formats is to show notes and durations as horizontal lines or bars of varying lengths (often called *piano-roll notation*). In this format, velocities can be shown as vertical lines, colors, or shadings. Controllers, Pitch Bend, or Pressure may be shown as graphs of value versus time. Graphic displays often allow different magnification scales for examining data closely. Graphic editors usually require a mouse (with which you can select individual events or regions for editing).

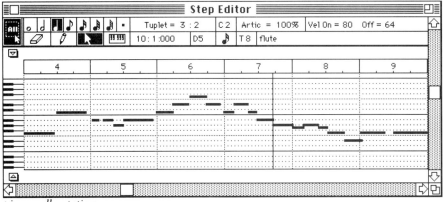

piano-roll notation

An event list displays a sequence of MIDI data as a list of numbers. Editing an event list (called *numerical editing*) is not as intuitive a process as graphic editing, but it is usually more precise. Numerical editing is preferable when editing events that have to be aligned with certain timings, such as music or sound effects that need to coincide with visual events. Thus, most numerical editors display data in musical time (measures, beats, and ticks), as well as SMPTE/MTC time (hours, minutes, seconds, and frames).

Event List Editor

Goto... | Filter | Insert: ♪ | PC | ⌨ | ⬒ | ↓ | ↓↓ | T8 | flute

Event	Measure	Chan	Data				
♪	4: 1:004	9	F3	!73	i64	0: 1:204	
♪	4: 2:238	9	C4	!73	i64	0: 1:204	
♪	5: 1:030	9	A#3	!73	i64	0: 0:108	
♪	5: 1:187	9	A#3	!64	i64	0: 0:154	
♪	5: 2:104	9	G#3	!73	i64	0: 0:153	
♪	5: 3:001	9	A#3	!64	i64	0: 1:192	
♪	5: 4:238	9	C4	!64	i64	0: 1:007	
♪	6: 1:233	9	D#4	!100	i64	0: 0:235	
♪	6: 2:228	9	F4	!73	i64	0: 1:003	
♪	6: 3:227	9	D#4	!60	i64	0: 0:207	
♪	6: 4:234	9	C4	!82	i64	0: 0:146	
♪	7: 1:136	9	D#4	!73	i64	0: 0:210	
♪	7: 2:102	9	C4	!73	i64	0: 0:127	
♪	7: 2:221	9	A#3	!60	i64	0: 1:011	
♪	7: 3:225	9	G#3	!56	i64	0: 1:017	
♪	8: 1:003	9	G3	!64	i64	0: 0:169	
♪	8: 1:159	9	G#3	!56	i64	0: 0:217	
♪	8: 2:133	9	G3	!60	i64	0: 0:136	
♪	8: 3:026	9	F3	!60	i64	0: 1:008	
♪	8: 4:024	9	D#3	!60	i64	0: 1:014	
♪	9: 1:012	9	F3	!64	i64	0: 1:120	
♪	9: 3:000	9	F3	!64	i64	1: 3:000	

an event list

Some sequencers allow you to view tracks in standard music notation. As we'll see later in this chapter, notation is often an awkward way of depicting MIDI data. However, many composers and arrangers prefer to work in standard music notation.

Tempo Control

All sequencers allow the user to specify a tempo at which to start a sequence—and most also allow the tempo to change during the course of the sequence. Tempo values are set in beats per minute (*bpm*), or in tenths, or even hundredths of a beat per minute. Depending on the sequencer's design, tempo changes may go into effect only on barlines, only on beats, or on any designated subdivisions of a beat.

Tempos (and often time signature or meter changes) are stored in a sequence in a *tempo map*. Some sequencers let you view the tempo map in its own window and edit it graphically and/or numerically. Other sequencers do not represent tempos graphically. Many sequencers allow the same type of changes to be made to tempos as to other musical parameters such as percentage or fixed-amount changes, changes over time, and so forth.

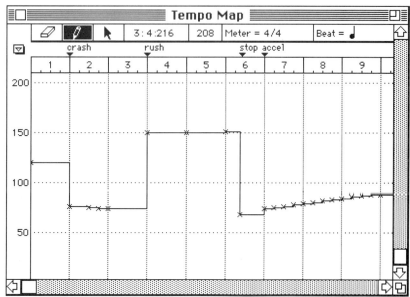

a tempo map

Some sequencers can record tempo maps in real time when locked to external M<small>IDI</small> Clocks. As the speed of the Clocks changes, the sequencer notes the difference in time between them, and records it. That tempo map is now part of the sequence. When the sequence is played back using the sequencer's internal clock, the tempos will change according to the recorded map. (This is not a recommended method for achieving synchronization between a sequencer and another device however.)

Another way to record a tempo map into a sequence in real time is to use a feature called *tap tempo*. This feature allows the sequencer to record the tempo map from a different kind of incoming signal: a M<small>IDI</small> note played on a keyboard or drum pad, an audio trigger, or the tapping of a computer key. Each "tempo tap" can be interpreted as a beat, a half-beat, or any rhythmic value the user specifies. This feature is useful when a rhythm track has already been recorded on tape—and the sequencer is now being used to record additional tracks. The kick-drum track is commonly used as the trigger (through an audio-to-M<small>IDI</small> convertor) for constructing the sequencer's tempo map. Used in a different way, this feature also allows a composer to play a free improvisation into a sequencer and tap in barlines after the fact, for editing, overdubbing, or notation purposes.

Time Fitting and Scaling

Time fitting is a feature that makes it possible to create tempo maps in a sequence automatically, so that musical events can match visual events on a film or video. *Time scaling* allows you to change the relative speed of all or part of a track without changing the tempo map. Since tempo maps are global for all the tracks in the sequence, time scaling is the function to use when you want to change the tempo of one track without disturbing the others. To rush a passage, simply scale it faster by a small amount. To double the speed of a passage, scale it up by 200 percent. The time scaling function sometimes allows you to determine whether or not note durations will be lengthened or shortened in the same proportion as the timings.

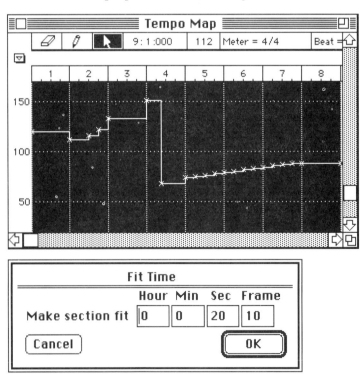

before time scaling

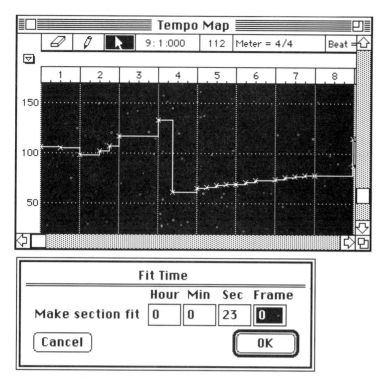

after time scaling

Additional Sequencer Features

Besides recording and manipulating recorded data, many other features have been developed to make sequencers effective creative tools. Here are a few.

Controller and Program Change Chasing

Because MIDI is a linear data stream, when you edit a sequence, it is possible for the synthesizers controlled by the sequencer to become confused. This is best illustrated by the following example of *Program Change chasing*. Say that you have a sequence that is three bars long. In the first bar, a Program Change message tells the synthesizer on Channel 1 to play a horn sound, and this instruction is followed by some notes. The second bar has no notes, but it does contain a Program Change message telling that same synthesizer to change to a flute sound. The third bar has more notes.

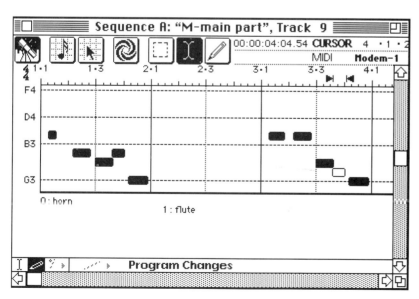

When you play the sequence normally, the synthesizer will play the horn notes, fall silent for a bar, and then play the flute notes. But imagine starting the sequence, stopping in the middle of the first bar, and then telling the sequencer to start playing at the beginning of the third bar. The notes in measure 3 will sound, but they will be horns, not flutes, because the sequencer never sent out the Program Change in bar 2. In a complex, multisynth setup, this can lead to a tremendous amount of confusion.

The same problem can occur with other types of MIDI data. For example, let's say you have a guitar lick with a big Pitch Bend sweep in it, and you stop the sequence during the sweep and jump to a place where there isn't any Pitch Bend information. The sequencer has no way of knowing that the Pitch Bend wheel was supposed to return to zero, because you skipped over that point. Thus, the track will play out of tune.

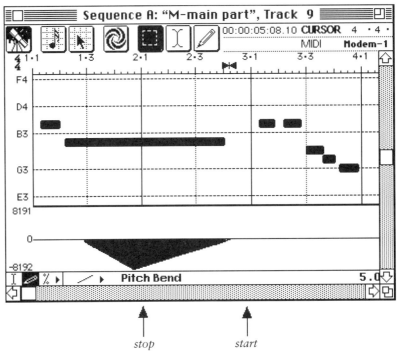

stop   start

Similar problems can crop up with Sustain Pedal, Channel Pressure, and especially MIDI Volume: Say you've played a sequence to the end, with a nice MIDI Volume fade on the track, and then you jump back into the middle of the sequence (where there is no Volume data). The track won't sound at all. *Chasing* eliminates this problem. When you start a sequence in the middle, the sequencer looks back over each track from that point. Before it starts playing, it executes the last Program Change, Channel Pressure, and Pitch Bend commands, as well as the command for each numbered Controller it encounters. This way, wherever you start playing the sequence, all of the instruments will be set properly for that point.

A few sequencers will also chase Note On messages. Thus if a note is supposed to be sounding, the sequencer recognizes this and plays it. This is most useful in sound-effects work, where there may be many ambient tracks from samplers playing at the same time. However, it is less useful in music composition, because it can cause a big chord to play every time you start the sequencer.

Scrubbing and Fast Play

Although finding a particular place in a sequence is easy if the sequencer provides good visual feedback, sometimes audio feedback can be helpful as well. This is particularly true when you are looking for wrong notes in a complex passage. On a tape recorder, you can cue precisely to a particular spot by rocking the reels back and forth with the playback head engaged against the tape. Some sequencers offer a similar function (usually accomplished by pressing a special key combination and dragging the mouse or cursor). In this way, you can *scrub* through a track at any speed you want, often backward as well as forward. However, when you play a track backwards, Note Offs have to be interpreted as Note Ons and vice versa.

A tape recorder will also let you engage the playback head while in fast forward or rewind, so that you can quickly find a particular spot by listening. Some sequencers offer a similar feature, allowing you to move through a file quickly while listening to playback. This feature is generally only possible in a forward direction, as the accurate recognition of Note Ons and Note Offs in reverse order at high speed can tax the capabilities of even the best sequencer.

Resolution

The *resolution* of a sequencer is the number of segments into which it can break down each beat (usually a quarter-note beat). These subdivisions are called *ticks*, *ppq* (*pulses per quarter*), or *ppqn* (*pulses per quarter note*). (They're also sometimes erroneously referred to as "clocks.") Typical sequencer resolutions range anywhere from 24 to 480ppqn, but some go as high as 1024ppqn.

It's very important to realize that a sequencer's resolution is not limited by the fact that Midi Timing Clocks occur only twenty-four times per quarter note. Instead, resolution is based on how finely the sequencer's own internal clock can be read, which theoretically can be as fast as a single instruction cycle of the computer or CPU chip the sequencer is running on. This same principle applies whether a sequencer is running from its own clock, or it is locked to external Midi Sync or Midi Time Code. When it is synced externally, the sequencer should be able to interpolate events between the incoming Timing Clock or Quarter Frame messages, and still resolve to the limit of its internal clock.

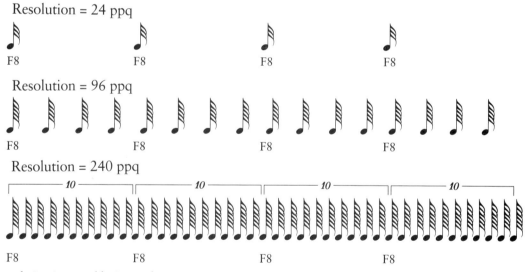

resolution increased by interpolation

Looping and Patterning

A lot of music, most notably dance-oriented music, is made up largely of repeating patterns. A *looping* function lets you create each pattern once, and then specify that it should repeat (either a specific number of times or until it is told to cut off). A loop can be a few notes or many bars. It can encompass one track or several. Many sequencers offer multiple loops of different lengths, and *nested loops*, in which loops repeat inside other loops.

Patterning is a variation on looping. This feature is an expansion of the track/pattern concept of drum-machine programming. In patterning, different sections of the composition are created as patterns (again, on one track or several). These are then called in the proper order by a master playlist. Patterning lets you restructure a composition very quickly—for an extended mix, for example, or a film cue whose timing has changed.

In some sequencers, the pattern/playlist structure is the primary mode of operation—and the more linear, tape-recorder-like model is a secondary mode. Many of these sequencers allow patterns (sometimes called *chunks* or *modules*), to trigger each other, or permit several patterns to nest within each other. Another feature lets the user select patterns at random and have them queue up—with each pattern waiting until the previous one is finished. This allows the order of a composition to be changed on the fly.

Markers

Many sequencers let you place *markers* in a sequence. These markers may denote the start of a verse, the entrance of a new instrument, or indicate a visual cue that's supposed to match up with a point in the sequence. Markers are generally placed with respect to musical references such as bars, beats, or ticks. However, when working with visual media it can be helpful if the sequencer can anchor markers to specific SMPTE times. In this way, if the sequence's tempo map changes, the marker still shows the placement of the visual event.

Like tab stops in a word processor, many sequencers provide a simple keystroke combination that lets you jump to a specific marker and start recording or playing.

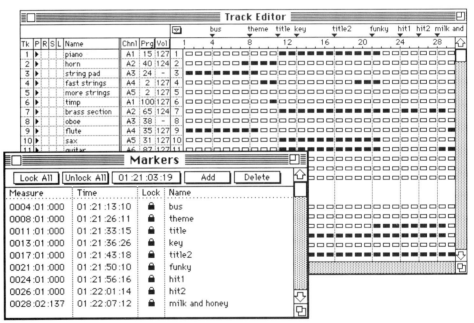

markers in a sequence

On-Screen Faders

Some sequencers provide *on-screen faders* that can be moved by a mouse as a sequence is playing, or while it is stopped. These control the volume of a track. Some sequencers provide real-time control for many more functions. For example, assignable faders may be used to control other Continuous Controllers, tempo, or relative velocity of one or more tracks. The faders can be moved by the mouse during recording—and will then move by themselves when the sequence is played back. They may also move when any MIDI data that they are programmed to respond to comes into the sequencer.

		Faders			
F1	120	▷	Modem-1	Volume (7)	▶
F2	14	▷	Modem-1	Modulation Wheel (1)	▶
F3	90	▷	Modem-1	Pan (10)	▶
F4	106	▷	Modem-2	Volume (7)	▶
F5	118	▷	Modem-2	Foot Controller (4)	▶
F6	26	▷	Modem-2	Pan (10)	▶
F7	110	▷	Modem-3	Volume (7)	▶
F8	80	▷	Printer-1	Volume (7)	▶
F9	106	▷	Printer-2	Volume (7)	▶
F10	38	▷	Printer-2	Modulation Wheel (1)	▶
F11	64	▷	Printer-3	Balance (8)	▶
F12	112	▷	Modem-4	Volume (7)	▶
F13	118	▷	Modem-13	Volume (7)	▶
F14	78	•			
TEMPO F14	40 – 360	○ Rcv ⊙ Send		1 17	⊡

on-screen faders

Often the receive and send functions of the faders can be set independently, so that incoming data can be output as something completely different. This output can be produced in real time, as part of the sequencer's Thru function, or at playback. For example, a keyboard that doesn't put out MIDI Volume (Controller 07) but does have a Foot Pedal (Controller 04) can be used to control the Volume on a receiving device if you set up a fader to receive Controller 04 and send it as Controller 07. This *remapping* function is not limited to Controllers: it can also be used for tempo, or for velocity. For example, you can set up a fader that will respond to Data Slider (Controller 06) on Channel 1—and that uses the current value of the Controller to determine the velocity byte of all Note Ons on Channel 12. The Controller value might be used to control the velocity bytes directly—or to scale the existing velocities of the notes by a positive or negative factor.

System Exclusive

As discussed previously, System Exclusive (SysEx) messages can be used to do bulk dumps of individual synthesizer programs or processor setups. SysEx messages can also facilitate dumps of entire device memories—or make individual sound changes beyond the capabilities of standard Controllers. Sequencers handle System Exclusive messages in various ways. Some can record System Exclusive messages in real time and play them back. They can receive small amounts of SysEx—enough, say, to change a voice parameter—store it, and play it back within the sequence at a particular time. Some units also allow you to examine the individual bytes and edit them as you would numeric MIDI data.

Some sequencers can record entire bulk dumps from a device and play them back later—restoring the programs that were in the device at the time of the original dump. This is a very useful way to store the contents of a synthesizer or processor—or even a room full of equipment. You can record and store all the banks of sounds and processor settings you've used in a certain sequence, then download them to your studio devices to restore the sequence's setup quickly and accurately. This lets you switch back and forth between projects without relying on a special librarian program. This type of dump is best done when no music is playing (such as at the beginning of a sequence). Generally speaking, synthesizers that require handshaking routines in order to dump sounds do not work well in this context.

Other sequencers can deal with SysEx in an "off-line" way, accepting bulk dumps and storing them in a library (usually on disk). These can then be called up and sent back out to a particular synth. This operation can only be done when the sequencer is not playing.

Variation Generators

A few sequencers include *algorithmic* or *variation* functions, which change existing data in real time according to rules defined by the user. These can be very powerful compositional tools, but they can also drive you quite crazy. (There are also programs that specialize in algorithmic composition, which are not sequencers.)

Multiple Ports

Although the MIDI specification allows only sixteen simultaneous channels, there is often a need for many more data channels. This need is met by allowing a sequencer to address multiple MIDI data streams. Many personal computers are fast enough to handle several MIDI lines—and sequencers are now available that can transmit anywhere from 32 MIDI channels (two cables) to 512 channels (thirty-two cables). Of course, special interfaces are needed to deal with such configurations, and the software must be designed to work with these interfaces. In some cases, special computer operating systems are required to accommodate large numbers of cables. Some hardware sequencers can handle multiple MIDI lines as well.

Mark of the Unicorn's Midi *Time Piece*

Multiple MIDI lines can also help to limit "MIDI choke," where so much data is being moved down the line that timings get fouled up. This can be avoided by putting controller-hungry tracks (such as mix automation) on different MIDI cables from rhythm-sensitive tracks (like drums or bass).

Midi Machine Control

Some more recent MIDI sequencers are able to transmit *Midi Machine Control* (*MMC*) commands. These allow the sequencer to control mechanical transports (such as audio or video tape decks and hard-disk recorders) directly from its own front panel. Some of the commands available with MMC include *Play, Record, Shuttle, Search, Punch,* and *Record-Enable.* Some sequencers are designed with built-in Midi Machine Control commands. Others let you customize MMC commands so that they can be sent in the background during normal sequencer functions.

Hardware and Software Sequencers

As described in the chapter "Midi Equipment," a sequencer may take the form of hardware or software. Each of these formats has its advantages and disadvantages.

Sequencers Built In to Synthesizers

Many multitimbral synthesizers (and some drum machines) have built-in sequencers that let you use the instruments as stand-alone compositional systems. These instruments have the advantage of being relatively portable and easy to set up (and the sequencer adds very little to the cost). These synths are good for beginners who cannot afford a separate sequencer or computer—or for traveling musicians who want to be able to do some composing in a hotel or dressing room.

Some synth-based sequencers allow storage of sequences on RAM cards or cartridges—while others have built-in disk drives. Some limit their track and channel capability to the number of multitimbral channels that the synthesizers themselves can handle. Others have greater capabilities, and can be used to control other MIDI synthesizers. Built-in sequencers have several important

limitations. Their displays are usually limited to small LED or LCD screens—
which means that editing operations can be clumsy and complicated. Editing
features in general are also limited—as is their memory capacity for recording
notes and other events.

Hardware Sequencers

Stand-alone hardware sequencers provide a good degree of flexibility
without requiring a large financial investment. Early hardware sequencers were
fairly limited as to the number of tracks and notes they could handle. However,
today's units normally have at least sixteen tracks and enough RAM to make
them practical for professional use. Editing features are generally fairly comprehensive, although small displays are still the rule. These devices are usually
quite portable, and, because they have few breakable parts, they are well suited
for stage and road use.

Most hardware sequencers cannot be upgraded. Thus, the size of song files
is limited by the capacity of the system's installed RAM. Due to manufacturing
costs, the resident operating systems of many hardware sequencers usually
reside on ROM chips that are not designed to be upgradeable. However, some
manufacturers distribute their operating systems on disks—allowing their
sequencers' software to be upgraded periodically with little trouble and minimal cost.

Computer-based Software Sequencers

Sequencing programs for personal computers provide the greatest flexibility and capacity. In fact, many advanced sequencer features can be found only
in software sequencers. Sequencing programs can be found for just about every
computer in existence—but the most popular platforms for sequencers are
Apple Macintosh, Atari ST, Commodore Amiga, and IBM PC (and clones).

Software sequencers can take advantage of many features of a computer,
including large displays, color graphics, mice, and *keyboard macros* (in which
several operations are combined into a single keystroke). The user has a choice
of what kind of computer to buy—as well as how much memory and what
type of disk drives to include.

Because sequencing software is distributed on floppy disk, it is easy to
install and upgrade. Many software manufacturers release several new versions
of their programs each year. Upgrading the product is merely a matter of
mailing out new disks to all registered users.

A single computer can be host to several different sequencing programs, so
a user can select a program to fit the needs of a particular project. In addition,
it becomes quite convenient to transfer data from one system to another: just
carry your sequences with you on disk.

Historically, the disadvantages of software sequencers are that they are
expensive and require a costly and bulky computer to run. Setting up a computer, monitor, keyboard, mouse, MIDI interface, and all of the necessary cables
can be a big job for a musician playing a different venue every night. Computers and monitors do not stand up well to travel—although the development of
powerful laptop computers from many manufacturers in recent years has
ameliorated this problem to a degree.

MIDI Files

MIDI files, formally known as *Standard MIDI Files,* provide a format
through which different sequencing programs can exchange MIDI data, especially sequences. The MIDI file specification was added to the MIDI 1.0 Spec in
July, 1988. Just as the ASCII format allows for transfer of text data among
different word processing and page layout programs, MIDI files allow you to
create a sequence in one program, and play, display, or modify it in another.
Most modern sequencers that run on computers handle MIDI files. Some hardware sequencers with disk drives can also generate and/or read MIDI files.
Sequencers don't normally save sequences in MIDI file format, but in their own
particular *native* formats. They use special export and import commands to
convert sequences to and from their native formats.

You can record all types of MIDI data in MIDI files, including System Exclusive commands. Each event in a MIDI file contains a *delta-time* indicating the time since the previous event—either in beats and fractions or in seconds and fractions. A *header chunk* at the beginning of the file contains resolution information and other global parameters.

MIDI files can also contain non-MIDI data, known as *meta events*, which may include sequence names, lyrics, markers, cue points, track names, time signatures, and key signatures. Unfortunately, the MIDI spec allows so much flexibility in how these events can be stored in the file, that a marker in one sequencer may be a cue point or text event in another. When MIDI files are exchanged between sequencers, these non-MIDI events often end up getting lost or put in the wrong place. Manufacturers are beginning to communicate more with each other to help alleviate these problems, but they may remain with us for a while.

Tempo maps can be stored in a MIDI file as well. In fact, a MIDI file may consist of nothing but a tempo map—which can be very useful in film and video applications. MIDI files express tempos in microseconds per quarter note, as opposed to beats per minute. This can help to insure accuracy when synchronizing to SMPTE timecode–based systems.

MIDI File Types

There are three types of MIDI files. *Type 0* files put all MIDI data on a single track. Each event maintains its channel number (1–16), so Type 0 files can still be fully multichannel. *Type 1* files put the data on one or more simultaneous tracks, any of which can be single-channel or multichannel. *Type 2* MIDI files use multiple tracks, each with one or more MIDI channels. These channels are sequentially independent of each other—that is, they don't necessarily share the same starting time or tempo map. These can be used to denote different patterns or subsequences which can be combined later into a single piece. Practically speaking, Type 2 files are very rare.

There is unfortunately no standard for cable assignments in a MIDI file, so files of more than sixteen channels cannot be readily exchanged among different programs. This is not to say that it's impossible to do so. If you have a sequence that uses multiple cables, you can send it as a Type 1 file to another sequencer that also can handle multiple cables. But when you open the file up in the new sequencer, you will have to set up the cable assignment for each track by hand. Fortunately, if you then save the file in the new sequencer's native format, the cable assignments get saved for future use.

MIDI files have also made it possible to exchange sequencer files across different computer platforms. Although an Apple Macintosh cannot read an Atari ST disk, a MIDI file created with a Macintosh program can be sent to an Atari over a serial cable or a modem, using any standard communications software capable of handling binary files. The Atari saves the file to disk, from which it can be read into a sequencer program. Some hardware sequencers can read MIDI files directly from disks created by Atari or IBM computers.

A recent addition to the MIDI specification simplifies this cross-platform exchange by allowing a MIDI file to be sent over a MIDI cable. This may sound not much different from simply playing a sequence on one sequencer and recording it on another in real time—but there are important advantages. With this method, there is no possibility of timing errors caused by MIDI's limited bandwidth (remember, a sequencer file may show two events taking place simultaneously, but on a MIDI cable there's no such thing as simultaneous events), non-real-time data is also transmitted as part of the file, and this type of file dump can often be much faster than playing and recording the sequence in real time.

MIDI Files and Nonsequencing Programs

Like MIDI itself, a wide variety of interesting uses have emerged for MIDI files since their introduction. Algorithmic composition programs can record their own output as they work and save the result as a MIDI file. The file can then be imported into a sequencer for study and editing. Some edit-list programs designed for audio post-production provide the ability to import MIDI files, so that sequences can be played along with sound effects and MIDI-based studio automation.

Many programs that combine hard-disk audio and MIDI cannot create their own MIDI data. They need to import MIDI files from other programs, like sequencers. Hit-list programs designed for film scoring use MIDI files to send tempo maps to sequencers—or to import existing sequences and fit them into their tempo maps.

In addition, MIDI files have created a genre of MIDI *records,* or recorded sequence files on disk. Many musicians make use of recorded sequences of popular tunes so that they can have the latest hits in their performance repertoires. Recorded sequences also make excellent material for students, who can practice soloing while playing along with a MIDI jazz combo, pop band, or symphony orchestra. The adoption of the MIDI file standard means that the providers of these sequences do not need to prepare different versions for every sequencer on the market; they can just create MIDI file versions for the most popular computers, and they will be able to accommodate most users.

Finally, recorded MIDI files, especially in the new *General MIDI* format, are a crucial element in the development of multimedia. These files provide a universally acceptable method of storing musical data—and they do so in a fraction of the space needed for true digital audio.

Generating Music Notation

MIDI equipment can be used to produce printed music scores. With the right software and hardware, a musician can play a piece on a keyboard, and the computer will interpret it and print it. Many musicians prefer this method to writing each note on paper by hand—or to using an unwieldy music typewriter. With the advent of PostScript-based typesetting machines and high-quality music fonts, printed output derived from MIDI data can be publication quality. Most notation programs can also act as at least a rudimentary sequencer. If the composer has the appropriate synthesizers or samplers, he or she can hear a fully orchestrated version of a composition while writing it.

There are other reasons why notation is valuable in a MIDI studio. Most classically trained composers have a well-developed eye-to-ear correspondence—and many feel most comfortable editing music presented in standard notation. Also, many composers who work with MIDI use their setups as electronic scratch pads, to work out arrangements that are designed to be played by live musicians. If they are able to print out scores and parts directly from their MIDI setups, they can work more efficiently. However, integrating MIDI and music notation is not as easy as it may appear at first glance. The core of the problem is that the correlation between music notation and how a piece sounds is very loose and open to interpretation. On the other hand, the correlation between the data in a MIDI sequence and how it sounds is exact with no room for interpretation. For example, a whole note in a measure on a printed score means one thing to a bassoon player: blow for four beats. A whole note means something quite different to a percussionist playing the chimes: strike it once and let it ring. If these actions were performed on a MIDI keyboard—holding a key for four beats as opposed to hitting a key and letting it go quickly—and subsequently interpreted by a notation program, the bassoonist's note would be transcribed as a whole note and the percussionist's would come out as something like a thirty-second note.

Many problems similar to the instance described above crop up when a computer tries to interpret the many and varied aspects of a musical performance. For example, a computer cannot readily differentiate between a staccato quarter note and an ordinary eighth note. Or consider the case of a fermata over a whole note. A human musician might interpret this by holding the whole note for one extra beat. If such a performance were played into a computer, it would simply be interpreted as a five-beat note. Thus, every subsequent measure would be off by one beat. For these types of reasons, turning a MIDI performance into printed music involves second-guessing the intentions of the performer, and that is something a computer finds very difficult to do. Although producing printed notation from MIDI data is a challenging procedure, manufacturers continue to improve their products in this important area.

Quantization

High resolution is a desirable feature in a sequencer. It allows you to play back a performance with a corresponding degree of accuracy. However, high resolution is not such a desirable trait in a notation program. If a notation program faithfully reproduced a performance with a resolution of ninety-six parts per beat (which is not a particularly high resolution for a computer sequencer), the result would be a completely unreadable mess of flags, dots, and microrests. *Quantizing* is thus an important key to successful transcription.

unquantized notation

notation quantized to eighth notes

A transcription program also needs to know what the minimum acceptable resolution of a piece is to be. This allows it to make decisions about note placements and lengths that will be logical to the eye and that will also make musical sense. The resolution of quantization should be adjustable on a track-by-track and passage-by-passage basis, so that, for example, a flute solo rich in sixteenths and triplets can be displayed at one resolution, while the quarter-note bass line underneath it is at another.

It is also essential to keep the MIDI data and the notation data separate from each other. The amount of quantization needed to make a good transcription will rob a MIDI performance of any human qualities when played. For example, sounds that have long attacks (like string pads) should start before the beat, so that they seem to come in on time. However, if you notate these anticipated attacks, each note will seem to start on a pickup—while if you quantize the tracks to produce appropriate notation, the string pads will consistently sound late when you play back the sequence. This is why notation-based sequencers are more useful for executing large structural edits (such as moving whole phrases around) than for microediting individual events (such as adjusting the relative timings of notes on different tracks).

The Art of Notation

Music notation itself is an art, honed by centuries of use and development. Like magazine or advertising page layout, a computer can do the work, but it can't necessarily produce aesthetically correct output all by itself. To create a publishable score—or even to print out parts that will be comprehensible to other musicians—requires an understanding of the art of notation that software notation packages are simply not capable of. Knowing how to tweak the output from a notation program to turn it into truly publication-quality pages is therefore a valuable skill. Designing a single program that can satisfy both performance and notation needs is difficult. It is safe to say that there is no program available that can be both a full-featured sequencer and a professional-quality notation generator. The tasks are just too dissimilar. Fortunately, since the adoption of Standard MIDI Files as a method of transferring data between programs, it is possible to use a specialized program for each task.

Algorithmic Composers

Algorithmic composition is a process by which music is generated according to a set of rules, or *algorithms*. The process has its roots in the work of such composers as Schoenberg and Messiaen. Computers are ideally suited for such work—and the acceptance of MIDI, in which musical events are represented by simple numbers, has made the concept very popular. Algorithmic composition programs are sometimes known as *intelligent instruments*. They are designed so that a small action on the part of the user—moving a mouse or pressing a key—can have a large effect, such as starting a new sequence of notes, changing orchestration, or transposing the music. In other words, you control the patterns and parameters that determine the way the music is being produced, while leaving the mundane task of actually playing the notes to the computer. Some programs include elements of chance, which add a degree of randomness and unpredictability to a performance.

There are stand-alone algorithmic composition programs—and some sequencing programs include certain algorithmic functions. The patterning functions of some sequencers referred to earlier can be considered a form of algorithmic control. More elaborate control can be found in the *Generated Sequences* feature of Opcode's Vision or the *Programmable Variations Generator* in Dr. T's Keyboard Controlled Sequencer (KCS) Level II. The best way to explain algorithmic composition is to describe three of these programs.

Music Mouse

Music Mouse, was created by computer-music pioneer Laurie Spiegel, and is distributed by Dr. T's. It is a seemingly simple (but actually quite rich) program for generating MIDI data and is available for the Macintosh and the Amiga. In addition to using MIDI, it can also use the computer's internal sound-generating capabilities (although it sounds much more interesting with MIDI instruments).

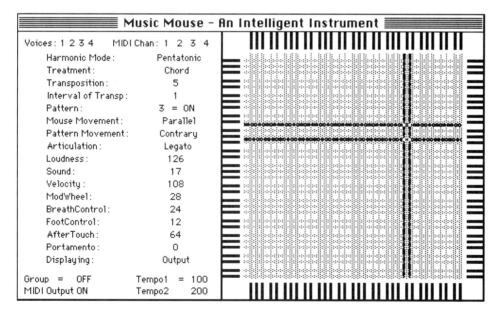

Music Mouse requires no MIDI keyboard (although a Thru function is available to the user). Instead, the user "plays" the program by moving the mouse around the screen. Music Mouse produces four simultaneous voices, which can be assigned to the vertical or horizontal axes of the mouse movement. The voices can move in parallel or contrary motion. You can choose different modes (chromatic, diatonic, quartal, and so on). You also can specify the speed with which the mouse responds. Play can be turned on and off with the spacebar. Various computer keys change Volume, Velocity, Program Change numbers, and articulation, as well as MIDI Modulation Wheel Controller (01), Breath Controller (02), Foot Controller (04), and Channel Pressure. In addition, the program has ten built-in pitch patterns. These are not notes, per se, but patterns of up and down movement that produce notes in accordance with the current settings of mode, harmony, counterpoint, speed, and pitch. These patterns can be switched on and off—and the notes they produce can be changed in real time by mouse movement or any other active keys.

Although Music Mouse is inexpensive and easy to use, it is actually a powerful performance instrument, and can produce some fascinating music. It is also an excellent tool for teaching the basic principles of melody, rhythm, and counterpoint.

M

M, by David Zicarelli (originally published by Intelligent Music), is a far more complex program. It is available for Macintosh (now distributed by Dr. T's) and IBM (distributed by Voyetra Technologies). It can record notes played on a MIDI keyboard, but rather than just play them back, it uses them as raw material for musical permutations and improvisations generated by the computer. There is room for twenty-four such note patterns, with four active at any one time. The pitches and durations of the patterns are treated as separate entities, and can be controlled independently. When you click on "Start," the four patterns start to play and repeat.

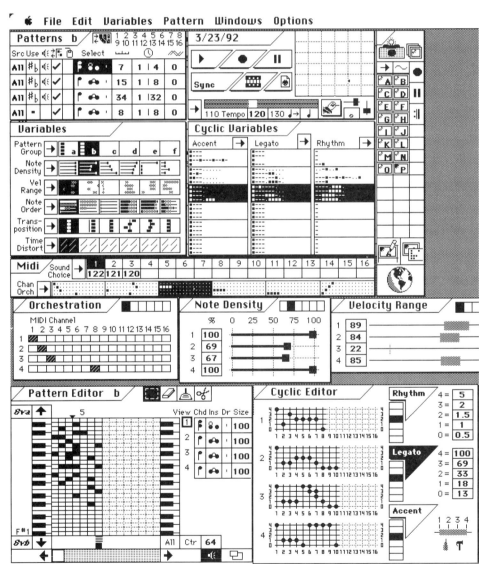

various windows in M

Patterns can be changed, with notes added, altered, or deleted as they play. Tempos, rhythms, and note densities (what percentage of the notes will play during a given iteration) also can be changed. You can alter the order of the notes in a pattern, introducing varying degrees of randomness. The voices can be transposed, sped up, or slowed down independently or as a group. Each of the four voices can be sent to one or more MIDI channels. You can set up Program Changes on all sixteen MIDI channels, and change them instantaneously, individually or as a group. MIDI Note Velocities are controllable, using *accent patterns,* which increase or decrease the velocity within a specified range on certain notes in the pattern. Similar patterns are used to vary note durations and articulations.

The program responds to incoming MIDI notes in a variety of ways: It can record them, use them as transposition points, or respond to them as if they were specific computer commands. In addition, M features a *conducting grid,* which lets you assign any of the program's variables, in either a positive or negative direction, to the *x* or *y* axis of the mouse's movement. Moving the mouse around the grid then changes all those variables together, which can have very dramatic effects.

When a screen is set up to your liking, you can take a "snapshot" of it. Up to twenty-six snapshots can be stored in one file. Each snapshot recalls the settings of all the variables, so changing snapshots can effect a radical change in the music. Snapshots can be arranged into a "slideshow," which will automatically switch snapshots after a certain amount of time. A performance on M can be stored in real time as a "movie," which can then be saved as a MIDI file and imported into a sequencer for further refinement. M is a highly complicated program, with a very dense and involved user interface. Not for the faint of heart, it is nevertheless an intriguing and educational program—and one capable of creating fascinating performances if the user is patient and perseveres.

Band-in-a-Box

Band-in-a-Box (by PG Music) is a very different type of algorithmic program. This program is designed as an automatic accompanist for a human instrumentalist, either in the studio or in live performance.

The principle behind this program is that it is a real-time performing lead sheet. The user enters a chord progression, tempo, rhythmic style, and structure for a song, and then identifies which MIDI channels are assigned to drums, bass, and accompaniment instruments (piano, guitar, and/or strings). (It may also be necessary to set up a MIDI-note-to-drum-sound correspondence chart, but this need only be done once.) When used with a General MIDI instrument, you don't even need to put in Program Changes. The program then creates the rhythm tracks for the sounds, playing them over and over like tireless sidemen. Rather than repeat the patterns exactly, the program introduces variations as it plays, including chord inversions, bass lines, and drum fills, so as to keep it interesting. Style templates can be edited and new ones created as well. The output of the program (as well as what the soloist plays on top of it) can be saved as a MIDI file, for later editing. The algorithms that Band in a Box uses for creating accompaniments are very clever and natural sounding. It's not really a composition program, but it makes improvising easy and a lot of fun.

Chapter 4
Composing Techniques

The previous chapter highlighted various MIDI composing tools and their basic application in the MIDI studio. This chapter explores many important techniques used by professionals to create music using these tools. There are as many ways to compose with a sequencer as without one—and your own preferences are primary. Here are some guidelines and techniques for composing in a MIDI environment.

Setup

Whether your sequencer is a high-end computer application, a simpler workstation sequencer, or a dedicated "box"—you must connect it to one or more MIDI instruments. Unless you're happy with hearing only one track at a time, you will want to connect the sequencer to at least one multitimbral synth. This will allow you to play many notes on several different patches over multiple MIDI channels. A more complex type of setup features a number of instruments, each playing notes on one patch and each receiving on only one channel. (Some instruments fit somewhere in the middle, and can play on a few channels but not enough to act as your entire orchestra.) The more instruments and sounds you have, the more potential there is for confusion. When you're ready to write music, the very last thing you need is to spend your time and attention programming instruments, repatching MIDI cables or downloading sounds. However, if you are working with a big set of sophisticated instruments, chances are that you'll need to give them this attention. For this reason, it's a good idea to develop the simplest possible setup of instruments and sounds for use during composing sessions. This way you can start writing when the inspiration hits—and not lose your ideas swapping cables on the floor behind your instrument rack. When you have come up with a score that is musically satisfying, you can start digging around for the sounds that work best with the piece. Some people even like to compose using just one instrument that has fairly low-end sounds, but a reasonable number of multitimbral voices. It's easy to program all the patch names of an instrument like this into your sequencer to make all the standard instrument sounds available quickly. This way, you need pay almost no attention to getting timbres right while you compose, and concentrate rather on the music.

By contrast, some people prefer to explore sounds at the beginning of a composing session. They use patch editors and librarians to browse through their sound collection and try out different sounds. Finding even one interesting timbre can often inspire a new figure, phrase, or even an entire piece.

MIDI Thru and Local Control

When you record, you will usually play your music on a MIDI keyboard connected to your sequencer. In order to be able to hear all the instruments and timbres you have available, you need to route your keyboard's MIDI output through the sequencer to your other instruments.

Most sequencers have a programmable Thru function that you can turn on and off, and set either to one specific channel or to an "auto" mode. The latter sends your performance data through the sequencer on the MIDI channel of whatever track you put in Record mode. So, for example, if the bass track is assigned to Channel 2, when you put this track into Record your performance data automatically goes to the synth you've set to sound like a bass and assigned to receive on Channel 2. Thus, when you play the keyboard, you hear the bass sound.

Once MIDI Thru is active, set your keyboard synthesizer's Local Control to off. If you don't, your synth will play every note twice: once when it hears the MIDI data directly from its own keyboard, and again when the same data stream goes from the keyboard to the sequencer and back to the sound-generating side of the synth. While you may find this gives you a nice thick sound, there are two disadvantages to this kind of doubling: Playing each note twice cuts the instrument's polyphonic capability in half. Also, the sequencer isn't actually recording twice the number of notes you're playing. When you play the part back, you'll only hear one set of notes: the ones you actually played on the keyboard.

Initial Program Change and Volume

Since synthesizers can sound like anything from a French horn to an electric oud, they give you a lot of options. But of course this means you have to keep track of more things. If you decide to use one synth as a bass in a sequence you're composing, you have two choices. You can reach over to the instrument and punch its buttons until the bass sound comes up, or you can send it a MIDI Program Change message that does the same job. The next time you load that sequence though, you may not recall which bass patch you used. To help you out here, most sequencers allow you to specify a Program Change command at the beginning of each track. When you start playing the sequence, the software sends this message to the synth, which then produces the sound you want. (This will work provided that you haven't edited the sound in the synth or loaded the instrument with other sounds.)

Another MIDI message you can sometimes tell a sequencer to send when it starts to play is MIDI Volume (Controller 07). Many software sequencers present a set of on-screen sliders that look and operate like their hardware equivalents. These allow you to see the relative volumes of the tracks at a glance.

Tk	P	R	S	L	Name	Chnl	Program Name	−	Volume	+	
1	▶			♪	new Tymp	A2	MT32 Tympani				1
2	▶			♪	Bass	A3	MT32 Acou Bass				2
3	▶			♪	Counter	A4	MT32 BrassSect 1				3
4	▶			♪	Counter 2	A9	MT32 Elec Guitar 1				4
5	▶			♪	Lead	A5	MT32 Fr Horn 1				5
6	▶			♪	organ low	A7	MT32 Elec Organ 3				6
7	▶			♪	organ hi	A8	MT32 Elec Organ 3				7
8	▶			♪	Pizz	A6	MT32 Koto				8

A sequencer can let you set initial program and volume of each track.

Once the initial volume and program numbers are set, you can change either the program or the volume of any track at any point in the sequence. Different sequencers implement these functions in various ways—but they all amount to inserting a Program Change or Volume message in the MIDI data stream along with the notes. When the sequencer sends these messages, the synths respond accordingly.

Click Track

Most sequencers offer a *click track,* or metronome pulse, to help you play in tempo. A software sequencer can tell the computer to use its internal speaker to click in time to the tempo you set for a song—or it can send out a MIDI message that makes one of your instruments (typically a drum synth) play the click track. The more sophisticated the sequencer, the more control it gives you over the channel, pitch, duration, accent, and loudness of the click. Even a sequencer that lacks a true metronome can send out MIDI Clocks to control the tempo of a drum machine playing a simple pattern, which can serve as a click track.

```
┌─────────────────────────────────────────────┐
│            Click Settings                      │
│  ═══════════════════════════════════════      │
│        ○ Internal      ◉ MIDI                  │
│                                                │
│         Port  Chan  Pitch  Uel   Dur (1-8)    │
│ Bar click  [A]   [1]   [C6]  [127]  [3]        │
│                                                │
│ Beat click [A]   [1]   [C6]  [64]   [2]        │
│                                                │
│  [ Cancel ]              [  OK  ]              │
└─────────────────────────────────────────────┘
```

a click setup window

When you are creating a sequence, a click track is important for a number of reasons. First, much of the editing power of sequencers is bar- and beat-based. These editing features become much less useful when you try to apply them to rhythmically free playing. What is more important, in most music the need for all the parts to work together rhythmically becomes increasingly crucial as the tracks proliferate. Since it's so easy to add more tracks in a sequencer, you can quickly create an awesome heap of rhythmic figures. If these are not all marching to the same drummer, the overall effect can be mush. This is not to say that free or experimental music can't be done with a sequencer. In fact the multitude of ways in which a sequencer allows you to make many musical changes easily and quickly makes it a great tool for those who want to "see what happens if . . ."

The click track is also a great help when you use one of a sequencer's most basic features: slow tempo recording. As you are composing or recording a piece, you may come across a particular passage that's too difficult for you to play well. The sequencer offers the perfect solution to this problem. Set the sequencer's tempo slow enough to allow you to play the passage. Once you have recorded the perfect take, set the tempo back to normal and you will hear the passage played up to speed. Playing a passage with the right articulation and phrasing at slower tempos can be tricky, but the results are invariably much more musical than using step-time recording. An audible click will be a great help in giving you the feel of the slower tempo. Be sure to set it for at least one measure of count-in. Some sequencers allow you to double the number of clicks per beat, which can help make playing at extremely slow tempos feel more natural.

Looping

Even the most primitive sequencer has the ability to *loop*—that is, the ability to play back a given selection of MIDI data repeatedly. In fact, the more limited a sequencer's memory, the more it must rely on this function. Nearly all sequencers allow the user to loop an entire sequence, or some section of it. Some allow looping of individual tracks or sections of tracks—or let the user specify a number of iterations for a loop. Some even allow *nested loops* within loops.

There are sequencers that do not strictly follow the multitrack tape metaphor—but treat sequences as modules that can be linked into a whole. This approach can encourage complex compositions, where multiple modules stop, start, and loop against one another at various times and through different iterations. The loops can be programmed to play in a certain order by a master sequence, or they can call each other singly or in groups. It is also possible to start the loops in real time from a MIDI device or computer keyboard.

Looping in record is a function distinct from playback looping. A loop record function repeatedly plays a specified section of music with one track in record mode—and is intended to assist recording and composition. The function has two basic variations: *looped overdub*, in which everything the user plays on every pass is cumulatively added to the track, and *looped replace*, which erases everything recorded on each iteration as the next iteration begins.

looping

The looped overdub function is akin to the way drum machines historically operate (even before MIDI). The user can hear the tempo, then record the kick drum on one pass, the snare on another pass, the hi-hat on another, and so on until an entire part is built up. In a sequencer, looped record can be used exactly the same way for drum parts—and in similar ways for other parts. Those users not overly endowed with keyboard technique can record a series of fast-paced piano chords by recording individual chords on separate passes.

Looped replace is more like the traditional tape-machine punch-in function. The player has the opportunity to replay the part until satisfied—but with a MIDI sequencer, there's no waiting for the tape to rewind. Some sequencers create a new track with each loop, so that you can select which portions of which takes you would like for the final version.

Creative Quantization

Quantization can make a rhythmically sloppy passage sound metrically perfect. While this feature has allowed more people with less technique to record more music, it has also been responsible for the production of a lot of rhythmically stiff, and ultimately boring, music. The problem is that even the best of musicians does not play with metronomic accuracy. Before sequencers came along, no form of music simply ticked along at a mechanically locked, absolute tempo. Instead, musical tempos breathed; pushed and pulled the meter in relation to the melody, dynamics, lyrics, phrasing, and other performance elements. These variations, in part, create the feel of a performance and help make music the personal and expressive art that it is. Quantizing a piece of music removes its natural rhythmic feel. It's important to note that quantizing doesn't remove all feel from music—but it does give it a feel of being quantized: rigid, stiff, and mechanical. Not surprisingly, certain inventive musicians and composers have developed forms of music (such as techno-pop) that effectively use this quantized feel. However, in most musical styles people tend to prefer the rhythmic nuance imparted by a human player to absolute, computerized precision.

Today, many sequencers let you set the degree with which quantization acts on notes. Instead of pulling all the notes completely on to a beat or subbeat, you can tell the sequencer to move them towards the beat by a certain percentage. This lets you tighten up the sloppy parts while keeping the overall feel of the original performance.

Another quantization parameter that a good sequencer lets you set is *sensitivity*. This can work in one of two ways, depending on the sequencer you're using. If you tell the sequencer to quantize to quarter notes, for example, in effect it lays a grid over the music. The lines of this grid fall on every quarter-note beat. In one method of quantizing, the sensitivity control tells the sequencer how far away from each grid point to look for notes to quantize—if they are too far away, don't touch them. For example, if the sensitivity is set to thirty percent, a note that falls a sixteenth note after a beat (twenty-five percent) will be quantized to the beat, while a note that is almost an eighth note away (say, forty-eight percent) will be left alone.

In the other method, all of the notes that are in the track are quantized, but the sensitivity parameter controls which direction they are quantized in. The parameter sets up a dividing line between the lines of the grid. This line can be equally distant between the grid lines (fifty percent), or it can be moved earlier or later than the midpoint. If the line is earlier, say thirty-three percent, then any notes that are less than one-third of a beat late are quantized to the previous beat—while notes more than one-third of a beat late are quantized to the following beat. In the same way, if the sensitivity parameter is set to sixty-seven percent, notes that are up to two-thirds of a beat late are quantized backward—while only notes more than two-thirds of a beat late are quantized forward. This type of control is more helpful than ordinary even-grid quantization when players find themselves playing consistently ahead of or behind the beat. Some sequencers even manage to provide combinations of both of these types of sensitivity settings.

Quantizing to too fine a grid often creates problems with consistently late or early playing. In fact, it's rare that you'll find a quantization algorithm that works to your satisfaction perfectly every time. In almost every case, you'll have to go to the individual notes and tweak some of them manually. It's usually easier to try a different approach than to hunt down the exact, byte-sized flaw that makes a given algorithm not work with a given piece of music. As a rule of thumb, use the finest grid you can that moves the notes the way you want. Also, never be afraid to repeatedly undo and redo quantizations with different settings until you achieve the desired effect.

When writing music with a sequencer, you not only have to be careful not to overquantize your music, but you have also to contend with tracks that have been entered in step time, where every note is automatically recorded exactly on the beat. Drum tracks are often recorded in step time because there are more MIDI keyboardists than drummers out there—and it's easier for a nondrummer to step in a drum part than try to play it in real time on a keyboard. The other common method for getting a drum track into a sequence is to develop a phrase a few bars long, then to copy it repeatedly to fill up the rest of the piece. Even if the initial phrase is played in with feeling (and not edited and quantized to death), its constant repetition throughout a song makes for a feel only a little more satisfying than a stepped-in track. This situation has resulted in a number of sequencer features and techniques aimed at putting the feel back into tracks. They are useful not only with drum tracks, but also to enhance the musicality of any track in a sequence.

Randomizing

Music that's been recorded in step time or absolutely quantized can sometimes benefit from a *randomize* feature. When you randomize quantized or stepped-in music, notes are randomly pulled away from the beat, forward or backward, by an amount whose limit is specified by the user in ticks or percentages. This can help to a degree, but it only goes so far. Studies show that the performances of skilled musicians, while not metrically perfect, are not random: They have pattern and context that add up to the feeling the player lends to the performance. Randomizing can remove some of the stiffness of music that sounds too perfect, but it can't reproduce the many nuances of expression with which a good instrumentalist colors a performance.

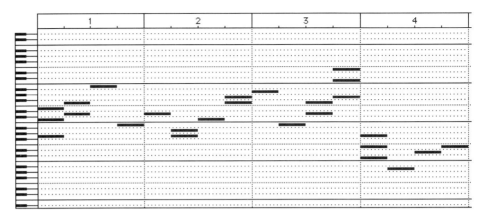

before randomizing

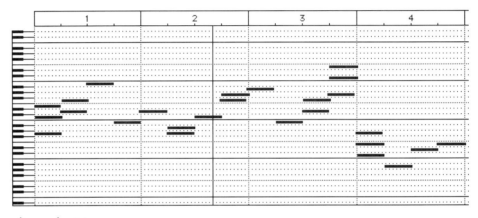

after randomizing

Randomizing algorithms produce the best results when applied to very fast or dense passages. This feature is particularly effective in string passages (especially those recorded at slow tempos or in step time). In this context, randomizing can remove some of the overly mechanical feel and make the passage sound more human. It also can be applied to other parameters such as velocity and duration—the latter application being particularly effective with stepped-in passages.

Push and Pull

Another way to achieve a more lifelike feel is to move groups of notes or entire tracks slightly forward or back in time. To use a drum set as an example, moving all the backbeat snare notes a few milliseconds later can make a groove funkier, or more laid-back. Moving a sixteenth note hi-hat a little earlier than the beat can give the groove a little more impetus. Other instruments may be *pushed* or *pulled* in this way to alter the character of the sequence. Moving a track a few milliseconds one way or the other can often create amazing differences—and may add just the right touch to a sequence. (Just remember not to get so bogged down in numbers and software features that you forget to use your ears and follow your musical instincts.)

Pattern Quantize

Some sequencers can quantize to a one- or two-bar (or even longer) pattern in which notes on different beats are rushed or delayed by various amounts. The concept here is that a particular feel or groove is created, at least in part, by such patterns of variation. In the one-bar example below, the downbeat is a little early, the second beat a little late, the third beat is right on the beat, and the fourth is very late.

notes quantized to a feel-oriented pattern

Imagine that this quantization pattern is applied to a sequence in which the kick drum plays on beats one and three and the snare plays on beats two and four. This quantization would add an urgent and somewhat funky groove to an otherwise square drum pattern.

Velocity Patterns

Changes in dynamics can also influence the feel of a sequence. Particularly where percussion instruments are concerned, the relative volume of notes can be very important (and is often overlooked). A good example of this is the typical sixteenth-note hi-hat pattern. Using a combination of step entry and copy/paste commands, you can enter an entire track's worth of perfectly regular notes. But such a figure will sound pretty dead if every note has the same loudness. This will happen if the step-entry feature ignores incoming velocity and assigns the same velocity to every note. With the right dynamic variation though, the pattern can come alive.

MIDI Velocity is the parameter usually used to describe the loudness of individual notes. Here is an example of the velocities that a drummer might create in playing a bar of sixteenth-note hi-hats. (The vertical lines represent the MIDI Velocity level of each note.)

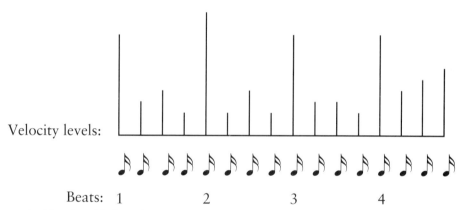

note velocities played in by a drummer

The simplest way to record a pattern like this would be to have an experienced drummer play it on a MIDI drum transmitter with good velocity sensitivity. If this is not practical, you may choose to record the pattern in step time, with this result.

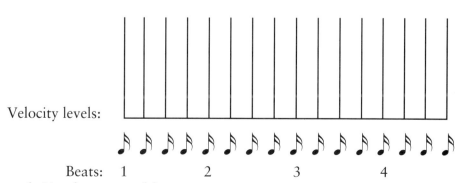

note velocities of a step entered drum pattern

Once the pattern has been recorded in step time, there are several ways to get it to sound more like the real-time performance of a practiced drummer. Most software sequencers offer a command that changes the velocity (or other parameters) of individual notes or groups of notes. By changing the velocities of each of the notes in the pattern above, you can get it to approximate the first pattern. Such note-by-note editing can be tedious, but the results are often worthwhile. Another way to accomplish the same end is to globally change the velocity of the notes, but specify rules as to which notes get changed and in what way. (See "Constrained Editing" below.)

Continuous Controllers

Since the very first days of electronic music, an ongoing challenge has faced synthesists: how do we turn electronically generated tones into musical notes—with all the plasticity, character, and expressiveness that make music what it is? The MIDI spec includes a number of elements specifically designed to add expressiveness to synthesized sounds. You've seen how editing the velocity of stepped-in drum notes can add life to a passage. MIDI also provides specific messages for Pitch Bend, Key and Channel Pressure (Aftertouch), and over 100 Control Change messages that can continuously change modulation, stereo pan position, pedal functions, chorus, and other musical parameters. As MIDI instruments get more complex, the possibilities for real-time timbral control over filters, envelopes, sample layers, modulators, effects, and so on are increasing dramatically. These controls allow the musician to take a very active role in almost all aspects of MIDI music-making.

Of the 128 possible Continuous Controllers in the MIDI spec, many are defined either in terms of being part of a transmitter, a receiver, or both. As explained earlier, Controllers 120 and above are reserved for Mode messages. Although these Controllers can be used for real-time expressive purposes, it's best not to, for this may confuse receiving devices. (Some of the slots immediately below 120 may be used in the future for other mode-type messages; for example, 119 is currently being considered as a *Mute* message.)

During MIDI's ten-year history, some of the Controller definitions have been updated or altered slightly. This means that some older MIDI devices may use certain Controllers differently from newer devices. There is also a separate class of Controllers that includes *Registered Parameters* and *Non-Registered Parameters*. These have the effect of increasing the available Controller set enormously.

Although the definitions of the Controllers are part of the MIDI specification, they are not absolutely carved in stone. They are provided as a guide to manufacturers and programmers. Many of the more sophisticated transmitters allow their physical controllers (wheels, sliders, pedals) to be assigned to any Controller number. Similarly, many receivers allow a variety of incoming Controllers to be assigned to their various timbre-modifying parameters. In reassignable devices, the MIDI spec's table of Controller definitions should serve as the default assignments: what the Controllers do without any intervention on the part of the user.

The First 64 Controllers

The first 64 Controllers were originally designed so that they could be sent in pairs, as fourteen-bit Controllers. When Controller pairs are used, the lower-numbered Controller is sent first, and its value is considered the *Most Significant Byte (MSB)* of the command (that's the leftmost two digits of the four-digit hex number). The higher-numbered Controller follows immediately afterwards, with the *Least Significant Byte* (*LSB*) (the rightmost two digits). Combined, the two Controllers constitute a single message with a resolution of 16,384 discrete values (as opposed to the 128 available with a single Controller). The MIDI specification says that an MSB can be sent without an LSB. With the exception of Bank Select (where it is probably the least useful), few fourteen-bit Controllers have been implemented in any hardware or software. Although the practice is still outlined in the Spec, it is considered essentially moribund—and today Controllers 21 through 3FH (33 through 63 decimal) are more or less up for grabs.

Here's how the first 64 Controllers are defined and used.

Decimal Value (MSB/LSB)	Hex Value (MSB/LSB)	Name	Applications and Notes
00/32	00/20	Bank Select	Should use LSB (32) first, but some manufacturers use MSB only.
01/33	01/21	Modulation	Transmitter is a wheel or lever; receiver usually controls LFO depth.
02/34	02/22	Breath	Transmitter is a breath controller originally made by Yamaha or part of a wind controller; receiver is usually related to loudness or timbral change. Also, many early Korg keyboards used this to transmit information from one axis of a joystick.
03/35	03/23	undefined	Original Yamaha DX7 used this for Aftertouch.
04/36	04/24	Foot Pedal	Transmitter is a foot pedal; receiver controls loudness or timbral change.
05/37	05/25	Portamento Time	Transmitter is a slider; receiver controls time to glide from one note to the next when Portamento switch (65) is on. (See also the discussion of Legato Footswitch in this chapter.)
06/38	06/26	Data Entry	Transmitter is a slider; receiver may control any parameter change. Used in conjunction with Registered and Non-Registered Parameters (98–101).
07/39	07/27	Volume	Transmitter is a slider or pedal.
08/40	08/28	Balance	Transmitter is a slider; receiver controls the balance between two layers of a sound—or the wet/dry mix of an effects device.
09/41	09/29	undefined	
10/42	0A/2A	Pan	Transmitter is a slider; receiver changes stereo pan position of sound.
11/43	0B/2B	Expression	Transmitter is a pedal; works in conjunction with Controller 07 (Volume) to make temporary volume changes or performance inflections. Volume can be thought of as a fader on a console, while Expression the pedal on an organ.
12/44	0C/2C	Effect Control 1	Transmitter is a slider or knob; receiver is a control on an effects device—reverb, delay, equalizer, etc.—which might be send, wet/dry mix, or any other parameter of the effect
13/45	0D/2D	Effect Control 2	same as Effect Control 1
14/46	0E/2E	undefined	
15/47	0F/2F	undefined	
16/48	10/30	General Purpose 1	Transmitter and receiver can be anything; designated as General Purpose essentially to prevent them from being defined for anything specific. General Purpose 1 is used by some transmitters for the x-axis position of a joystick.
17/49	11/31	General Purpose 2	Used by some transmitters for the y-axis position of a joystick.
18/50	12/32	General Purpose 3	
19/51	13/33	General Purpose 4	

The remainder of the set, 20 through 31 and 52 through 63 decimal (14H through 1FH and 34H through 3FH) are, at present, undefined.

The Switches: 64 through 69

The next set of Controllers was originally reserved for binary switched functions, transmitted by momentary-contact or locking pedals, and could have one of only two values: 0 (off) or 127 (on). The MIDI spec says a receiver is supposed to consider any values between 0 and 63 to be *off*, and values 64 and up to be *on*. (However, some older receivers interpret any value above 0 as *on*.) Although these Controllers are still used as switches for the most part, the restriction has been eased—and designers are free to use them for full-value (seven-bit) Controllers.

Decimal Value	Hex Value	Name	Applications and Notes
64	40	Sustain	Also known as Damper or Hold 1. Retains Sustain portion of sound's envelope on all notes played, until turned off. Sometimes used to turn on a special Release segment that allows the sound to die away more slowly.
65	41	Portamento	Turns on and off Portamento Control (see 05 and 84).
66	42	Sostenuto	Sustains notes that are being held when the control is turned on; subsequent played notes (unlike 64) are not sustained.
67	43	Soft Pedal	Lowers volume and/or softens timbre by a preset amount.
68	44	Legato Footswitch	Puts receiver into Legato mode: only one note can sound at a time; overlapping notes result in change of pitch with no attack.
69	45	Hold 2	A second hold pedal that sustains a portion of the sound, like the middle pedal on an upright piano; sometimes triggers an alternate Release segment (like 64).

Sound Controllers: 70 through 79

These ten Controllers, officially known as *Sound Controllers 1* through *10*, have recently been set up to allow manufacturers to provide users with a common and easy way to accomplish real-time control over a variety of timbral characteristics of a sound without having to deal with System Exclusive commands. Exactly how these Controllers work is entirely up to the manufacturer. For example, to an FM-synthesis module "Brightness" may mean increasing the level of a modulating operator, while to a wavetable synth it may mean raising the cutoff frequency of a low-pass filter. Ideally, the user doesn't have to know how this is done—all he or she needs to know is that increasing the value of Controller 74 makes the sound brighter.

Only the first half of the set is defined so far. Manufacturers are free to use the remaining ones for any parameters they like (although it's possible that more formal definitions of the undefined Controllers will appear in the future).

Decimal Value	Hex Value	Name	Applications and Notes
70	46	Sound Variation	Deliberately vague (Once upon a time, this Controller was Velocity Replace, but it was never implemented by anybody.)
71	47	Harmonic Content	Richness or intensity of timbre
72	48	Release Time	Length of release portion of envelope
73	49	Attack Time	Length of attack portion of envelope
74	4A	Brightness	High-end content
75–79	4B–4F	Sound Controllers 6–10	Undefined

Controllers 80 through 97

Decimal Value	Hex Value	Name	Applications and Notes
80–83	50–53	General Purpose 5–8	Similar to 16–19 and 48–51 (10–13H and 30–33H)
84	54	Portamento Control	When Portamento Switch (65) is turned on, and Portamento Time (05) is not zero, the value of this Controller is the number of the note at which the glide will start.
85-90	55-5A	undefined	
91	5B	Effect 1 Depth	Most commonly used as an effects send, but like 12 and 13, can be used for any effects-related control. (Formerly called External Effects Depth.)
92	5C	Effect 2 Depth	Similar to 91; formerly Tremolo Depth.
93	5C	Effect 3 Depth	Similar to 91, formerly Chorus Depth
94	5D	Effect 4 Depth	Similar to 91, formerly Celeste Depth
95	5E	Effect 5 Depth	Similar to 91, formerly Phaser Depth
96	60	Data Increment	The transmitter is a button, usually labeled +1 or Yes, so this is a unipolar controller, with only one value: 127=On. Similar to Data Entry (06), the receiver may execute any parameter change, and this can be used in conjunction with Registered and Non-Registered parameters (98–101).
97	61	Data Decrement	The opposite of 96, the transmitting button is labelled 1 or No.

Registered and Non-Registered Parameters: 98 through 101

Even though no manufacturer takes advantage of the entire list of MIDI controllers in any one piece of equipment, the flexibility of the MIDI spec continues to evolve. Provisions were made a few years after the adoption of MIDI 1.0 to increase the available number of Controllers by an enormous amount by using a new type of data format. Several new universal Controllers were also defined under the new format in order to standardize access to various old and new functions of many MIDI devices. These new Controllers are known as *Registered Parameters* (RPNs) and *Non-Registered Parameters* (NRPNs). Rather than sending a single Controller command followed by a Controller value, these Parameters combine three commands (a total of nine bytes; seven with Running Status).

The first two commands define which Parameter is to be changed: the first is the Parameter number's Least Significant Byte (LSB), and the second its Most Significant Byte (MSB). The third command sets the value of the designated Parameter using either a Data Slider (06) followed by the desired value—or else a Data Increment or Decrement (96 or 97), which increases or decreases the current value of the selected Parameter by 1. By using two additional commands, the number of Parameters accessible by Controller commands is increased by a factor of 16,384. That should be enough to satisfy anybody. While 14-bit Controllers increase the resolution with which you can control a synth parameter, RPNs and NRPNs increase the number of parameters you can control.

Decimal Value	Hex Value	Name
98	62	Non-Registered Parameter Least Significant Byte (LSB)
99	63	Non-Registered Parameter Most Significant Byte (MSB)
100	64	Registered Parameter Least Significant Byte (LSB)
101	65	Registered Parameter Most Significant Byte (MSB)

Although an RPN or NRPN can theoretically be identified by only one command (either the LSB or the MSB), it's considered good practice always to send both commands. After the two commands are sent, any Data Slider or Data Increment or Decrement commands sent on the same channel will affect the same RPN or NRPN. In this way, further changes in a Parameter don't require all three commands to be sent. All three commands only need to be sent if you want to change the RPN or NRPN you're addressing.

Non-Registered Parameters can be anything a manufacturer wants them to be. Basically, any parameter that is remotely addressable in a synthesizer, sampler, effects device, mixing console, lighting controller, or any other Mɪᴅɪ device can be set up as a Non-Registered Parameter. In the manual that comes with such a device, the manufacturer tells what NRPNs exist, and what they do. The user can then access them however he or she wishes. Here's an example: your synthesizer's manual tells you that the LFO speed of a program can be controlled by Non-Registered Parameter 8. Therefore, to change the LFO speed of the program on Channel 1 to the middle of its range, you send the following hex bytes:

B0 (Control Change, Channel 1)
62 (NRPN LSB)
08 (Parameter number)
B0 (Control Change, Channel 1)
63 (NRPN MSB)
00 (there is no MSB)
B0 (Control Change, Channel 1)
06 (Data Entry)
40 (the value of the LFO speed)

The second and third B0s can be eliminated under Running Status, as long as these commands are sent all together. Further changes in the LFO speed can be made merely by sending B0 06H and the desired value.

Registered Parameters have certain functions, which are defined in the Mɪᴅɪ specification.

Decimal Value (MSB/LSB)	Hex Value (MSB/LSB)	Name	Applications and Notes
00/00	00/00	Pitch Bend Sensitivity	Range of the Pitch Bend wheel, with the MSB referring to semitones and the LSB to cents (1/100s of a semitone)
00/01	00/01	Fine Tuning	Tuning of the receiving device, with each increment of the LSB equal to 1/8192 of a semitone, and an overall range (using both MSB and LSB) of 1 to +1 semitone
00/02	00/02	Coarse Tuning	Tuning of the receiving device in semitones, with a range of 64 to +64
00/03	00/03	Tuning Program Select	Selects a scale tuning that is stored in the device's RAM
00/04	00/04	Tuning Bank Select	Selects a bank of tunings, which is then followed by selection of a particular tuning program (RPN 03)
127/127	7F/7F	Null Function	This "turns off" the last RPN or NRPN so that the Data Slider and Data Increment/Decrement switches can be used for something else. Its use is optional, but it can help to avoid confusion in very complex data streams.

The rest of the list of Controllers is undefined, up to 119 (77H), but they will not all remain so. Stay tuned!

Aftertouch

The common term *Aftertouch* actually refers to two separate MIDI Channel Voice messages: Channel Pressure and Key Pressure (also known as *Mono Aftertouch* and *Poly Aftertouch*). Key Pressure, though much more rarely implemented, is the more powerful of the two. A device that uses Key Pressure can simultaneously send or receive different pressure values for each key, while Channel Pressure messages affect all the notes of the instrument identically.

Depending on the capabilities of the synthesizers being used, Channel Pressure can be useful in a number of ways. Many people, for example, find pressing a key provides smoother control than using a Pitch Bend wheel, which may have a dead zone around its center position. Or they find Key Pressure preferable for creating an even Control Change data curve. This data can be even more useful if it will eventually be translated to affect another controller.

Perhaps the most common use of Aftertouch is to open and close a low-pass filter. However, many synthesizers can be programmed to respond by changing the depth of a vibrato or tremolo or the speed of an LFO, or to crossfade between sounds or create other effects that require a smooth curve.

An obvious use for polyphonic Key Pressure is bending only one note in a chord. However, if this controller is routed to control pitch—or to an LFO that in turn controls pitch, loudness, or timbre—it can create very interesting chorus, vibrato, and tremolo effects. One of the drawbacks of using Key Pressure is that it can generate huge amounts of data in a sequence.

System Exclusive

If you are adventurous, you can use System Exclusive data for expressive control. Many synthesizers let you change parameters within a program while the voice is sounding. (These are parameters that are not accessible with ordinary Controllers.) To use this feature, however, you need a thorough understanding of the device's SysEx structure (including how checksums, if they are used, are calculated). You also must have a sequencer that lets you record, edit, and/or create little chunks of SysEx data for playback at specific times in the sequence.

Some sequencers let you create SysEx-generating faders or macros that can help take advantage of this capability. For example, some sequencers let you set up an on-screen fader to change a single program parameter in real time. To do this, you first designate a string of non-variable SysEx bytes which the fader will generate every time it is moved, including the SysEx header, manufacturer's ID, model sub-ID, parameter number(s), and EOX. Then you specify the variable byte or bytes (which are the values of the parameters you want the fader to change). Now each time the fader moves, it sends out a complete SysEx message changing only the parameter(s) you designated. If the program allows, you can create a complete custom patch editor this way. There are also transmitters that can generate custom strings of SysEx data—either from their own sliders or pedals or by translating incoming Controller command—to achieve the same purpose.

Be warned, however, that System Exclusive can be hazardous to your system's health. If you send a bad SysEx message down a MIDI line, it can scramble not only the brains of the device you're trying to control, but possibly everything else on the system as well. Also, SysEx messages take up a lot of room—the simplest command will require at least six bytes—and so sending great gobs of them on multiple channels down a MIDI line is an invitation to trouble.

The new Sound Controller additions to the list of designated MIDI Controllers can go a long way towards eliminating the need for custom System Exclusive messages in a sequence (as can the increased use of Non-Registered Parameters). The coming years will see more manufacturers take advantage of these changes to help make our musical lives easier and more productive.

Using Controllers in a Sequence

Having all these Controllers and other real-time parameters at your disposal sounds wonderful, but taking advantage of them poses some practical problems. Midi keyboards, guitars, and wind controllers provide us with a few ways to translate various human gestures into these midi messages that modify the music. However, these interfaces can only transmit a few gestures at a time. Most keyboards usually offer only a Pitch Bend wheel, Modulation wheel, Aftertouch, and a pedal or two at most, leaving the user far short of total control over the broad palette midi offers. Even the most advanced keyboards add only a handful of sliders. The fact that many keyboard performances require both hands just to play the notes is also a limiting factor. Highly trained keyboardists can also find it difficult to modify years of technique training to incorporate pitch- and mod-wheel twiddling. In addition, most factory patches in synthesizers and samplers take advantage of very few of the timbre-modifying possibilities of Controllers and Pressure. Therefore, you have to tweak those sounds if you want to use them to their full potential—always keeping in mind the expressive possibilities of your particular setup.

Fortunately, there are a number of ways to get Controller (and Pitch Bend and Pressure) information into a sequence for expressive purposes beside playing it in along with the notes. In the following section, the term "Controllers" most often refers to Pitch Bend, Channel Pressure, and Key Pressure as well as Continuous Controllers such as Modulation, Volume, and so on.

Controller Overdubs

One way to use midi Controllers to liven up a sequenced performance is the overdub method. This consists of first recording a straight, notes-only performance on one track of a sequencer, with no attempt at generating Controller data whatsoever. Then you assign a second track of the sequencer to the same midi channel as the first, and put the second track into record mode. When you begin recording, the first track will play back as recorded, leaving both of your hands free to move the pitch or modulation wheels, or to hold down a key and exert pressure. This new data will be sent to the synthesizer at the same time as the note data in track one. When you play both tracks back, you will hear the original performance played with the Controller changes that are recorded on the second sequencer track.

Of course you can record as many takes of the Controller movements as needed for a satisfactory performance. Once this is done, the Controller data can be cut and merged into the track that contains the original note data, if desired.

You can overdub Controllers much more accurately if you slow the tempo down before you record. The sole drawback to this technique is that it causes the controller data to become quite dense. This can be remedied by using the sequencer's data-thinning function, as described later in this chapter.

Controller Drawing

Even the simplest of sequencers allows the user to enter a series of Control Change messages into a track. However, some sequencers require that each message be entered individually by such methods as typing the controller numbers and values on the computer keyboard. This is a tedious task for most people.

The musical expressiveness offered by midi Controllers is often a continuous change in some aspect of an instrument's tone. Taking this into account, one of the most powerful functions a sequencer can offer is *Controller drawing*. This feature bypasses both the mechanical controller devices such as pitch and mod wheels (which not everyone finds easy to use) as well as the computer-keyboard data-entry method. Instead, it allows the user to enter data by drawing a curve on the screen using the computer's mouse. This method of data entry can be accomplished in an instant, and it has proven to be quite popular. Although you are sending a large number of discrete, digital midi messages, the curve looks and feels continuous. The curve is also intuitively analogous to the musical effect you want to achieve. In this way, Controller drawing gives you a lot of control over the instrument. Very often you can determine the density of the controller data you generate by specifying a resolution for the curves.

Translating Controllers

Even if your keyboard controller doesn't generate every MIDI Controller you'd like to use, you can still add any kind of Controller data to a track using your existing hardware and software. A sequencer can translate the data generated by any controller keys, wheels, pedals, or levers into any other MIDI Controller. For example, you can record a smooth sweep of the Pitch Bend wheel from value 127 (all the way sharp) to value 0 (all the way flat) while beats 1 through 4 of bar 10 are playing. While it's being recorded, this would simply change the pitch of that track, but once that series of data values is in the sequencer, it can be modified to send not Pitch Bend data, but Controller 07 data, resulting in a four-beat fadeout in bar 10.

Different sequencers perform this data translation in different ways. Some provide a separate window for each controller and allow the copying and pasting of data from one window to another. Others offer specific commands that allow the user to change the controller addressed by the recorded data while leaving the values untouched.

Controller Editing

After a stream of controller data has been recorded, it's often necessary to edit it in some way. The simplest way to edit a graphic display of controller data is to redraw all or part of it with the mouse. This is usually possible regardless of whether the data was entered from the MIDI keyboard or on the computer screen. Any or all of the data curve can be reshaped with mouse movements to achieve the desired rate and amplitude of change.

In some situations, the changes desired in a stream of controller data may be more easily conceptualized and changed by a mathematical function than by mouse drawing. An entire section may need to be globally altered by a consistent amount or a percentage, or to be limited to a minimum or maximum. Most sequencers allow you to select a section of a track or tracks and alter the controller data in it according to a user-defined algorithm. The values on any selected series of Pitch Bend, Pressure, or Controller messages can be modified by a number of simple algorithms: They can be increased or decreased by a given amount, scaled by a percentage, or randomized. The results of these modifications can be limited to a range of values.

Constrained Editing

When editing with algorithms, various sequencers allow the user to limit, or *constrain,* the process in different useful ways. Starting from the top down, an edit can affect all the data in a sequence, one or more specific tracks, one or more specific measures (on one or more tracks), a subdivision of a measure, notes within a limited pitch range, or, finally, a single note or other event. Notes or regions can be selected graphically or from event lists. Some sequencers allow specified regions to be nonadjacent (or *discontiguous*).

Other constrained editing functions allow the user to a select a group of notes to be edited by certain of their attributes. For example, an edit constrainer might allow you to specify the pitch, velocity, and/or duration ranges of notes to be edited. Any notes not meeting the specified criteria will be ignored. The proximity to certain beats or subdivisions of beats may also be designated as a constraining factor. In addition, specific measures or groups of measures can be skipped. These constraints let the user select a large amount of music, then zero in precisely on what notes are to be edited: for example, all notes longer than twenty ticks that fall within ten ticks of the third beat of every other bar.

Constrained editing allows very sophisticated control over musical parameters. If you specify that a quantization take place every four bars on the bass track, only the fills at the end of each four-bar phrase are quantized. By specifying a downward velocity scaling that only affects notes above a certain velocity, a kind of limiting can be imposed on a track. By specifying that only notes within ten ticks of the downbeat and third beat are to be quantized, a drum part can be cleaned up so that it locks solidly to the beat (yet retains some fluidity on the backbeats). The list of possibilities is nearly infinite.

Thinning the Data Stream

A Continuous Controller curve is not really a curve, but a series of individual messages. The higher its resolution—that is, the more messages per time unit—the closer we approximate an actual analog event (such as a continuous fade out). If a curve is drawn with a low enough resolution, the illusion of a continuous event disappears—and each message is heard as an instantaneous change. As desirable as a smooth, high-resolution Controller curve seems, there is a tradeoff. If enough Control Change messages are recorded simultaneously in a given period of time, they can clog the MIDI data stream, and compromise timing. To ameliorate this, many sequencers have a data-thinning algorithm that will delete some of the messages in a series. The user can usually specify that the software delete any messages that occur more closely together than a given number of ticks. Alternatively, the software may provide an option to delete any messages containing changes in value finer than a certain number, or simply to decrease the message density by a given percentage.

A good thinning algorithm needs to be fairly intelligent—and needs to be used intelligently. To preserve the overall intent of any Controller movement, an algorithm must leave the initial and ending values alone. Local high and low points of the Controller movements must also be maintained, regardless of how close together they are. MIDI Volume and Pitch Bend changes should be thinned with care, or there will be audible jumps in volume or pitch. Modulation wheel or Channel Pressure changes, on the other hand, can be relatively well spaced out (especially if they are mapped to LFO parameters). The goal is to keep Controller streams as thin as possible without losing apparent smoothness. Each situation will be different, so let your ears be the judge.

Some sequencers will let the user filter incoming Controller data. When this option is in effect, whether a Controller curve is drawn in or played from a keyboard (or another Controller), the resolution of the curve will not exceed a specified amount. Other sequencers only allow data to be thinned after it is recorded or drawn in.

Using Wind Controllers

Many musicians are much more comfortable playing some kind of wind instrument than a keyboard. For these users, a MIDI *wind controller* can be a great asset in composing and performance situations.

One of the limitations of these devices is that they don't really come close to the expressiveness of their acoustic equivalents. The tones from a wind instrument are continuously shaped from attack to decay by breath pressure, tongue articulation, lip pressure, and even the angle at which the player holds the horn. MIDI wind controllers don't offer nearly as much control as the real thing. This is due not only to limitations in their own design, but in some degree to the keyboard orientation of most MIDI receivers (and of MIDI itself). Specifically, velocity sensitivity, envelope generators, LFOs, and pitch and modulation wheels are all designed to add the motion and life of an acoustic instrument to the essentially static output of a keyboard event. But input from a wind controller is dynamic, so it's usually necessary to program the synthesizer in a way that disables many of the devices designed to make it work well under conventional circumstances: envelopes, LFOs, and so forth. The result is that only a handful of MIDI instruments have been found to be especially friendly to wind controllers. By and large, simpler synths and digitally controlled analog synths seem most compatible. In any case, patches must almost always be custom designed to work with wind controllers. Here are some basic guidelines to programming a useful and realistic-sounding synth patch for a wind controller.

- Disable the operation of envelope generators entirely.

- Don't assign Velocity directly to patch volume, but rather to a small portion of a sound's attack that ends quickly and won't affect breath-to-volume on the bulk of the note. (The "chiff" operator in an FM patch will produce the desired effect.)

- Set up the patch's volume so it is controlled either by Channel Pressure or Breath Control (02), depending on what your controller sends when you blow into it. Make no breath equal to zero volume and maximum breath equal to maximum volume.

- Assign the filter cutoff point to the same Controller as volume, but allow the filter to change only a small amount. Set the maximum Pitch Bend to a minor third.

- Disable all automatic LFOs. This reserves as much control as possible for the player's wind, tongue, and lip.

These guidelines should produce a fair simulation of the response of an acoustic wind instrument. Use this as a starting point to create other responses.

The extensive use of Continuous Controllers, Pitch Bend, and Pressure by MIDI wind devices generates a lot of MIDI data. While this is not much of a problem in live performance, it can slow down the operation of a sequencer. To overcome this, it's a good idea to thin out the data you generate as you play.

Mono Mode

Under normal circumstances, an acoustic wind instrument can play only one note at a time. To simulate this in the MIDI environment, it's best to put the synth you're playing with your wind controller into Mono mode (Mode 4). As occurs with most wind instruments, this means that playing a note will always cut off the previous note. This will make a wind controller sound and feel more like an acoustic horn as you play it. Perhaps some new instruments will include the new Legato Footswitch (54H) and Portamento Control (44H) commands to make Mono mode easier to use and to provide more control. If not, you may be able to use a mapper to create these commands using data from existing Controllers—and send them to receivers that understand them.

Chord Layering

Unlike their acoustic counterparts, most MIDI wind controllers allow for some kind of polyphony. The simplest of these implementations allows you to program a series of intervals above and/or below the note you play. As you play, this programming adds additional notes—sometimes up to four or five—to your line. These notes are always in a fixed relationship to the note you play. The parallel harmony this creates adds some harmonic interest to your line, but does not resemble the kinds of shifting harmony a composer normally includes in a piece. More sophisticated controllers let you program harmonies appropriate to a certain scale, and to control by embouchure the number of notes that sound for each note you play. This is a much more useful and flexible scheme. The third approach uses a form of Sustenuto—either the real thing (Controller 42H) or a sustenuto effect created by keeping track of Note Ons and Note Offs. If you press a particular button on the wind controller and then play a note, when you release the button the note will continue to sound. You can then play a monophonic line over the sustaining note. More than one note can be held this way, so you can play a melodic line over a chord pad. Optionally, the held note can define a harmonic interval, rather than an actual note. The controller will accompany any note you play with a note that is the same interval away as the original note you played was from a specified constant (such as middle C).

Zipper Noise

A good wind controller should allow the player to perform wide dynamic sweeps and smooth timbral changes. When a player attempts this however, the 128-step Controller resolution implemented in the vast majority of MIDI instruments is sometimes coarse enough to make changes from one step to the next audible. This results in a stepwise change (rather than a smooth sweep) commonly known as *zipper noise*. Some players use outboard effects such as digital delays to disguise zipper noise. Another approach used on some wind controllers is to translate some of the player's gestures into control voltages. These are then sent over a special multiconductor cable to voltage-controlled amplifiers and filters in a dedicated synthesizer. While this provides perfectly smooth, analog control over those elements, it controls only the dedicated synth. These controls cannot be recorded in a MIDI sequencer for use with other synths. In addition, since so much of the true sound of the instrument is reliant on these control voltages, recording and playing back what MIDI data the controller does produce will result in only an approximation of the original performance.

Orchestration

When orchestrating a MIDI composition, your goals are the same as in any other musical environment, but there are many different considerations and techniques. This section briefly explores the use of MIDI instruments and their interactions when combined in an arrangement.

MIDI Instruments

As synthesizers have evolved, their ability to produce more dynamic and musically interesting sounds has continued to develop. Nonetheless, no matter how a given synth is programmed, its overall sound has characteristic strengths and weaknesses. Analog synths are noted for "fat," buzzy sounds and the "gronk" of hard-synced, detuned oscillators; L/A instruments are often used for light, shimmering pads; FM synthesis creates excellent bell-like and pitched-percussion sounds, and so on. Even sample players differ, depending on how their creators decided to program them. Some are relatively genteel and polite—suitable for symphonic music. Others are more "in your face," lending themselves better to rock and roll. Today's synthesizers shine most in the area of dynamics. Synths now have more voices, and they combine them in different ways using different sound architectures. They can make use of complex, multistage envelopes to produce very lively sounds.

Samplers are the other important source of sound in your studio. A sampler's strong point is realism, but there's a qualifier. A sampler plays back a replica of a sampled sound—but a replica of that sound only. In performance, a musician almost never plays two notes exactly the same, while the sampler is limited to a single version of a given note. The line between samplers and synthesizers is getting very gray. Samplers are acquiring more and more synth-style programming capabilities—and synthesizers are using sampled sounds for their waveforms. Older (or less expensive) samplers tend to produce realistic, but static, sound—and this remains a limitation.

Combining Instruments

Although some synthesists spend large amounts of time tweaking their sounds looking for the "perfect patch," there are other ways of achieving interesting and unique textures. One of the simplest ways is to double instruments. By sending a sequencer track out on more than one MIDI channel, you can have several instruments playing the same line. The important consideration here is to combine instruments so that their strengths complement one another. The channelizing and Program Change capabilities of your sequencer will help you to add instruments freely. Also, don't be content to play a chord (or even a solo line) with just one patch from one instrument. Mixing voices—either from different MIDI instruments or different multitimbral parts of the same instrument—can add a lot to a sequence.

If a chord or line sounds too static—like a blat from a car horn—there are a number of ways to enliven it.

- **Detune patches:** Use the synthesizer's fine pitch adjustment to put each of the instruments slightly out of tune—no more than a few cents up or down. Keep the patch that plays the bottom voice right on key to act as a harmonic anchor, and move the other voices to add life.

- **LFOs:** Another way to accomplish this is to use an instrument's Low Frequency Oscillator to add vibrato to a patch. All by itself, the repetitive nature of an LFO can sound boring, but it can be effective when a little is added to an already detuned patch. If you can change the vibrato rate in real time using a pedal, slider, or Channel Pressure, so much the better.

- **Sample+Synth:** A chord played by a sampler—sampled brass, for example—can sound too static to emulate a real section. Mix a synthesized brass sound with the sampler to add life, or to clean up the sound. In much the same way, analog string sounds can fatten up sampled strings—and actually make them sound more realistic. These techniques can be especially effective if each patch has its own unique (but subtle) vibrato characteristics. If you have voicing problems, and can't double everything, use sampled instruments in the outside voices of the chord and synthesized sounds for the middle voices.

The overall color and dynamics of a line can also be spiced up by doubling. Here are some further considerations.

- **Timbre:** Chords with different timbres assigned to different harmonic voices will generally add depth and texture to harmony lines.

- **Instrumentation:** When a section of music that you're playing with two or more instruments plays again at a later time, change the voice of one or more instruments playing at lower volume levels (or in the lower voices of the chord). Subtle changes in instrumentation will add a lot to a piece—even if they don't jump out at the listener.

- **Envelopes:** Use two sounds whose envelopes change in different ways, at different times. If one goes up while the other goes down, the overall timbre will be more interesting. The attack of a sampled sound will often have the most interesting timbre, but a loop later on in the sample may be a real dog. Layer the sample with a synth sound with an attack slow enough to let the sampled attack stand out—and the sustain portion of the synth sound will mask the bad loop. Keep in mind that when you double instruments in a chord or unison line, differences in the envelopes of the two patches can make the sound sloppy. Differences in the attack or release times may need to be adjusted to maintain the illusion that one instrument is playing. Either the attacks and releases should be similar enough to work together or they should be different enough to create a specific effect. Anything in between may sound mushy.

- **Volume:** Playing the same line with two instruments can also accomplish a less subtle effect: the line gets louder. If an instrument is at the top of its effective dynamic range, you can make its line stand out by adding another instrument.

- **Octaves:** Some patches are weak in specific frequency ranges. For example, a given sound may have a good bass, but a bad high end. Doubling such a patch with another that sparkles at the top can remedy this weakness—especially if the added sound is played an octave higher.

- **Panning:** When you mix (or if your synths have Pan control), the placement of sounds in the stereo field can help make them to blend or complement each other in various ways. For example, if you have a stereo string sample that is spread out over the entire spectrum, doubling it with a synthesized brass sound that comes right up the middle makes for a highly dramatic effect. For added interest, place two similar sounds on opposite sides of the stereo spread, and then mix up their attack times so that the one that sounds first keeps changing. Sweeping an instrument across the field while it's playing can also be a striking effect (as long as it's used relatively sparingly).

Drums

- **Live Drums:** Whenever possible, play in drum lines from a controller rather than drawing or stepping them in, or loading them from a drum machine. A drum controller is best, but a keyboard will work too. It's easier to tighten up sloppily played parts with quantization than to add the right feel to a mechanically played part.

- **Cut, Paste, and Overdub:** Even if you have limited chops, try recording one or two bars of your drum part at a time. Use rhythmic placement and dynamics to make the part solid, but expressive. When you get a few measures right, copy these to create the rest of the part. If you have very limited chops, step in the kick drum, then overdub each instrument on top of that, a few bars at a time. When everything else is there, try rerecording the kick to see if you can improve on the stepped-in part of the pattern.

- **Echo:** Copy every occurrence of a specific instrument for an entire section (for example, all the snare drums). Paste it back into the track about fifty milliseconds later (that's 1/10 of a beat at 120bpm). Or, move the original notes about 50ms earlier, and paste the new notes where the original notes were. Then reduce the velocities of the new notes by about twenty percent. This makes for a tight, slap-back drum effect. Use looser timings for less subtle effects.

- **Fills:** After the basic drum part is laid in, add fills at such logical divisions as the ends of parts; every four, eight, or sixteen bars; and wherever else they can complement the lead or other lines. Explore the different sounds available to you. Remember, there's nothing wrong with playing a cowbell fill once in a song and never repeating it.

- **Rhythm Parts:** If your drum machine responds to Program Change messages, use these to play variations on the basic pattern—or to access different sets of sounds. This can keep a good part from getting stale.

Chapter 5

Live Performance

Although one of the original aims of MIDI was to help simplify on-stage keyboard setups, that aspect has been eclipsed by the advances MIDI has allowed in music composition and arranging, studio automation, and film and video scoring. Nonetheless, live performance remains an important part of the MIDI world, and this environment is constantly changing and expanding. A new addition to the MIDI specification, *MIDI Show Control*, takes the concept of live performance control out of the musical realm completely and into entirely different areas.

Solo Performance

The one-person orchestra has replaced many a lounge piano player (not necessarily for the better). With one keyboard, a single performer can simulate a large ensemble. If the keyboard is a relatively sophisticated synthesizer, it can split its range into various parts—such as bass, piano, guitar, and trumpet. If there is a sequencer on board, it can be used to play back drum patterns, a rhythm section, or even an entire arrangement. With the press of a button, the performer can move from song to song and orchestration to orchestration quickly. If a sequencer is involved, there may be enough memory in RAM to hold an entire set's worth of songs—and they too can be called up quickly. If memory is limited (which is often the case), songs can be loaded in from RAM cartridges. If the instrument has a floppy disk drive, songs can be loaded from slower, but less expensive, high-capacity disks.

A more complex solo-performance setup might include a master keyboard and one or more sound modules. The master keyboard could be programmed to split its range into several parts, each assigned to a different MIDI channel. Each module, tuned to its own channel, then receives only a certain range of notes. If the keyboard can't be split, all of the modules can be set to the same channel—and each limited to respond only to a certain range of notes. With multiple modules, it is important to set up *Program Change maps* within each one, so a Program Change message coming from the master keyboard calls up the right sound for the right song in every module. For example, a module may come from the factory with Acoustic Piano assigned to Program Change 1. However, if you want to use that sound in song number six, and get the right sounds by pressing the 6 button on the master keyboard, you have to configure the module's program map so Program 6 calls up Acoustic Piano. You can also put redundancies in these maps so that, for example, Funky Bass is assigned to Program Changes 1, 2, 4, 13, and 16—and so can easily be used in more than one song.

Adding various external controllers such as pedals, breath controllers, slider boxes, and so on can enhance the performer's capabilities. A real-time MIDI data processor can also help, as described later in this chapter. Adding a drum machine to this setup is easy enough. It can run on its own, while the performer plays live. Or it can be slaved by way of MIDI Clocks to the synthesizer's internal sequencer—or the drum machine can drive the synth. You can select the internal song memory in many drum machines by Program Change, so the press of a single button will change the drum machine as well as synth modules.

A hardware sequencer (preferably with large RAM and a disk drive) can be added to this setup to allow more elaborate orchestrations. It is also possible to add a computer-based sequencer (preferably a portable or laptop computer with a built-in or simple MIDI interface). The higher the capacity of the sequencer, and the faster it can load in new files, the more interesting and smooth the performer can make a set. One-man bands are not the only ones who can benefit from these techniques: they can also help a duo or small ensemble, where a keyboardist accompanies one or more singers, guitarists, monologists, storytellers, or other instrumentalists.

Rock Bands

Keyboardists in rock bands face problems similar to those of solo performers—and they choose similar solutions. Keyboard splits, multiple modules, and the ability to change from one song to another quickly are all important. Multiple keyboard players often share modules, making a programmable MIDI patch bay very helpful.

A rock band usually has a live drummer, although he or she will often not be playing the drums the audience actually hears. The drums may be equipped with trigger-to-MIDI converters, or may simply be drum pads, triggering the sounds from a drum machine or a sampler. Sequencers are sometimes used to add additional instruments to a band. (In some cases where sequencers have been used to replace an entire band lawsuits have resulted.) When a sequencer track is used to add instrumental parts to a live performance, it plays a click track through the monitors, so the band can follow along. In many cases, the click track is fed only to the drummer's headphones. This allows the drummer to follow the sequencer and keep the rest of the band locked up. (If you've ever wondered why so many rock drummers wear headbands—it's not just to look cool, it's also to hold and cover up their headphones.)

Another approach is to program the sequencer to follow the band. This is accomplished by feeding the sequencer a steady rhythm track—like a kick drum or tambourine—and telling it to calculate the song's tempo from that. This is actually quite a tricky practice, and it is not widely—or wisely—used.

Many bands use MIDI-equipped saxes, brass, or string instruments wired to synthesizers to enhance their overall sounds. Not even singers escape MIDIfication: Pitch-to-MIDI converters can create instrumental sounds that follow a voice and fatten up its texture, and real-time pitch shifters can create vocal harmonies from a single voice input. Pitch shifters vary in complexity. The simpler ones create new pitches at fixed intervals or fixed frequencies, while more sophisticated units can create complex multipart harmonies that can change with time. These harmonies can be based on the input pitch or changed with a footswitch. They can even be determined by incoming MIDI data. Although these devices are often referred to as *harmonizers*, that word is actually a registered trademark of Eventide, Inc., and cannot legally be used to refer to products made by another company.

Guitarists and bassists can take advantage of MIDI-controlled preamps and effects units which memorize settings for different types of sounds and instantly recall them by way of Program Change messages. A simpler setup is to store patches in sequential memory locations, following the changes needed for a song or a set. The player calls up the next patch simply by stepping on an *increment switch*. MIDI-controlled patch bays designed for guitarists are also popular. These can instantly change signal routings through a forest of *stomp boxes*, making the job of switching, for example, from a solo sound to a rhythm-guitar sound much easier.

The engineers running sound systems for live rock bands also have many MIDI-based tools at their disposal. The most common are effects units that respond to MIDI Program Changes. When the band is ready to start a song, the engineer sends out a MIDI Program Change (from a keyboard, sequencer or other transmitter), and all of the reverbs, delays, compressors, pitch shifters, and so on in the effects rack go to the correct programs. Of course, Program Changes, Controllers, or any other data can also be used to make instant changes in the middle of a song—just as in the studio. If a sequencer is driving the band, it can just as easily drive the effects as well—and make any necessary changes in effects parameters at exactly the right points in the song with no help from the sound engineer.

More elaborate live-performance systems, just like larger MIDI-based studios, have mixing consoles that can store level settings and even automated eq and effects send and return levels for individual songs These can all be controlled by standard MIDI commands from a sequencer or a manual source. MIDI commands can be used to drive lighting equipment as well.

Finally, MIDI can be used to record a live performance. Some bands (most notably the Grateful Dead) not only record their concerts on tape, but also into a sequencer. Every instrument on stage feeds data to some kind of MIDI converter, which may or may not be used to produce sounds heard by the audience. This gives the band an extra editing tool: If they want to release a live album and correct some mistakes or substitute some voicings, they can just edit the MIDI data in the sequencer and use it to generate the sound they want. The edited section can then be dropped into the tape mix at precisely the right time—with everything, of course, synced together using SMPTE timecode.

MIDI in the Theater

MIDI technology has come to the theater world in a major way, affecting everything from elementary-school pageants to major Broadway shows. Augmenting the ubiquitous piano with a synthesizer is the simplest way the technology has impacted the art. Replacing an entire pit orchestra with a couple of players hooked up to banks of synths and samplers represents the other end of the spectrum.

MIDI has enabled smaller groups of musicians to have access to a huge variety of sounds. The same techniques used by lounge and concert performers—splitting keyboards, mapping programs and effects changes, and even using sequencers—are finding their way into theatrical productions. Having one or two players handle multiple synth modules from one or two keyboards is a common way to fill out (or even replace) a pit orchestra.

The Virtual Orchestra

Theatrical synthesists usually need to handle far more orchestration changes than their rock-band counterparts. Very often, they must continue playing through these orchestration changes, and can't even afford to let go of a note long enough to press a program-change button. Therefore, many theatrical players depend on foot-operated devices that increment Program Changes (often on multiple channels). In rehearsal, of course, when songs and parts of songs are repeated, the progress of programs is not linear. Some provisions must thus be made for moving backwards, either by including a decrement switch, or letting the user call up a particular step in the progression by hand. Such devices need to have prodigious memories: It's not unusual for a single show to have hundreds of orchestration changes—and designing devices large enough and flexible enough to be used in professional theater pits has been a problem. In addition, synthesizers that produce audible glitches or experience response delays when they get a Program Change need to be handled very carefully when the Program Changes are flying thick and fast.

Controlling other types of MIDI data in nonstandard ways is often useful in the pit. *Mappers* which reconfigure Controllers, Pitch Bend, Aftertouch, and even notes are useful. A simple example is a volume pedal that crossfades two synths—so the volume of one goes up while the other goes down. For a scene change, it might be great to have the brass come down in volume while the ethereal strings get louder and rise in pitch—all controlled by moving one pedal.

Computerized Performance Maps

Mappers have not been very successful on the MIDI market for various reasons. A recent development that shows more promise is mapper software for use with a computer equipped with a MIDI interface. This offers a tremendous amount of power to the player willing to learn a bit of simple programming.

Here's a description of how performance maps are created and applied by Michael Starobin, a Broadway theater composer and orchestrator, using a Macintosh computer and a program called Max (distributed by Opcode Systems). Starobin uses up to three *control layers* for a show's mappings (which can number in the hundreds). Within each map, each MIDI synthesizer in the system has a *device window*. This determines the channel on which the device will respond, the range of notes to which it will respond, the internal program it will load when the map is called up, and the volume at which it will play.

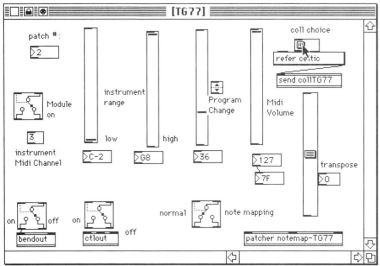

a device window

In addition, the user can either specify a transposition of incoming MIDI notes, or call up a *notemap* (the second control layer). The notemap is a lookup table that tells the synth to play specific MIDI notes or even chords when it receives certain notes. When used to play chords, this setup adds greatly to the player's flexibility. For instance, the left-hand pinky can be used to play full-chord pads, leaving the other nine fingers to play moving parts.

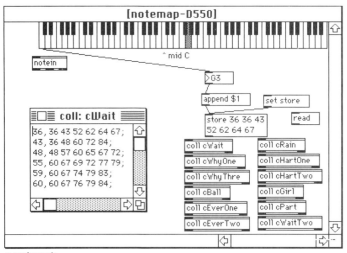

a notemap

The third layer is the *control window*, into which all of the device windows are loaded. The control window also contains the name and assigned number of the map.

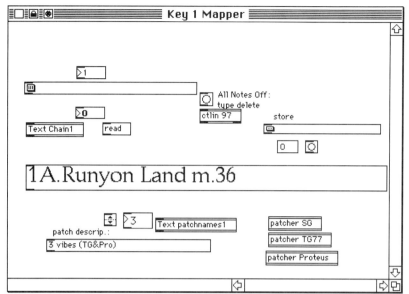

a control window

The names of the various maps are collected into a text file, and then executed in a chain in the order in which they appear. During the performance, the player steps on a pedal switch to advance through the chain. Each device window is set to send Note Offs for any notes being held when the switch pedal is pressed; the new Program Changes and Volume messages are sent when the pedal is released. This prevents notes being held through Program Changes (which can cause a glitch, or abrupt volume changes that may sound clumsy).

A manual switch is set to send a Controller message that will step backwards through the chain for rehearsal purposes. Another acts as a panic button, sending a complete set of Note Offs, Controller 01 (Modulation wheel) zeros, and Pitch Bend centers (40H) to every device. These switches are duplicated by keys on the computer keyboard. In addition, Program Changes sent from the master controller can call up a particular map, regardless of its position on the list. Random access through the chain is also available using the mouse in the control window. An entire show can consist of a single chain—or chains for individual songs can be loaded in as the performance progresses.

In addition to the mappings, Starobin has created three *objects* in Max to do specific musical functions. One is a *sequencer window*, which plays a short sequence when a particular map is called and stops when the next map is called. Another is a *repeater* which sends out repeated notes quickly while a key is held down. The third object is a *redundancy filter*, which remembers the last Program Change and Volume command sent to each module. If the same command is supposed to be sent when a map is called up, it doesn't send it. This helps prevent unnecessary delays in modules that are slow to respond to these commands.

Orchestral Optimization

Not only individuals, but small companies composed of musicians with extensive theater experience are working on extending the capabilities of MIDI in the pit. An example is Counterpoint Musical Arts Technology whose 2-T Orchestral Optimization System is a complete system for performing fully orchestrated music with a minimum of players. This professional system is also aimed at school, community, and amateur theater groups, who can use it to produce music of a quality far beyond what their resources would otherwise allow.

The 2-T Orchestral Optimization System consists of controller and synthesis hardware, as well as software. It allows keyboard and other control commands to be constantly redefined according to the software—which itself is dynamically controlled in real time. It consists of a couple of rack-mountable black boxes, which constitute a synthesizer, sampler, and MIDI processor. These are designed to be controlled by two players, each equipped with standard eighty-eight-note keyboards. With the 2-T system, the two musicians can perform a fully orchestrated show.

The company rents the hardware for particular productions, much like a publisher rents a score and orchestral parts. The system comes with software designed for a specific show, as well as a specially modified printed score for playing the show. The software contains complex maps or *orchestration points* (a typical show will have perhaps 300 of these). These maps are accessed sequentially by the players from foot pedals, or nonsequentially from any of a number of sources (including a numeric keypad or specific MIDI commands). Each map contains keyboard splits, Program Changes, Controller settings, and other processing algorithms appropriate to that point in the score. When a map is called up, the notes played on the keyboards (dictated by the printed score) produce the notes that a full orchestra would be sounding at that moment in the score.

The system's processing algorithms can be highly complex. A single note can play a fully orchestrated chord. Moving a volume pedal will change the volume relative to where it is currently (instead of making the volume immediately jump to the current position of the pedal, as would a normal Controller 07 command). Different volume response curves can be sent to different synth voices, allowing for complex balance shifts and fades. Hitting a note or moving a controller wheel can turn on vibrato for a predetermined number of subsequent notes, and then automatically turn it off. A single note can trigger a harp glissando or very fast string passage. To ensure that the tempo of the minisequence matches the tempo of the performance, the performer must tap out the correct tempo on a nonsounding key just prior to the event. (Eventually, the designers hope to make the system able to analyze tempo automatically from notes that are part of the score, so that this won't be necessary: The system will calculate the tempo so that when the glissando is triggered it will be executed at precisely the right speed.) Finally, to free up the players' hands, a note or chord that needs to be held underneath a long passage can be programmed so that once played it will continue to sound until some other predetermined event takes place. The possibilities go on and on.

The emphasis of this system is on live performance. Except for things like harp glissandos, no sequencing is used. If a group wants to have one or more other musicians in the pit playing acoustic instruments, the software can be adjusted by the user to eliminate specific voices from the score. The scores are marked so that performing groups can easily choose the combinations of instruments they want. In most cases drums and bass are left out of the scores to encourage the use of a live rhythm section.

Sequencers in Performance

Although some theater musicians wouldn't be caught dead using sequencers, others swear by them. Sequencers have the advantage of providing virtually unlimited orchestral textures and palettes. Their main disadvantage in theater work is that they don't respond to conductors too well. For instance, shouting at a sequencer to skip twenty-four bars when a dancer twists an ankle doesn't work as well as it does with live players.

Here's a description of how New York composer and arranger Jeremy Roberts uses Opcode's Vision software as the sequencer in a theatrical production. This program allows instant recall of up to twenty-six sequences from a computer keyboard. By breaking each song up into component parts and making each part into a separate sequence, the player can jump around from section to section as necessary. A certain section of a song may be set up as a loop for a "vamp until ready" cue—or in case a singer wants to hold out a note for a few extra beats. In this case, the player must hit the key to change sequences at exactly the right point, or the rhythm will jerk.

Another Opcode product is the Studio 5, which is a combination Macintosh MIDI interface and real-time MIDI processor. This device can be extremely useful in this type of system because it can handle multiple-channel Program

Changes, controller mappings, and so on. The setups in the Studio 5 (which has room for 128) are programmed using special Macintosh software. The setups can then be recalled using standard Program Change commands.

Roberts feels strongly that actors and singers appreciate consistency in tempos from one performance to the next. For this reason, he has no qualms about using sequencers for about thirty to forty percent of the music in a show. He has programmed macros in Vision that can slow down or speed up the tempo in increments of one or two beats per minute at the touch of a button. If, for some reason, the music gets ahead of or behind the singing or stage action, the sequencer can be made to mirror the way a conductor would subtly change the tempo of music played by a live ensemble to follow a singer.

Midi on the Air

The amount of live music heard on the airwaves these days is very small. There is the occasional classical or rock concert broadcast on radio or cable or network television. However, there are other aspects of broadcasting that depend significantly on a live element, and here MIDI has a number of uses.

Disk jockeys who use sound effects during broadcasts (usually for comic relief) rely on random access to a library of sounds. Tape cartridges are fine for commercials and other recorded announcements, but they are a little slow for executing a perfectly timed rimshot. Midi-based samplers give the DJ a much higher degree of spontaneity. Triggered from a small keyboard in front of the DJ's console, a sampler can be used to play effects, musical stings, IDs, and even short spots. A small MIDI setup can play background music for live commercials. This gives the DJ or engineer immediate control over the timing of the *donut;* that is, the music before, during, and after the spiel. MIDI-controlled effects can also be used to add color or weirdness to a DJ's voice or to the voice of a telephone caller. The type and amount of the effect may be controlled by Program Changes sent from the same keyboard used to control the sampler.

A Case History—*What's the Score?*

One of the authors of this book (Paul) was involved in a radio project that used MIDI technology on the air to a great degree. Allow us now to switch into a first-person narrative to provide a description of the show and how MIDI made it happen.

Hi, Paul here. I was asked to help design a new radio show, *What's the Score?*, produced by WGBH-FM, a major public station in Boston, Massachusetts. It was a call-in musical quiz program where listeners were asked to identify pieces of music played on the air, and tested on musical trivia in various categories. A host talked to the callers and did the general chatter, and my job was to be the equivalent of the in-studio live band: to play musical examples, fill space, and comment aurally on the proceedings with both music and sound effects. A typical segment consisted of the host asking a caller a series of questions like "Who lived longer, Mozart or Schubert?" or "Who wrote the lyrics to *West Side Story?*" If the caller did well, he or she was awarded a prize, which could be anything from a coffee mug to a pair of concert tickets.

The music I added under these segments served to help (or sometimes confuse) the caller, or provided entertainment for the listeners while the caller struggled with the answer. For the first question, for example, I played an original, classical-sounding piece that wove together tunes by Schubert and Mozart, and for the second I played a jazz arrangment of "Tonight,"

The producers of the show wanted more than just a piano player, or even a synth player—they wanted fully orchestrated music. Besides the underscoring, they wanted opening and closing themes, bridges between segments, fanfares, and sound effects like cheers, boos, and, vaudeville-style rimshots. The challenge was to come up with a way to jump instantly and randomly from cue to cue, making the jumps sound natural and at the same time maintaining live control over as many elements as possible.

Live Versus Sequenced

Playing all the music live was not a viable option: it would have involved shuttling a lot of printed sheet music, designing keyboard splits with the orchestration for each cue, and then playing everything note-perfectly. An average thirty-minute show would have about three dozen cues, ranging from five to sixty seconds, and keeping them all straight and smooth while we were on the air promised to be a logistical, technical, and musical nightmare.

The solution was to sequence as many of the cues as I could, and use a single, multitimbral keyboard synthesizer to play them back. The instrument I chose was the Kurzweil K2000, a combination synthesizer, sampler, and effects processor. Recorded sequences would be played on MIDI Channels 2 through 16, while Channel 1 (with Local Control turned On) was reserved for live playing of short cues and sampled effects.

A conventional sequencer would not be able to provide random access to the many different cues, so I used HyperCard for the Macintosh, designing a custom program or "stack." I used a series of extensions to HyperCard designed by Opcode Systems that allow playing of Standard MIDI Files from a stack. I used a conventional sequencer to record all the cues, including initial Bank Select (Controller 20H, 32 decimal) and Program Change messages for each track, to access the more than nine hundred programs that can be stored in the K2000. The Program Changes also controlled the effects, so I could go from a concert hall for a Beethoven symphony to a small nightclub for the Thelonious Monk trio instantaneously. These sequences were then saved to disk as Standard MIDI Files.

The HyperCard stack contained a set of on-screen buttons, one for each MIDI file. When I clicked on a button, it first sent out an "All Notes Off" message (Controller 7CH, 123 decimal), to cleanly cut off the sound of any cue already playing, and then started the designated cue.

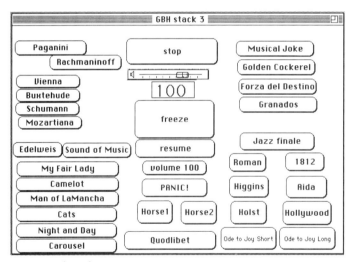

HyperCard stack

The overall MIDI velocity and tempo of a sequence can be changed right in HyperCard, either in real time, using on-screen faders, or as part of the "script" of the button that calls up the file. Since HyperCard lets you reprogram a stack literally as it is running, this feature allowed me to make last-minute adjustments to the files in the studio to make sure they all played at similar volumes.

The tempo-scaling feature let me create a "freeze" button, which set the tempo of the currently-playing file to 1% of its nominal tempo. This let me stop a sequence at any time and hold the notes, the way a real bandleader would get his orchestra to pause while waiting for something to happen. After the freeze, I could tell my virtual band to stop entirely, resume playing (a "resume" button set the tempo back to 100%), or go instantly to another cue.

Sound Effects

The live keyboard was used primarily for sound effects, which I recorded into the K2000. Like most samplers, the K2000 loses its memory when the power is turned off, and so I saved all of the sounds on a SyQuest removable 44-megabyte hard drive, which I would reload into the K2000 through its SCSI port for each show.

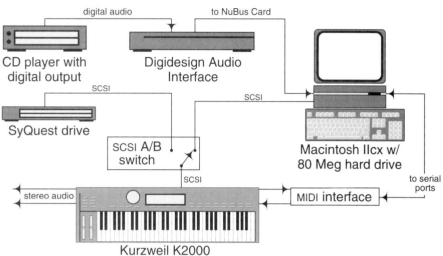

the production setup

Every key or group of keys had a different effect. These included the crowd at a rock festival, a New Year's Eve party, a bunch of kids booing, breaking glass, a maniac laughing, an orchestra tuning up, and of course a complete drum set. Some of the effects were assigned to multiple keys so that I could thicken them by playing two or more, or lengthen them by playing one and then the other.

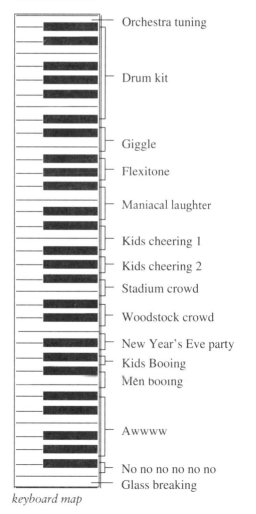

Orchestra tuning

Drum kit

Giggle

Flexitone

Maniacal laughter

Kids cheering 1

Kids cheering 2

Stadium crowd

Woodstock crowd

New Year's Eve party

Kids Booing

Men booing

Awwww

No no no no no no

Glass breaking

keyboard map

Besides the sound effects, I set up several other programs for use on the "live" channel, including brass with timpani and cymbals for fanfares, marimba and wood block for a clock-ticking effect, and a wah-wah trumpet for when a contestant blew an answer.

Name Those Tunes

Each show also featured a different musical puzzle, which consisted of various musical fragments strung together in odd ways. Listeners had to identify the fragments, and send in their answers on postcards to win prizes. For one of the puzzles, I put together a sixty-second piece containing fourteen classical, jazz, and theatrical themes, played on inappropriate instruments, and laid on top of a schlocky, big-band, pseudo-disco beat. The week after we played the puzzle, I was asked to "dissect" it for the listeners. I broke the original sequence, recorded with Passport Designs' Master Tracks Pro 5, into fourteen shorter sequences, each one containing a single theme, and increased the velocity of the track containing the theme to make it clearer. I then played the sequences using the program's Playlist feature—this lets you set up as many as sixteen files and play them one at a time, in order. Between songs, the sequencer waits for you to press a computer key (or anything else you specify) before it plays the next song. I would play one sequence, identify the theme, and hit a key on the Mac to start the next one instantly.

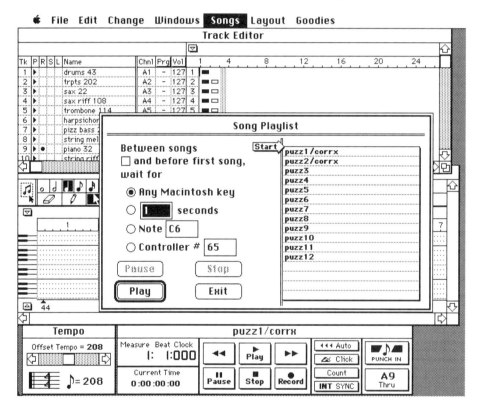

Besides being a lot of fun, *What's the Score?* was a unique opportunity to explore the use of MIDI in a medium that hasn't yet used it nearly as effectively as It could—and maybe someday, will.

Chapter 6

Sound Editing

One of the things that is most attractive about MIDI as a compositional tool is the enormous palette of sounds readily available to the composer. MIDI instrument technology is continually evolving to provide new models and methods of sound synthesis. Software and hardware using MIDI System Exclusive commands are constantly being refined to make it both faster and easier to include these timbres in a MIDI-based composition. This chapter covers the various types of synthesis commonly available in commercial MIDI instruments, as well as the ways both synthesized and sampled sounds are edited, saved, and loaded into these instruments. The different sounds a synthesizer or sampler makes are commonly referred to as "sounds," "patches," "timbres," "programs," or "voices." We'll use all of these terms here except "voice," since that word is often used for something else: an individual note in a polyphonic synthesizer, as in "twenty-four-voice polyphony."

System Exclusive

MIDI System Exclusive commands are primarily used to modify a synthesizer's sounds. SysEx commands were designed to enable manufacturers to create MIDI messages that work with any specific instrument, regardless of its sound architecture. By sending SysEx to an instrument from an external source—such as a computer application—a person can edit any parameter of any sound stored in the synthesizer. MIDI samplers work similarly, but the process has some different dimensions.

Patch Editors and Librarians

Along with sequencers, patch editors and librarians are among the most useful kinds of MIDI application software developed for the personal computer. A *patch librarian* is the simpler of the two. It receives and stores SysEx data that define the parameters of any or all sounds (or banks of sounds) stored in a synth. Depending on the structure of the synth, the patch librarian can receive the data when a button is pushed on the synth's front panel, or it can request the synth to send the data. The librarian can save the sounds or banks to disk, and send them back to the instrument on demand. Since a computer is usually outfitted with a much greater storage capacity than a synthesizer (although the recent inclusion of floppy drives and SCSI ports on MIDI instruments is changing this), the user can accumulate a vast assortment of sounds that can be easily uploaded to the synth.

A *patch editor* can also download sound data from an instrument, save it, and send it back. Where it exceeds the librarian is in its ability to let the user edit the instrument's sounds using the computer. This capability became very important as manufacturers realized that they could cut costs by including fewer hardware controls on the instruments themselves. As a result, a large number of synthesizers have few or no onboard sound editing controls, and rely completely on computer-based patch editors in this respect.

When the user selects a sound in a patch editor—whether the sound has just been downloaded from the instrument or loaded from the computer's storage—the software sends the SysEx data defining that sound to the instrument's *edit buffer* or *edit register:* that's the area of the synthesizer's memory where its current sound is loaded. This is identical to what occurs when a sound is edited with the instrument's controls (if it has any).

The editor usually provides one or more ways for the user to play the sound:

- Keyboard Thru

- On-screen keyboard

- Sequence record and playback

The *keyboard Thru* feature is similar to those found on sequencers: The user plays the main controller, and the MIDI data generated is passed on to the instrument being edited, which plays the sound. An *on-screen keyboard* display plays the selected synth when the user clicks the mouse on the keys. Alternatively, some programs allow notes to be sounded when computer keys are pressed. Some editors let the user record a short sequence of notes that can be played back at any time. This sequence may even play back automatically when a parameter is edited, letting the user hear the results of the edit.

The editor presents a display that describes the parameters of the instrument's sound-generating capabilities. When a sound has been edited to the user's satisfaction, it can be saved to any of the computer's storage devices—by itself, as part of a bank, or as part of an open-ended library of patches. Patch editors can also send sounds, either individually or in banks, directly to the instrument's memory.

Early editors simply displayed a set of labels and numbers ("Volume = 24," for example). To edit a parameter, the user typed in a new number. The Apple Macintosh, with its graphic user interface, changed this by inspiring software developers to design screens that give the user a graphic overview of the instrument's sound architecture This often incorporates on-screen equivalents of such standard controls as faders, knobs, push buttons, and numerical readouts. In addition, these programs have developed a number of useful conventions that represent quite clearly some of the more abstract elements of synthesizer architecture, such as envelopes, matrix modulation grids, and keyboard splitting/layering.

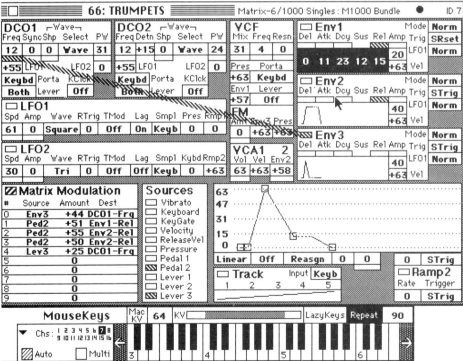

A patch editor uses interactive graphics to display elements of a synthesizer's sound architecture. (Oberheim Matrix-1000 module from Galaxy+ Editors by Opcode Systems)

Let's take a close look at how an envelope may be displayed. Just above the lower right-hand corner in the illustration above, a standard *ADSR (Attack/Decay/Sustain/Release)* envelope is graphically depicted as a grid. The y axis represents the amplitude (the degree to which the envelope is open) and the x axis represents time. Like most of the elements of this screen, the envelope display is interactive. Each segment of the envelope, for instance, has a *handle* (shown as a small square) at each end. Clicking and dragging these handles sends SysEx data to the synth that changes the amplitudes and time values of the envelope segments. In addition to providing an informative display and offering easy control over such details, the graphic nature of the patch-editor display provides an immediate and intuitive overview of all the sound's parameters.

The above illustration also provides an example of how programming a complex modulation matrix can be made clear. The shaded line going diagonally from the right center to the upper left of the window connects an envelope generator (Env 3) to one of the instrument's digital oscillators (DCO1). When this line is visible, either end of it can be dragged to any of a number of the timbre's elements. In this way, the user can route the output of MIDI velocity, envelopes, LFOs, pedals, and other sources to destinations such as oscillator pitch, filter settings, or envelope segments. (Some elements can act as either a source or a destination. That is, they can either send a signal that affects another element or be affected themselves by another element's output.) The panel in the lower left displays the other modulation matrix routings active in this particular timbre. Each of these can be edited in the same fashion. A graphic depiction and mouse-based control of a structure as complex as a synthesizer's sound architecture is invaluable. It offers both control over the details and an overview that helps the user to conceptualize the structure of the sound—and work with it in a meaningful way.

Configuring Synthesizers

In addition to timbre programming, a patch editor can help configure global aspects of a synthesizer. The complex voice and output assignments of multitimbral instruments particularly benefit from a good graphic editing interface.

1: 4 horns				TX81Z Performance : Strings&H... ● ID 4			
Assign mode	**Normal**	Effect	**Off** ▶	Microtune table	**Oct.**	**Key**	–
	1	**2**	**3**	**4**	**5**		
Notes	1	1	2	2	2	0	0	0
MIDI Ch.	3	4	5	6	7	–	–	–
Voice	Int 4	Int 8	Int 12	Int 18	Int 1	– –	– –	– –
	1 : Horn		3 : Sy.Brass 4		5 : Flute 1			
	2 : Sax 2		4 : Trumpet 1					
Volume	95	99	89	92	99	–	–	–
Out Assign	I	II	I & II	I & II	I & II	–	–	–
Low Limit	C0	G#1	C-1	C-1	C-1	–	–	–
High Limit	G1	G#2	G9	G9	G9	–	–	–
Note Shift	0	0	0	+12	-12	–	–	–
Detune	+1	0	-1	+1	0	–	–	–
LFO Select	2	2	Vib	Off	Vib	–	–	–
Microtune	Off	Off	Off	Off	Off	–	–	–

This window lets you organize the various elements of a multitimbral synthesizer. (Yamaha TX81Z module from Galaxy+ Editors)

The above illustration shows a screen that configures an instrument with five multitimbral parts, indicated by the large numbers 1 through 5 across the top of the window. Working down from each of these numbers, you'll see boxes for setting the following parameters for each part.

  • The number of notes available

- The MIDI channel on which the part receives data

- The patch used (Yamaha calls it a "voice")

- Volume

- The audio output(s) the part uses

- The lowest MIDI note number to which the part will respond

- The highest MIDI note number to which the part will respond

- Transposition in half steps of incoming MIDI notes

- Detuning in fractions of a half-step

- The type of LFO used

- Microtuning (non-tempered scale) table on/off

While this window is not a particularly striking example of a graphic interface, it illustrates the concept of instrument configuration beyond just patch programming. Most of these parameters are regularly used in configuring multitimbral synthesizers. Individual parameters are simultaneously visible—and each can easily be edited by clicking and dragging the number.

Universal Editor/Librarians

Early editor/librarians were designed to work with just one model of synthesizer. By around 1990, *universal editor/librarians* appeared that consolidated control over an entire studioful of instruments. These universal programs are continually updated to accommodate new instruments, and make the "online MIDI studio" much closer to reality. One feature offered by the better universal editor/librarians is control over MIDI patch bays. Many large studios use a MIDI patch bay to route MIDI signals. One of the benefits of these devices is their ability to instantly reconfigure the studio's MIDI routings by calling up a configuration the user has already programmed and stored in the patch bay. Calling up a program on a patch bay is an infinitely superior alternative to repatching cables.

Often the cable routing needed for using an editor/librarian is different from that needed for a sequencer. A synth whose parameters are being edited normally needs to both send and receive SysEx, so both its MIDI In and Out jacks must be connected to the computer. On the other hand, when a sequencer is running, only the studio's main controller should be sending data to the computer. The rest of the studio's sound modules should only receive data from the sequencer or from the main controller via the sequencer. A MIDI patch bay can be programmed with a number of different routing configurations to serve both the sequencing and the editing requirements of each instrument in the studio. To the uninitiated, this may sound like a trivial matter, but even the most casual experience trying to control a multimodule MIDI studio will confirm that simple, fast reconfiguration (without the drudgery and confusion of constantly swapping cables) is an important element in the studio's functioning.

As a result of this need, the most useful universal editor/librarians have the following capabilities:

- They can be programmed to recognize which instruments receive on which MIDI channels in any studio.

- They remember the programs in the MIDI patch bay that connect both the MIDI In and Out of each instrument to the computer.

- They remember which patch-bay programs connect the studio controllers to the computer for sequencing.

If all the connections are properly made, and the programming and channelizing properly set up, a user can go from composing to editing or uploading a patch on any instrument, then back to composing without losing the thread. Unfortunately, a flaw in any one of those links can snap the chain and create serious delays in the process. In fact, many experienced MIDI users find it necessary to separate editing sessions from composing sessions. Each task requires a kind of concentration and creativity specific to itself—and very few people can readily switch from one to the other. For this reason, composers will often set aside one session for creating new sounds and a different one for composing with a stable and familiar set of sounds.

Algorithmic Patch Generation

Several approaches are available to users who want to develop new patches. If you are adventurous, you may choose to start from scratch with an *initial* patch and create something totally new. Or, you can modify patches programmed by others (either the ones that come with the instrument or ones available from other commercial or noncommercial sources). Some editors offer a third option: automatic patch-generating algorithms. These functions can create a new bank of patches, ranging in size from one to hundreds or more, in a matter of seconds. Here are some of the ways in which these algorithms accomplish their task.

- *Random patch creation:* The software assembles a bank of patches built on completely random parameter values.

- *Constrained random patch creation:* As above, but you can set limits to the randomization of certain parameters.

- *Parameter shuffling:* A new bank of patches is created by randomly mixing the parameter values in an existing bank of patches.

- *Parameter transition:* A new bank is created that consists of patches whose settings gradually change from those of one patch to those of another.

Parameter shuffling and parameter transition require source patches from which to start. These functions are very useful when you work with commercial patch libraries and want to create sounds that are just a little different. The first two work with no raw material whatsoever (except for any constraints you may set). Generally speaking, a bank created with these functions will contain a very high percentage of junk. However, all you need to justify your efforts are a couple of really good, original sounds. Sorting through a bank of sounds created by a random generation algorithm is usually a very fast process—just don't expect to strike gold right away.

Types of Synthesis

Patch editors work with all the major kinds of synthesizers: analog, digital, additive, FM, wavetable, and the many hybrid architectures now available. Some instruments use analog technology under digital control. The digital-control aspect simply means that the instrument can be controlled by MIDI. Otherwise the elements of its sound architecture, its operation, and its timbres are those of any purely analog synth. The editing window of a patch editor for this type of synth displays analog-style elements such as oscillators, waveforms, filters, envelopes, LFOs, and voltage-controlled amplifiers (VCAs) as shown below. You can, for example, set either of the instrument's two (digitally controlled) oscillators to generate sine, square, pulse, or sawtooth waves, and the frequency at which they will do so. The display makes setting the frequency easy by referring to it as half steps in relation to concert pitch. In the illustration below you'll see *12* under the word *Freq*. This setting means both oscillators will play an octave (twelve half-steps) above whatever key you press. Entering *-12* would set the oscillators an octave below concert pitch, and so forth. At the right of the detail—under *Shp*, *Select*, and *PW*—you can select various waveshapes and modify their pulse widths (*PW*) to get a wide selection of basic sounds.

details of analog synth editing

In the same way, the *VCF* (*voltage-controlled filter*) box lets you set the frequency and resonance of the low-pass filter the Mix of the two oscillators that is fed to it. The ADSR settings of Envelope 1 appear to the right, as do the delay before the envelope kicks in, its amplitude, and its sensitivity to key velocity.

FM Digital Synthesis

FM digital synthesis was first popularized by Yamaha with its DX7 synthesizer, and has been incorporated in many other Yamaha devices since then. FM synths particularly benefit from graphic editing interfaces, because programming FM sounds can be highly counterintuitive. Having all of the *operators*—the individual waveforms that act together to affect the patch's amplitude and timbre—laid out graphically makes it much easier to understand how they act on each other. The figure below illustrates how a DX7II/TX802 editor displays a block of parameters for each of the instrument's six operators, including controls for the following.

- turning the operator on and off

- configuring the amplitude envelope by numeral or click-and-drag graphic

- configuring the scaling curve, so the operator level increases or decreases as you move up and down the keyboard

- adjusting output level, velocity sensitivity, envelope rate scaling, and amplitude modulation (*tremolo*) sensitivity

- adjusting pitch with coarse, fine, and detune settings

In addition, the window offers controls over a sound's overall pitch envelope, range, LFO settings, choice of algorithm and other settings. A separate window, accessed by clicking on the graphic icons on the left side of the window just above the algorithm selector, sets up routings for the instrument's real-time controllers: Modulation Wheel (Controller 01), Foot Pedal (Controller 04), Breath Controller (Controller 02), and Channel Pressure.

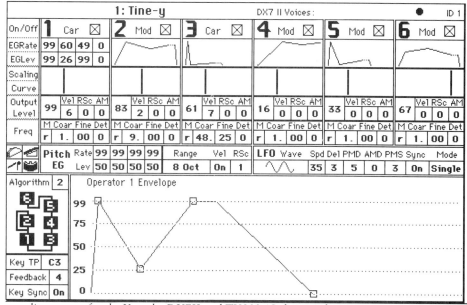

an editor screen for the Yamaha DX7II and TX802 (Galaxy+ Editors)

Sample Players

Sample players use recorded samples of real instruments and other sounds, burned into nonvolatile *Read-Only Memory* (ROM). The samples themselves are not editable and are designed to be as useful as possible when played in their natural state. The samples are usually multisampled to cover a wide musical range. In the interest of consistency of performance, the divisions and layout of the multisamples is not user-definable. However, many sample players allow real-time modification of the samples when they are played back, so that new sounds that combine the realism of recorded samples with the flexibility and creativity of a synthesizer can be created. These modifications include:

- layering multiple samples, to thicken textures or create hybrid sounds that combine elements of different sources, such as strings, bells, and human voices

- imposing user-defined envelopes on the samples, which can result in effects like bowed pianos or plucked choirs. Envelopes can be used for pitch control as well, and different envelopes can be laid onto different layers, so that the sound evolves over time.

- velocity control over the sound's attack time—or over the starting point of the sample playback—so that the sample's natural attack can be emphasized or eliminated

- velocity-switching between layers, so that a hard keystroke can produce a completely different sound from a soft one.

- the creation of LFOs that affect pitch or amplitude to give the samples motion

- affecting the balance between layers to allow timbral changes under live or sequencer control

The Kurzweil 1000 and 1200 series include some good examples of high-end sample players. This line has featured several models of keyboards and sound modules—each specializing in different families of sampled instruments. The illustration below shows a program for editing sounds on a Kurzweil 1000. As you can see, it is a complex program. (These windows do not all appear simultaneously, but open and close as various functions are called up.)

At the top of the screen is the program window, which assigns up to four sample layers to the program. A limit to the number of polyphonic voices used by the program can be specified. The instrument is capable of twenty-four-voice polyphony, although the actual number of voices available varies depending on the number of layers used in each program. Clicking on the Edit button next to one of the layers opens up an editing window for that layer. Two, or even all four, layers can be viewed at the same time (if you have a large enough screen). The editing window lets you choose the source sample—and set the layer's volume, pan position, and MIDI range. There are also sections for amplitude control, pitch control, LFO design, and envelope design—each of which can open its own subwindow when clicked on. The Pitch section, for example, lets you tune the layer in coarse and fine increments and determine the Pitch Bend range. Clicking on the musical-note icon opens the Pitch Control subwindow, where pitch-based LFOs can be defined as to the source, the depth controller, and the minimum and maximum pitch change. In this case, the depth is controlled by Modulation Wheel, and the source of the pitch change is LFO1 (each layer has four independent LFOs). LFO parameters, in turn, are accessed by clicking on the LFO1 box, and opening its subwindow. This subwindow gives control over waveshape and phase, as well as minimum and maximum rate values, and what type of control will determine the rate (in this case, Channel Pressure).

Yet another subwindow controls envelopes, both a main amplitude envelope and up to five auxiliary envelopes. The envelope shown can have any number of segments, while the others are simple Attack/Sustain/Release envelopes. These envelopes can then be assigned to volume, pitch, LFO, or various logical functions that interact with each other and the sound parameters.

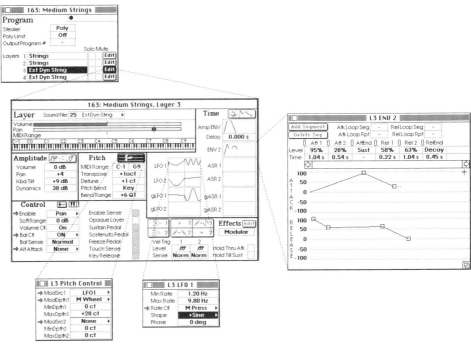

Kurzweil 1000 editing screens (Opcode K1000 Editor Librarian)

Sample/Synth Hybrids

Some MIDI instruments use both recorded samples and waveform-generating oscillators to produce their sounds. The architectures of these synths take advantage of the psychoacoustic phenomenon that when you hear a sound, most of the important information your ear and brain will use to try to identify it will occur during the first few milliseconds of the attack. These hybrids therefore, will do a credible job of emulating the sound of a violin, for example, by splicing the sampled attack of a violin onto a simple sawtooth wave. This technique allows for the creation of convincing sounding new instruments that sound real, but would be quite impossible to actually build. In addition, these sounds can be stored in a fraction of the space that complete samples require.

The following illustration shows the editing window for a Roland D-50—and the sophisticated way that a sample and synthesized waveform work together in the device. Like the Kurzweil editor, the D-50 editor gives you access to different aspects of the instrument's architecture in different windows. The screen shows the wave-generating aspects of the instrument. In the upper left, under *Struct* (structure), you can choose from seven different ways that the sampled wave (labeled *P* for PCM, the sampling technology used) and synth wave (labeled *S*) relate to each other—as well as the way each is routed through the D-50's onboard reverb (*R*). Towards the upper right of this window, under Pulse Width, is a graphic indicating the name of the PCM sample (Kalimba) and the shape of the synth waveform used in this patch (a sawtooth wave). Below this is a set of programmable numbers that allow you to set the waveform's pulse width, how it responds to Velocity and Aftertouch, and the LFO depth. These parameters do not affect the sampled part of the sound—just the synthesized part of the sound. D-50 samples always play exactly as they were recorded. This window also lets you edit the LFO depth and how Modulation Wheel and Channel Pressure affect pitch modulation. Here, you can also set the shape, rate, and delay of the LFO wave, and determine whether it will *sync* (start from a zero point) to each Note On command.

wave generating editor for the Roland D-50 (Opcode Galaxy+ Editors)

The illustration below depicts the envelope editor for the D-50 from the same program. In Roland's nomenclature, a filter and its envelope are called a *Time Variant Filter* (TVF). A volume envelope is referred to as a *Time Variant Amplitude* (TVA). The left side of the window offers control over the filter's initial level, resonance, keyboard tracking, and bias—and how the LFO and Channel Pressure change the filter. (*Bias* sets a point on the keyboard above or below which these controls take effect.) Below this are controls for the filter envelope, a graphic that displays the shape of the envelope, as well as velocity sensitivity and keyboard scaling controls. On the right are the controls for the amplitude envelope, which operate in the same way as the filter controls.

an envelope-editing window for the Roland D-50 (Opcode Galaxy+ Editors)

Sample Editors

The basic, theoretical distinction between a synthesizer and a sampler is the original source of their basic sounds. Synthesizers create sounds from scratch by generating a waveform with one or more analog or digital oscillators, and then modifying it with envelopes, LFOs, and the like. Samplers play back sounds that have been digitally recorded. A *sample editor* allows the user to alter those samples in various ways.

Synthesizers and samplers have been crossbred quite a bit. The differences between the two have thus become blurred—and this trend will continue as the technology evolves. Sample players are a good example: They often have synthesizer-like functions (envelopes, filters, LFO control, and so on) to add character to the samples they play. Their samples cannot be edited, but the sound-modifying functions can be handled with an editor that performs very much like a synthesizer editor. True samplers allow sounds to be recorded into their memory, and many of these also include sophisticated synth-style functions. In addition, they have their own sample-oriented modifiers, such as cutting and pasting and loop editing.

Sample-editing programs generally do *not* address any of a given sampler's synthesizer-type controls. Although early sample editors were designed to work with specific instruments, the sample editors available today generally don't address the controls of any particular sampler (except for some generic features like keyboard splits) Instead they modify only the sample itself. As samplers become more loaded with synth elements, it is possible that we will see a return to sampler-specific programs, which will incorporate patch-editor/librarian functions in addition to sample-editing features.

Sample-editing software loads sampled sounds—either from a computer storage medium or directly from a sampler. Most sample editors allow editing of sounds from a large number of different models of samplers, and so *profiles* of popular sampler models are included in the software to facilitate interchanging the sounds in formats that these individual models can deal with. The sample-editing application may also have the ability to record and play back sounds with specific hardware inside the computer—independent of any stand-alone sampler.

Once a sample is recorded or loaded, the software typically displays a graphic depicting the sound's waveform on the computer screen. It will play the sound back through the computer's speaker or through dedicated hardware—but not through the sampler. The software provides the user with an array of commands for editing the sound. You can alter volume, pitch, duration, and timbre using digital equalization or filtering. The software also typically allows extensive cut, copy, paste, and mixing functions. It may also allow mapping of one or more samples to any number of ranges and/or layers of the sampler's keyboard. The program will then allow the user to save the sound to the computer's storage media or to upload it back to the sampler.

Hardware

Unlike patch editors, sample editors do not typically play the sample being edited via the external sampler. Instead, the sample is played back through hardware associated with the computer. Patch editors can send all of the parameters that determine a sound down a MIDI line in a fraction of a second. However, samples are big files, and they require a long time to transfer from one device to another. If you want to hear an edit right away, the computer itself has to play it.

One method is to use the computer's native sound-generating circuitry and speaker. This is adequate under some circumstances, but the limitations of such circuitry make for poor sound quality (normally it is only eight bits, and operates at relatively slow sampling rates). A more useful approach is to use an expansion card installed in one of the computer's slots that plays sixteen-bit samples at a full sampling rate through an external amplifier and speakers. If an editor has a sample-recording function, it can often work with such a card if the card is equipped with analog audio inputs and onboard *analog-to-digital converters* (*ADCs*)—or digital inputs (*AES/EBU* or *S/PDIF*). In the latter case, sounds in the proper digital format can be recorded directly, but recording analog sounds (like from a microphone) requires digitizing the sounds with ADCs in an external device (like a DAT deck).

Loading a sample for playback and editing is implemented in two different ways, depending on the size of the sample and the way the software is structured. The most basic is to load the sound into the computer's RAM. The other common method is to load information about the sound into RAM and place an image of the sound waveform on the screen, but play it directly from (or record it directly to) the computer's hard disk. RAM-based methods provide faster edits and retain the disk version as a backup. However, they only allow you to load sounds of limited length; typically a few megabytes. (One megabyte can hold roughly twelve seconds.) Disk-based methods can let you work with longer sounds (up to the capacity of the disk). Since they perform edits to the sound directly on disk, you need twice as much disk space if you want to maintain a backup copy of sound that is being edited. Also, edits on disk files usually take longer than those done in RAM.

Seeing and Selecting

Sample editing requires both extreme close-ups and zoomed-out views of a sound. As with patch editors, the graphic interface of the Macintosh was instrumental in the development of sample editors (although a number of applications for the PC, Atari, and Amiga have also appeared).

The illustration below depicts an editor screen where the top third of the window shows an overview of the entire sample (a cello playing C♯4). The long white rectangle above the left end of the overview represents the portion of the wave shown in the lower display. The reverse-video section at the extreme left indicates a portion of the sample that has been selected for some kind of editing. The lower display is a close-up view of the first 600 or so milliseconds of the sample (and also shows the selected area in reverse video). If the lower display were zoomed in to a small area *within* the selected section, you could still look at the overview to see how much of the sample was selected. Clicking and dragging across any portion of the overview immediately fills the lower window with that selection. The user can select a portion of a sample by dragging the mouse across the section in the lower window. Not every sample editor has all these features or implements them in exactly the same way. However, a well-designed editor will always give you several ways to view the parts of a sound and move among those parts in order to edit the sound most effectively.

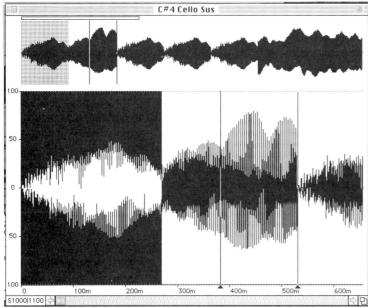

This window has an overview at the top, and a larger area below that can zoom into any part of a sample, select part of it and loop it. The numbers at the bottom give the sample's duration. (Sound Designer II by Digidesign)

Cut and Paste

One of the most powerful aspects of sample editing software is that it lets the user select any portion of a sound, with precision of up to a single sample. This can be as short as 1/48,000 of a second long. A selected area can be cut or copied out of the sample, and pasted back into it (or any other sample) at any point. In the figure, the overview area at the top shows that the attack portion of this note (the section selected in the lower area) has already been pasted three times into the middle of the note. The first of these pasted attacks appears at the right of the lower area, for that well-known "stuttering" effect.

A very common use for cut-and-paste editing is to splice the attack of one sound onto another very different sound to create a new timbre. An example of such sound design would be pasting the first 200 milliseconds of an iron door clanging onto a sustained cello note. To create a smooth transition in such a splice, good sample editors provide automatic *crossfades* between sounds pasted together. This feature allows the user to set the duration of the crossfade from a millisecond or two to a second or more.

Pasting one sound into the middle of another creates a gap in the target sound and inserts the new sound into the gap. A similar practice is mixing sounds rather than splicing them end-to-end. A copied sound can be mixed into another sample at any point—and the volumes of each controlled. The result will be the same as if they were blended in a mixing console. The more sophisticated user of this type of software will commonly paste and mix a number of samples to design a single sound.

Looping

Looping is a technique that allows a sampled sound to be sustained indefinitely—without recording enormous amounts of the sound into memory. When you play back a looped sample, it will play from the beginning, through to the end of the looped section, then instantaneously replay the looped section from its beginning to end, and continue looping in this way until the sampler's key is released.

Although the process of setting up a loop using an editor is fairly easy, creating a really good loop can be far from simple. Unless you don't mind an audible glitch every time the sample loops, a loop should be undetectable. This requires three things.

- The transition from the end of the loop to the beginning must sound seamless.

- The loop must not have any drastic dynamic, pitch, or timbral changes. For example, looped sounds typically should not have any heavy built-in vibrato: The sampler's LFOs should be used to create this effect.

- When the loop plays, it should sound enough like the rest of the sample to give the impression that the note is sustaining naturally.

Of course, these guidelines assume that the user wants to create a natural sound. A loop that violates any or all of the above rules can be quite useful for special effects or for experimental or consciously rude music.

The most basic problem with a loop is an audible click or pop where the end loops to the start. This can often be partially or completely solved by using the loop window provided by most editors. This window displays an extreme close-up (up to a few cycles) of the end and the beginning of the loop. When a loop plays, the end point of the loop immediately precedes the start point. For this reason, a loop window displays the end point on the *left* and the start point on the *right*, showing how the waveforms match up (or don't).

By scrolling each side of the window left and right, you can change the loop points so the start and end points have the same amplitude and are going in the same direction (up or down). Making both points occur at a *zero crossing* is also a good idea. A zero crossing is any point where the amplitude of the wave is zero (i.e., where it crosses the *x* axis). At points with zero amplitude, problems from any mismatch between loop points are minimized. It's also important to loop at points where the waveform looks the same, for this implies a similarity in timbres at these points. This will avoid an abrupt timbral change in the loop. The bad loop and the good loop in the figures below illustrate these concepts.

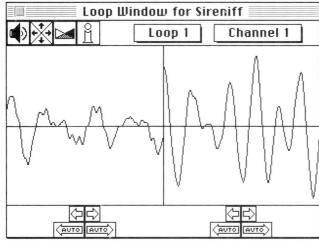

bad loop

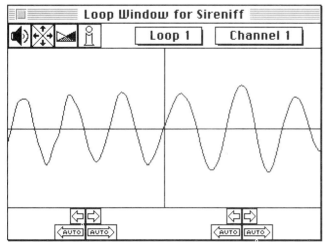

good loop

The loop points in the bad loop do not match in a number of ways and will create an audible sound. The loop points in the good loop match and should provide a noiseless loop. (Alchemy by Passport Designs)

The next consideration is the overall volume of the sample at the loop points. Even a small difference between the volume of the start and end points can produce an abrupt jump or drop as the loop cycles. The best way to avoid this is to find a section of the sample that is naturally level. If that's unavailable, some editors have a dynamic compression function that may help the situation. A problem may also arise from a related phenomenon. While the amplitude around the loop points may be identical, there may be a dip or peak in the middle of the loop. If such a situation results in an obvious, regular cycle, similar repairs will be necessary.

The pitch or timbre of the loop may also require editing. While the software may have pitch shifting or eq functions, it's not usually practical to modify these parameters at the loop level. Here, the best answer is often simply to find another section of the sound to loop.

Basically there are two kinds of loops: short and long. A short loop consists of anywhere from one to perhaps ten cycles of the wave. A short loop will work only if you can find a section whose sound fits in with the rest of the sample—and whose period doesn't change the pitch of the sound. A short loop functions more like a synthesizer wave than a sample. In fact, its effectiveness will usually depend on the synthesizer functions of the sampler. If the instrument has a good set of envelopes, filters, and LFOs, there's a better chance a short loop will work.

A long loop is typically a second or more in duration. A long loop is used when the sampler has enough RAM to allow you to loop a long chunk of sound. It can also help when there is no stable section available for looping. If this is the case, look for a loop where there is a pulsing in pitch, volume, or timbre, but where the changes are subtle, irregular, or musical enough to actually add life to the sample. This choice is a matter of experience (and opinion)—and the result will not work in every context. If the editor has a crossfade function, this can be a big help. This function interpolates data from the beginning and end of the loop so as to create a smooth loop point. The crossfades can be set up to be any length. The longer the crossfade, the smoother the loop (but long crossfades also tend to dull the tonal characteristics of a sound).

Crossfade Looping

Crossfade Type: ⦿ Linear
               ○ Equal Power

Loop Type: ⦿ Forward
          ○ Backward/Forward

Maximum Length: 19091 Samples

Crossfade Length: [19091] Samples

[Cancel]   [Continue]

---

crossfade loop editing

Sample looping is almost never as simple as it may seem. It relies on trial, error, experience, and not a small amount of blind luck. In some cases it may just not work at all—and a good loop may simply not be achievable in a given sample. On the other hand, sometimes one intuitive swipe of the mouse defines a loop so good it actually improves the sample. When this happens, have enough confidence in your ear not to change it out of sheer disbelief and lose it forever.

Digital Signal Processing

Many sample editors offer a host of *Digital Signal Processing* (*DSP*) functions such as pitch and time shifting, dynamic compression, equalization, and time-based effects. As sample editors have matured, they've developed the ability to process sounds in many of the same ways that traditional signal processing devices do. In addition to performing graphic and parametric equalization, dynamic compression, limiting, gating, and expansion, these programs can change the pitch of a sample without affecting its length Or, they can lengthen or shorten a sound's duration, without affecting the pitch. This feature, more than any other, has allowed sampling technology to expand beyond the needs of musicians into the realm of audio post-production.

Most sample DSP is handled *off-line*; that is, you define a processing function, let the computer crunch the numbers, and listen to the results. Most often, you have the option of undoing the effect if you don't like it. A few editors have functions that let you preview certain processing features (usually eq-related) before you commit to changing the sample. They can play the sample (or a section of it) repeatedly while you fiddle with on-screen controls and parameters. The internal playback hardware changes the sample "on the fly" so you can hear what the controls are doing. When you get the settings where you want them, you tell the program to execute the change, and the sample is permanently altered.

In some cases, you can store DSP parameters separately from the sample data. In this way, you can have the DSP applied to the sample when it plays, but the settings won't be an integral part of the sample itself. This feature can only be used when you are playing the sample from the computer, not from the external sampler that will ultimately be responsible for playing the sample.

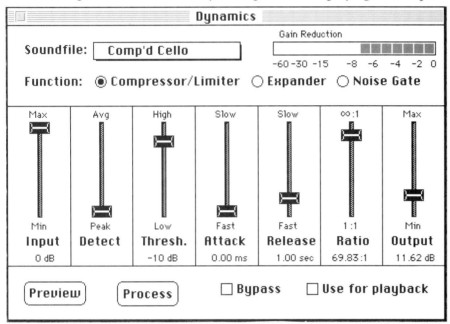

This display offers all the parameters common to compressor/limiters, expanders, and noise gates. (Sound Designer II)

Mapping, Multisampling, and Layering

After a sample has been edited to perfection, it must be sent to a MIDI sampler where it can be played. Theoretically, it can be played from any key of the sampler's keyboard (or another MIDI keyboard) and transposed appropriately. For example, if a sample of a piano's middle C is assigned to the sampler's middle C as its *root key*, then pressing middle C will play that sample back exactly as it came from the editor. Pressing the C below middle C will play that same sample transposed down an octave—and playing the C above middle C will transpose the sample up an octave.

This doesn't mean that one string sample will a full orchestra make. One of the limitations of digital sampling is that transposing a sample more than about a major third distorts its sound. Transposing can make a sample longer or shorter—or can add *aliasing* and other unwanted digital noises. Usually the most obvious problem is that the transposed timbre sounds as if it's being played on a tape recorder at the wrong speed, resulting in the "chipmunk" or "Donald Duck" effect (formally known in hip sampling circles as "Munchkinization"). The solution to this problem is multisampling; that is, taking a number of samples of a source at various pitches, then assigning them to different ranges in the sampler. So, for example, you might sample the piano notes C1, G1, C2, G2, C3, G3, and so on up the piano's keyboard. After editing each of these samples, you would assign C1 to that same key on the sampler (its root key)—but limit the range of notes that would play that sample from A0 to E1. Assign the G1 sample to a root key of G1, limit its transposition range to betwen F1 and G♯1, and so on.

This means most of the samples will be transposed no more than a major third (often the highest and lowest samples are excluded). The more multisamples you load into a sampler, the less distortion you'll get from excessive transposition (but the more sampler RAM you'll use).

Samplers can also assign samples to two or more *layers* of the keyboard. For example, playing with a velocity from 0 to 64 might play one sample, while playing with a velocity from 65 to 127 would play a different one. Sometimes the distinction is not so abrupt, and samples can blend into each other as velocity changes (a feature called *velocity crossfading*). Of course, any appropriate MIDI message can be assigned to control layered samples: Mod Wheel, Aftertouch, or any continuous controller.

Getting and Sending Samples

Most sample editing programs can communicate with most samplers—and editor manufacturers continually update their software to accommodate new instruments. There are four methods in which samplers and computer-based editors can communicate with each other. These are listed here roughly in order of their introduction.

1. MIDI System Exclusive
2. MIDI Sample Dump Standard, which uses "Universal System Exclusive" commands
3. high-speed serial communication, such as the RS-422 protocol used to connect computers with peripheral devices like modems and printers
4. SCSI, for *Small Computer Systems Interface*, which is a very high-speed protocol used by personal computers to communicate with hard disks and other storage media

The problem with SysEx is that the editor had to know the System Exclusive implementation for every sampler it might be used with. Such an editor must also make provisions for adding SysEx information for new devices as they came to market. The Sample Dump Standard alleviated that problem, but did not change the fact that transferring samples over MIDI can take a very, very long time. A sample consists of individual sixteen-bit *words* occurring 44,000 or 48,000 times per second. MIDI only passes 31,250 bits per second (and only seven out of every ten bits can be used for data—remember, the high bit must be zero). Thus, transmitting a sample over MIDI will take, under the most favorable of circumstances, at least thirty-two times as long as the sample's real-time length.

Serial communication can occur at speeds of up to 1MHz, and the seven-bit restriction does not necessarily have to be followed (since it's not MIDI). This method improves performance by a factor of thirty-five or more. However, no standard has been set for this kind of transfer—and only a handful of samplers from one manufacturer (E-Mu Systems) ever used it. This puts us back in the situation where a sample editor needs to know the correct protocol for every sampler it deals with.

SCSI can be very fast. It can pass several megabytes of data per second using a high-speed parallel interface. But SCSI is its own protocol—and an incredibly complicated and often vague one, at that. SCSI also requires specific hardware (cards, plugs, jacks, and cables) and software. It was first implemented in samplers as a way to use hard disks, with their large capacity and high speed, to store samples. Some sample editors adopted SCSI protocols as well, but there naturally was great concern that conflicting usages of SCSI would emerge, with all of the attendant problems.

SMDI

A protocol has been developed expressly for transferring sampled sound that essentially follows the format of (and can work in conjunction with) the MIDI Sample Dump Standard, but runs within the framework of the SCSI protocol. Called SMDI (for SCSI *Musical Data Interchange* and pronounced "smiddy"), this format was originally developed by Peavey, but is available to anyone who asks without charge. It was adopted early on by Passport Designs (makers of Alchemy), Kurzweil, and Turtle Beach Softworks (makers of software and hardware for IBM-compatible computers), with other manufacturers soon to follow.

Like MIDI, SMDI outlines a set of procedures and specifications that can be used by both hardware and software. Also like MIDI, even though there are no governing boards for its specification, manufacturers are being very careful to implement it correctly in their products. This will ensure universality and avoid problems in transferring data. Even so, it is a tricky protocol, and there are occasional glitches that have to be addressed by the user.

SMDI cannot, of course, become part of the MIDI spec, but there is some discussion going on among the governing bodies of MIDI concerning putting their approval on it, in one form or another. Whether or not that happens, it is quite possible that, before long, SMDI will be almost universally recognized by sampler and sample-editor manufacturers.

Using Patch and Sample Libraries

When the first synthesizers appeared, since their purpose was to create new and different sounds, it was assumed that each owner would produce his or her own patches. Creating original sounds was considered to be a very important part of the creative process of making electronic music. Indeed, until onboard digital memory came to the synthesizer, making your own patches was the only way to program a synth. Today, however, the majority of synthesizer users don't have the time or motivation to create all of their own patches. The role of the synthesizer itself has largely changed, as well. Rather than being used solely to produce new and original sounds, a synthesizer is very often used to imitate acoustic instruments, or even another synthesizer. (Just as one example of the latter, we have several dozen DX7 patches labeled "Jump" in honor of that Van Halen hit, which featured an Oberheim synth. Some of them aren't bad.) A number of companies offer preprogrammed, named, and organized patches for nearly every synthesizer ever sold, as well as sampled sounds for samplers.

Commercial Synthesizer Patches

Since synthesizer patches consist of SysEx data, they take up relatively little disk space. Collections of patches are comfortably packaged on floppy disks, typically in the format of a popular editor/librarian. Some instruments have built-in floppy disk drives—or slots for ROM or RAM cards that store magnetic data. The synthesizer manufacturer may even market disks or ROM cards of sounds in their instruments' native formats.

Although many commercial patches are quite good, it is often valuable to modify them to fit your own needs. One of the areas in which commercial patches often leave room for improvement is real-time control. This is also an area where you can effectively add musicality and naturalness to your sounds. Here's a general checklist to use when assessing the quality and usefulness of a given patch. If the patch is weak in any of these categories, try tweaking it as suggested.

- **Velocity.** Does velocity affect more than just volume? If the instrument allows for it, try routing velocity to the filter. This will give the sound some action independent of the filter envelope. With FM synthesizers, you can sometimes make one or more operators wholly controlled by velocity to give a wide range of character to a sound's attack.

- **Channel Pressure.** Does the patch use Channel Pressure to good advantage? In addition to changing volume or filter level, Channel Pressure is very useful in patches comprising two or more simpler layers ("timbres," in some manufacturers' nomenclatures). In these situations, you can assign Channel Pressure to change the relative level of the different layers or waves. This can make the sound change radically, or subtly, depending on how you modify the patch.

- **LFO.** The shape, rate, and depth of an LFO on a given store-bought patch will rarely be perfect for the piece you're composing at the moment. Setting the LFO to pulse with the beat (or at some regular division of the beat) can make a line sound as if it was played by a musician listening to the rest of the band. Deepening the LFO depth can make a solo line stand out; lessening the depth can make an instrument fit in better with an ensemble. Making the LFO rates slightly different among the various patches playing an ensemble line can make a synthetic sounding group seem more lifelike.

- **Modulation and Pitch Bend.** The range of the wheel controls may be much too wide or too narrow for your playing style (or for a given context). Make these greater (or smaller) for more impact (or more subtlety).

Commercial patch libraries are perfect candidates for the algorithmic patch generation functions discussed earlier in this chapter. These functions can create a new bank of patches in a matter of seconds—and quickly turn a good library into several good libraries.

Databases

Finding small bits of data on disk is never easy, and a personal patch library is no exception. Some librarian programs let you attach tags to patch or bank files, and search for them according to those tags. If you have a database program, you can develop your own file of patches that lets you find them by various criteria. These might include:

- date

- synth

- instrument type or sound category (multiple categories or keywords can be helpful)

- transposition

- number of voices or layers

- real-time controllers

- a short description of the sound

You will find this an invaluable tool when you need a sound quickly. If you don't have a database, a simple word processor or spreadsheet program will work just fine. A list on paper doesn't have the expandability, search capabilities, or easy storage of a computerized list—but it's better than nothing.

Commercial Samples

Commercial sample libraries come either as plain, unprocessed samples, or they are configured for particular samplers. In theory, these sounds are sampled under the finest studio conditions: the best musicians playing the best instruments recorded by the best engineers using the finest microphones, mixers, and recording devices. If the samples are processed with reverb, chorus, or other signal processors, the gear used for this is also theoretically much better than the average Joe or Jane can afford. And all of the above is supposedly supervised by a producer who understands the needs of the sampler owner in need of fresh sounds. In reality, of course, not all of these elements are always evident in the production of every sample. Use care and research when choosing a commercial sample library, and make sure that it is manufactured and distributed by a reputable company.

Since samples take up so much more storage space than synth patches, floppy disks are not the medium of choice for exchanging them. Even though some libraries are still available on large sets of floppies, providers are now more likely to put their libraries on CD, CD-ROM, magneto-optical disks, or SyQuest cartridges (44-megabyte removable hard disks).

Audio Compact Discs

Conventional compact discs contain audio information in the format known as *Red Book audio*. To get this sound into a sampler or sample editor, you must route the audio output of the CD player into the audio input of a sampler. Or, if the editing software can record sounds using an internal audio card, you can route the CD audio to the computer. If your CD player has a digital output and your sampler (or audio card) has a digital input of the same format, you can route the sound digitally. In this way, you can avoid converting the digital data on the CD to analog, and then back to a digital format again in the sampler or editor.

The digital outputs on CD players most often come in the S/PDIF or AES/ EBU Consumer format (also called *IEC Type II* or *CP-340 Type II*). This format uses a single RCA connector for two channels of audio. Some professional CD players have an *AES/EBU Professional* (sometimes called just *AES/ EBU*) digital out, which can be identified by its XLR connector. Still others have an optical-fiber digital output. All of these connectors can also be found on different samplers. In most cases, signals from one type of connector cannot be sent to a different type. Thus, if a CD player advertises "digital outs" and a sampler advertises "digital ins," the two machines will not necessarily work together. The formats and connectors have to be the same as well.

The major advantage of a digital transfer is that it will prevent any buildup of noise or distortion. This is not to say that analog transfers should be avoided. In practice, one or two digital-analog-digital transfers (with properly referenced levels, good cables, and solid contacts) will not produce any discernible ill effects.

CD-ROM Libraries

Libraries that come on CD-ROM are recorded as data files in one of the following formats.

- a format specific to a particular sampler, in which case the samples may also include key mappings, control matrices, and other performance parameters

- a format specific to a particular sample-editing program, in which case the samples will be raw samples

- a universal format such as *AIFF* (for *Audio Interchange File Format*). This standard was developed by Apple Computer for exchanging sound files of all types (music, sound effects, speech, and so on) among different applications. Most sample-editing applications can readily deal with this class of raw samples.

A CD-ROM is not meant to be read by an audio CD player, but by a CD-ROM player that is connected to a computer or sampler (usually through a SCSI port). CD-ROM sample files are not audio files and could possibly harm your speakers or amplifier should you try to play them on a CD player. However, CD-ROMs can also contain Red Book audio, and some companies include Red Book versions of their samples to provide flexibility. CD-ROM players normally have audio outputs through which these tracks can be heard, although in some cases the quality of the output is not very high. If you cue up the disc properly you can play back the Red Book audio tracks on a conventional CD player. However, improper cueing can cause actual damage to your audio equipment, so it is recommended that you play CD-ROMs on CD-ROM drives only.

With the advent of CD-ROMs and universal formats like AIFF, sample libraries on SyQuest cartridges and magneto-optical disks are becoming increasingly rare. Libraries distributed in these formats are generally designed for specific samplers.

Choosing a Library

Regardless of format, the quality of a sample library can be evaluated by common sense criteria such as potential usefulness and uniqueness. Sample libraries are available that concentrate on individual instrumental sounds from distinct musical genres, such as classical, pop, or electronic music. Others focus on specific sound types such as percussion hits or orchestral chords and stabs—or on longer sounds such as harp glissandi. There are also plenty of sound-effects libraries available, which may include natural or industrial sounds or both. These are most often to be found on audio CD but can also be obtained as samples on CD-ROM for both musical and post-production work. An increasingly popular form of sample library consists of rhythmic loops to be used in dance music—either in the recording studio or by club DJs. Obviously, the type of music you make will determine what type of library to buy. If the library consists of samples of musical instruments, consider the following features.

- The sounds should be organized into banks for multisampling—with groups of notes, no more than a fifth apart, covering at least the natural range of the instrument being sampled.

- Each note in a bank should be played and recorded at levels essentially identical to other notes.

- There should be separate banks for notes played at normal, high, and low intensities. Also helpful are separate banks for notes with varying articulations, depending on the capabilities of the instrument.

- Notes should have no vibrato, tremolo, pitch bend, or other ornamentation. (These effects should be added by the end user in the sampler as performance options.)

- The miking should be appropriate to the instrument. Close-miking a snare drum or guitar amp might sound fine, but violins, bassoons, and steel drums need some space between them and the microphone to sound natural.

- Unless the samples are already processed for a sampler, they should be long enough to give you room to find a loop—but not so long as to eat up all your sampler's RAM. (Remember: A minute of sixteen-bit 44.1kHz stereo sound needs about ten megabytes of RAM or disk space.)

The following considerations apply to samples of any kind.

- **Audio quality.** Each sample should have the highest level possible without distortion. This helps keep the signal-to-noise ratio low. In fact, no noise should be present in any sample. This includes hiss, hum, buzz, sounds not part of the sample, or noises produced by a musician's poor instrumental technique.

- **Production quality.** Listen for consistency in miking technique. Miking too close creates a proximity effect (boomy bass). A wrong placement can distort the sound. Placing the mike too far away can introduce room noise.

- **Frequency range.** Sounds should come across in their full frequency range, with no unwanted peaks or valleys at different points in the spectrum.

Customizing Samples

Samples require effort to make them usable. Each multisampled bank of sounds you acquire will need to be customized to accommodate the capabilities of your sampler. Libraries that contain completely unprocessed samples will require the most work, while sampler-specific libraries will require the least (but may also perhaps offer less flexibility). Here are some techniques you can use to customize the sounds in a sample library.

- Use the filter (and any envelopes controlling it) to make a multisample more realistic or to change it radically to produce an entirely new sound.

- Layer different multisamples together to create new sounds. Use fast-acting envelopes to create percussive sounds and slow envelopes to create pads and string simulations.

- Make envelopes sensitive to pitch (shorter at higher pitches) and/or velocity (faster attacks at higher velocities) to simulate the natural envelopes of acoustic instruments.

- Detune layers to produce chorus effects.

- Include as much real-time control over LFO rate and depth, filter depth and frequency, sample starting point, and envelope speed as possible. This can help to create expressive instrument sounds from static samples.

Samplers are coming out with more and more processing capabilities that allow you to exercise your creativity. Read the manual and talk to other users of the unit to learn its power. This will help you to produce a surprising number of sounds from a limited number of samples.

Databases

As with large patch libraries, a good database can help you find the right sample in a hurry. As of this writing, there are no sample librarian programs with built-in data-organizing functions, so if you want to keep track of what's where, it's up to you to create your own database. Categories appropriate to organizing a sample library could include the following

- date

- instrument or sound category (multiple keywords are helpful)

- sampler

- sample rate

- note range

- length (in seconds and kilobytes)

- loops

- short description

Again, even if you don't have a database program, just organizing your samples and writing up a list on paper can be a big help in finding a particular sound when you need it.

Chapter 7

Synchronization and Audio Production

In music, audio, and video, the term *synchronization* refers to two or more devices playing (or recording) simultaneously in a consistent time relationship. When we hear a symphony orchestra, the strings and woodwinds are synchronized to the visual cues given by the conductor. When we watch a movie, the sound and picture are synchronized on the film itself.

There are many reasons to synchronize sequencers, drum machines, and other MIDI composition and production tools to external timing signals. Here are just a few.

- To expand the capabilities of a small multitrack studio by using a sequencer to play virtual tracks. That is, vocals and acoustic instruments are recorded on tape and all other musical parts are handled by sequenced synthesizers or samplers.

- To expand the capabilities of a small MIDI studio by using a multitrack tape deck. By recording multiple passes of a sequencer on one or more tape tracks, each synthesizer may eventually play two or more distinct tracks.

- To minimize the memory demands on the main sequencer by syncing it to a drum machine playing its own internal patterns.

- To use a sequencer to compose, edit, and "spot" music, effects, and dialogue tracks for film, video, or multimedia presentations.

- To use a sequencer or other MIDI-based compositional tool to enhance a live performance.

Synchronization of electronic music systems requires the exchange of three types of information.

- **Start/Stop:** whether a device is running or not

- **Location:** where each device is within a piece of music

- **Tempo:** how fast each device is running

This information is handled in MIDI systems in several different ways.

MIDI Sync: Clocks and Pointers

A basic form of MIDI synchronization uses *MIDI Clocks*. MIDI Clocks are single-byte commands (F8H) that are sent on a MIDI line at the rate of twenty-four per quarter note. MIDI Clocks are a direct descendant of the timing pulses and Frequency-Shift Keying (FSK) employed in pre-MIDI synchronization schemes. These were known variously as "pulse," "clicks," "drum sync," "TTL sync," or "DIN sync." These signals were used both to link different sequencer and synthesizer modules together, and to lock sequencers to tape.

Since there were no standard methods of producing these signals, the various schemes that different manufacturers came up with were utterly incompatible with each other: They used different signal levels, pulse widths, shift frequencies, and/or number of pulses per quarter note (*ppq*). Needless to say, this drove users nuts. In fact, a number of small companies and consulting engineers did quite well designing and operating boxes that could translate from one manufacturer's sync method to another.

MIDI Clocks were included in the original MIDI specification to provide consistent guidelines for synchronization. Where a drum machine is synchronized to a sequencer, the sequencer (acting as the master) sends Clocks at a rate determined by its own tempo map. The drum machine (acting as a slave) plays along in lock step with the timing of the incoming Clocks. If the sequencer speeds up, so does the drum machine; if it slows down, the drum machine follows. When the Clocks stop, the drum machine stops. A large jump in tempo will put the drum machine behind for only as long as it takes the second Clock at the new tempo to be received: 1/24 of a beat. As long as no Clocks are garbled in transmission or missed by the receiver, this scheme works fine. Alternatively, the drum machine can act as master, in which case it generates the Clocks according to its tempo map, and the sequencer follows.

A slave device following MIDI Clocks may have a tempo map of its own, but it can't use that tempo map while it is acting as a slave. The internal tempo map would conflict with the incoming Clocks, and so the device would not be able to synchronize to the master.

Interpolation

It's a fairly common myth that, because MIDI Clocks are transmitted at the rate of twenty-four per quarter note, any sequencer under external control can only resolve its MIDI events to twenty-four per quarter note. This is quite far from the truth, thanks to the principle of *interpolation*. A sequencer receiving a string of Clocks can use its internal processing power and timing circuits to interpolate much shorter time intervals between those Clocks. For example, if a note is supposed to happen 1/96 of a beat after a quarter note, the sequencer listening to the Clocks makes a reasonable guess when the next Clock (1/24 of a quarter note) is supposed to arrive. It then sounds the note when one quarter of that time interval has passed. Obviously, if the tempo is changing rapidly, there will be some errors, but in most circumstances, this works just fine.

The maximum resolution of a sequencer under external control is therefore not dependent on the speed of MIDI Clocks, but on how finely and accurately the sequencer can divide up the times between Clocks. In other words, the speed of the sequencer's internal processor and the precision of the software determine the sequencer's resolution.

Start, Stop, and Continue

MIDI Clocks are almost always used in conjunction with Start and Stop messages. *Start* (FAH) tells the slave to go to the beginning of the current sequence or file and get ready to start playing. As soon as the first incoming Clock is received, the sequence starts playing at the tempo determined by subsequent Clocks. *Stop* (FCH) tells the slave to stop playing wherever it is (and if any more Clocks come in, to ignore them). The *Continue* message (FBH) tells the slave to start playing from its current position. This may be where it was stopped by a Stop message, where the user has told it to go by setting a dial, or where a Song Position Pointer message has told it to go.

With appropriate conversion hardware, MIDI Clocks can be used to control pre-MIDI sequencers and drum machines. The hardware converts MIDI clocks into a form of sync that can be read by the older devices. Of course, since there was no standardization of sync formats prior to MIDI, different converters are needed for different manufacturers' products.

Pointers

If a sequencer synchronized to an external source receives a Start message, it will play from the beginning of the sequence. This is O.K. if you are working on the first part of the sequence. However, if you want to work on a section in the middle—and don't want to wait for it to play through from the top—you need a *Song Position Pointer* message. This type of message allows remote control of a sequencer's current position. The Song Position Pointer (*SPP*) message is not sent in real time, but only when a master device is started and/or stopped. The message (F2H plus two data bytes, with the least significant byte sent first) contains the current position of the master in sixteenth notes. As with all MIDI messages, the maximum value of a data byte is 127 (7FH), so the maximum length of a sequence that relies on Song Position Pointers is (128×128)÷4, or 4,096 quarter notes (1,024 measures in $\frac{4}{4}$). This is about thirty-four minutes of music at a tempo of 120 bpm. Of course, Song Position Pointer doesn't know anything about barlines or time signatures, but merely counts each sixteenth note individually. Another way to calculate Song Position Pointers is to take the number of MIDI Clocks that have passed since the beginning of the piece and divide them by six. This formula is derived from the fact that there are twenty-four MIDI Clocks per quarter note, and four sixteenth notes per quarter note.

If the sequencer is set to start at the beginning of the piece, the data bytes of the SPP message will all be zero, and the message will be F2 00 00. If the sequencer is set to the beginning of the third beat in the fifth measure (assuming $\frac{4}{4}$ time—four beats per measure and a quarter note gets one beat), the data bytes will be:

> (4 measures × 4 beats × 4 sixteenth notes/beat) + (2 beats × 4 sixteenth notes/beat)=
> 64 + 8 = 72
> 48H = 48 00 (Remember, LSB first.)

If the sequencer is set to the third beat in the thirtieth measure, the arithmetic is:

> (29 measures × 4 beats × 4 sixteenth notes/beat) + (2 beats × 4 sixteenth notes/beat) =
> 464 + 8 = 472

This translates to 1D8 in hex, or D8 01 in proper form (LSB first). However, this won't work, because D8 is not a valid data byte—the first digit of a data byte cannot be higher than 7. You must therefore subtract 8 from the first digit of the least significant byte and carry it over to the second digit of the most significant byte. So, the actual message will be 68 02. It's a little confusing, but it works, and fortunately this sort of thing is normally completely invisible to the user.

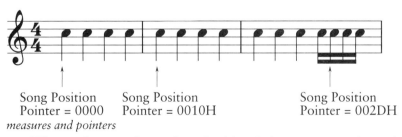

Song Position   Song Position   Song Position
Pointer = 0000   Pointer = 0010H   Pointer = 002DH
measures and pointers

When a slave receives a Song Position Pointer message, it sets its internal counter to the position indicated, and then waits for a Continue message and a Clock. It then starts to play, following the Clocks to determine its speed. Sometimes it takes a few moments for the receiving device to locate the appropriate position. To avoid losing any data that may come in during that time, many SPP transmitters put some "pad time" in between the SPP and the Continue. It's not called for in the spec, but it's a courtesy to the user. The Song Position Pointer message with data bytes of zero followed by a Continue is often used instead of a Start command. This prevents any possible ambiguity.

As mentioned earlier, Song Position Pointer should not be confused with Song Select (F3H followed by one data byte), which is used to choose from among several sequences that may be stored in a device's memory. This confusion may arise from the fact that both messages are sometimes referred to as *Song Pointer* interchangeably.

Bar Markers and Time Signatures

Song Position Pointers merely indicate beats (or portions thereof). They do not indicate barlines or contain any time-signature information. A recent addition to the MIDI specification allows for both of these types of information to be transmitted using Universal System Exclusive messages. These are of interest mainly to programmers who are developing sequencers and other programs that are based on standard music notation.

The B*ar Marker* message tells the receiver that the next Clock it receives is to be considered the downbeat of a measure. The measure number may be sent as part of the message (or not), and negative numbers are allowed for count-in beats. The Bar Marker message is not supposed to be a substitute for a Song Position Pointer, but it may find use in systems that sometimes lose MIDI Clocks due to clogging of the MIDI stream or in longer compositions where SPPs are inadequate. It can also be useful in situations where a device has come on line after a piece has started playing—and no more SPPs are being sent. An example of this would be a computer jam session when a new electronic "player" joins in and needs to know where it is.

The format of the Bar Marker message is (in hex):

F0 7F <device ID> 03 01 aa *aa* F7

Here, aa *aa* represents the bar-number bytes, LSB first. A bar number of 8129 (01 40—LSB first) or above indicates a negative (count-in) bar. Therefore, the total number of bars addressable using this message is eight times greater than that using Song Position Pointers.

The T*ime Signature* message is designed primarily for notation based systems. It comes in two versions.

- **Immediate:** in which the time signature changes instantly upon receipt of the message (or, if it is receiving MIDI Clocks, with the next Clock)

- **Delayed:** in which the time signature changes after the next Bar Marker message is received

The Time Signature message is very flexible, in that it can describe any simple or compound time signature as long as the denominator of the signature is a power of two. (Sorry, Michael Colgrass fans—those $\frac{12}{5}$ time signatures are not available.) It can also specify the number of MIDI Clocks in a metronome click. That number is usually twenty-four, but it can be changed if the user wants the metronome to beat eighths, triplet sixteenths, or whatever. In addition, a Time Signature message can specify how beats will be divided notationally.

Syncing to Tape: FSK

If you could record a MIDI signal consisting of Clocks and Song Position Pointers on magnetic tape, synchronizing MIDI systems with tape decks would be a breeze. Unfortunately, life isn't so kind. MIDI is a digital signal with a baud rate far higher than the frequency response limit of any analog or digital tape deck. It's essentially a 31.25kHz square wave, interspersed with intervals of DC (0Hz). However, there are several ways to record the timing information needed for MIDI synchronization on tape.

Frequency-Shift Keying, or FSK, is a popular tape-synchronization technique. In the MIDI studio, FSK uses an audio signal whose pitch changes in step with MIDI Clocks. This signal is produced by an audio oscillator with a fixed nominal frequency—for example, 1,000Hz. The generator has a MIDI input jack, and when a MIDI Clock is received, it changes the frequency to 2,000Hz. Depending on its design, it then either waits a few milliseconds and changes the frequency back to 1,000Hz, or it changes back when the next Clock is received. When a MIDI sequencer putting out MIDI Clocks in step with its own tempo map is connected to the generator's MIDI input, the audio signal will change in step with the sequencer's tempo. If this signal is recorded on tape, the tape will contain a precise representation of the sequence's tempo map.

To read the audio signal from the tape, a device senses the changing frequency of the audio signal. It then immediately sends out a MIDI Start message followed by MIDI Clocks in step with the changing audio frequencies. When these signals are sent to a sequencer that is set to follow external Clocks, the sequence will begin to play back when it receives the Start command. It will continue to play synchronized to the tape, following the tempo map recorded on the tape. If the tape should slow down or speed up, the rate of the Clocks will change, and the sequencer will follow right along.

FSK was actually developed many years ago for radio-teletype as a way to send digital information on a standard radio signal that was much faster than Morse code. FSK is a very inexpensive way to accomplish tape sync—and has been popular since quite early in the MIDI era. FSK converters normally do double duty as encoders and decoders. Usually there's a switch that tells the device whether it is writing the FSK tone or reading it. FSK converters are available from a number of manufacturers—and many hardware sequencers and even drum machines also have FSK generating and reading capability built in.

Disadvantages of FSK Sync

FSK has several important limitations. Since there is no standardization of what frequencies or levels a FSK signal should use, different manufacturers use different schemes. These schemes are rarely compatible with each other—so a FSK signal recorded with one maker's box cannot be read by a different maker's box.

Once the tempo map in a sequence has been recorded on a track of tape, it cannot be changed without restriping the entire track. Attempting to punch in and out on a FSK track can create serious timing errors. If other tape tracks have been overdubbed since the sync track was striped, the new sync track has to start exactly where the old one started. Matching the starting points of the old and new tracks can be difficult. Therefore, making any changes in the tempo of the music after the sync track is recorded is not practical. Because FSK readers are "tuned" to a small band of frequencies, FSK sync cannot be read at speeds much higher or lower than normal playback. So, there is no way to fast-forward a tape and keep the slave sequencer locked to it—or "rock" the reels and keep sync. It is also not possible to read FSK sync backwards.

If there is a dropout on the sync track, a Clock may be missed. This would cause the sequencer to go out of sync (and it will stay out, because there is no way to recover that lost Clock).

FSK is finicky about audio quality. Some devices like hot levels, while some prefer the signal to be recorded at a fairly low level. Noise reduction can make the signal difficult to read—and so multitrack tape decks that have undefeatable noise reduction on all tracks may not be usable with FSK sync. This is why many such decks allow you to shut off the noise reduction on one track. It possible, use a guard track between a FSK track and any music track to prevent crosstalk that might interfere with reading the sync track (and/or allow the sync track to be heard in the audio).

FSK is perhaps most significantly limited by the fact that it contains no location information. It generates a Start command and Clocks but no Song Position Pointers. This means that it covers only two of the three types of information needed for true sync: It tells you when to start and how fast to play, but not where you are. Therefore, a sequencer slaved to a FSK track must always be started at the beginning.

Smart Fsk

A number of manufacturers have developed FSK formats in which location information can be placed in the audio signal along with the Clocks. This *Smart FSK* uses more complex frequency-shifting algorithms to encode beat information at regular intervals into the taped signal. When the tape is played back, the beat information is decoded and sent out as a Song Position Pointer. This is followed by a Continue message and then Clocks at the tempo dictated by the frequency-shifts. This location encoding generally takes place every quarter note. Thus, the amount of time it takes the sequencer to lock to a Smart FSK signal is slightly longer than with more sophisticated synchronization techniques. However, most users do not notice the delay. Unfortunately, Smart FSK has never been standardized any more than ordinary FSK—and different manufacturers' techniques are not generally compatible.

SMPTE and MIDI

SMPTE timecode is the standard method of synchronization in today's video and audio studios. For this reason, several ways have been developed to link SMPTE and MIDI together. SMPTE timecode was developed by the Society of Motion Picture and Television Engineers, from whom it gets its name. (It is formally known as SMPTE/EBU timecode, because it is also used in Europe, where the equivalent organization to SMPTE is the European Broadcast Union.) It is an audio signal consisting of a square wave that shifts irregularly between approximately 1,200 and 2,400Hz. SMPTE timecode is quite different from FSK, which shifts regularly. The timings of these shifts represent digital bits that denote the hour, minute, second, and frame number of a particular point in time. There is also other information including the type of code; *user bits* for encoding text information (such as reel names) into the signal; and a *sync word* which precisely locates the beginning of the SMPTE message, and can be used to tell whether the tape is moving forwards or backwards.

When a timecode signal is recorded on the audio track of a video tape, the numbers in the signal correspond to individual frames of the video signal. When they are recorded on a track of a multitrack audio tape, they simply serve as a timing reference for the rest of the tracks on the tape.

SMPTE Types

There are several forms of SMPTE timecode in common use. All of these use 80 bits per frame. Two types of timecode (with subtle differences) are in common use in the U.S., Canada, and Japan. The standard in North American is *NTSC* video, which stands for National Television Standard Committee (not, as some chauvinistic Europeans would have it, "Never Twice the Same Color"). NTSC runs at 29.97 frames per second. To avoid dealing with fractional frames, SMPTE timecode numbers assume exactly 30 frames per second. This makes for a discrepancy between a frame's SMPTE number and the actual elapsed time of the program to that point.

One form of NTSC-compatible SMPTE timecode, called *Non-Drop-Frame,* counts 30 frames per second. This means that a SMPTE *minute* is actually longer than an actual minute by 0.1%, or 60 milliseconds, and this error is cumulative: thus at the end of an hour, the SMPTE time differs from the actual elapsed time by 108 frames (3.6 seconds).

Drop-Frame is another form of SMPTE timecode. This format leaves out frame numbers 00 and 01 at the beginning of each minute—so that SMPTE time and elapsed time match more closely. Frame 00:01:59:29 is followed by frame 00:02:00:02. However, if this were done every minute, it would lop off 120 frames per hour (which is 12 frames too many). For this reason, the 00 and 01 frames are not dropped when the minute count is divisible by 10—therefore, 00:09:59:29 is followed by 00:10:00:00. In this way, Drop-Frame timecode is self-correcting: The frame number and the actual elapsed time are always within 66.6 milliseconds (two frames) of one another.

A variant on SMPTE timecode, which is used when video synchronization is not an issue, runs at exactly 30 frames per second. Many SMPTE-to-MIDI converters with SMPTE-striping capabilities generate this type of code. (Naturally, you would expect that this "true-30" SMPTE is the Non-Drop-Frame type, but there actually are fairly esoteric circumstances in which 30 Drop-Frame is needed.) Using true-30 fps timecode is an acceptable practice as long as the tape striped with this code is never used in conjunction with any video equipment. When scoring a film or video—or even producing a song that may eventually find its way into a music video—it is far preferable to use 29.97 fps timecode.

Professional SMPTE equipment (and the more sophisticated SMPTE-to-MIDI converters) have an input for a video signal. The converter's SMPTE-generating circuitry uses this signal as a timing reference. Therefore, the code generated by the converter is based precisely on the video frame rate (29.97 fps). In addition, the beginning of the SMPTE word coincides exactly with the beginning of the video frame, which can avoid a lot of confusion at the post-production stage.

In Europe, television runs at 25 fps—and so European timecode does too. (Since it runs at exactly 25 fps, there is no need for a Drop-Frame SMPTE version.) Most equipment also allows for timecode running at 24 frames per second, which would make it compatible with edge numbers on film. In practice, this is almost never used with audio. (It is sometimes used when converting special effects from film to video.) When film is edited on a SMPTE-based system, especially if audio is involved, it is usually first converted to videotape.

Linking SMPTE and MIDI Sync

There is no one-to-one correspondence between SMPTE and MIDI, as there is between FSK and MIDI Clocks. The problem is that SMPTE is an absolute, constant format for designating time without regard to musical tempo. On the other hand, MIDI Clocks and Song Position Pointers are completely tempo-dependent. Therefore you can't just send a SMPTE number to a MIDI sequencer and expect it to interpret it as a Song Position Pointer—or send a stream of SMPTE numbers and have them interpreted as Clocks. The sequencer won't have the slightest idea what to do with the information. You need a *SMPTE-to-MIDI Converter* to link together SMPTE data streams and MIDI sequencers. At its simplest, this is a device that reads SMPTE timecode and converts it to timing information that the sequencer can understand: Clocks and Song Position Pointers. (Some people refer to these devices as *synchronizers* rather than *converters*. However, to avoid confusion, the term "synchronizer" is best left to equipment that physically controls the speed of tape machines.)

The converter must be programmed with two essential pieces of information. The first of these is the starting time for the sequence; that is, what SMPTE hour, minute, second, and frame corresponds with the first beat of the first measure of the sequence (Pointer 00 00). This starting time is also known as the *SMPTE offset time*, or *SMPTE start time*. When tape is rolling and the converter is reading SMPTE numbers, it compares the incoming numbers with the offset time and decides whether to tell the sequencer to start playing or to wait. If the SMPTE frame number is lower than the offset time, the converter does nothing. If it is the same as the offset time, it sends out a Start command, followed by Clocks. If it is higher than the offset time, it sends out a Song Position Pointer, followed by a Continue, and then Clocks.

The second basic piece of information with which the converter must be programmed is the sequence tempo. Without this information, the converter does not know how fast to send MIDI Clocks once it has sent its Start or Continue. Converters stay constantly aware of the speed of the incoming SMPTE numbers by continuously clocking the SMPTE bits. They use this information as a *timebase* to calculate the speed of the outgoing MIDI Clocks. If the tape should slow down or speed up slightly, the converter will adjust the speed of the Clocks to keep the sequencer in sync with the tape (just as when using FSK).

SMPTE-to-MIDI Arithmetic

Since the converter knows the tempo of a sequence, when it reads a SMPTE frame number that is later than the offset time, it can calculate the exact beat of the sequence that corresponds to that SMPTE number. The converter then sends that information to the sequencer in the form of a Song Position Pointer, so that the sequencer can jump to the measure and beat that corresponds to the current tape position. For example, a converter is programmed to start a sequencer on SMPTE frame 00:01:00:00 and cause it to play at a tempo of 120 bpm. If the converter reads a SMPTE number of 00:01:08:00, it knows it is exactly eight seconds after the starting point; that is, sixteen beats, because 120 beats per minute equals 2 beats per second. The converter will send a Song Position Pointer message for the sequencer to start on the seventeenth beat (the data bytes will be 40 00). This message is followed by a Continue message, followed by Clocks every 1/48 of a second.

In practice, this operation is not instantaneous. The converter is likely to send a Song Position Pointer for the next beat (or even perhaps a beat or two after that). It will probably then pause for a second or two to allow the sequencer time to get itself set, before sending the Continue. Contributing further to this delay is the fact that it takes at least a few frames for the converter to read an accurate SMPTE number from the tape once it starts.

Tempo Maps

A sequencer locked to a SMPTE-to-MIDI converter does not have to run at a constant tempo, because the converter can contain a tempo map of its own. Most converters have dials, buttons, and/or keypads that allow you to insert tempo changes at any point in a sequence. You must specify the new tempo, and the exact beat (or sub-beat) where the tempo will change. Although Song Position Pointer messages don't actually contain information about time signatures or barlines, many converters will allow you work with them for convenience' sake. For example, if you tell a converter that a sequence is in $\frac{4}{4}$, it can let you specify the location of a tempo change in terms of measures and beats. The converter will then automatically calculate the correct SPPs. (Future converters may well incorporate the new MIDI Bar Marker and MIDI Time Signature messages, but, as of this writing, none exist that do.)

A complex tempo map may contain many tempo changes. The converter will take into account all tempo changes when making its Song Position Pointer calculations. It will also send the correct tempo for that measure and beat when it starts sending Clocks. Here is a breakdown of the information contained in a tempo map for a forty-four-measure MIDI sequence.

- start time of 01:45:33:12

- tempo of 120 bpm in $\frac{4}{4}$ for measures 1 through 25

- 160 bpm in $\frac{3}{2}$ for measure 26

- 92 bpm in $\frac{4}{4}$ for the first two beats of measure 27

- 84 bpm for the last two beats of measure 27

- 60 bpm in $\frac{6}{8}$ for measure 28 through the second eighth-note of measure 44

Converters differ as to how many tempo changes they will allow in a sequence: some allow only a few, while others have enough memory for several hundred. Some converters can learn a tempo map from a sequencer. This is accomplished in much the same way that a tempo map can be recorded on tape with FSK signal: Play a sequence containing the tempo changes on the sequencer and send the MIDI Clocks to the converter. The converter will note the timing of all the Clocks and store them as a tempo map. This way, complex tempo maps can be programmed without the tedium of entering each tempo change by hand. (Of course, when the sequence is played back, the sequencer's internal tempo map must be disabled, or it will interfere with the Clocks coming from the converter.)

Many converters can store just one tempo map in their internal memory, while others can retain several. Some converters have memory cards or cartridges for off-loading tempo maps. It is even more convenient to store tempo maps on a computer (or other device with disk storage). There are several ways to do this. Tempo maps may be encoded as System Exclusive dumps—or made into an actual sequence (in which notes and velocities correspond to beat numbers and tempos). The most elegant method is to store the tempo map as a Standard MIDI File. In fact, there is no reason why a MIDI file must actually contain any notes or other MIDI events—it can consist only of tempo information. Within a single computer running multiple applications that need the same tempo map, the information can in some circumstances be transferred instantaneously through a RAM *clipboard*. In other situations, or with multiple computers, the file containing the tempo map can be written to disk by one program and read by any other. Multiple devices connected by a MIDI cable (for example, computers, dedicated sequencers, or synchronizers) can also share a tempo-map file using the newly accepted MIDI File Dump Standard. However, few devices have yet to implement this last technique.

Advantages of SMPTE-to-MIDI Sync Converters

Besides its universality in the non-MIDI world, there are many advantages to using SMPTE timecode for MIDI-to-tape synchronization (versus using FSK). First of all, tempo maps in a SMPTE-to-MIDI converter can be reprogrammed without restriping the tape. This means that a sequence can start earlier or end later without much fuss (as long as there is enough timecode on the tape to cover the extra length). It also means that adjusting the tempo of a sequence after the tape has been striped is relatively simple. More significantly, it makes it possible for the user to adjust the tempo of a segment or cue to correspond with a visual scene. On the other hand, because SMPTE is a square wave and FSK uses sine waves, FSK is kinder to the tape and the tape recorder, and will survive a couple of generations of dubbing, while SMPTE will not.

Because SMPTE is a standard, the practices and techniques of recording timecode signals and distributing them around a studio are well codified. Theoretically, timecode generated by one device can always be read by any other device, regardless of its manufacturer.

A tape recorded with FSK sync must always be the master in a studio. But, a video or audio tape striped with SMPTE can itself be a slave to another SMPTE source. (This is only possible if the playback deck is equipped to function in that way—that is, if it will accept external speed control from a SMPTE-based synchronizer.) During this process (called SMPTE *chasing*), the synchronizer constantly compares a timecode track on the slave deck with the incoming timecode from the master deck. If the numbers should not match up, it speeds up or slows down the slave deck's drive capstan by minute amounts, until the numbers coincide. This type of multimachine synchronization allows, for example, an audio deck and a sequencer to both be slaved to a video deck, with the SMPTE-to-MIDI converter reading timecode from either the slave or the master.

SMPTE-to-MIDI converters can handle other timing related chores as well. Many can generate and read FSK sync signals, produce metronome clicks, or generate non-MIDI timing signals for various kinds of non-MIDI hardware. Some can also accept finger taps or audio triggers for constructing tempo maps. Others can even act as synchronizers for tape decks.

MIDI Time Code

Most sequencers (especially computer-based ones) include sophisticated and user-friendly tempo editing and tempo mapping capabilities. These features provide many advantages—even when the sequencer is being synchronized to an external timing source. In addition, sequencers store tempo information along with all other information in a sequence, eliminating the need for separate storage media and facilities for tempo maps. To accomplish this, the sequencer needs to be able to read SMPTE numbers directly, in a way that is not related to tempo.

Proprietary SMPTE Conversion

Some manufacturers (notably developers of sequencing software for Atari computers) use converters that encode SMPTE information into proprietary digital data. This data is sent to the computer through its serial (non-MIDI) or cartridge port. While this is a workable solution, it is not ideal in that the data format is exclusive to that specific program. Besides being counter to the entire philosophical basis of MIDI, this technique requires that if the studio wants to use a different sequencer, it also needs a different converter.

A solution more in the spirit of MIDI would be a method of encoding the SMPTE information in real time into a MIDI data stream. This was first attempted by two Macintosh developers, Mark of the Unicorn and Southworth Music Systems, who collaborated on *Direct Time Lock,* (or *DTL).* In this system, when the converter reads an initial SMPTE number, it sends out a System Exclusive message to the sequencer with that number encoded in it. The sequencer—which contains its own offset time and tempo map—calculates from the number where it is supposed to start. Then MIDI Clocks are sent at a constant (non-tempo-dependent) rate of one per SMPTE frame (30 per second). The sequencer uses these Clocks as a timing base to play its internal tempo map. A later version of DTL, known as *DTLe,* sends MIDI Clocks every quarter frame for increased timing resolution.

Direct Time Lock is an interesting synchronization method, but it was never adopted as part of the MIDI spec. For location data, it uses Southworth's System Exclusive ID (and that company is now out of business). Understandably, other software manufacturers would be extremely reluctant to implement a system using another manufacturer's ID number. However, a number of hardware manufacturers have implemented DTL in their SMPTE conversion boxes, although these will only work with Macintosh computers. Implementing DTL ensures that their boxes will work with Mark of the Unicorn's popular Performer sequencer, which still uses DTL or DTLe.

The MIDI Time Code Specification

MIDI Time Code was developed primarily by two individuals: Chris Meyer (during the period of time he was working for Sequential Circuits and Digidesign) and Gerry Lester (who was working for Adams Smith). It became part of the MIDI specification in 1987. MIDI Time Code consists of four types of messages: Full, Quarter Frame, Cueing, and User Bits. The Full and Quarter Frame messages are used for synchronization, while Cueing messages are used for automation. User Bits are designed to convey the information contained in the User Bits portion of a SMPTE signal (but so far, no one has found a use for them).

The *Full* message consists of ten bytes and is sent when a tape starts, stops, or repositions itself. This message contains the entire SMPTE number—hour/minute/second/frame—as well as the SMPTE type (Drop, Non-Drop, 25 fps, or 24 fps). The format is as follows (in hex).

F0 7F 7F 01 01 *hr mn sc fr* F7

The *hr* byte specifies both the hour and the timecode format or type. The first bit is zero (as it always is for a data byte). The next two bits specify the type: 00 is 24 fps, 01 is 25 fps, 10 is Drop Frame, and 11 is Non-Drop. The last five bits specify the hour. So the hour byte for 6 hours, in 30-frame drop-frame would be 0 10 00110, or 86H. The hour byte for 17 hours in 25-frame format would be 0 01 10001, or 31H.

The *Quarter Frame* message contains the entire SMPTE number as well, but not all at once. Instead, the number is "nibblized" over eight messages—that is, it takes eight messages to transmit the SMPTE number, and each message contains a part of the whole number.

The format is F1 *nx*, where *n* goes cyclically from 0 to 7, and *x* is the "nibblized" SMPTE number (which ranges between 0 and FH, or 0 and 15 decimal). When *n* is 0, *x* is the least significant (LS) nibble (the rightmost hex digit) of the Frames number. When *n* is 1, *x* is the most-significant (MS) nibble (the leftmost digit) of the Frames number. When *n* is 2, *x* is the LS nibble of the Seconds number, and so on.

> when *n*=3, *x*=Seconds MS
> when *n*=4, *x*=Minutes LS
> when *n*=5, *x*=Minutes MS
> when *n*=6, *x*=Hours LS
> when *n*=7, *x*=Hours MS (which can only be 0, 1, or 2, and
> therefore requires only two bits) and SMPTE type
> (using the remaining two bits, following the same
> format as the Full message)

As their name implies, Quarter Frame messages are sent every quarter frame (or from 96 to 120 times per second, depending on the format). The F1 0*x* message occurs on the SMPTE frame boundary. When eight messages (starting with an F1 0*x*) are received, the receiver knows what the SMPTE time is. Therefore, it takes at least two frames to communicate an entire SMPTE number using Quarter Frame messages.

Here's an example of a string of Quarter Frame messages. The SMPTE time is 01:23:30:15, and the format is 30 fps drop-frame. The Quarter Frame messages (all in hex) are as follows

F1 0F F1 10	15 + (0 × 16) frames
F1 2E F1 31	14 + (1 × 16) seconds
F1 47 F1 51	7 + (1 × 16) minutes
F1 61 F1 78	one hour, 30-frame drop-frame

Besides transmitting the SMPTE number, the Quarter Frame message serves as the timing reference for the receiving device. As messages come in faster or slower (due to variations in the speed of the SMPTE coming off the tape) the sequencer follows accordingly. Besides having a tighter resolution than MIDI Clocks (at tempos below 300 beats per minute), MIDI Time Code has an important added advantage: The receiving device can constantly check its position against the incoming SMPTE numbers, and if there is a dropout or other error, it can correct it by minutely slowing down or speeding up the sequence. This technique is called *slewing*—and imitates the way a tape recorder controlled by a synchronizer can chase timecode.

Notice that there is no provision in MIDI Time Code for differentiating between 29.97 fps and 30 fps frame rates. This is true of SMPTE timecode itself as well. In situations involving video synchronization, it should be assumed that the frame rate is 29.97, but in audio-only situations, there can be some confusion. This is particularly true if the SMPTE from which the MTC is derived was striped *wild*, without reference to a video signal. It is up to the receiving device (and the user) to know the frame rate of the incoming MTC. Otherwise, slight—but significant and cumulative—timing errors can result. Regrettably, not all manufacturers of MTC hardware and software recognize this problem.

Converting SMPTE to MIDI Time Code is a relatively straightforward process. The converting hardware does not need any controls at all—although many converters also generate SMPTE for tape striping, and therefore have a read/write switch. Many converters also generate DTL, and so need a switch for that option. The MTC being produced goes over an ordinary MIDI cable to the sequencer or other receiver. In many cases, MTC converters are built right into computer/MIDI interfaces, saving a cable. SMPTE-to-MTC converters have no displays and few buttons—and they need no internal RAM for tempo maps. This makes them considerably less expensive to make than SMPTE-to-Clocks-and-Pointers converters.

Advantages of MIDI Time Code

The biggest advantage of MIDI Time Code is that it allows tempo maps to be contained within a sequence. Thus, no external hardware is needed to construct or store them. When it comes to programming tempo changes, it's easier to work with a well-designed computer sequencer than a hardware converter box. The computer's keyboard and large graphic display are naturally preferable to the converter's small keypad and a single-line alphanumeric display. Most good sequencers let you perform useful tricks like creating smooth accelerandos or ritardandos—or designing a complex tempo and beat pattern that runs over several bars and having it repeat many times. Some sequencers even let you run different tracks at different tempos. When using MIDI Time Code, you can continue to use all these features—and let the computer worry about making sure the numbers are exactly right. In applications where knowing the time is more important than knowing what bar and beat you are in, like sound-effects spotting and studio automation, MIDI Time Code allows the MIDI user to work with SMPTE numbers directly.

A sequencer reading MTC does not need a Start message to start playing. It can simply begin as soon as it has received a Full message and a couple of Quarter Frame messages (or, in the absence of Full messages, a complete set of eight Quarter Frame messages). This simplifies hardware and software design and operation. Another important advantage provided by the MIDI Time Code system is that it can easily recover from a momentary loss of sync. If a SMPTE dropout occurs, lasting anywhere from a single bit to a couple of seconds, some MTC converters can *flywheel;* that is, they can continue to generate MTC for a period of time until the SMPTE resumes. When the SMPTE starts coming in again, the sequencer can speed up or slow down (slew) to match the SMPTE. This chasing ability also means that when several devices reading MIDI Time Code are running simultaneously, they will always stay in sync, even if there are dropouts somewhere in the system.

Some software sequencers also have flywheeling capability built in. In most cases, it doesn't matter whether hardware or software flywheeling is used—they both work equally well. However, it is possible to buy a combination of hardware and software from different manufacturers and end up with no flywheeling capability (because each expects the other to have it). This usually occurs because the software manufacturer also happens to make a box that does flywheeling—and the hardware manufacturer also makes software that has flywheeling capability. SMPTE dropouts are very common, especially on consumer video decks and low-end multitrack audio decks, so be sure that at least one device in your studio is capable of flywheeling.

Disadvantages of MIDI Time Code

MIDI Time Code does have a few drawbacks. When it was first proposed, there was a lot of discussion about the problems it might create. MTC has the potential to use up about eight percent of MIDI's available bandwidth. Since timing problems can result when a MIDI signal is pushed to its limit, it is conceivable that the extra load presented by MTC could make the situation worse. However, if you are running a MIDI line that close to the edge, you would probably have problems whether MTC is there or not. It's also quite likely that the MTC would suffer more than the note and controller data, since it is even more time-sensitive than the musical data. For this reason, it is recommended in the MIDI specification that MIDI Time Code be carried on its own MIDI line, separate from conventional MIDI data.

Different devices perform SMPTE-to-MTC conversion in different ways. A number of converters just send Quarter Frame messages, and never send Full messages. If MTC is only being used to lock a sequencer to a moving tape striped with conventional, linear-recorded SMPTE timecode, this presents no problem. However, when using a videotape that has *Vertical Interval Timecode* (or *VITC*), there can be some confusion because the timecode number is imbedded in one or more lines of the video signal itself.

Unlike linear timecode (known for comparison's sake as LTC), VITC can be read while a tape is standing still or while it is moving at a wide range of speeds. For this reason, interpreting VITC solely in terms of Quarter Frame messages may not be appropriate to the needs of the studio. Sequencers cannot normally run backwards except in a special scrub mode. However, they can certainly locate backwards—and for this purpose, Full messages are far easier and faster to deal with. The same is true when fast-forwarding tape: the sequencer will have an easier time locating itself if the converter sends at least one Full message when it arrives at its destination. Better still, the converter could periodically throw off Full messages so that the sequencer doesn't have to jump an enormous amount in a single bound. This is also an issue when jogging or shuttling the tape: When the tape stops, if a Full message is generated, the sequencer will know exactly where it's supposed to be (and will not be confused by strange, constantly reversing, weird-speed Quarter Frame messages).

Some sequencers are a bit lazy. They read the first set of Quarter Frame messages—and then merely follow the data stream without checking the messages themselves. When confronted with a stopped tape, some LTC-to-MTC converters will continually generate Quarter Frame messages that contain the same frame number. In the same situation, some VITC-to-LTC converters will continue sending the same LTC frame number over and over (which the MTC converter will gleefully continue to convert). The combination of these two practices can cause serious problems: The sequencer will play as soon as it reads the first set of Quarter Frame messages—and will continue to play even when the tape is no longer moving. There are two methods of solving this problem. Tell the LTC-to-MTC converter not to send any MIDI Time Code when tape is not running—or tell the VITC-to-LTC converter (if you're using one) not to send LTC when the tape is not running.

Individual sequencing programs deal with MTC in different ways. MTC-based sequencers (the ones that aren't lazy) can catch up with lost data, but just as different tape synchronizers behave differently when they are dealing with off-speed tape decks, different sequencers use different algorithms to chase MTC. Some devices may check the code every ten frames, while some may check it every beat, or only once each measure. If the algorithm is designed well, its action should be inaudible. However, if you happen to be using two MTC-based programs simultaneously that use dissimilar algorithms, it is possible that they would go in and out of sync audibly.

MIDI Time Code is always running behind. This is something that makers of MTC receivers—hardware and software—have to keep in mind. Since it takes two frames (eight Quarter Frame messages) to send a complete SMPTE number, by the time the number is received, it's already two frames later. This constant offset must be built into any device that reads MTC, or else it will never line up correctly with other devices.

Theoretically, MIDI Time Code can be used to synchronize a tape deck to another device. This is possible only when the code is produced by a device with an extremely high clock resolution (like a computer). There have been periodic rumors that tape decks that sync to MTC are being developed, but the practicality of such a machine is questionable. MIDI-compatible tape decks use MIDI for transport control, but synchronization is achieved by converting SMPTE on a tape track to MTC. This practice has now been standardized as the MIDI Machine Control portion of the MIDI specification as described in the following chapter.

The Accuracy of MIDI Time Code

It may surprise a lot of people to learn that MTC is actually accurate enough to lock up a tape transport. MIDI's bandwidth is relatively limited, but the ceiling on the number of commands a MIDI line can handle in a given time period has nothing to do with how accurately it can send individual events. The bandwidth limitation only becomes a problem when you are sending a lot of MIDI data down a line—such as when you are controlling sixteen synthesizers, each with its own Pitch Bend, Modulation Wheel, Pressure, and other data-intensive parameters. When you exceed the capacity of 1,000 or so commands in one second, some of the commands will be delayed. If MIDI Time Code is on its own MIDI cable (as the MIDI specification recommends), this should never happen.

MIDI Time Code can be extremely accurate because MIDI is an asynchronous protocol—meaning that it doesn't follow any kind of master clock. A MIDI command can be transmitted and received at any time. (If it were a synchronous protocol, its messages would have to fall on arbitrary boundaries of 1/3,250 of a second.) The limiting factor to accuracy is not MIDI itself, but the transmitter and receiver. If the device generating the MIDI command feeds the UART in the MIDI interface with a master clock running at 500kHz (a very normal practice), then the accuracy of an individual MIDI byte can be predicted to one clock cycle, or 2 microseconds (abbreviated μs). The SMPTE specification allows 4.2μs deviation in the length of time between SMPTE bits, so in this case MTC is actually twice as accurate as SMPTE.

While MTC can only resolve down to quarter-frames, SMPTE can resolve to 1/80 of a frame (one bit). Again, because of the ability of MTC receivers to interpolate incoming timing data, this distinction is not relevant. Although only four MTC messages arrive per frame, a sequencer can interpolate times between those messages to whatever degree its designers wish. That's why there are MIDI sequencers that let you specify the SMPTE times of events down to 1/80 or 1/100 of a frame. An added bonus of MIDI Time Code is that, unlike MIDI Clocks (which are tempo dependent), MTC is sent at a constant rate. The errors in interpolation that might occur in MIDI Clock–based systems when lots of rapid tempo changes are encountered are not an issue in MTC-based systems. This is because the MTC itself is always coming in at the same rate. Therefore, any interpolations made between MTC Quarter Frame messages will always be equally accurate, regardless of changes in tempo.

Using MIDI Time Code With MIDI Clocks and Pointers

Sometimes it's desirable to be able to run MTC, MIDI Clocks, and Song Position Pointers simultaneously within the same system. For instance, you may want to run two sequencers together, one of which doesn't respond to MTC. Or, perhaps a studio wants to use one drum machine, and a client has another favorite one, and so both of them need to be run off the same sequencer using MIDI Clocks. In such situations, it is best to make sure that there is only one source of MIDI Time Code and only one source of MIDI Clocks. Good practice says that the MIDI Time Code converted from the master SMPTE signal should be distributed around the system (not reconverted at each point where MTC is needed). In the unlikely event of error or slippage during the conversion, this will prevent the individual devices from drifting apart due to different units coming up with different numbers.

Converting MTC to MIDI Clocks and Pointers is basically the same process as converting SMPTE to MIDI—except that the input is a MIDI signal, not an audio signal. Again, once the Clocks are generated, they should be distributed around the system, and not regenerated from the MTC at each point they are needed. This is far more crucial with MIDI Clocks than it is with MTC because of the many different ways that MIDI Clocks may be generated. For example, if one unit only deals with whole-number tempos, while another can handle tempos in 1/10 of a bpm, there will be drift between these two devices. Or, one unit may allow tempo changes on beats, while another allows them only on barlines. Making sure that just one converter is responsible for generating all MIDI Clocks will ensure that all the units in the system reading MIDI Clocks will stay in sync.

Several manufacturers have come up with devices that can sync MIDI to video without a SMPTE stripe on the entire videotape. This is useful when you are working with a video that has audio on it that you want to keep, and your video deck (like most consumer models) doesn't allow you to overdub timecode without destroying the existing audio. The device has two inputs, an audio input for the timecode and a video input for the video signal coming from the deck. To use this device, you print a few seconds of SMPTE timecode on the audio track at the head of the videotape, just before the program starts. The device reads the timecode, then starts sending out MTC messages. When the SMPTE stops, instead of shutting off the MTC, the converter continues sending it. The device uses the timing information imbedded in the video signal (the vertical sync pulse) as a timing reference. This timing is always going to be dead accurate—and so the device works perfectly as a SMPTE-to-MTC converter. The compromise is that you must always start the videotape from the beginning, or else the converter will have no idea what MTC numbers it is supposed to send out. This method is practical only for short videos, like commercials, where you can do without the ability to start in the middle.

Drop-Frame and Non-Drop

Drop-Frame and *Non-Drop* timecode formats are both used widely throughout the industry. Drop-Frame is used more in broadcast applications, where correspondence to real time is important. Non-Drop is found more often in industrial and nonbroadcast video production. Generally, the choice of whether a MIDI studio will use Drop-Frame or Non-Drop will be made by default: whatever format the original source uses is what the MIDI studio should use. Communication between the MIDI studio and the video production and post-production facilities is essential: If one place assumes that a tape is in one format and the other thinks it's in the other format, all the edit lists sent from one facility will seem to be wrong to the other.

If a MIDI studio has to choose a format, it's important to know there are advantages and disadvantages to each. Drop-Frame code is not the most intuitive of formats. If a sound effect is to start at 03:59 and end three frames later, its stop time must be 04:04, not 04:02. If a tempo-stretching function in a sequencer is used to make a musical cue fit a specific period of time, and the cue happens to cross a minute boundary, the real time of the cue will be two frames shorter than the difference in frame numbers would indicate. Non-Drop also has its drawbacks. If one follows such a program with a stopwatch, the duration of a cue computed by the edit list and the elapsed time shown on the stopwatch are not going to be the same. The longer the cue, the greater this difference will be.

30 Versus 29.97

In recent years, MIDI equipment has become extremely common in the preparation of music and effects tracks for television and film. This has led to an interesting and confusing controversy based on the fact that 30-frame SMPTE timecode does not actually run at 30 frames per second. The reason why 30 doesn't equal 30 is historical. When television in the U.S. was all black-and-white, TV broadcasts were actually run at exactly 30 frames per second. When color was adopted in the late 1950s, however, it was determined that there would be problems receiving color signals at this rate, and so the frame rate was changed slightly, to 29.97 fps (actually, the true figure is 29.97002617). This is now known as the NTSC television standard. As it happens, the engineering assumptions that led to the 29.97 standard proved to be mostly erroneous, and so the whole thing was probably unnecessary. However, by the time this became apparent, it was too late, and 29.97 (or "slow 30") had irreversibly become the standard. Today, all television signals—broadcast, cable, or recorded on tape or disk—in the U.S. (as well as in Canada and Japan) are based on the NTSC frame rate of 29.97, regardless of whether they are color or black-and-white.

S<small>MPTE</small> timecode came along after the NTSC color standard was adopted. The initial research into it began in the 1960s, and it was formalized in 1972. Therefore, S<small>MPTE</small> timecode as applied to video has always been based on a standard of 29.97 fps. While 30-fps timecode does exist, calling it "black-and-white S<small>MPTE</small>" is a serious misnomer. It exists primarily in the world of M<small>IDI</small>, and it apparently came about largely due to misunderstandings and poor judgment on the part of manufacturers of some audio console automation systems and early S<small>MPTE</small>-to-M<small>IDI</small> converters. Many console automation systems with their own internal computers use a timecode track on tape for time-stamping automation "moves." Some automation system manufacturers were not well versed in the true nature of S<small>MPTE</small> and assumed that tapes used with their systems would not be used in conjunction with videotape (probably a safe bet at the time). These manufacturers reportedly designed their hardware so that the timecode was striped onto the tape at exactly 30 fps. Some makers of early S<small>MPTE</small>-to-M<small>IDI</small> converters, out of the same innocent ignorance, also assumed that they should be striping code at 30 fps. Software manufacturers at this time similarly assumed that the code they would be reading would be at 30 fps, and that S<small>MPTE</small> time and real time could be counted on to be the same.

When 30-fps systems were interfaced with 29.97-fps video systems, there was trouble. The first problems that users encountered were fairly minor: a piece of music recorded in a studio using 30-fps S<small>MPTE</small> as a reference and played back in a video studio will play 0.1% slow. If the music is being played directly from a sequencer, it will play very slightly slower, but at the correct pitch, and this is usually of no consequence. If the piece is recorded on tape with a 30-fps S<small>MPTE</small> track, however, the music will play slow and will be slightly low in pitch. This may likewise be of little consequence, unless the music is supposed to match pitched sounds recorded on the videotape—such as sung vocals that are part of the dialogue track—in which case it will be out of tune. If the rhythm of the music is supposed to match a click track recorded on the videotape (for example. to guide a dancer), it will drift noticeably.

More serious problems will occur if a M<small>IDI</small> studio user receives a videotape from a producer for which he or she is to compose a score—and the tape has not been striped with S<small>MPTE</small> timecode. If the M<small>IDI</small> studio has an inexpensive S<small>MPTE</small>-to-MTC converter with striping capabilities, the composer can record a S<small>MPTE</small> stripe that runs at 30 fps on the videotape's audio track, and then compose the music locked to that stripe. As long as the tape is played back in the same studio, the music and picture will appear to be synchronized. However, since the S<small>MPTE</small> stripe and the video frame rate are running at two different speeds, any music cues timed to specific video frames will be off when the music is played back locked to the correct video frame rate. Whether the music is played from a sequencer or a tape, none of the cues (except maybe the first) will be in the right place—and the timing errors will get worse as the music continues. When working with video, it is therefore essential to use a S<small>MPTE</small> track that is not only at the proper 29.97-fps rate, but is also locked to a real video signal. More sophisticated S<small>MPTE</small>-to-M<small>IDI</small> devices now available have a video input to perform precisely this task, which is known as *genlocking.*

Here is another nightmare scenario: A M<small>IDI</small> studio creates a multitrack audio tape with a 30-fps S<small>MPTE</small> stripe on one track, and brings it into a postproduction studio. The studio engineer records a 59.94Hz signal on another track on the same piece of tape. This is known as *vertical drive* or *resolve tone,* and it is designed to help the deck synchronize to the master video deck. (The frequency 59.94 is equal to 29.97 × 2, and is known as video *field rate,* because each video frame consists of two fields of alternating lines.)

The hardware synchronizer controlling the multitrack deck looks at both the resolve tone and the SMPTE stripe: the resolve tone to keep the speed of the tape capstan constant, and the timecode stripe to detect any errors or slippage. Because the resolve tone and the timecode are based on different timing sources, they immediately start battling each other. Within seconds, the synchronizer detects that the frame number it's reading is too high, and it slows down the deck. The resolve tone reader, however, sees the deck is running too slowly, and speeds it up. The result is constantly changing speed that renders the tape useless. (Digital audio, which needs an incredibly precise master clock for synchronization, presents even more serious potential problems, but we won't get into that here.)

Syncing to Live Sources

Adding sequenced tracks to a piece of music already on tape can be a tricky task. Perhaps a great vocalist has recorded a track with a lousy band, and rather than redo the whole track with other musicians, the producer wants to save some money by sequencing the instruments and keeping the vocal. Or, perhaps a band that has recorded a live concert wants to flesh out the sound for the album release with synthesized horns—or replace the drums with samples. As with all MIDI-meets-tape situations, some form of timecode track on the tape is required for these situations. Because of its flexibility, SMPTE is almost always the choice. Unfortunately, unless the original recording was done to a very accurate click track (which is still on the tape), the tempo of the music will vary over time. One way of solving this is to play the MIDI tracks "live" along with the tape track, recording data into the sequencer as the tape runs. However, because there is no tempo map relating to the music—and therefore no correlation between the sequenced notes and the sequencer's bars and beats—many of the advantages of working with a sequencer are lost with this method. For example, an entire verse or chorus of sequenced data cannot be easily copied and pasted elsewhere because the section will probably not start on a measure boundary. In addition, if the tempo is not exactly the same the second time around, the sequenced tracks won't match up with the tape. Quantizing is out of the question as well.

To take full advantage of a sequencer's capability, a tempo map must be derived from the recorded music. This map must then be routed to a SMPTE-to-MIDI Clocks-and-Pointers converter or an MTC-locked sequencer. A *tap button* on the converter provides a simple solution. The musician listens to the recorded track, and the converter listens to the SMPTE track. Every time a beat happens, the musician hits the tap button. The converter notes the SMPTE time of each tap and constructs a tempo map based on that information. While simple, this method is not necessarily very practical. The tapping must be extremely accurate (probably more so than most humans are capable of). The converter must also be able to detect the taps and perform the tempo calculations with a great deal of precision. (A unit that is capable of storing tempos only in whole-number bpm values will not be very useful for this task.) Some tap devices will average a series of taps, instead of following each one slavishly, but many of theses averaging algorithms are less than perfect. Also, the nature of such converters makes correcting mistakes very difficult.

A more common method of creating a tempo map for recorded music is to use an audio input to a converter instead of a tap button. The audio input used is some rhythmically constant track, such as a kick drum or tambourine (or if you're really lucky, a click track). Again, the converter notes the SMPTE times of the audio triggers, and constructs a tempo map from them. The track must often be fed through a noise gate before it reaches the converter so that other instrument sounds that might have leaked onto the track do not create false beats. Because no guesswork is necessary, this technique has a much higher success rate than "live" tapping (although, again, a high degree of precision is required from the hardware, and editing can be tricky). Tap-tempo entry is also a feature of several MTC-based sequencers. The disadvantage of potential inaccuracies caused by the human tapping remain, but editing the resulting tempo map is generally easier to deal with than it is with a hardware converter.

Some sequencer manufacturers are beginning to implement what is probably the most elegant solution to this problem. This technique combines audio triggering with recalculation of the tempo map based on recorded MIDI notes. It works like this: As the tape plays, audio triggers are fed to an audio-to-MIDI converter (such as those found in many drum pads) and possibly through a noise gate. These are recorded as MIDI notes in a sequencer that is locked to the tape's SMPTE track via MTC. The sequencer is then told to assume that each of the notes it has recorded is to be considered a quarter note (or eighth note, or whatever). It will then construct a tempo map that will cause the notes to fall exactly on beats without changing their SMPTE times. The tempo map that remains is a perfect replica of the tempo played on the tape, and the original beat track can now even be discarded. Reclock, a clever Macintosh shareware program written by Doug Wyatt, performs this trick with MIDI files—and can be used to give any MIDI-file compatible sequencer this capability. It is available on PAN and other public music networks and is also a feature of Opcode's Vision sequencer (version 1.4 and later).

Chapter 8
Automation and Post-Production

The use of MIDI is not confined solely to composing music for recording or performance. Because MIDI is a standardized, easily implemented communications protocol, it is also an excellent tool for automating many functions in the music studio. Before MIDI, effects units could only be adjusted by their front-panel controls (or, at best, with dedicated remote controllers). Console automation systems were controlled by expensive (and usually unfriendly) internal computers. Today, MIDI can be used to perform just about any studio function, using common, easy-to-learn, off-the-shelf tools. MIDI may also be used in video post-production—that complex and demanding activity where sound is married to picture. One of the newest additions to the MIDI specification is MIDI Machine Control. Although it may be some time before we realize all the potential of this new tool, it can provide control over such hardware as tape and video decks. Thus, MIDI provides a single language for controlling every aspect of the audio (and even some aspects of the video) in any production environment.

Effects Processing

Effects processors are an important MIDI tool in recording and post-production, as in live performance. A wide variety of effects devices respond to MIDI commands and can be remotely operated by a controller or sequencer. If the sequencer is locked to tape via SMPTE and MIDI Time Code (or even FSK and MIDI Clocks), you can achieve full effects automation.

Effects devices such as reverbs, delays, pitch shifters, equalizers, compressor/limiters, and the like generally respond to Program Changes and/or Continuous Controllers. A Program Change calls up a specific program or register stored in the effects device's memory. This can be anything from a particular reverb, to a flanger, ducker, or eq curve. Continuous Controllers can adjust individual parameters within those programs: shortening the RT60 (reverb time), speeding up a flanger's LFO rate, changing the shelving frequency of an eq band, and so forth.

Individual parameters are assigned Continuous Controller numbers (or other continuous MIDI commands). For example, Program Change 14 might call up a delay program, then Controller 10 will adjust its delay length, and Controller 11 its feedback. At different points in a mix, different programs can be called up, so that one effects device can serve several purposes. MIDI Parameter Control then further enhances the creative control by letting you alter or tweak individual parameters at specific times without changing the entire program.

One useful feature often found in MIDI-controlled effects is a range limit. If you have MIDI control over delay feedback for example, the feedback should never exceed 95%, for this would put the unit into self-oscillation. Therefore, the unit might allow you to specify that a maximum value for Controller 11 (127) sets the feedback to only 95%. Similarly, to keep the range of delay times fairly small, the unit would assign a delay time range—for example, 40 ms and 150 ms corresponding to values 0 and 127 of MIDI Controller 10.

You can also invert a parameter map so that a minimum Controller value sets up a maximum delay time, and vice versa. One MIDI Controller can also handle two different parameters. For example, a Modulation wheel might control both LFO rate and depth of a flanger simultaneously. This can create very dramatic real-time effects changes. You can also set limits on MIDI ranges in an effects program. For example, you can set the program so that only Controller values between 40 and 100 will adjust the parameter, and values of less than 40 or higher than 100 are not acted upon at all. This function has two important purposes. In a multiparameter setup, this could set a ceiling on one parameter (e.g., feedback level) while not limiting the range of another (e.g., LFO rate). In a different scenario, MIDI limitations can allow a single MIDI Controller to handle two different parameters independently (by setting one to respond only to low Controller values and the other only to high ones).

Using Program Changes combined with Controllers is the most common way to automate effects, but there are alternative methods. Some devices allow the same functions to be controlled by MIDI notes and velocities, Channel or Key Pressure, or Pitch Bend. A common and exciting use of delay that is found quite a bit in dance music links delay times to MIDI Clocks: the faster the sequence plays, the shorter the delays, and vice versa. Some devices don't need complex control. These respond only to Program Changes and have no parameter adjustments. Other devices do not need program registers. For example, a simple compressor may only require real-time Continuous Controller parameter adjustment. The number of individual parameters that can be mapped to Controllers varies among different units: some allow one or two, while others allow ten or more. The flexibility of these mappings also varies: some allow range limitations (as explained above), while others use fixed ranges. Some devices assign the same Controller to the same parameter in every program, while others allow each program to have its own custom parameter map. Some popular effects units have the same kind of computer-based editing programs as synthesizers. These allow for the display of System Exclusive data and the adjustment of parameters and MIDI maps (that can be stored in the computer for later retrieval).

Here's an example of an elaborate effects setup under MIDI control. The device is a multi-effects unit—and the program involved incorporates reverb, eq, delay, and flanging (short delay).

Effect	Controller or Source	Minimum Value/Maximum Value
Reverb Time (RT60)	Data Slider (Controller 6)	1.0 sec./60 sec.
Reverb HF Ratio (reverb brightness)	Channel Pressure	60%/150%
EQ Center Frequency (a wah-wah pedal)	Foot Pedal (Controller 4)	100Hz/1,200Hz
Delay	MIDI Clock	800ms(75 bpm)/300ms(200 bpm)
Flange Delay (resonant frequency of the flange —goes up as note numbers go up)	Note Number	800 /90
Flange Feedback	Note Velocity	25%/95%
Flange LFO Rate	Mod Wheel (Controller 1)	0.2Hz/6Hz

As you can see, multiparameter mappings of complex effects programs offer some amazing possibilities. A look at the manual for any MIDI-controlled multi-effects device should give you many more creative ideas. Some Continuous Controller commands are defined with effects control in mind: 0CH and 0DH are "Effects Control" 1 and 2. These can be used as sends or parameter controls—as can 5BH through 5FH, which are known as "Effects Depth" 1 through 5. In addition, Balance (08) can be used to control the wet/dry mix in an effects unit. More specific assignments for individual parameters within a multipurpose effects unit may be adopted in the future. It is likely that such assignments would be along the lines of the "Sound Controller" assignments already in place for instruments (numbers 46 through 4FH). In fact, these new assignments may use those very same numbers.

While equalizers tend to change programs smoothly, and reverbs more or less smoothly (depending on how important that feature was to the designers), delays are usually fairly uncooperative. Changing the delay time drastically can cause an audible "clunk" in some units (whether you're doing it from the front panel or through MIDI). To avoid this, fade down the signal to the delay before sending a Program Change message. In some units, changing some parameters works beautifully, while other parameter changes cause problems. As a rule, you'll get a smoother transition if you change one or more parameters with Controllers from within a single program, than if you change registers with a Program Change.

Audio patch bays also use MIDI automation to good effect. Often a number of your sound sources (synthesizers or tape tracks) need to be rerouted among a number of effects devices during a mix. You may not have enough effects devices, so some must do double duty. A MIDI-controlled patch bay that responds to Program Changes can help greatly here. Like effects devices, some patch bays are smoother than others in handling changes. Some switch silently, some automatically fade or mute sounds before executing a rerouting, and some cause glitches if a signal is present when the switch occurs.

Level Control and Mixing

Although effects control was the first use of MIDI automation to gain wide popularity, level control and mixing were not far behind. Adjusting MIDI velocities is one way to control audio levels, but it is no substitute for true level control. This is because Velocity often affects the timbre of a sound as well as its volume. A trumpet played loudly a long way away sounds very different from a trumpet played softly close by even though their absolute volumes, or SPLs, may be the same. In addition, since velocities only affect how a note starts, you can't use them to fade or swell sustained sounds.

MIDI Controller 07: Volume

MIDI Controller 07, Volume, is useful for changing volume in many synthesizers. This Controller is invaluable in some circumstances, but, like Velocity, it is not always a sufficient substitute for true automated mixing. This is because many synthesizers use a digital-to-analog converter at their output stage to change the digital "model" of the sound created by the synth's circuitry into an audio signal that can be amplified and monitored. While an audio volume control (such as on a mixing console) would adjust the signal from this converter, in many cases Controller 07 lowers the input to this converter by lopping bits off the signal while it is still in its digital form. This certainly turns down the volume, but it also reduces the instrument's dynamic range. Even worse, it often doesn't change the noise component of the resulting audio signal. It's almost as if you were to fade down a trumpet track by moving the trumpet further away from the mic, allowing the mic to pick up more room sound in relation to the trumpet's sound. Expression, Controller 0AH (11 decimal), is also often used for the same purpose as Volume, especially in the new General MIDI devices. The difference is that Volume is supposed to be considered similar to a fader movement, while Expression is used for temporary dynamic changes that would be under the control of a pedal.

MIDI Control of Audio

There is still a need for true audio-level controllers that respond to MIDI. The simplest of these consist of one or more *voltage-controlled amplifiers* (VCAs) that raise or lower an audio signal in response to MIDI Controllers (or note velocities). These are used "in front" of a conventional mixer's inputs or in the mixer's insert loop. Some users feel that VCAs adversely affect sound. They prefer resistive networks that respond to MIDI by attenuating the audio—providing a potentially quieter audio path.

One problem to watch out for in level controllers is "zipper noise," which is generated when levels of a steady sound source are changed in discrete steps. This occurs either because of the nature of the digital signals controlling the VCA or because of the design of the circuitry itself.

Some lower-end units act as mixers as well as individual level controllers. They offer stereo mix outputs, and sometimes even effects sends and returns. However, they do not offer the extensive user interface of a large console. Other units are controlled by dedicated, graphic-oriented software running on a personal computer (which adds considerably to their power and attractiveness). There are also dedicated controllers for working with such devices, consisting of sliders, knobs, and/or buttons that send out Midi Controller or Note commands. On some of these units, the Midi identity of each physical controller is predetermined. More sophisticated units allow the user to define each controller for optimum performance with the device that they are controlling.

Midi Controlled Mixers

On the other side of the automation coin are full-blown mixers that respond to Midi. So far, however, manufacturers have been squeamish about implementing full Midi-controlled mixers. Most of these only use Midi to mute inputs and/or effects sends and returns. These *mute maps* are stored in RAM in the mixer itself, and are recalled by Program Changes. While they're a far cry from complete level automation, they can go a long way towards cleaning up a mix by making sure that channels (from synths, mics, or tape tracks) are automatically shut off when they're not needed.

Several third-party manufacturers have developed aftermarket automation systems that fit into consoles made by major manufacturers (and are supported by the manufacturers). These implement complete control, although many of them are designed to be "invisible." Still, none yet include such truly high-end features as moving faders. Other manufacturers have tried to market full-featured Midi-controlled mixers, but their acceptance rate has not been high. Like Midi-controlled effects units, these mixers use one or both of two types of control. *Snapshot control* is used for gross changes—and *continuous control* is reserved for more subtle adjustments. Snapshots (or "scenes") read the entire control surface of the mixer and store all of the knob settings in RAM. These settings can then be recalled with Program Changes. The amount of time it takes the mixer to go from one snapshot to the next (often called *fade time*) is usually adjustable. With continuous control, each fader or knob is assigned a Midi Controller number or note—and is adjusted by sending different Controller or Velocity values. Scaling input or output values is not normally necessary in mixers.

The ultimate Midi-controlled mixer uses both snapshot and continuous control. So far, only a couple of manufacturers have dared to produce such a unit. The Yamaha DMP7 (which first appeared in 1987) responds to Program Changes and continuous control of levels. It also allows full Midi control of pan and three-band, fully parametric eq on each of eight inputs. In addition, it has three internal effects devices with every individual parameter, as well as send and return levels controllable with Midi. It also has moving faders and completely digital internal circuitry.

The full-featured DMP7, and its successors, the DMP7D (which features digital inputs and outputs) and the Yamaha DMP11 (which lacks the moving faders) were actually designed for the low-end market. Although they are expensive by home-studio standards, they are a small fraction of what a full-blown professional automated console normally costs. Yamaha followed the DMP series with a Yamaha DMR8, geared at the very high end of the market. It includes a proprietary-format eight-track digital tape deck. A version without the tape deck, the DMC1000, is available, however, this unit actually costs almost as much as the DMR8 because of its extra features.

The more recent (and more modest) DCM100 from Fostex is a rack-mountable, control-less mixer with eight stereo inputs. It features high and low eq and two effects sends on each input. All control settings respond to Midi. It can be used by itself, or with the Mixtab, which is a dedicated control surface for the mixer. Instead of moving faders, the Mixtab features the next best thing: faders with nulling functions. When you move a fader, LEDs turn red, green, and/or flash to tell you how the fader position relates to the current setting of the parameter it controls: too high, too low, or right on the money. This eliminates the guesswork in determining whether the physical controls match the virtual controls.

MIDI Mixing of Non-MIDI Music

MIDI-controlled mixing can be used with non-MIDI sources, like multitrack tape. A SMPTE stripe on a multitrack tape can allow a sequencer to follow in sync with the tape. The sequencer can then be used for automating effects and mixing of the tape tracks. It's important to note that if the studio is not synthesizer-based, there's no reason for the sequencer to be used for anything else. Therefore, there is no reason for it to have a musical user-interface. In fact, some MIDI-based automation systems are actually sequencers in disguise, with user interfaces that resemble a mixing console and/or a meter bridge.

Problems With Using MIDI for Mixing

Traditional console automation systems have onboard computers that keep track of updates. This means that multiple passes over a piece of audio in which different fader moves are made complement rather than conflict with each other. When using a MIDI sequencer for automation, this process is not automatic. Ideally, each Controller should be placed on its own sequencer track, so that you can punch individual movements in and out. However, this method is not often practical. If multiple Controllers share a track, then punching a new pass in the middle of a previous one will erase all old Controller data in that section. On the other hand, if you merge the second pass with the first, there will be conflicts between the old data and the new.

One solution is to use a fader box that is also a MIDI processor. It will pass MIDI data from a previous mix unchanged until you move a fader. At that point, all old data corresponding to the fader's assigned Controller is blocked—and new Controller data generated by the moving fader is sent. The combined new and old data (from all the other Controllers) are recorded on a new sequencer track, and the previous track is erased. Moving faders, nulling functions, and "update modes" are extremely helpful in these situations. *Update mode* indicates that no data be sent until the physical fader passes the point corresponding to the current Controller value. This will prevent abrupt changes in volume caused by a fader starting its move from a place very far from where it's supposed to be. In addition, the sequencer you use to do automation must have Controller chasing or you will continually be hopelessly lost.

Samplers

With the growth of high-fidelity, high-capacity samplers, MIDI has become an important tool for processing sound effects, Foley, ambience, and dialogue in the post-production studio. Here, a specialized sequencer locked to a SMPTE-striped audio tape or videotape provides the link to the sampler. Sequencers can fire MIDI notes with very high precision: the theoretical limit is on the order of two microseconds. Even with an ordinary sequencer, capable of dividing a quarter note into 240 ticks and playing at 180 bpm, the resolution is a thoroughly usable 1/24 of a frame (or better than 1.4 milliseconds).

A big reason to use sequencers and samplers to handle effects is that it is very easy to edit their timings. Subtle changes in the timing of a sound effect can make a great deal of difference in the effect's impact. Effects that slightly precede a visual event elicit a different response than those that occur slightly after it—and the ability to tweak that timing without actually having to re-record anything is a great advantage. In addition, the modification tools in most samplers and in computer-based sample-editing programs can alter, clean up, and change the emotional value of sound effects in very creative ways.

MIDI makes effects production more efficient in several other ways. It allows volume changes to be part of the actual sample—or programmed into a sequencer using Controller 07 (saving a step at mix time). Using a sampler also saves computer memory. You can use the same sample as many times as you need without taking up any additional tape tracks or hard-disk space. If you need variations on the effect, you can play the sample at a different pitch or velocity. Or, if the sampler allows it, use MIDI Controllers to change the envelope or filter characteristics of the sound.

Effects

Car tire squeals, phaser blasts, windows breaking, screams in the night, and all manner of audio effects can be handled with samplers. Actual sounds can be recorded on location with a portable cassette or DAT machine—or sounds may be taken from sound-effects libraries on CD or tape. You can load these into a sampler's RAM, and have the sequencer play them on cue. Many advanced samplers have a time-compression algorithm, so you can create alternate versions of samples at the same pitch, but running slightly longer or shorter. You can also layer effects samples with other samples or synthesized sounds to create completely new sounds.

Ambience and Natural Sound

A sampler's ability to loop sounds of varied lengths makes it well suited for creating ambience tracks and natural sounds, such as street noise, forest sounds, and so on. You can thicken an ambience by playing the same ambient loop from two different sampler keys simultaneously, thus creating two different pitches. Many samplers allow untempered scales with small differences between the pitches. If the sampler is multitimbral, you can play the sound on two channels using the same note, and add a small amount of Pitch Bend to one. A time-compression feature can also create alternate versions of loops without obvious pitch changes (which can be very useful for layering).

Foley

Foley effects are ordinary sounds like footsteps, doors closing, and chairs squeaking that accompany a picture. These are traditionally laid in by hand by a sound editor who matches the frame numbers on a reel of magnetic sound film containing the effects to the frame numbers on a visual reel. Or else, the sounds are painstakingly recorded by a Foley artist walking through sand, lighting a match, or doing whatever the film calls for while watching the actor on screen do the same thing. With MIDI and samplers, this process is much easier. If a selection of footsteps is loaded into a sampler and laid out on a keyboard, a sound editor can literally play the footsteps on the keyboard while watching the scene. Then the editor can go back and tighten up the sounds by adjusting their times within the sequence. Again, different pitches and Pitch Bend can create variations in the sound—like the Doppler effect that indicates something moving away from the listener. An entire library of Foley effects can be loaded into a large sampler to make the process of assembling tracks very efficient. Adding and changing room ambience or Foley effects can be handled at the same time as the recording (that is, if the same sequencer is used to control a reverb or delay unit through which the sampled sounds are fed).

Dialogue

You can even create dialogue with a MIDI sampler (although sampling even a single reel of a film's script would require an awful lot of memory). *Looping*, however, is a perfect application for a sampler—that's when background voices are used to create an atmosphere of a given locale in a film. (Don't confuse this with looping a sample, as described earlier.) Samplers can also come in very handy when individual pieces of dialogue need to be rerecorded—particularly if they need some kind of pitch change or time compression.

In some cases, foreground dialogue can be handled with a sampler. In a rerecording session that follows the shooting of a scene, if an actor reads his line too slow, a sampler can speed it up (with or without pitch change) to fit the picture exactly. There are expensive, professional time-shifting and hard-disk-based processing systems dedicated to these kinds of tasks. However, ordinary samplers can handle these tasks if they are equipped with the right features (and as long as they are working with sounds on a relatively small scale).

Edit Lists

Sequencers that allow notes and other events to be specified in SMPTE times as well as musical times are quite useful for post-production sound editing. Specialty programs that serve as *Edit Decision Lists* (*EDLs*) for MIDI-based effects systems are actually sequencers, but with front ends more suited to effects editing. Q-Sheet A/V, a Macintosh program from Digidesign, is such a tool. It lets you create an effect and move it around in time using any kind of MIDI data input—whether recorded from a MIDI device or typed directly into the program. The program locks to SMPTE via MIDI Time Code, and deals with SMPTE time rather than musical time. You can tell the program that certain MIDI keys are assigned to specific sound effects. Whenever one of those keys is played into a track, the name of the effect (not the MIDI note) shows up on the list. This makes it easy to edit the effect.

An *event backtimer* is a feature that allows the editor to align the end or middle of a sound cue (like the peak volume of a train passing by) with a visual event (the locomotive zooming past the camera). It will then calculate where the beginning of the cue should start. Another feature automatically repeats events for ambient loops, creates random spaces between the events, and even plays them at random velocities.

MIDI events are recorded in tracks. Each track can address multiple MIDI channels and different tracks can be used at different times. This has many practical applications. For example, a client may want to hear a variety of different effects tracks or mixes—and the sound editor can switch among them instantly. Or, if a commercial is to be used in various foreign-language markets, and the different versions use a common background track, the background track needs to be recorded just once. Preparing the different versions simply means recording and switching among different voice-over tracks.

Q-Sheet A/V will also play Standard MIDI Files recorded with other sequencers along with its effects tracks. This allows music and effects to be mixed and printed in one pass. It can import video Edit Decision Lists from CMX (a popular editing system) and compatible systems. Placing the EDL directly into a Q-Sheet track simplifies the editor's task by eliminating the need to record or calculate any cue timings by hand—they're already in there. All the editor has to do is decide what MIDI-controlled sound effect to put with each edit.

Synchronizing Music

So far our discussion of post-production has concentrated on effects. But music also plays an important part in the audio palette accompanying a film.

MIDI Time Code

MIDI Time Code is the key to synchronizing a sequencer to videotape and audio tape machines. Consider a situation where you have completed the score to a film—and the director decides to cut three seconds out of a two-minute scene. If your sequencer reads MIDI Time Code and has a *time fitting* feature, you can select the original two-minute piece of music and tell the sequencer to make it three seconds shorter. The software recalculates the music's internal tempo map and the music plays at a slightly faster tempo. No matter how complex the tempo map, it will be rescaled to reflect the difference. It will also maintain all relative tempo changes, even though the total tempo has been increased by 2.5%.

Another advantage of MIDI Time Code is that it always uses the sequencer's internal tempo map. This allows you to play the sequence without the tape running and hear exactly the same thing as you would with the tape running. When you're editing a sequence and you don't need to see the picture, it's much easier to use the sequencer's autolocating functions than it is to rewind the tape, roll it, and wait for the synchronizer to catch up each time you want to hear what you've done.

Finally, MIDI Time Code allows complete slaving of a sequencer. Most sequencers can be told to start automatically as soon as they read a complete set of valid Quarter Frame messages. This may seem trivial at first glance, but it can prove to be a major convenience when tape is being continuously stopped, rewound, cued, and restarted. With MTC sync, you only have to worry about starting the tape (and not the sequencer). You can even start an MTC-controlled sequencer after tape starts rolling. This is impossible to do with MIDI Song Position Pointers and Clocks, because in that form of sync, location information is normally not sent once the tape has started.

Tempo-Matching and Hit List Programs

MIDI helps the professional film and video composer conform tempos to visual events. In a given scene in a film, a number of film scoring *hits* (or visual events) will be linked with musical events, such as a downbeat, a key change, a frozen chord, or the entrance of a new instrument. Unless the film is a music video, it will be rare that the film editor will cut it so that all these moments happen on even beats at a constant tempo. Rather, it's up to the composer to find the tempos that will cause as many hits as possible to land in musically logical places. The traditional tool for this task is a *clickbook*, which is a compendium of numbers showing the length of time, in film or video frames, of a given number of beats at various tempos. Since a computer can easily generate such numbers on the fly, clickbook replacement programs are common. There are a number of advantages of having a computer do this work.

- While a clickbook always starts beat 1 on time 0, a computer can use any frame number as a starting point.

- A computer can compute non-whole-number tempos with great precision. A clickbook would have to be ten times larger just to add one digit past the decimal point.

- A computer can deal simultaneously with different frame rates, like 24, 25, or 30 fps (or even *feet per minute*, which is a common reference in the film world).

Beyond simply generating tempo and frame numbers, a clickbook replacement program can be given a list of the timings of the hits and instructed to scan the possible tempos within a given range. It then produces a report that tells how many hits are made at each tempo and how far off the misses are (in SMPTE or musical time). The composer can use this report to change the tempo at any point in the hit list—and even program in accelerandos and ritards to see how they affect the percentage of hits and misses. You can set priority levels for different hits so that the program sees some as more important than others. The program also lets you set different tolerances for what constitutes a made hit (that is, how many frames off it can be). People normally perceive a music cue that comes slightly ahead of the visual event as being more "off" than one that is slightly behind. For this reason, some programs allow different tolerances to be specified for early and late hits.

The connection to MIDI here is that the program can create a tempo map reflecting the process of searching and changing tempos. This map can then be used directly in a sequence. Hitlist programs can often import a piece of music from a sequencer in the form of a Standard MIDI File and play it back with the tempo map it has created. It can also work the other way around: the hitlist program can store the tempo map itself as a Standard MIDI File; you can then import it into a sequencer and compose the music on top of it. You can easily generate multiple tempo maps and use them with the same sequence of notes to audition different versions of the tempo map.

When the composer transfers a tempo map to the sequencer, the list of hits that created the map is often transferred as well. The description of each hit will show up in the sequencer as a *text event*, *cue*, or *marker* at the appropriate time. The composer can use the tempo map and the markers as a framework on which to compose the music. Some hitlist programs allow their tempo maps to be transferred into older-style SMPTE–to–MIDI Clock and Pointer converters. This is accomplished using System Exclusive dumps tailored for the particular converter. Obviously, this method isn't as flexible as working with an MTC-compatible sequencer, but it works.

Composers who work with live orchestras on scoring stages can also make good use of these programs. Instead of generating a tempo map that controls a sequencer, they generate a click track which is fed to a conductor's head-phones. Some of these programs can even hook up to video processors to superimpose visual markers—known as *punches* (along with the audible tempos)—onto the picture as it plays. These punches, which flash when the film reaches a hit point, are so named because they used to be actual holes punched in the work copy of the film. A *streamer* is a visual count-off preceding a punch that moves laterally across the screen to prepare the conductor for the punch.

There are several hitlist programs on the market. Some of the features described above have been incorporated into general-purpose sequencers as well. Special mention should be made of Opcode's Cue. Designed for high-echelon Hollywood professionals, Cue performs an amazing number of tasks.

On the basis of the hitlist, it can print out a blank score on one or several staves, complete with clefs, instrument names, time signatures, and tempo markings. To finish the score, the instrumental composer only needs to fill in the blanks with the notes. Cue can also generate a compendium of all of the sound and music cues for a film, organized by reel. This book goes to the sound editor, along with copyright registration forms and performing-rights organization forms. In this way, the composer can be sure to get his royalties when the film plays on Brazilian or Indonesian TV.

MIDI and Digital Audio

MIDI systems are wonderful for processing synthesized and sampled sounds, but there are many types of sounds that MIDI equipment can't handle well (if at all). Speech and singing (unless the phrases are short enough to fit into a sampler) pose problems for MIDI. Certain expressive instruments like violin and saxophone—and ethnic instruments, such as bagpipes and gamelans—are also difficult to emulate using MIDI.

These sounds are best recorded on tape. That is why it is so important to be able to synchronize sequencers to tape machines. An increasingly important alternative to tape is digital audio. The development of this technology, combined with the ever-falling price and ever-increasing speed of personal computers, has made it possible for the computer to become a low-cost digital recording system. The recording medium can be either a hard magnetic disk or a high-speed magneto-optical or phase-changing optical type disk. Since sixteen-bit stereo digital audio sampled at 44.1kHz requires 10MB per minute of audio, such a system requires a good-sized storage device. It usually also requires a dedicated card installed in one of the computer's expansion slots. The card will contain at least a processor chip and possibly A/D and D/A converters. However, some cards connect to external units such as DAT decks. Several computers are now available that have this capability built in.

Such systems have several advantages. Because they're digital, the resulting fidelity can be extremely high. Generation noise and signal loss associated with mixing, copying, and bouncing tracks of analog sound can be minimized or even eliminated. Disk-based audio systems are truly random-access in that any piece of audio can be played back at any time in relation to any other with no physical editing required. Tape, on the other hand, always plays back sounds in the order they were recorded, unless it's physically cut with a razor blade and spliced. Once it's striped with SMPTE timecode however, splicing a tape is no longer an option.

The digital audio system can exist in the same computer as the MIDI sequencer. This makes it possible to design a common user-interface that can record and play both MIDI and digital audio tracks. It can display both tracks simultaneously and keep them in sync both aurally and visually. This allows you to slip or cut and paste them together as you wish. Such hybrid programs are available for most systems, including Macintosh, IBM, Amiga, and Atari. Some of these programs concentrate on the digital audio side of things, and rely on sequencing software to create Standard MIDI Files. The audio program can then play the MIDI data back (usually at specific SMPTE times) while it records and plays back the audio. To control the audio, these programs often present the user with a mixing console simulation and/or an audio layout screen in which MIDI events or sequences are placed in time alongside audio events. Some of the audio-oriented programs have rudimentary MIDI recording and editing facilities as well.

Edit list programs such as Q-Sheet A/V or Passport Designs' Producer let you construct a list of audio and MIDI files recorded with other programs—and direct them to play at specific SMPTE times. In addition, these programs offer some limited MIDI recording capability.

The truly integrated system attaches equal importance to both MIDI and digital audio. These look essentially like MIDI sequencers with extra tracks for audio recording and editing. Like MIDI tracks, the audio tracks in these programs can be cut, pasted, moved around, faded, and panned from within the program. The audio tracks are displayed on the screen as waveforms right along with the MIDI Note and Controller data. Generally speaking, the audio editing functions in these programs are *nondestructive*. They don't actually affect the audio data on disk, but merely provide pointers to the audio files and instructions on how to play them. These instructions include volume and panning controls, and sometimes equalization and rudimentary effects processing as well.

More elaborate audio editing functions are *destructive*, in that they physically alter the files on disk. These functions include complex equalization and effects, noise and click removal, or mixing many files into one. These processes are generally handled by a separate, dedicated digital-audio editing program. This type of program is similar to the sample-editing programs described earlier. Some MIDI/audio programs have hooks into the audio editing program that let a user automatically move files between the two programs to provide an all-purpose front end.

There are also now available a number of dedicated hard-disk audio recording and editing systems at prices comparable to the computer-based ones. Many of these can deal with MIDI by playing sequences loaded in as Standard MIDI Files—or by outputting MTC or MIDI Clocks and Pointers to drive an external sequencer.

Synchronizing Midi and Digital Audio

When you're working with MIDI and digital audio together in a computer, syncing is no problem—as long as the computer's internal clock is being used as the timing reference for all your sound sources. The computer's clock determines the playback speed of the MIDI data and the digital audio card's sample-rate clock determines the playback speed of the audio. Even if these clocks are not linked, if the same computer, card, and clocks are used for both recording and playback, there should be no discrepancies at any point.

Things get a little more complicated when using external synchronization, such as playing a combined MIDI and audio file locked to videotape. Naturally, SMPTE timecode or MTC is used to drive the program. However, there are different ways of using these timing signals, and this can create problems. A sequencer following MIDI Time Code will always follow any changes in the speed of the master source (for instance, the tape with the SMPTE stripe). This is because the sequencer's playback rate is determined by the speed of the incoming Quarter Frame messages. If the tape speed changes, the sequencer will follow it and change the tempo of its MIDI playback. Of course, the pitch and tuning of the music (whether it's coming from synthesizers or samplers) will remain the same.

Digital audio, however, when synced to external clocks, can be handled in one of two ways. It can be used in *edge trigger mode* or *continuous resynchronization mode*. In edge trigger mode, the SMPTE (or MTC) numbers provide location information only. An audio file will start to play at its specified time, but once it starts, the audio system's own sample-rate clock takes over to determine the playback speed. Any changes in the incoming timecode are then ignored. In resynchronization mode, the timecode provides both location and speed information. The file starts at the specified frame, and then plays back as the audio system's sample-conversion circuitry constantly monitors the incoming timecode. If the system detects any change in the speed, it slows down or speeds up the playback.

Each of these methods has pros and cons, especially when they are used in conjunction with MIDI playback. In edge trigger mode, the audio is always played at the correct pitch and speed. However, if the tape providing the master timecode should slip, the hard-disk audio and the tape will go out of sync, and so will the audio and the MIDI data. Since the MIDI sequence follows the changes in speed, and the audio doesn't, they will start to "walk away" from each other.

Continuous resync ensures that the master tape, the audio, and the MIDI notes are always locked together. It's like an audio tape deck that uses its own SMPTE track to resolve itself to SMPTE coming from another deck. Any speed variation or jitter in the timecode, however, will cause the audio to experience pitch fluctuations (which we might hear as wow or flutter). The MIDI tracks will experience the same fluctuations, but only in tempo, not in pitch. Thus, the MIDI and audio will be in sync, but out of tune with each other. In most situations, timecode sources and commercially available audio MIDI systems are stable enough so that this problem never arises. In addition, short video cues (such as thirty-second and sixty-second TV spots) are usually not long enough for these discrepancies to become apparent.

Manufacturers are just now getting around to implementing the best solution—that is, to make sure everything in the entire studio is locked to a very stable and consistent master clock. Preferably, it is a clock that has even better timing resolution than SMPTE. This may be either a video signal known as *blackburst* or *house sync*, which comes from a super-stable source. Or, it might be some other form of standard digital word clock that all the systems can read. (Even samplers could benefit from word-clock synchronization: it would make them more useful for longer sounds in a post-production environment.)

Stable sync sources, which once cost many thousands of dollars, are now available to the small studio for a few hundred dollars. An even cheaper source of good sync is a local broadcast TV station. Simply tune in a VCR to a strong station, and take the video out signal from the VCR into the house sync input on your master SMPTE generator. (Avoid using a station on a cable system as a sync source. Cable operators are notorious for ignoring good engineering practice when they do local "inserts"—and you may find your sync jumping all over the place.) Disk-based video is now becoming possible with new standards like Apple's QuickTime. The synchronization problems that this poses are even more complex than those already discussed. However, these systems are still in relatively early stages of development.

MIDI Control of Digital Audio

Some systems let you use MIDI controls to process an audio signal as it passes through the computer. Most of these use dedicated audio cards for the processing. An example is Opcode Systems' Max, a graphical programming language that lets you treat a digital audio file like any other object—and subject it to many of the same operations as MIDI objects.

Opcode's StudioVision combines audio recording and playback with MIDI sequencing on a Macintosh. This software allows real-time control over volume and pan position of the audio tracks, using the program's on-screen faders. An example of a more elaborate Macintosh-based digital audio system with real-time MIDI control is Kyma from Symbolic Sound Corporation. Kyma's hardware is based (like many audio processing systems) on Motorola's 56001 Digital Sound Processing chip—and can run from two to nine processors. As with earlier computer-music programs like Music V, Kyma's software is an *off-line* or compiled language. You write the program, then the computer takes time to figure out how to execute it. Unlike Music V, the program is graphics based, and each icon for an operation can graphically "explode" on screen into its constituent icons.

The software can define sound objects as complete audio events, and even entire compositions. MIDI can be used to work with the sound in real time. For example, incoming MIDI Note Velocity can be assigned to change the volume or pitch of a sound object—or controllers can be used to set the levels of multiple objects in real time. You can control the sound being generated from the program or the incoming audio signals that are being processed through the hardware in real time.

MIDI Transport Control

The traditional way of interfacing a tape deck and sequencer is to have the tape deck be the master to which the sequencer is slaved. This setup has served the MIDI community well for nearly a decade. However, there are situations in which it might be worthwhile to reverse this configuration. For MIDI users, control of physical tape transports is a logical extension of the computer-based studio. Synthesizers do the music, samplers do the effects, and processors process. All of these devices are under MIDI control, with a computer running a single, integrated program at the front. If you're used to that mode of operation, the idea of having a separate control panel for tape transports and other mechanical devices seems almost primitive.

In strict terms, the only way for the sequencer to really be the master would be if it were to generate SMPTE time code and/or house sync. In most studios, this would constitute an unnecessary duplication of hardware. Nonetheless, it's quite possible to construct a hybrid system that makes it seem to the user that the computer is in charge.

The first attempts at MIDI transport control were made by companies who built hardware interfaces that allowed a sequencer to issue commands that would operate the controls on a tape deck. When the user told the sequencer to start, it would send out a System Exclusive command that would close a contact connected to the deck's Start button, and the deck would start. Once the tape was moving, a SMPTE track on the tape would send timing information (usually converted to MTC) back to the sequencer. The sequencer would then follow the tape. Other System Exclusive messages were used for commands including stop, fast forward, rewind, record enable, punch-in, return-to-zero, and cue locating.

This type of system worked well. However, because it used the System Exclusive codes of individual manufacturers, one brand of device would not work with another. In addition, if sequencer developers wanted their products to interface with this transport-control system, they needed to include these System Exclusive codes in their software. As more manufacturers developed transport-control schemes, sequencer makers would be forced to choose among them (or else include all of the different codes in their products). This would require constant updates to the software and could create incompatibility problems.

MIDI Machine Control (MMC) takes this idea and codifies it into the MIDI spec, thereby making it universally available to all manufacturers of hardware and software alike. Any sequencer, tape transport, or controller that sends or recognizes MIDI Machine Control commands will have no trouble working with another such device. MMC can work alongside MIDI Time Code, SMPTE timecode (in either longitudinal or vertical form), or any combination of these. The authors of the MMC spec also expanded its capabilities considerably beyond what other manufacturers had devised.

In many ways, MMC emulates the ESbus standards developed for audio and video transport control. It's cheaper to implement than ESbus (especially if you already own a lot of MIDI equipment and don't want to buy a bunch of converters). In addition, it provides links to MIDI sequencers, computer programs, and instruments that ESbus cannot address.

MMC transmitters and receivers can be included in sequencers, computers, mixing consoles with internal computers, tape controllers and autolocators, transport synchronizers, disk-based audio systems, CD players, broadcast cartridge machines, and even musical instruments. Video decks and disk players can be addressed by MMC as well—either directly or through a separate device that translates MMC to ESbus (or some other video-control protocol).

MMC Systems

MMC systems can be broken down into three basic categories: *open-loop, quasi-open-loop,* and *closed-loop.* In an open-loop MMC system, a central transmitter broadcasts messages to all of the receiving devices. (This, of course, parallels the way most music-oriented MIDI studios operate.) In the quasi-open-loop system, MMC commands travel one cable, while MTC numbers travel another. In the closed-loop system, devices respond to the transmitter in some way and send messages back to it.

Open-Loop

The open-loop is the simplest of the three MMC systems. The tape transport (or its controller or autolocator) has a MIDI In jack. The MMC transmitter—an edit list program on a computer, for example—tells the transport in real time when to start or stop, rewind or fast-forward, or go in and out of record. Locating is the job of the tape deck itself, but the computer can act as a remote controller for the deck's own locating functions.

In one scenario, the computer might tell the transport to note the current location of the tape using whatever mechanism it has for a counter (tach pulses, capstan revolutions, or reel revolutions). Then the transport is told to record that number in a memory register within the deck. Any time after that, the computer can tell the deck to recall that memory location and cue the tape to it. Since the numbers are based on the deck's own counter, there doesn't have to be any SMPTE timecode involved. SMPTE timecode can be used with an open-loop system if the deck is sophisticated enough to use SMPTE instead of a tach-pulse system for its own location functions. In that case, the MMC controller can send frame numbers to the tape deck instead of just location-register numbers.

Regardless of whether it has SMPTE capability, the transport in an open-loop system sends no data back to the computer. Since there is actually no direct synchronization between the tape and the computer, this is not a very practical mode in a sequencing environment. Instead, this type of setup might be used in a simple production studio, when cues on multiple tape transports need to be lined up and fired remotely. This setup might also be found in a broadcast station that needs to get cartridge machines or CD players rolling at specific times.

Quasi-Open-Loop

A quasi-open-loop system is a bit more complex than the open-loop setup. It promises to be the most common setup in MMC-oriented music production studios where direct synchronization between recorded tape (audio or video) and MIDI is necessary, but only a single tape transport needs to be addressed. It's similar to the System Exclusive–based system described earlier: the transmitter sends MMC commands to the transport and the tape on the transport has a SMPTE stripe. A SMPTE-to-MTC converter sends MTC numbers back from the transport to the controller over a separate MIDI cable. In this case, the sequencer can act directly as the autolocator, and autolocate points can merely be markers in the sequence. When you move the sequencer to a marker, an *Immediate Locate* command with a SMPTE/MTC frame number is sent to the deck. The tape deck's own controller either knows SMPTE or is able to translate this frame number into its internal counter numbers. The converter tells the deck to go to that spot and stop. Then when the sequencer is told to start, it immediately commands the tape deck to start playing first. MTC is sent back to the sequencer, and only then does it start to play (locked to the tape).

One nice potential feature of this system is that, when used with a multi-track tape deck, the sequencer can operate and display the tape tracks in the same way that it handles MIDI tracks. The sequencer can turn on and off individual track record-enables. It can also handle punch-ins and punch-outs, either precued or in real time. Therefore, the sequencer can keep track of which tape tracks have had music recorded on them (as long as the tape deck is only operated from the sequencer and never manually). These tracks may be displayed in the same window in which MIDI tracks appear. Instead of using MIDI tracks as "virtual tape" tracks, we now have a situation in which tape tracks are "virtual MIDI" tracks!

Closed-Loop

A closed-loop environment is the most complex and also the most flexible of the MIDI Machine Control systems. Closed-loops allow the use of multiple transports under one controller, including analog, digital, cassette, disk-based, and video formats. The master controller can periodically send an inquiry message to the various machines. During this process, called *strobing,* the controller finds out the location of each device. It records the statuses of individual tracks, and even what types of commands each device will respond to, using a special message called a *signature message.* This means that the controller will know what to send to each transport. The divisions between the machines can be invisible: they can be controlled together as one giant "virtual" deck, with up to 317 tracks per machine.

Both MMC and MTC messages can be sent back from the transports in real time—either as they run or just when they're stopped. This way, the controller has a constant picture of where every machine is and what it's doing.

An MMC Studio Session

Let's take a close look at MIDI Machine Control in action during a hypothetical studio session. The heart of the system is a device that translates MIDI Machine Control commands into serial commands that control a specific multitrack tape deck. Let's assume the translator is designed to be used in closed-loop mode and that it receives MIDI Time Code on the same cable as the MMC responses. Let's also assume that, in addition to handling MMC-to-serial conversion, the translator also handles SMPTE-to-MIDI conversion. The device also has some internal memory for storing information about the transport that it's connected to. In addition, there is a sequencer that transmits MMC commands as it locates within the sequence, enables and disables tracks for recording, and starts and stops the sequence.

The first thing to do is to stripe a track of the multitrack tape with SMPTE timecode. If the deck does not use a SMPTE-based autolocator, it needs to know how SMPTE numbers correspond to the numbers in its tach-pulse or capstan-revolution counter. This often requires some kind of intelligent setup routine, which is handled by the translator. The translator keeps in its memory the relationship between SMPTE times and counter numbers, so it can use it later to calculate cue points.

Now the tape deck is ready to be controlled by a sequencer. A SMPTE *offset time,* the spot on the tape corresponding to the beginning of the sequence, is programmed into the sequencer. When the sequencer locates any point in the sequence, it calculates the SMPTE frame number based on its internal tempo map and the offset time. It then sends this information to the MMC translator in the form of a special MMC command that contains the frame number. The translator calculates the equivalent number for the deck's internal counter from the SMPTE number. It then tells the tape deck (using the deck's own serial protocol) where to locate to.

When the sequencer is told to start, it doesn't play immediately. It first sends an MMC Start command to the translator, which in turn starts the tape. As the tape runs, it sends SMPTE to the translator, which converts it to MTC. The MTC goes back to the sequencer, which starts to play and locks to the tape. If you have a quick-responding tape deck and SMPTE reader, this can all be accomplished in the time it takes to send eight Quarter Frame MTC messages (or 1/15 second).

At any time, the sequencer can tell the translator to set up record-enable switches on any track. It can also load punch-in and punch-out points into any of several registers for any track or combination of tracks. Alternatively, the sequencer can perform these punches in real time. The deck itself can communicate back to the sequencer, telling it which tracks are in record, as well as any errors it encounters. This indicates to the user whether things are going the way they're supposed to. The sequencer can display the tape tracks right alongside the MIDI tracks. This shows which portions of which tracks on the tape have had audio recorded on them—and which portions are available for recording additional material.

MMC Message Set

The MIDI Machine Control specification is comprehensive. It is designed to accommodate every conceivable function that a studio would need now or in the foreseeable future. It consists of over one hundred messages, including master operations, responses from slaves, and information fields. These permit data such as track record-status, tape speed, or timecode numbers to be sent and received.

The specification breaks its messages down into ten general categories:

- control, such as Play or Stop

- communications, such as Wait or Group Assign

- events, or "do this at the designated time"

- timecode generator controls

- memory read/write and error-handling commands

- synchronization, such as Offset or Chase

- timecode arithmetic operations, such as adding or subtracting constants

- turning on and off MIDI Time Code

- procedures, or defining and executing predefined command strings

- information about the timecode, such as its type

Not every MIDI Machine Control–compatible device will send or recognize every message in the set. In fact, it's difficult to conceive of any device that would need to handle the entire message set. Most will deal with a subset (guidelines for which are offered in the MMC specification).

It's exciting to think of the potential complexity and flexibility of transport handling available under MMC. With MIDI Machine Control, the production studio of the future may bear no physical relationship to what we see today. Not only can tape machines be located in another room, even their controls can be out of sight. MIDI Machine Control should make it possible to create custom-designed, instantly configurable, user-friendly "virtual studios" for doing any kind of audio or video production.

Chapter 9
Multimedia

Multimedia has been around for a long time, at least since sounds and visuals were linked together in the first talking movie. But the growth in power and availability of the personal computer spurred many people to believe that audio/visual productions could be produced on a platform such as the Apple Macintosh, IBM PC, Commodore Amiga, or Atari ST. Not only would this put production into the hands of many more people than ever before, but these productions could be interactive, and respond to input from the viewer in ways traditional media such as film or tape could never duplicate.

MIDI plays a central role in desktop multimedia. It provides the ability to record, edit, and play back synthesized or sampled events with stable timing and the ability to be synchronized to changing visual images. That it does this within the context of a personal computer makes it a natural fit to the goals and practices of multimedia. In fact, many of the issues confronting the development of desktop multimedia have already been addressed and effectively implemented by MIDI technology. These include event sequencing, on-screen editing, synchronization, continuous digital control over analog events, digital control over hardware, and so on.

By definition, multimedia constitutes a marriage of visual and auditory events. The new desktop version of multimedia—universal and interactive—adds implicit new requirements. These include:

- Both the production and playback processes should be more accessible to more people than those of traditional media.

- The production values of a given presentation must be competitive with other popular media such as television and film.

- The elements of a production must be well fitted to the interactive nature of multimedia, allowing facile transitions, as well as continuity.

The digital nature of MIDI makes it particularly suited to these requirements. Prerecorded sequences can be provided for non-musicians to use in productions. Any sequence can be easily edited to fit various scenarios. It can be started and stopped at any point, sped up or slowed to fit a specific time or mood, looped indefinitely, and changed according to key, range, instrumentation, and other parameters. A sequence can sound as good as the instruments that play it back, and MIDI sequences can be easily manipulated by software to fit the demands of nonlinear, interactive playback.

In this chapter, we will discuss some of the ways in which MIDI accomplishes this—and some of the applications in which it is used.

Why MIDI?

If you want to enhance a desktop multimedia presentation with sound, you have a number of choices. You can play whatever audio you have available on external devices such as CD, CD-ROM, or laser disk—or you can digitally record sound in the computer, and have the presentation play these files on cue. Both techniques are limited.

Many presentation applications can start and stop a CD-ROM drive to get high-quality audio to play along. If you use the music on a commercially available CD, copyright law says you have to get the permission of the artist and the record company (unless you're only going to use it to entertain yourself and your friends). This can be very expensive, if not downright impossible. Music is also available on music library CDs, but these too are expensive—and often involve paying a separate royalty each time you use a cut. This payment is called a *needle-drop fee* (although this should probably now be renamed "laser flash fee," or something like that). Finding a piece of music from any existing source that complements your presentation in tone, tempo, and length is no trivial job.

The other audio path is digitized sound. On the Mac, many models have built-in microphones. For those that don't you can use Macromedia's MacRecorder. On the PC (running Windows 3.1 or later), you can record audio to the hard disk via the microphone input on an audio card. Your presentation software can play this audio back at any given time during the production. Two things diminish the desirability of this solution. One is file size. Even with the eight-bit digitizing schemes and low (22kHz maximum) sampling rates both platforms offer, these sound files take up over 1MB per minute of monophonic sound. (Double that size for stereo, and double it again for sixteen-bit audio.) This can add up. MIDI files are minuscule by comparison. Even a ten-minute-long MIDI sequence can be as small as fifty kilobytes. If a MIDI file is used in conjunction with an outboard sampler, you can even enjoy the advantages of sampled sound without inundating your computer's hard disk.

The other problem is audio quality. Eight-bit audio will give your sound track a quality akin to what comes out of an inexpensive cassette deck or AM radio. If your listeners are used to the kind of quality they get from their home (or even car) stereos, or from movies, eight-bit audio will sound cheesy and old-fashioned by comparison (particularly for music). Though it can be acceptable for voice or sound effects, it pales in comparison to the production values we all hear almost daily in Hollywood films, on network television, and on CDs. With little or no alteration to the MIDI file, you can play any MIDI instrument from a single compact General MIDI module or card to a bank of the best synthesizers and samplers on the market. The range of cost, portability, and quality is very broad, and you can position your presentation at any point in this range. Nor is this point carved in stone: you can play the presentation one way one day—and another way when you want to deliver it differently. The flexibility is tremendous.

Standard MIDI Files

Before the advent of desktop multimedia, the ability to exchange time-stamped MIDI data (MIDI sequences) among different sequencers and computers was added to the MIDI spec. Today, virtually any sequencer can save a sequence as a Standard MIDI File that can be loaded and played by any software acquainted with the standard. In terms of desktop multimedia, Standard MIDI Files serve a fairly well defined role. Principally, they provide a way for the MIDI-based composer to create music on a sequencer, then to export it in a form that can be played back by another program (such as a multimedia presentation program). This exportability was a big step in making sequences created by the MIDI professional available to more people than ever. It was first necessary for some other pieces to fall into place, however. One of them was General MIDI.

General MIDI

One area of keen competition among synthesizer manufacturers has always been the claim to superior sounds. No manufacturer ever wants to admit its sounds are anything but the most creative, original programs ever loaded into a play buffer. Each one approaches the creation and implementation of these sounds with a near-religious attitude. There is at least one unfortunate result of this situation: when you play a sequence through a synthesizer straight out of the box, you have no idea what it's going to sound like.

Assume a person composes a sequence, using a half-dozen or so synthesizers. This composer painstakingly chooses the individual patches from the various instruments, tweaks each track to take best advantage of each sound, and loads the sequence with custom-designed Velocity, Volume, Aftertouch, and Program Change data. Now dump that sequence to disk and load it into the sequencer in the studio next door, and a whole new set of instruments, sound banks, and programs react quite differently to produce something totally unrecognizable.

General MIDI (GM), a "Recommended Practice" ratified by the MMA and JMSC in 1991, is designed for those who compose music sequences intended to be played on other systems. It consists of several parts. The first is a specifically defined *Patch Map:* every one of the 128 available Program Changes calls up a predefined instrumental sound. How the manufacturer creates that sound is completely up to him—but program number 5 is always an electric piano, program number 41 is always a solo violin, and so on. The second part of the spec defines how to play percussion sounds: drums are always played on Channel 10, and each note is defined. C1 (Note 36) is a kick drum, D1 (Note 38) is a snare, and so on. Again, how the percussion sounds are created is up to each manufacturer.

Now a composer can use a General MIDI instrument to record a sequence that's portable between studios. For the piano track, the composer tells the sequencer that the initial Program Change is 1 (which is defined by the spec as Acoustic Piano). When the sequence is played through another General MIDI synthesizer, Program Change 1 calls up a piano patch. It could be a brilliant Bösendorfer grand taking up all the memory in a 32MB sampler—or it could be a wimpy piano created on a two-operator FM synth card—but at least it's a piano.

General MIDI is an option. No manufacturer is required to utilize it, and many high-end synthesizers and samplers do not implement it. However, synthesizer and synth card manufacturers who wish to sell to the multimedia market will use it—and will include a bank of preset sounds in ROM that match the General MIDI map. Many synths will be designed to be used in both General MIDI and non–General MIDI modes. In this way, they will fit into situations demanding either compatibility or creativity—and so a General MIDI map will be one of several that exist in the synth. The General MIDI spec defines messages for turning General MIDI on and off to cover just this kind of situation. They are Universal Non–Real Time SysEx messages (all numbers are hex):

> F0 7E <device ID> 09 01 F7 turns on General MIDI mode.
> F0 7E <device ID> 09 02 F7 turns off General MIDI and returns
> the synth to its previous mode of operation.

Many older multitimbral synthesizers can be programmed so that their Program maps more or less conform to General MIDI. Some intrepid programmers are making General MIDI maps commercially available for older instruments. These are designed for users who want to take advantage of the new practice without the drudgery of constructing the map themselves. Older synths may not fully comply with General MIDI, either because they're not flexible enough to handle all of the sounds or because they don't meet the polyphony requirements.

General MIDI allows people using multimedia products, such as games and CD-ROM products, to play the MIDI music created for the product on inexpensive synthesizers installed in or attached to their computer. The standard patch map enables them to do this without dealing with Program Change maps or channel assignments. Obviously, no two synthesizers' piano or guitar patches will sound exactly the same. However, if you create a score sequenced according to General MIDI's guidelines which is used in a CD-ROM travelogue soundtrack, anyone playing that CD-ROM with a General MIDI synth chip in their computer will hear a reasonably good representation of what you scored.

With General MIDI, video producers, commercial directors, broadcasters, and multimedia producers have a new, flexible, inexpensive source of high-quality music. It's similar to the "music library" principle, but with an important twist: While conventional libraries are on vinyl or CD, GM libraries are distributed on floppy disk and CD-ROM. Thus, users with only minimal knowledge of music can edit the files as to length, tempo, or even orchestration to customize them for their particular applications. GM also has great potential in the home market, where amateur musicians can experiment and learn with prerecorded music. It also has a bright future in music education, where interactive theory, orchestration, ear-training, and "Music Minus One"–style practice courses can exist without the expense of creating and stocking multiple versions for different synths.

General MIDI Instruments

A basic definition in the General MIDI specification is that of the General MIDI instrument. A General MIDI instrument is defined as "a synthesizer, sound module, card, keyboard or any other physical device that features sounds stored according to the General MIDI specification." Here is the Program Change map to which this specification refers:

General MIDI Program Change Map

1. Acoustic Grand Piano	33. Acoustic Bass	65. Soprano Sax	97. FX 1 (rain)
2. Bright Acoustic Piano	34. Electric Bass (finger)	66. Alto Sax	98. FX 2 (soundtrack)
3. Electric Grand Piano	35. Electric Bass (pick)	67. Tenor Sax	99. FX 3 (crystal)
4. Honky-tonk Piano	36. Fretless Bass	68. Baritone Sax	100. FX 4 (atmosphere)
5. Electric Piano 1	37. Slap Bass 1	69. Oboe	101. FX 5 (brightness)
6. Electric Piano 2	38. Slap Bass 2	70. English Horn	102. FX 6 (goblins)
7. Harpsichord	39. Synth Bass 1	71. Bassoon	103. FX 7 (echoes)
8. Clavichord	40. Synth Bass 2	72. Clarinet	104. FX 8 (sci-fi)
9. Celesta	41. Violin	73. Piccolo	105. Sitar
10. Glockenspiel	42. Viola	74. Flute	106. Banjo
11. Music Box	43. Cello	75. Recorder	107. Shamisen
12. Vibraphone	44. Contrabass	76. Pan Flute	108. Koto
13. Marimba	45. Tremolo Strings	77. Blown Bottle	109. Kalimba
14. Xylophone	46. Pizzicato Strings	78. Shakuhachi	110. Bagpipe
15. Tubular Bells	47. Orchestral Harp	79. Whistle	111. Fiddle
16. Dulcimer	48. Timpani	80. Ocarina	112. Shanai
17. Drawbar Organ	49. String Ensemble 1	81. Lead 1 (square)	113. Tinkle Bell
18. Percussive Organ	50. String Ensemble 2	82. Lead 2 (sawtooth)	114. Agogo
19. Rock Organ	51. SynthStrings 1	83. Lead 3 (calliope)	115. Steel Drums
20. Church Organ	52. SynthStrings 2	84. Lead 4 (chiff)	116. Woodblock
21. Reed Organ	53. Choir Aahs	85. Lead 5 (charang)	117. Taiko Drum
22. Accordion	54. Voice Oohs	86. Lead 6 (voice)	118. Melodic Tom
23. Harmonica	55. Synth Voice	87. Lead 7 (fifths)	119. Synth Drum
24. Tango Accordion	56. Orchestra Hit	88. Lead 8 (bass + lead)	120. Reverse Cymbal
25. Acoustic Guitar (nylon)	57. Trumpet	89. Pad 1 (new age)	121. Guitar Fret Noise
26. Acoustic Guitar (steel)	58. Trombone	90. Pad 2 (warm)	122. Breath Noise
27. Electric Guitar (jazz)	59. Tuba	91. Pad 3 (polysynth)	123. Seashore
28. Electric Guitar (clean)	60. Muted Trumpet	92. Pad 4 (choir)	124. Bird Tweet
29. Electric Guitar (muted)	61. French Horn	93. Pad 5 (bowed)	125. Telephone Ring
30. Overdriven Guitar	62. Brass Section	94. Pad 6 (metallic)	126. Helicopter
31. Distortion Guitar	63. SynthBrass 1	95. Pad 7 (halo)	127. Applause
32. Guitar harmonics	64. SynthBrass 2	96. Pad 8 (sweep)	128. Gunshot

If you look carefully, you'll notice the Program Change map is broken into instrument groups. This is not accidental, but conforms to the specified Instrument Group map, as shown:

General MIDI Instrument Group Map

1–8 Piano	65–72 Reed
9–16 Chromatic Percussion	73–80 Pipe
17–24 Organ	81–88 Synth Lead
25–32 Guitar	89–96 Synth Pad
33–40 Bass	97–104 Synth Effects
41–48 Strings	105–112 Ethnic
49–56 Ensemble	113–120 Percussive
57–64 Brass	121–128 Sound Effects

The specification says that a General MIDI instrument will contain forty-seven percussion sounds, all available on Channel 10. These must be named and mapped to MIDI note numbers, according to this list:

General MIDI Percussion Map

35. Acoustic Bass Drum	51. Ride Cymbal 1	67. High Agogo
36. Bass Drum 1	52. Chinese Cymbal	68. Low Agogo
37. Side Stick	53. Ride Bell	69. Cabasa
38. Acoustic Snare	54. Tambourine	70. Maracas
39. Hand Clap	55. Splash Cymbal	71. Short Whistle
40. Electric Snare	56. Cowbell	72. Long Whistle
41. Low Floor Tom	57. Crash Cymbal 2	73. Short Guiro
42. Closed Hi-Hat	58. Vibraslap	74. Long Guiro
43. High Floor Tom	59. Ride Cymbal 2	75. Claves
44. Pedal Hi-Hat	60. Hi Bongo	76. Hi Wood Block
45. Low Tom	61. Low Bongo	77. Low Wood Block
46. Open Hi-Hat	62. Mute Hi Conga	78. Mute Cuica
47. Low Mid Tom	63. Open Hi Conga	79. Open Cuica
48. Hi Mid Tom	64. Low Conga	80. Mute Triangle
49. Crash Cymbal 1	65. High Timbale	81. Open Triangle
50. High Tom	66. Low Timbale	

The spec also lists a number of *Performance Requirements* indicating that a General MIDI instrument must include:

- a minimum of twenty-four fully dynamically allocated voices available simultaneously (Manufacturers have the option of dividing the voices into sixteen for melody and eight for percussion sounds—but few, if any, have chosen this method.)

- the use of all sixteen channels for multitimbral, polyphonic operation

- the availability of at least sixteen different timbres, playing various sounds

- a minimum of 128 preset MIDI program numbers

It also states that an instrument must respond to Velocity and Channel Pressure. The instrument must also respond to a subset of defined MIDI Controllers: Modulation (1), Main Volume (07), Pan (10), Expression (11), Sustain (64), Reset All Controllers (121), and All Notes Off (123). It is supposed to respond to these Controllers in "the most natural (expected) way." In other words, the instrument should not use Pan to speed up the vibrato. GM instruments must also respond to the Registered Parameters for Pitch Bend Sensitivity (00 00), Fine Tuning (00 01), and Coarse Tuning (00 02). If an instrument follows these (and a few other) guidelines, then any sequence produced on it and saved in the Standard MIDI File format can play back properly on any other General MIDI instrument.

A Word About GM Controllers

Expression (11) and Main Volume (07) are more or less equivalent in their effect. In general practice, Volume is considered more suitable for initial level settings and fader-like moves, while Expression is used for crescendos and diminuendos. (This is pretty much the same way these Controllers are used in non–General MIDI settings. The difference is subtle.)

Pan works differently on different synths. Some units let you move a note across the stereo field in real time while it is sounding. On other synths, the command determines the placement of the next note on the channel. Some synths also allow you to pan the drums on Channel 10. On others, the drum positions are fixed.

Pitch Bend range is assumed to be ±2 semitones. You can change it using Registered Parameter 00 00. As with all Registered Parameters, you accomplish this by sending Controller 100 with a value of zero, followed by Controller 101 with a value of zero, followed by Controller 06 (Data Entry) with the value of the range you want (in semitones). Maximum Pitch Bend ranges are not specified, so you may run into trouble if you want to use a value of 24, but the device playing the file will only bend a maximum of one octave. Reset All Controllers (121) and All Notes Off (123) are good things to have at the end of a sequence to make sure the device is properly set up for the next file it will be playing.

Roland GS Format

Roland's first General MIDI instrument, the SC-55 Sound Canvas, was a small standalone multitimbral synthesizer/sample player with stereo outputs. It was followed closely by the SCC-1, a PC card containing the same sound engine. Several variations on this model were then released. Besides ease of use, good sound, and GM compatibility, Roland added something extra to the pot. These instruments follow a format that the company calls GS—a kind of superset of General MIDI. Roland's GS architecture has two built-in effects generators (for reverb, delay, chorus, and so on) with effects send controls on each channel. This architecture adds a number of extra instruments to the percussion map—and includes a mode that emulates the MT-32 (an earlier inexpensive multitimbral synth). The map also includes extra "variation" patches in addition to the basic GM Sound Set. The variation patches are accessible via the MIDI Bank Select command (Controller 00), although strictly speaking they should be using Controller 32.

Other GM Instruments

Other manufacturers have taken Roland's lead and are implementing new instruments that are either always in GM mode, or can be switched into GM mode through software. In the first year of GM's existence, Yamaha and Korg introduced GM-compatible models. E-Mu Systems, Ensoniq, and Kurzweil/Young Chang offered entire synthesizers on a chip that can be played in GM mode. Because of the Sound Canvas's head start, some GM manufacturers use its sounds as a model on which to design their devices. Still, all modules do not sound exactly the same. The more you tweak your files to sound good on one instrument, the more likely it is that they will not translate well to another platform.

IBM-PC Sound Cards

One of the important ways in which General MIDI has been implemented is in expansion cards that fit into the slots of an IBM-PC or compatible computer. Before we get to the GM cards though, let's take a look at the history of sound cards in general. In the late eighties, IBM and Yamaha collaborated in producing the IBM Music Feature based on the central chip in Yamaha's four-operator FB01 synth module. The product was met with little enthusiasm in the marketplace. In the same period, Creative Labs came out with the Sound Blaster, a card that had an onboard Yamaha synthesizer chip. This chip was based on a two-operator FM architecture and could play eight-bit digital audio. While the sound quality of the synth chip was primitive, it had eleven voices and could play eleven multitimbral parts. Combined with the audio and a few other features, this capability made the Sound Blaster a huge success as a sound generator for PC-based computer games. The card became the ad hoc standard for a number of years, spawning a plethora of competitors.

The FM chip on the Sound Blaster, the OPL2 (alternately called the YM3812), has far fewer abilities than a conventional synthesizer. Two-operator FM is severely limited in the types and number of timbres it can produce. Whatever percussion it produces is also produced by FM programming. The best thing about this situation is that there are no specific limits as to note allocation from one part (or channel) to another, but notes are allocated more or less as they arrive at the chip. Since it was designed to be operated not by a sequencer, but by an application such as a computer game, it does not actually understand MIDI. Instead, it has its own set of performance instructions. Therefore, it needs a software program, generically called a *driver*, to interpret MIDI data. The usual procedure for getting these cards to play music is that the composer writes the music on a sequencer, and saves it as a Standard MIDI File. The game developer then must write a driver for every sound card it wants the application to support. When the game runs, the MIDI file is read by the appropriate driver, translated into the chip's native language, and finally sent to the chip, producing the appropriate notes.

This clumsy situation was addressed in grand fashion by John Miles of Miles Design. Miles created a large library of drivers and development tools that interpret MIDI to the OPL2 and its four-operator descendent, the OPL3 (YMF262). The Miles library is typically licensed to people who are developing software such as games, who want to use these chips. The library has drivers for DOS as well as Windows and other DOS extenders. It serves not only the Yamaha chips, but cards like the Roland LAPC-1 (a card version of the MT-32), the Tandy three-voice card, the internal PC speaker, and the Roland SCC-1 General MIDI card. The Miles library brings coherence to an otherwise free-form situation.

To play the synth chip on one of these cards with a MIDI sequencer, the sequencer must include its own drivers. These drivers are not usually available for use in applications you may develop. It's important to note that (with the exception of the SCC-1) none of these cards truly meet the GM spec. As we'll see later in this chapter, under certain circumstances you can treat them as GM instruments.

GM Scores: Writing Music for General MIDI Applications

This section will provide a look at some of the potential stumbling points presented by the GM spec as it stands today, and will offer some real-world tips for producing a General MIDI score. Like MIDI 1.0 before it, General MIDI is taking a while to settle down. The official "General MIDI System Level 1" document, which formally defines all the rules, is only eight pages long. Thus, there are many aspects of using GM that it doesn't cover fully. The MMA and JMSC are considering writing new documents that will be more specific, both in defining how the hardware behaves (e.g., relative levels and envelope speeds), and the way in which scores are created. In the meantime, there are substantial variations in the way different GM devices handle data. This means that it's not yet enough to write something that sounds good on just one synth.

A large part of the General MIDI composer's job is to make sure his or her music sounds good on all General MIDI devices in all possible contexts. While General MIDI doesn't yet make this automatic, it does make it possible.

Rule number one is to always follow the Program Change map and the Percussion map. Rule two is to keep in mind how many simultaneous notes a device can play. The spec calls for up to twenty-four, but some manufacturers may yet opt for the "split polyphony" scheme, in which case only sixteen pitched notes would be allowed. In addition, some devices sneak around the spec a little and actually only produce twenty-four timbres. If a particular sound you're using uses two or more of these timbres, your available polyphony will be diminished accordingly. In other words, the more conservative you are, the better your chances of the music sounding good on all GM platforms. The hardware dynamically allocates voices, so you needn't worry about how many voices are playing on any one channel at any time, as long as the combined total is less than twenty-four (or sixteen). You can use all MIDI channels (each with a different timbre) except Channel 10, which is reserved for key-based percussion in accordance with the percussion map. So, if you want five octaves of tom-toms, you can have that (melodic toms are program number 118), but not on Channel 10.

Crossing Platforms

While all GM patches are supposed to be musically equivalent across platforms, in practice, some are more equivalent than others. French Horn may be reliable, but Goblins (number 102) can throw you a curve, so be conservative.

When using a Roland GS instrument, the Bank Select command will slightly change some (but not all) of the sounds in the GM patch map. When played back on a non-GS instrument, the sounds will not be the same. GS also includes extra percussion notes beyond the GM specification. Again, if your file is going to be played back on a non-GS instrument, don't use those sounds.

As we mentioned earlier, some GM instruments have built-in effects. The GM spec says nothing about effects, so manufacturers are free to implement them their own ways. The effects on the Korg 03R/W, the second GM module to appear on the market, are of the same high quality as Roland's, but they are structured completely differently. Roland's effects sends are set with Controllers 91 and 93; Korg's are adjustable only with System Exclusive commands. The Yamaha TG100 General MIDI module uses the same effects structure as Roland's, but doesn't include the entire set of effects. E-Mu Systems has developed a Proteus chipset for sale to other manufacturers (Turtle Beach Systems' Multisound card for the IBM uses it). This chipset includes a General MIDI mapping, but has no effects at all.

Here are some suggestions for using your instrument's effects in a General MIDI composition. Putting some Controller 91 and 93 commands into the sequence is probably not too risky. Devices that respond to them will probably do so in a predictable way—and those that don't will simply ignore them. Just make sure your mixes don't depend on the effects, because they often will not be there. If you're writing on a Korg, leave the effects off—they may sound nice in your studio, but they won't help make your files transferable.

MPC and MIDI

A whole other can of worms is opened if your scores are going to be used in an *MPC* (*Multimedia Personal Computer*) environment. MPC is the specification that attempts to turn IBM-compatible machines into multimedia presentation devices. Although the MPC spec mentions the General MIDI program and percussion maps, it is a long way from being GM-compatible. The MPC spec looked backward at the large installed base of sound cards compatible with the Sound Blaster and similar cards. Thus, the minimum number of voices required by the "base spec" is only six pitched sounds plus two percussion—all playing multitimbrally on MIDI Channels 13 through 16. The extended MPC MIDI spec is much closer to General MIDI, except that it uses only channels 1 through 10. Therefore, a General MIDI score that will be MPC compatible must actually be two scores in one. Channels 1 through 10 must contain the regular version of the score. Channels 13 through 15 contain a stripped-down version of the material scored on Channels 1 through 9—and Channel 16 is a drummer. This means you have to put the essence of your piece on four channels for worst-case scenarios (that is, the base spec). Regarding Channels 11 and 12, use them if you want, but for the least important tracks. An instrument that strictly follows the MPC spec won't play them.

The best news in this area is that, unlike MIDI, the MPC spec was considered just a starting point from its inception, and sound cards exceeding its base requirements began appearing immediately. There is little doubt the original boundaries will be irrelevant before long.

Preparing a General MIDI Score

Nothing in the Level 1 document dictates how to structure a GM file, but some practices are emerging out of necessity and common sense.

Polyphony. Don't push instruments to their polyphonic limits, because some voice allocation schemes may react sluggishly. Even letting a note sustain too long and overlap another note can eat up voices.

Controllers. Use as few as you can get away with and cancel all controllers at the end of a file: set Sustain, Mod Wheel, 91, and 93 to 0; set Pitch Bend to 64 (or 0 if your sequencer uses positive and negative values); set Volume to 100 (the default according to the GM spec), not 127; and include a Reset All Controllers (Controller 121) command. Be sure all envelopes are completely decayed before you reset the Volume at the end of a sequence, or you may encounter an unwelcome little leftover. Also initialize all of the above parameters at the beginning of every track.

GM On. It may be a good idea to put the General MIDI On command (defined earlier) at the beginning of every file. This will ensure that the receiving device is actually in General MIDI mode (although this may delay the synth's response to subsequent data). If you know the synth is already in GM mode (or it has no other mode), and you need it to play instantaneously, you can omit this message.

Labels. Pepper your files with lots of labels to make user editing easier. Include instrument names, beginnings of verses and choruses, and other hit points. The Standard MIDI File spec provides seven different ways to insert text into a file or track. Since no two sequencers use the same combination of track names, cue points, markers, lyrics, and so on, include labels and cues in several different formats. Make the information as complete as possible: including channel number, patch number, and instrument name at the beginning of each track in some retrievable form of text.

Sections. Be sure the first notes of every section of a sequence do not start before the downbeat of that section. If a Note On command occurs even one clock before the beginning of a measure, and the user wants either to play or move the file at that measure, that Note On may get lost.

Setup. Some folks like to put a *setup bar* at the beginning of every sequence to give devices time to receive Program Changes and Controller defaults. This can prevent glitches and small initial timing errors. If your setup bar is very short, the delay it creates won't be too bad: a ♪ bar at 300 bpm, for example, will delay the music only 1/10 of a second. If there is a pick-up (one or two eighth-notes) at the beginning of the sequence, make the first bar only as long as the pick-up—and set up Programs and Controllers on all the other tracks while the pick-up plays. Make the last measure the same number of eighth notes shorter, so the sequence can loop smoothly. Remove any extra empty bars at the end of the sequence so that your user doesn't encounter any mysterious pauses when looping.

Program Changes. Because you're restricted to fifteen instrumental tracks (fewer if you're MPC compatible) it's tempting to vary the orchestration with Program Changes. The GM Program Change map lets you assume these orchestrations will be compatible, but there are still dangers. Program Changes in the middle of tracks make editing tricky. If you delete a section with a Program Change in it, the instrumentation following it will be wrong. Also, not all GM *playback engines* (the little programs buried in multimedia applications) will chase Program Changes. Thus, if you start a track in the middle, and there was a Program Change earlier in the track, it may be missed.

Tempo Changes. For similar reasons, make tempo changes carefully. A gradual accelerando over a whole sequence can create a sense of excitement, but if a user moves or removes sections, the sequence will exhibit abrupt and seemingly random shifts in tempo.

Voices. The GM document assumes that voices will be allocated democratically among the different MIDI channels. However, this is not always the case—especially in older instruments that are reprogrammed for General MIDI. You will often find that notes on Channel 10 will get first priority, followed by Channel 1, and the rest in ascending order. Unless drums are the most important aspect of a piece, keep percussion tracks relatively simple so they don't steal voices from other sounds. Your most complex or important parts should be on Channel 1, with less important ones on subsequent channels.

Tracks. Depending on who will play your music, you might want to put the left and right hands of a piano piece, or the four parts of a Bach fugue, on different tracks, even if they're on the same channels. The same goes for individual drums: Put each instrument on its own track, so users can change the drum sounds easily.

Formats. Type 0 (single-track, multichannel) files are easier to use in multimedia and other extra-musical applications, but they provide no way to edit parts. Type 1 (multitrack) files allow the user to change orchestrations and bring individual instruments in and out more easily. Fortunately, because MIDI files are small, you often don't have to choose: you can do two versions. But when disk space is tight, and you only have room for one, keep your intended audience in mind.

Universality. Above all, play your files back on as many different GM systems as you can to ensure that they sound acceptable. Take the player piano approach: make it so simple that if you play the bass line back on a glockenspiel it still sounds okay.

All these important considerations might make it seem that writing General MIDI sequences involves one compromise after another. However, working within such a tight context can actually be a highly creative, even liberating, experience. With only half a dozen guitar or brass sounds to choose from, you spend a lot less time hunting around looking for just the right sound, and a lot more time making music. Working in a conventional MIDI studio is like writing for an infinitely large and varied orchestra. Working with General MIDI is like writing for a resident chamber group: you know who your players are and what they can do. Your goal is reduced to getting the best out of them. Although it may not be totally wild and nouveau, the music that today's General MIDI tools can make is pretty darn good.

Media

The multimedia industry can provide a new market for the MIDI composer, producer, and musician, so it's important to understand how desktop multimedia works (at least in broad terms). As opposed to linear media, such as film and tape, computer-based multimedia is interactive. That is, since a computer is controlling the order of events, the viewer can change that order, and make a presentation go in a different direction. To accomplish this, a multimedia presentation must be delivered in a computer-compatible medium.

CD-Rom

The most common medium for the multimedia presentation is the CD-rom (Compact Disc–Read Only Memory). Physically, a CD-rom is exactly the same as a common audio CD. In fact, it can contain, in part, the same Red Book audio used on CDs. The difference is that a CD-rom can also contain computer files, just like a floppy or hard disk. A CD-rom also requires a CD-rom drive (which usually includes stereo audio outs) attached to a computer that is equipped with a software driver that can read it. In multimedia, the program playing the presentation reads in files from the CD-rom, then plays them back on the computer. If the files hold graphic images, these are displayed on the screen. If they contain midi or digital audio data, they are played back as the presentation calls them.

A CD-rom can hold up to 650MB of data and it is a much sturdier medium than its magnetic cousins, the floppy or hard disk. You can no more easily lose or corrupt the data on a CD-rom than you can on your audio CDs. The principal reason for this is that the CD-rom is an optical, rather than a magnetic, medium. Data is recorded onto it by means of a laser that literally melts microscopic pits into its surface. Another laser can then read the melted and non-melted parts of the disc (called *pits* and *lands*, respectively) as the ones and zeros on which computer languages are based.

CD+Midi

An interesting, but largely unimplemented, phenomenon is that midi data can be recorded as *subcode* onto an audio CD in such a way that it can be read back in real time. This means you can record music and midi data onto a CD so that both play back in sync. To do this, of course, requires a playback machine that's fitted with a Midi Out port. There are lots of possibilities for this technology. The midi data can contain control information for an effects processor, changing the acoustic space of your living room in real time. Or, it can contain tracks from the music itself, so you can actually reorchestrate the music as you are listening to it. It's going to be a while before any of this becomes reality. The first use of this technology is implemented in the new Sega Genesis CD system.

Platforms

While there are multimedia applications for every personal computer, the two platforms that have taken hold of the industry are the IBM-PC and compatibles (especially using Microsoft Windows) and the Apple Macintosh. There is a welter of both hardware and software available that give users of both systems the ability to develop and play back multimedia presentations.

The MPC Spec

At the same time the MMA and JMSC were developing General Midi, the makers of computers and software were taking steps to put multimedia on the desktop. In 1991, the Microsoft Corporation issued its own specification, defining its concept of a Multimedia Personal Computer, or MPC. The Microsoft spec defined the *baseline* configuration of an IBM-PC compatible computer that could run multimedia productions. It stated that the MPC must possess at least a 80286 processor (subsequently upgraded to a 80386), 2MB of RAM, a 30MB hard disk, an internal or external CD-rom drive, a VGA graphics monitor, and an audio card in one of its expansion slots.

The standard audio card is specified as able to record to and play back from disk 8-bit PCM digital audio at sampling rates of 11 and 22kHz. It has a microphone input, and contains an eleven-voice, eleven-part multitimbral, two-operator FM synthesizer chip (in other words, the equivalent of a Sound Blaster). In addition, it has Midi In and Out ports and a digitally controlled audio mixer that can mix any of these sound sources and send them out in stereo.

While these specifications are far below the level of professional music or audio, they did accomplish a few things. First, they established the presence of midi-controlled synthesis in the MPC. Secondly, they created a baseline from which manufacturers of both production tools and end-user products could begin (giving the previously unfocused multimedia industry a point of reference). Today, a number of companies produce MPC-spec audio boards—and others are making boards that greatly exceed the spec. Some sound cards are equipped with professional-level, sixteen-bit, 44.1kHz digital audio and top-quality synthesizer and sample-playback chips.

Windows

The Microsoft MPC spec operates in the context of Windows, the company's graphical user interface for the PC. Windows 3.1 offers a Mac-emulating interface that is more friendly to multimedia production and play-back than that of the PC's standard MS-dos operating system. In addition to its graphic interface, Windows has other elements of interest to the midi-minded.

The Windows *Media Control Interface (MCI)* is a set of software functions and commands that routes an application's output to video players, digital audio players, midi instruments, and other various hardware that can play back video, audio, and midi information. The MCI lays the foundation for synchronizing midi recording and playback with applications that play these other media. Midi sequencers, animation programs, and multimedia authoring programs that bring all the elements together can operate together under Windows and benefit from this system-level integration. In the MPC, Microsoft has set the stage for the development of multimedia—and has included at least the potential for all the necessary elements, including midi.

Multimedia Presentations Manager/2

Not to be outdone by Microsoft, IBM released Multimedia Presentations Manager/2 (MMPM/2) for its own operating system, OS/2. The purpose of MMPM/2 is to standardize the application interface in OS/2. It provides hardware and data format independence for applications—and can be extended by hardware providers and people with proprietary data formats. OS/2 is a true multitasking operating system, which could, for example, allow communication between a midi player and multimedia authoring application. If the right software is developed, and the market works in its favor, MMPM/2 could be a serious player.

Macintosh QuickTime

The Apple Macintosh is a natural for multimedia. QuickTime for the Macintosh functions as a part of the computer's operating system to play "movie" files that contain different kinds of *dynamic data,* each on its own track. Dynamic data includes still images, animation, video, midi, and sound. QuickTime creates a uniform way to connect software applications to such media-oriented hardware as laser disks, CD-roms, VCRs, or NuBus audio cards. The design of QuickTime addresses one of the principal problems of computer-based multimedia: synchronization. Different computers—even if the difference is as slight as the model of video card used—play back moving visuals at different rates. In a multimedia production, this destroys audio/visual synchronization.

QuickTime ensures synchronization by sending timing to each track of a movie directly from the computer's operating system. QuickTime defaults to getting its master time from the (digital audio) sound track, although the user can change this. The wisdom of this is that if the audio were not the master, and it was forced by whatever was the master to slow down, the drop in pitch would sound like a dying tape deck. Video, on the other hand, can lose frames occasionally and still maintain an acceptable appearance. The logic is that a QuickTime movie's master track—the sound track—will get priority access to the computer's timing services, and play back at its original rate regardless of anything else that's going on. If this should be too fast for the computer to display a visual track at its intended rate, QuickTime is designed to gracefully degrade the visual by dropping selected frames.

Another plus for QuickTime is that it is eminently extensible. The first release allowed for just two tracks—video and sound—but subsequent releases are slated to add MIDI to the list of track types. The first version of QuickTime plays a movie using only a small fraction of the Mac screen. The movie window can be enlarged, but resolution goes down concomitantly. While this, and a few other shortcomings, are present in the current incarnation of QuickTime, the fact remains that it is based on an extremely solid and intelligent foundation. For the MIDI musician or producer, it provides another potential demand for music in a MIDI format.

Apple MIDI Manager

Apple's MIDI Manager is a system extension that gives the Mac true, synchronized multitasking capability for applications that use MIDI. Without QuickTime compatibility, MIDI Manager is the only way that multimedia authoring applications can control different types of music software running on the same Mac at the same time. That is, it's the only way a multimedia presentation can communicate with a MIDI sequencer or digital audio application to play them in a multimedia presentation.

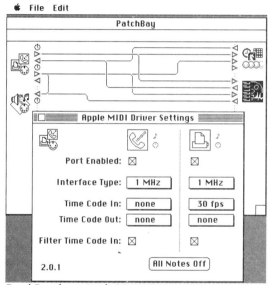

PatchBay from Apple MIDI Manager

MIDI Manager consists of three basic elements. The system extension (*INIT*) resides in the system folder. The Apple MIDI Driver does the actual communication between MIDI applications and the Mac clock and serial ports. Then there are two identically functioning versions—an application and a desk accessory—of PatchBay, MIDI Manager's user interface. When you launch PatchBay, it displays icons for all the MIDI Manager–compatible applications loaded in RAM at the moment. It also displays an icon for the MIDI Driver that talks to any MIDI interfaces connected to the serial port(s). You can draw lines between the icons to enable communication among the applications, giving MIDI Manager control over every application's use of the Mac's timing services. Since MIDI sequencers and multimedia presentation applications both demand rock-solid timing, running them together on a single machine was impossible until they all talked to MIDI Manager.

Multimedia Authoring and Playback Applications

Several applications on various platforms serve as authoring tools that allow you to create a multimedia production. Many, though not all, of these tools allow for the playing of MIDI files (or digital audio files) in the production—usually synchronized to the start of a visual event.

HyperCard

Although the multitasking granted by MIDI Manager is the only way MIDI and multimedia applications can pass control back and forth in the Macintosh, HyperCard (and its quasi-clone, SuperCard) provides another way to gain interactive, multimedia-style control over MIDI events in a Macintosh. HyperCard was originally distributed free with the Macintosh computer. However, in 1992, Apple started charging people for a development version of HyperCard, and only shipped a run-time player for free.

HyperCard is the Macintosh software that is part application, part programming language. It allows people to write programs in a relatively easy-to-learn language similar to English. These programs, called *stacks*, are chiefly designed to display various screens, called *cards*. The user maintains control over various computer functions via mouse buttons placed on these cards by the programmer.

HyperCard is an extensible language that can perform many functions that it was not originally designed for—thanks to external commands (called *X-commands* or *XCMDs*) and external functions (called *X-functions* or *XFCNs*). These are little applications, written (or compiled) in assembly language by third-party programmers, which you can install into a HyperCard stack to make it do what you want.

HyperMIDI

HyperMIDI, a product of EarLevel Engineering, is a set of MIDI-specific XCMDs, XFCNs, and utilities that can be installed into HyperCard to give it MIDI power. Using HyperMIDI, a HyperCard stack can give the user immediate control over any number of Standard MIDI Files. That is, without using an actual sequencer application, the stack can let the user load and play any stored MIDI file by clicking a HyperCard button. The stack can also do this automatically, so that one or more MIDI files can be played at particular times with or without user interaction. HyperMIDI allows you to modify files as they play. During playback, it's possible to filter particular data types, transpose one or more tracks, or change Velocity and Controller values. HyperMIDI also allows you to check up on the remaining time in a playing file to get timing data for other actions. You can change a MIDI file's orchestration, loop it, interrupt it, or jump to another sequence on the fly.

HyperCard is useful in a variety of multimedia situations, from kiosk-type setups that demonstrate products to museum exhibits. It can handle any type of MIDI data, including System Exclusive messages, and includes time-stamping capability so you can actually record sequences. With HyperMIDI assistance, HyperCard stacks can perform MIDI accompaniment, demonstrations of musical examples, and playback of sampled audio in multimedia productions.

MIDIPlay

Opcode Systems' MIDIPlay is a sequencer with a reduced instruction set in the form of a HyperCard stack. It plays MIDI files like any ordinary sequencer, and offers an editing interface that seems specifically designed for tailoring a MIDI file to fit a multimedia presentation. From one MIDIPlay card, you can set the music's duration in seconds, adjust its tempo, and establish start and stop points. The same card lets you set bar numbers that define the beginning and end of a loop. Another card lets you set both overall and individual track volume, change instrumental sounds via MIDI Program Change, and assign MIDI channels.

MIDIPlay can export MIDI files to Macromedia's presentation authoring program, Director, as a "cast member." This means that when you are finished editing a MIDI file in MIDIPlay, you can export it, and Director will play it without having a sequencer open in the background. (This can greatly simplify a Director session.)

MidiPlay is not a composing tool for a MIDI musician. Its editing features are far too few to put it in the class of even junior-level sequencers like Passport's Trax or Opcode's own EZ Vision. Also, it doesn't accept any MIDI input. But, for the multimedia producer using prerecorded MIDI files, it offers just the right level of editing power to conform a sequence to the needs of a multimedia presentation. Like HyperMIDI, MidiPlay contains XCMDs and XFCNs that can be exported to any other stack, so that you can use its capabilities in a custom application.

Producer

Producer is a Macintosh application (with a PC version planned) from Passport Designs that lets the user assemble QuickTime movies, videotapes, videodiscs, computer animations, graphics, sound, and music into a single multimedia production. Producer presents a visual "Cue Sheet" on which you develop a presentation by clicking and dragging icons representing various media elements ("cues"). These include MIDI files, animations, digital audio, and so forth. You can place these icons at specific SMPTE-based times on the Cue Sheet. A SMPTE time-line matches the timing of each element to indicate precisely when a MIDI file (or other element) will start and stop.

You can not only import MIDI files into Producer so they become a permanent part of a given presentation, but you can record and save a basic (single-track, single-channel) MIDI file from within the application. Then you can even do simple editing. Producer's MIDI editor includes controls for Volume, Pan, channelization, Program Change, Pitch Bend, and Pitch Bend range. For more in-depth editing, Producer lets you launch any of a number of Macintosh sequencers, including Master Tracks Pro, Vision, or Performer, and then edit the files in place. Once you place a cue representing a MIDI file on the Cue Sheet, various keyboard and mouse combinations offer even more options.

Producer synchronizes both sixteen-bit digital audio and Standard MIDI Files to SMPTE, according to the times on its Cue Sheet. In fact, an important goal of Producer is to provide real synchronization among the various elements of its productions. To do this, it automatically makes the digital audio track the timing master. If no audio track is used, a MIDI track is designated as the master. If desired, either of these tracks can be synchronized to incoming MIDI Time Code (typically generated by a MIDI device being fed SMPTE from a tape deck or similar source). Whether or not the MIDI or audio tracks are synced to MTC, all other events in the production—such as graphics, animations, or QuickTime Movies—sync to the MIDI audio.

Director

Director (from Macromedia) was the first major application for the Mac designed as a multimedia business presentation authoring tool. Director is essentially a sequencer that uses a scripting language to work with digitized video, computer animations, digital audio, and MIDI. It is designed to let the user assemble any number of these various kinds of events, arrange them in a score, and play them back as a presentation. This presentation can run on a Mac or be dumped to film or video. A Director score can also be interactive—and a viewer can make it branch to various portions of the presentation on command. It is used extensively for storyboarding and corporate presentations.

Director uses MIDI by controlling a MIDI sequencer (or player) application running on the same Mac via Apple's MIDI Manager. Its control is rudimentary, consisting of only Set Beat (Tempo), Start, Stop, Continue, Song Position Pointer, and Song Select commands. It has no synchronization capabilities. In practice, the connection is made by setting the sequencer to respond to an external clock, then connecting the sequencer to Director in the MIDI Manager Patch Bay. Putting the appropriate MIDI commands at various points in the Director score starts and stops the MIDI file at those points.

As an example, the following are the basic steps involved in putting a live MIDI sound track in a Macromedia Director desktop presentation.

1. Connect an external MIDI interface and a MIDI instrument to one of the Mac's serial ports (or Install a NuBus MIDI card such as SampleCell). Then connect the system to an amplification device.
2. In MultiFinder, start up Director and load a movie.
3. In the movie, find the start and end points of the scenes where you want to play your musical cues. (Use as many as you want.)
4. Start up a MIDI Manager–compatible MIDI sequencer.
5. Start up MIDI Manager's PatchBay. Connect the Director icon's output port to the sequencer icon's input port. Then connect the Sequencer icon's output port to the MIDI Driver icon.
6. Load the sequence(s) you want to use as cues into the sequencer.
7. Edit the cues to fit the scenes in your movie (saving the edits with new names as you go, of course).
8. Set the sequencer to respond to external sync.
9. In Director, go to the Score window and locate the sound channel. In cells representing the start and stop times you want, place MIDI beat, start, and stop commands.
10. If your sequencer loaded several numbered songs, use Director's Song Select command to select specific cues for specific scenes.
11. Roll the movie, and your MIDI instrument(s) will play your edited cues when it reaches the frames you specified.

Director can also play MIDI files via the use of XCMDs and XFCNs that operate similarly to those in HyperCard.

Asymetrix ToolBook

The presence of the Media Control Interface in the PC Windows operating system has allowed PC-based multimedia authoring systems relatively easy access to MIDI files. Asymetrix offers the sophisticated ToolBook, as well as the simpler product, Multimedia Make Your Point. Both can fire a MIDI file at any point in a presentation, and use the MPC spec as a basis for playing MIDI files. Since they play the MIDI file using the system-level MCI, there is very little fuss involved. For example, the multimedia application you create (called a *book*) and the Windows system both expect to have access to at least the MIDI synth on the MPC audio card. As a result, to access the MIDI file, you simply open a dialog box, select the MIDI file you want to play, and tell the application when to play it. The authoring application talks to MCI and MCI talks to the MIDI file—playing it on the MPC sound card (or any MIDI instruments connected to the sound card's MIDI Out).

Midi's Future in Multimedia

As the multimedia world continues to develop, MIDI will play an expanding role. Control of digital audio is necessary in multimedia, without a doubt, but a lot of the tasks one normally associates with audio can be handled by MIDI. MIDI's ease of use, minimal storage requirements, flexibility, and interactive potential make it ideal in an environment where speed, agility, and compactness are most valued traits.

Chapter 10

MIDI's Limitations and Inconsistencies

Although MIDI was recognized from the beginning as a remarkable idea, it also drew criticism for its built-in limitations. The criticism was not unjustified: MIDI is in many ways a compromise, and can't accomplish every task that every musician might like it to. But it does pretty well, and over the years clever designers have worked out ways around many of MIDI's limitations.

The Compromises

To ensure that it would gain universal acceptance, MIDI's creators built several compromises into the specification, mostly on the hardware side. If MIDI had been designed as a parallel protocol, rather than a serial one, it could have been made quite a bit faster. But this would have required more expensive hardware in transmitters and receivers. The cost of adding serial MIDI ports to a typical synthesizer at the manufacturing level when MIDI was introduced was around $5 to $10 per unit. Had parallel hardware been required, the cost would have easily been anywhere from three to ten times that, and that would have been multiplied further by the time the instrument reached the store. Even this relatively small extra expense, it was felt, might cause many manufacturers to balk at implementing MIDI in an instrument. Similarly, MIDI could have been designed to run at a higher data rate, but that would have required faster microprocessors all through the chain. This would have taxed the capacity and speed of the chips commonly available at the time—or forced manufacturers to use more expensive chips.

The cost of memory has dropped dramatically over the last decade, while the speed of data processing has increased. These factors have led some to say that MIDI is already obsolete—and that a new protocol that takes advantage of today's technology should replace it. However, the rumors of MIDI's demise are premature. MIDI still has plenty of life left in it, and there are ways to use it more efficiently in order to bring its capabilities up to par with today's computers and other digital gear. This chapter discusses some of the ways MIDI has overcome its own limitations, and dispels some myths that have grown up around MIDI over the years.

Channel Limitations

Once upon a time, sixteen channels felt like plenty to most MIDI users. After all, when MIDI was introduced, computer synthesis systems capable of more than sixteen simultaneous sounds were rare. Most commercial synthesizers could play no more than eight voices, and so sixteen channels with unlimited polyphony seemed more than enough. Within just a couple of years, however, the number of channels available on a MIDI cable became a handicap for many users. MIDI-controlled effects processors and mixers needed channels dedicated to them, lowering the number available for music. A MIDI guitar, if used in mono mode, takes up six or seven channels all by itself. The biggest impact came from the introduction of multitimbral synthesizers and samplers, which could respond polyphonically on multiple channels. A typical synth of this kind might have twenty-four voices, which it could dynamically allocate over all sixteen channels, with each channel playing a different sound. Many studios had more than one of these, but since the sequencer could only address sixteen channels, much of their usefulness was wasted.

Multiple Cables

In fact, some of the designers of the original MIDI specification knew that this was going to be an issue. This led to discussions of using MIDI "star networks," in which a source of MIDI data could address multiple, independent MIDI cables simultaneously. This could serve both to increase the number of MIDI channels and reduce the load on each cable. It took a while for the rest of the industry to catch up to the idea, however. (Although there was one early hardware sequencer, the Yamaha QX1, which did offer eight MIDI outputs. This wasn't very much of an advantage, however, because it could only transmit on eight channels and record on eight tracks.)

Once the need for multiple-stream systems was identified, they started to appear in the marketplace. For some designers, implementation was fairly easy. Macintosh programmers took advantage of the fact that the Mac has two serial ports: They could hang a MIDI interface off of each one, or combine two interfaces into one box. Their software could then assign each track a *port* as well as a channel (referred to as *modem* or *printer*), doubling the number of available output channels to thirty-two.

Similarly, IBM programmers could use two MPU-401 cards, independently addressable through software, or use cards that combined two MPU-401 chipsets on one chassis and provided two MIDI Out cables. Atari owners suddenly found their built-in MIDI port was not as much of an advantage as they thought—they needed a *breakout box* to provide additional channels. Most manufacturers built devices that attached to the expansion port. Fortunately, the ones made by the major Atari software suppliers—Dr. T's, C-Lab, and Steinberg—were all fairly similar to each other. Thus, manufacturers were able to support each other's hardware without too much trouble. Some other companies did find other ways of getting into the computer, but they remained outside the mainstream. The Amiga has a single serial port—and so has a problem similar to the Atari. However, a multiple cable box (with three outputs) is available from Blue Ribbon Soundworks.

Thirty-two-channel MIDI systems didn't solve everyone's problems, but they were a step in the right direction. Although a multitimbral synth might be capable of playing over sixteen channels, in reality it's often more useful playing over only four or six, so as to avoid running up against its polyphonic limits. It's also important to limit the number of channels according to the number of audio outputs on a device. This minimizes the number of different sounds that must be combined before they get to the mixer. So two (or three) cables were considered enough for a medium-size studio consisting of two or three multitimbral modules, a couple of processors, a drum machine, and a handful of single-channel synths.

But soon it became apparent that sophisticated MIDI users needed true star networks with a lot more channels. Soon, boxes with four, eight, and even fifteen MIDI-independent Ins and Outs appeared—with each jack capable of carrying its own set of sixteen channels. These boxes first appeared for the Mac, and then for the Atari and IBM. Some manufacturers allow you to connect multiple boxes so that you could end up with as many as 512 MIDI channels.

As with dual-port interfaces, these multiple-cable devices need a sequencer (or other software) that can address multiple cables. This means you don't just assign each track of your sequencer to a channel, but to a channel on a specific cable. It's not surprising, therefore, that the companies that make these boxes are usually MIDI software manufacturers as well. When the boxes first came out, they were optimized to work with each manufacturer's own software—and in many situations it was not possible to get one manufacturer's sequencer to work with another's multicable box. However, many companies have been willing to exchange the necessary information to ensure compatibility between products, so this is no longer such a serious issue.

Multiport devices also let you record multiple instruments at the same time (as long as the software allows it). This can be accomplished without using any external mergers, and without worrying about clogging the incoming data stream with tons of Controllers and Pitch Bend messages from an enthusiastic gang of MIDI jammers.

At the present time, there is still no way to designate multiple MIDI cables from within MIDI itself, or within a MIDI file. In other words, a sequencer can assign a track to a cable, but nothing in the MIDI command language or the structure of MIDI files can convey that information once it leaves the sequencer. For example, suppose that you create a sequence on one multicable system, and store it as a MIDI file, and then bring that MIDI file into a different multicable sequencer. Although the channel numbers will be carried over automatically, the cable assignments for each track will not. Thus, you will have to reassign each track to its proper cable by hand in the second program. If you have 512 tracks, that can be quite a chore.

This problem has been a topic of discussion among MIDI's governing organizations for a while. It's quite possible that a "cableization" scheme may be added to the spec soon. This would allow an event or string of events to be assigned to a MIDI cable, designated by a number and/or a name, as well as a channel. This scheme would be of particular help when moving MIDI files between multicable systems.

Resolution and Choke

Using multiple cables solves another common problem: MIDI's limited resolution. MIDI is a serial protocol, which means that the bytes follow one another in time, so there's no such thing as truly simultaneous events on a MIDI cable. Those bytes, however, can follow each other very quickly: a fully packed MIDI cable can handle about 1,000 commands per second, or one every millisecond. If Running Status is used, this improves the capacity to 1,500 commands/second, or one every 0.67ms. That means that a MIDI chord isn't a chord at all, but a very fast arpeggio, in which the notes occur at least 0.67ms apart. According to various studies, the human ear can't easily differentiate between sounds less than about 7 to 10ms apart, so we hear that arpeggio as a chord.

Furthermore, the response of MIDI devices to incoming MIDI events is often much slower than MIDI itself, so the data gets "smeared" more by the receiving devices, and MIDI's inherent speed limit becomes a less-important factor. Nonetheless, it is quite possible to overload a MIDI line with more data that it can handle, a phenomenon known as MIDI *logjam* or MIDI *choke*.

Here's a scenario of how MIDI choke can occur:

* A sequencer wants to send a thick load of data down a MIDI cable, and has it all queued up in its output buffer.

* During the first 0.1 second, the maximum amount of data is sent: 3,125 bits.

* If there is more data that is supposed to be sent during that first 0.1 second, it has to wait until the next 0.1 second.

* If there is still data waiting after 0.2 seconds has elapsed, it will be delayed too.

* The process continues until the sequencer slows down its sending of data sufficiently for the MIDI line to catch up.

* However, when the sequencer finally eases up, the MIDI data will actually start to come out faster than it's supposed to. The data will try to catch up to where it's supposed to be to make up for lost time.

The most obvious result of MIDI choke is a change in the rhythm of the music. The music slows down when the data is too thick, and speeds up again (sometimes too much) when the data thins out. The most common cause of MIDI choke is too much Continuous Controller, Pitch Bend, Channel Pressure, and/or Key Pressure data. Often, this kind of data is recorded by accident and is not actually being used. For instance, some early MIDI keyboards transmitted Channel Pressure all the time, whether or not there were any voices in the system that actually responded to it. Removing unnecessary data often eliminates MIDI choke.

When you want to keep all your controller and other continuous data, however, you can still relieve choke by thinning out the data. Most good sequencers allow you to reduce the density of continuous data so that fewer events per second are played. Setting the parameters for a thinning algorithm must be handled carefully: if too much data is removed, the effect can sound "stepped" as opposed to continuous.

A secondary cause of MIDI choke is too much data occurring right on a beat. You may find yourself creating a sequence in which every synth in the room is supposed to play a note or a chord on the downbeat. If there are too many notes too close together, the rhythm gets smeared, and the music loses its tightness. This is particularly true if you're making rhythm-oriented music and heavily quantizing everything. Unwanted changes may be unpredictable, and come out differently each time you play the sequence. This is usually a more subtle-sounding problem than too much controller data, because the MIDI line recovers right after the beat. Subsequent events are not affected until the next overload point. The cure for this version of MIDI choke is to limit the notes occurring on the beat to those that have to be there—such as kick drum and bass. Move notes whose rhythmic tightness is not as important, like string pads, guitar chords, or even scratches so that they occur slightly before or after the beat. Offsetting some of the rhythmic elements by as little as one tick may make the music tighter. Also, make sure that all of the notes don't have precisely the same duration so that the MIDI line won't get clogged with Note Offs.

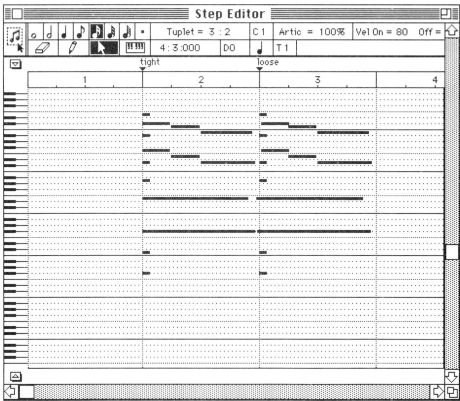

tight and loose beats

Using multiple cables is another cure for both types of MIDI choke. Instead of sixteen synthesizers sharing one cable, if you have sixteen different cables, each controlling one synthesizer, the capacity of the MIDI system to carry data is increased by 1,600%. (Any devices that are receiving data on only a single channel can take advantage of Running Status, thereby increasing the capacity of that cable another 33%.) A multiple-cable network can still be used to great advantage if you have fewer than sixteen cables, and need to double up synths on cables. In that case, it's important to combine the various MIDI-receiving devices on the different cables intelligently. For example, a synth that plays sounds using lots of Pitch Bend and Channel Pressure should not be put on the same cable as another similarly expressive synth. Instead, it could be paired with a drum machine, which only expects notes—or with an effects processor which only gets Program Changes and occasional Controller changes.

There's one situation in which multiple cables can't really be of much help, and that's when trying to send samples of any significant size over MIDI using the MIDI Sample Dump Standard. Ignoring for the moment any overhead, handshaking, or timeouts (which take extra time), the shortest amount of time a 16-bit, 44.1kHz sample can possibly take to be sent down a MIDI line is about forty times the length of the sample. SMDI was invented to facilitate this process. Although it is not part of the MIDI spec, it is becoming increasingly common in MIDI studios. Manufacturers are treating SMDI with the respect that they would give an officially sanctioned addition to the MIDI specification.

The Thru Delay Myth

Since MIDI cables cannot be split or joined together through a simple adapter the way that audio cables can, the MIDI Thru jack was invented. The Thru jack allows many MIDI devices to be linked together sequentially in a daisy chain, and driven from a single output. The source output goes to the MIDI In of the first device, then to its Thru jack, then to the In of the second device, and so on.

A myth arose at the beginning of the MIDI age (and has never quite disappeared) that this was actually a bad practice that introduced delays into the MIDI data stream. It was said that this delay was as much as three milliseconds per device in the chain. A synthesizer at the end of a long chain, so went the myth, would respond audibly later than a synth at the beginning. This myth is patently and categorically untrue. It is, however, worth looking at anyway for a number of interesting reasons. If there really were a three-millisecond delay in each device, it would indeed cause some serious problems. The actual delay of a MIDI signal passing through the In and Thru jacks of a properly designed MIDI device, however, is more like three microseconds (0.003 milliseconds). (This is essentially the amount of time it takes the optoisolator in the MIDI In jack to fire and tell the MIDI Thru jack that it's on.) Therefore, about 100 MIDI devices could be connected in a chain before a delay equivalent to a single MIDI byte would be encountered.

The origin of this myth can be traced to two different sources. One is a misprint in a *Keyboard* magazine article in early 1986. The other is that MIDI sequencers and other processors often do impose a relatively long delay when they are recording, filtering, mapping, and/or channelizing data—not just passing it along (which is all that a true Thru jack does). Early MIDI users may not have been aware that the Thru jack of a hardware sequencer was a very different animal from the Thru jack of a synth. When a 3ms delay was noticed coming out of the sequencer, some folks assumed that that's the way all Thru jacks worked.

There is, on the other hand, a very real problem associated with daisy-chaining many MIDI synths. It does not have to do with delay, but rather with distortion of the MIDI signal. As it passes through many optoisolators and their associated logic circuitry, the "on" time (logical 0) of the signal will actually start to get shorter relative to the "off" time (logical 1). (This is because the rise time of an optoisolator is not instantaneous.) If it gets sufficiently short, the bit may not be recognized by the receiver, and a start bit will be missed or a 0 will be misinterpreted as a 1. This will cause data to be missed or corrupted—and is definitely a situation to be avoided.

The exact point at which this kind of distortion occurs will be different under different circumstances. In the worst cases, daisy-chaining more than three devices will cause errors, while in other situations you might be able to get away with chaining as many as ten. The problem, unlike the timing delays discussed earlier, will be very obvious. So, if you hear a synth at the end of a chain missing notes, you can fix the situation by shortening the chain—or perhaps by using a Thru box.

Cable Length Limitations

MIDI cables are not balanced and use low voltages. For these reasons, they need to be kept relatively short. The MIDI Specification says that cables should be no longer than fifteen meters long (and speaking of misinterpretations becoming myths, a lot of people are under the impression that MIDI cables can only be fifteen *feet* long). Excessively long runs can cause the signal to distort, with disastrous results. Longer cable runs are necessary in large studio complexes, or live performance venues where MIDI must be communicated between stage and mixing or lighting control. These situations require special hardware. Putting a Thru box in the line every fifty feet or so can do the job. There are also dedicated devices for extending cable runs which boost the voltage and put the signal on a balanced line. Some manufacturers claim this allows runs of up to 4,000 feet.

A far more sophisticated (and expensive) solution is to use a *MIDI LAN*, such as Lone Wolf's MediaLink system. This device takes MIDI (as well as a variety of other signals) and converts them to a very high-speed protocol running over optical-fiber cable. These types of systems can literally run for miles.

Response Delays

Unlike the mythical Thru delays, there are true delays in many MIDI systems which can be a source of great frustration to the composer. These are *reception* or *response delays* in MIDI equipment: a lag between the time a device receives a MIDI command and the time it acts on it. First of all, a receiver must get a complete MIDI command before it can do anything. So for a standard three-byte command, any receiver automatically has a one-millisecond response delay. Secondly, all MIDI receivers can be considered computers, with clocks controlling their actions. Some clocks are faster than others. However, an incoming MIDI byte can only be recognized when the clock tells the receiver to be ready for it. This can lead to further delays. If the delay is short and relatively constant, it is not a problem. Most players can easily adjust to response delays the same way they adjust to other, more familiar delay factors. The action of a keyboard, the player's distance from amplifiers, or the acoustics of a performance space all can create delays.

When the delay gets very long—over 10ms or so—things start to get messy. When the delay is variable, it can be downright frustrating. A musician confronted with a response delay that keeps changing will have a hard time playing in any sort of consistent rhythm. In this situation, using expressive controllers (which are delayed right along with the notes) can become far more trouble than it's worth. Worse still, a performance recorded on a sequencer and played back on a synth with variable response delay will have small variations in the rhythm each time it's played back—so no two performances will be the same.

Variable delays can occur in a synth that has a long processing loop. Here, the keyboard, MIDI In jack, front-panel displays, waveform generator, and other functions are all serviced, one after another, by the CPU. This type of loop is relatively slow and has no provisions for being interrupted by incoming MIDI data. An incoming MIDI note that arrives just before the synth checks the MIDI port gets processed immediately. However, if the note arrives just after the synth has checked, it has to wait for the loop to come around again (which can be as long as tens of milliseconds).

In 1991, *Keyboard* magazine thoroughly researched the response times of a wide variety of synthesizers and samplers under various conditions and found huge variations. The results were published in their December, 1991, and January, 1992, issues. Many devices showed different response times depending on whether single- or multiple-oscillator voices were used. Multitimbral devices usually were slower in Multi Mode than in Omni (single-sound) Mode. The delays for single notes ranged from two to sixteen milliseconds, and the variations within a device were found to run from zero to more than 40%. As you might expect, newer designs, with faster clocks and interrupt-driven operating systems, fared better than older ones. If this subject is of particular interest to you, those articles make fascinating reading.

MIDI Misfits: Nonstandard Implementations

The MIDI specification is very straightforward, but it is possible to misinterpret it. In fact, over the years, a number of products that use MIDI in an odd way have appeared. Some have been honest mistakes, some can be traced to poor translations of the MIDI spec into foreign languages, and some were caused by otherwise well-meaning manufacturers who thought it was okay to bend the spec a little. Most of them were fairly benign, but some have had serious effects that other manufacturers have had to compensate for.

The Yamaha DX7 was the first extremely popular MIDI synth—and one of the most commercially successful musical instruments of all time. This synth originally did not send Channel Pressure information in the right form, but instead, sent it as Controller 3. It also sent the wrong command for Active Sensing, which confused just about every non-Yamaha sequencer on the market, and could actually cause some sequencers to freeze. The company changed the operating system fairly quickly to correct the situation, and most DX7 owners got their units upgraded. The long-term effect for the rest of the MIDI world has been that Controller 3 remains today essentially unimplemented in order to avoid possible conflicts with any un-upgraded DX7s that people may still be using.

There have also been some strange uses for the extra pins, 1 and 3, in MIDI jacks. According to the specification, these pins are not to be connected to anything. In the MIDI Out jack on Atari ST computers, however, those pins carry a MIDI Thru signal. A simple splitter cable could be made to turn this odd jack into conventional Out and Thru jacks, but Atari never made such a cable, and neither did any other major manufacturer. This would be of little matter since a sequencer doesn't usually need a Thru jack. However, some MIDI cables have appeared on the market in which pins 1 and 3 are shorted to pins 2 and 4 (one purports to provide extra copper for the signal path). Such a cable, plugged into an ST, could cause havoc. (Fortunately this feature has been eliminated on Atari's new Falcon.) There have also been suggestions that the extra pins be used to carry DC power, to cut down on the number of external transformers (or "wall warts") a studio might need. Imagine what this would do to the poor Atari.

Believe it or not, some manufacturers have not accepted MIDI speed as a standard to be followed—and have designed equipment that either runs not fast enough, or too fast. The specification is very clear about the maximum data rate of MIDI, yet some early synths would miss bytes or produce error messages when they received lots of data in a burst. To avoid this, some sequencer makers put a *Slow MIDI* switch in their programs to make sure there was enough space between the messages so that the amount of incoming data never exceeded that which these machines were capable of handling.

188 • Midi for the Professional

One sampler manufacturer was responsible for a well-meaning, but misguided, effort to reduce the amount of time it took to dump samples over a MIDI cable using System Exclusive (this was before the Sample Dump Standard). The manufacturer included a switch on the instrument that doubled the baud rate. As long as the only communication on such a line was between two identical samplers, or between the sampler and a computer equipped with an interface and software specifically designed to deal with the increased rate, this would work. However, what was being sent on that cable could no longer be considered MIDI. Any other MIDI synth on the line would, at best, encounter continuous framing errors. Fortunately, this idea died with the model.

Probably the most common compatibility problem in the MIDI world has been Roland's unusual use of the All Notes Off command (Controller FBH, 123 decimal). On many of this company's keyboards, this message is sent whenever the player releases all of the keys. While technically not a violation of the MIDI spec, it is not at all necessary—and it has created big problems for sequencer manufacturers.

Consider the following scenario. A player records a series of chords from a Roland keyboard into a sequencer, and at the end, lifts his hands off the keyboard. The sequencer dutifully records the notes and the All Notes Off command. Now the player wants to overdub a solo line on the same MIDI channel in which the last note is to be held longer than the chord that ended the first pass. As he does his overdub, when the last accompaniment chord ends, the solo note also gets cut off by the All Notes Off command that is already part of the track.

The solution to this problem has been for many sequencers, and synthesizers as well, simply to ignore All Notes Off commands. Unfortunately, this effectively removes from the MIDI language a useful command. All Notes Off is particularly handy during a live performance when notes are hanging. This command provides a convenient way to end a sequence abruptly.

Quite a number of other inconsistencies have shown up from time to time in MIDI products, but fortunately, MIDI has proven itself to be very robust and immune to serious abuse. Later in the book, we'll examine how MIDI can and will remain viable in the years to come.

Chapter II

MIDI in Music Education

MIDI technology has proven especially useful in music education. Even the simplest MIDI system—a personal computer and a good synthesizer—gives music students and teachers powerful tools for learning theory, composition, arranging, keyboard technique, and many other aspects of music. Using MIDI, students can integrate music skills—such as hearing, reading, writing, performing, and composing—along with the conceptual and theoretical aspects of music education.

Educational MIDI software generally reflects one of two models: drill and practice—or exploring and implementing. Drill and practice software typically shows the student a narrow body of information (e.g., intervals, scales, and key signatures). It then engages him or her in simple recognition or performance drills: What kind of triad is being played? Can you play the notes in an A Major scale? This software seeks to establish a vocabulary and context, and then apply the material.

The exploring and implementing model involves, thanks to MIDI, listening to actual music as the exploration process is pursued. Students working without a computerized MIDI setup tend to write out music on paper by the rules, and listen to it only after writing a complete line. They do little (if any) revision towards a more artful sound or aesthetic result. Conversely, in a MIDI environment, students hear their work virtually as soon as they create it. This changes the context for making musical decisions from the manuscript to the music itself.

The music software currently available for education can be considered as falling into two main groups: *dedicated* and *applied*. Dedicated software is designed to focus the user on a specific educational activity—such as playing scales on a keyboard or identifying the correct inversions of triads—and then drill him or her on this activity. Dedicated software is available for ear training, theory, skill development, repertoire practice, and jazz improvisation. Programs can be designed for use in a self-teaching environment, a single teacher-student situation, a classroom, or in many cases, all three contexts. Applied software is that which has been created for a more general musical purpose, such as composition or notation, yet can be used for educational activities. Applied software can be similarly appropriate in all three instructional contexts.

Dedicated software can be divided into three categories:

Theory software. Provides the user with a drill and practice environment for learning the basic elements of music theory and ear training.

Performance and practice software. Provides a performance environment such as a jazz ensemble, an orchestra rehearsal, or a piano lesson.

Exploration software. Creates an environment unique to computers and MIDI by providing either a visual musical interface the user can manipulate—or emulating procedural programming languages like BASIC or C.

Theory Software

Probably the most commonly used and most accessible music education software provides the tools to learn, integrate, and demonstrate a basic understanding of music theory. These programs usually present a straightforward drill and practice environment designed around the primary concepts of beginning music theory: scales, intervals, chords, melodies, key signatures, time signatures, and rhythms. To communicate these concepts, theory programs offer exercises and activities for fundamental theory, ear training, dictation, and functional keyboard skills. The computer can play a chord, for example, and ask the student to identify the chord form—or play a scale and ask for the mode, and so on. Other drills display some aspect of notation and ask the student to identify it: for example, the computer might display a key signature and ask the student what key it refers to. Ear training drills may focus on pitch or rhythm, using a set of exercises that build from simple to more advanced structures. For example, the drills may progress from scales to intervals, then to diatonic chord forms and extended tonal structures. Rhythm Ace from Ibis Software, for example, is an MS-DOS rhythm training program that offers rhythmic reading, dictation, and custom exercises.

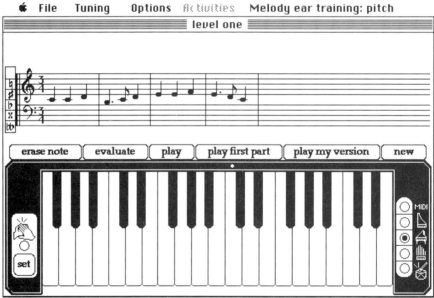

the Exercise Menu in Rhythm Ace from Ibis Software

Typical dictation drills play a melody, then allow the student to notate it in the computer. The student may be asked to notate the pitch, the rhythm, or both. Practica Music by Ars Nova Software provides melodic dictation drills. Such exercises are usually limited to short melodies that can be written in the space of a single screen.

a melody dictation screen showing a portion of a piece's melody in Practica Musica

Dictation software doesn't usually include drills for keyboard skills. However, notating scales, chords, and intervals may encourage (or even require) the student to play answers on the MIDI keyboard. This will provide him or her with some familiarity with mapping simple theoretical structures onto the instrument.

Theory applications also provide drills of such notational concepts as time signatures and the Circle of Fifths. MiBAC's Music Lessons is one such product.

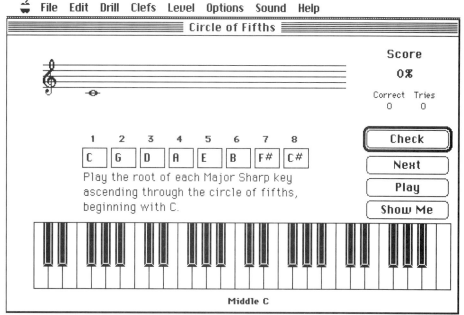

the Circle of Fifths drill in Music Lessons

The Environment

In establishing a drill and practice environment for basic theory, software needs to provide for the input and output of musical information. The student can input information using a MIDI keyboard, by clicking on the computer screen with a mouse, or by using the computer's keyboard. Software that allows for MIDI keyboard entry helps the student connect pitch concepts, theoretical concepts, and simple keyboard knowledge with actual sounding music. However, notational data usually requires mouse or alphanumeric keyboard entry. Information input with the mouse often involves clicking on a graphic keyboard displayed on the computer screen. Using this method, the student enters not only pitch information, but rhythms and notation as well. The program can also display a guitar fretboard or other instrument on the screen. Note these examples of different user interfaces from Rhythm Ace and Imaja's Listen.

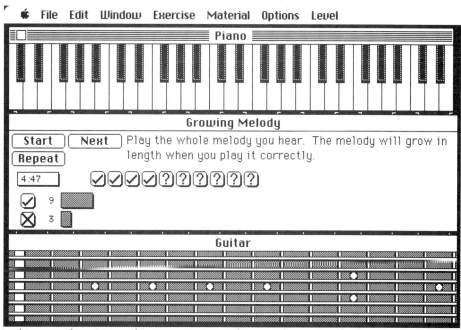

In this screen from Listen, the user can enter pitches on either a piano keyboard, or a guitar fretboard

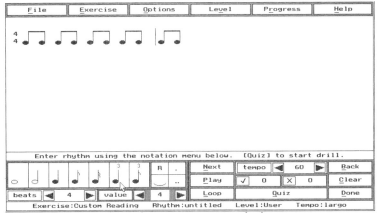

Rhythm Ace allows the student to enter custom rhythms.

Input with a mouse can also reinforce other associations, such as connecting grand-staff notation to a keyboard representation of the notes.

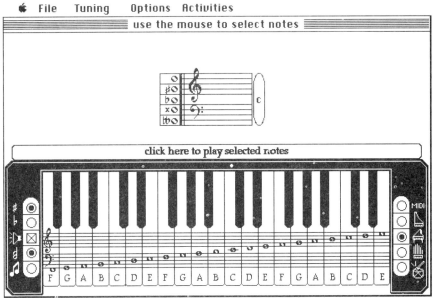

Practica Musica displays the grand staff on the keys of a keyboard.

Adjusting Skill Level

A feature usually found in dedicated theory software is the ability to set the range and difficulty level of the exercises. These controls allow the user to determine the scope and complexity of the material used to create a given drill or set of drills. In Rhythm Ace, for example, the student can select from single-handed or two-handed rhythms on twelve progressive skill levels—or set up custom exercises in time signatures from $\frac{2}{2}$ to $\frac{16}{16}$. This illustration shows the range of seventh chords in Ibis's Play It by Ear.

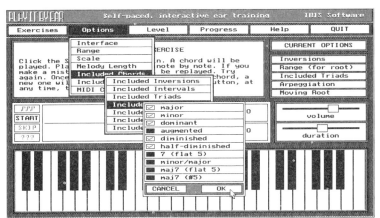

selecting a range of chords that Play It by Ear will use in a chord recognition exercise

When dealing with pitch-oriented exercises, difficulty options allow the student to include or exclude various scales, intervals, chords, inversions, and so forth. With these controls, the student can create focused and progressive drills. For example, a student having difficulty with intervals can limit the exercises played to perfect consonances. Another student, having difficulty recognizing scale types, might set the range to only a major/minor scale comparison before attempting to hear the differences among the minor scales. Once the student can identify all the major and minor scales by ear, he or she can expand the range to include the more difficult modal, jazz, or whole-tone scales. Here is a menu from an exercise in Music Lessons that allows the user to choose from a set of possible scales.

Material	
Pitch Set...	⌘P
Range...	⌘R
Included Inversions...	⌘I
Included Triads...	
Included 7th Chords...	
Included 9th Chords...	
Included 11th Chords...	
Included 13th Chords...	
Tones Per Random Chord...	
Melody Length...	⌘L

the range setting options for an exercise in Music Lessons

Dedicated software usually allows the student to begin at any range or difficulty setting. This allows the more advanced user to bypass unnecessary drills. In many cases, the software can be set to automatically increase the difficulty as the student solves the problems. This can help to create an environment that allows the student enough success to be encouraged. This learning environment fosters a sense of progress, while at the same time, maintains an appropriate degree of challenge.

Information

Programs often provide written theory information and simple help files. The latter work like the help files in other types of computer software. A student might use help to explain what a particular drill or feature does—or to expand upon a theoretical musical concept within the context of the exercise. Or, help may be used to provide a specific detail about the program's MIDI connections or options. This illustration shows Music Lessons' help screen for the Circle of Fifths. The help file here includes a fair amount of detail, with a list of available topics relating to the Circle of Fifths.

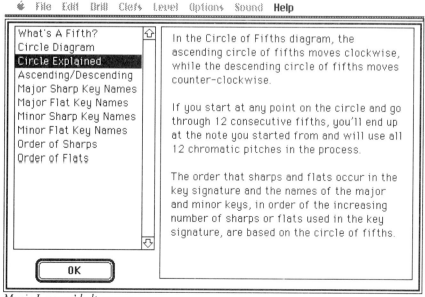

Music Lessons' help screen

Control and Feedback

Music theory applications may provide the user with classroom-oriented information and feedback. Often a clock or timer is built into the software with options for displaying the elapsed time spent on a given exercise. Or, a timer may be used to limit the time allowed to execute a particular drill or drill set. Such options may be displayed on screen in the form of a clock or counter. Most programs also provide a number of ways of keeping track of student's success and progress. Gauges or simple displays can show the number of correct and incorrect answers for a current exercise. In addition, progress reports and session tracking are common features. They summarize the current session and report the user's relative success in particular areas or drills.

** File Edit Drill Clefs Level Options Sound Help**

Untitled-2

MiBAC™ Music Lessons Progress Report

NEW STUDENT   Wednesday October 28

Drill	Treble Clef		Bass Clef		Alto Clef	
Note Names			Total: 81% (13 of 16) (3)			
Spaces:	81%	(13 of 16)	0%	(0 of 0)	0%	(0 of 0)
Lines:	0%	(0 of 0)	0%	(0 of 0)	0%	(0 of 0)
Staff:	0%	(0 of 0)	0%	(0 of 0)	0%	(0 of 0)
Ledgers:	0%	(0 of 0)	0%	(0 of 0)	0%	(0 of 0)
Key Signatures			Total: 80% (4 of 5) (4)			
Major Sharp Keys:	80%	(4 of 5)	0%	(0 of 0)	0%	(0 of 0)
Major Flat Keys:	0%	(0 of 0)	0%	(0 of 0)	0%	(0 of 0)
Minor Sharp Keys:	0%	(0 of 0)	0%	(0 of 0)	0%	(0 of 0)
Minor Flat Keys:	0%	(0 of 0)	0%	(0 of 0)	0%	(0 of 0)
Modes			Total: 100% (3 of 3) (2)			
Ionian:	100%	(3 of 3)	0%	(0 of 0)	0%	(0 of 0)
Dorian:	0%	(0 of 0)	0%	(0 of 0)	0%	(0 of 0)
Phrygian:	0%	(0 of 0)	0%	(0 of 0)	0%	(0 of 0)
Lydian:	0%	(0 of 0)	0%	(0 of 0)	0%	(0 of 0)
Mixolydian:	0%	(0 of 0)	0%	(0 of 0)	0%	(0 of 0)
Aeolian:	0%	(0 of 0)	0%	(0 of 0)	0%	(0 of 0)
Locrian:	0%	(0 of 0)	0%	(0 of 0)	0%	(0 of 0)

a progress report from Music Lessons

In a classroom situation, reports can often be stored in the program for later display on the screen or printout. This can help the teacher monitor and evaluate a student's progress, and structure further work. Progress reports can also help the student gain a sense of his or her relative strengths and weaknesses in the areas being drilled. In some programs, progress is tracked over more than one session. To accomplish this, the program may create individual files for each student. When a student starts a session, the software knows which drills to present to correspond with the student's current level of achievement.

Performance Software

Educational performance software is a logical evolution of an older technological tool in music education: "Music Minus One" records. These records provided an ensemble accompaniment for the student instrumentalist, either in a classical or improvisational setting.

MIDI performance software provides a more dynamic and sometimes interactive version of the same concept, and adds a high degree of flexibility. The software can be divided into two main categories: improvisation and practice. The improvisation applications are aimed primarily at jazz and pop idioms, while practice software is most often directed at classically oriented literature.

Improvisation

As compared with ordinary play-along records, improvisation software offers the student a higher quality and greater range of performance circumstances. MIDI instruments replace the instrumental ensemble—and the computer acts as the teacher and conductor. The software focuses specifically on improvisation and ensemble performance skills. It may also offer the student feedback on the relative success of his or her efforts.

To use performance software, the student or teacher first provides a set of performance instructions. The student can listen to the ensemble play, evaluate it, and modify the instructions to create a more desirable backup before joining in. This process offers the student great educational value, not only in the actual playing, but in creating the ensemble performance. To adjust the ensemble, the student must consider such issues as instrumentation, style, form, instrumental roles, tempo—and even details of pitch, rhythm, and articulations. Besides being more fun than just playing along with a record, all this can lead a student to a great deal of insight about performance situations.

Once the ensemble has been programmed to taste, the student can perform along with it, using either a MIDI controller or a conventional instrument. A beginning student of improvisation can use the software to prepare for the real-life situation of fronting a band—or as a substitute when other players are not readily available. While performing with real musicians is an irreplaceable experience, performance software can go a long way toward giving the beginning student the feeling that he or she is part of a larger ensemble.

There are two basic models for most improvisational software: a *dynamic lead sheet* and a *smart sequencer*.

Dynamic Lead Sheet

Dynamic lead sheet software is aimed at creating a coherent, stylized ensemble performance, requiring relatively simple instructions and options. Its principal educational value comes in the student's performance with the MIDI ensemble it creates. In this respect, this software comes closest to the original Music Minus One recordings, but adds the advantage of a flexible and dynamic performance environment.

Apart from his or her own performance, the student will typically enter little original music to the ensemble's performance. Similarly, the student does little direct editing of musical content, but instead uses preset choices of chord progression, meter and tempo, characteristics of the rhythm track, and so on. For example, a student could specify a standard twelve-bar blues chord pattern with a ⅜ swing feel, a fast Latin percussion background, and closed piano voicings. The results of these ensemble decisions are often stylistically narrow, but can usually be tweaked in some small ways. For instance, the student might set the drum part to play a little ahead of the bass player—or add fills every four bars. To provide variety, different types of instruments can be specified for the accompaniment track (e.g., acoustic or electric piano, fretted or fretless bass, or brushes or sticks on the drums). While the principal educational value of this software lies in the student's actual performance, creating the ensemble also provides some understanding of styles, score creation, and performance nuances typical of a given style.

Using dynamic lead sheet software involves creating a lead sheet, then arranging a performance around it. The student lays out the measures of the song form, and types in the chord changes. The student may use jazz chords such as sevenths, thirteenths, or other extensions. Or, the user may just enter triads and let the software determine what alterations to use. The lead sheet displayed is from MiBAC's Jazz.

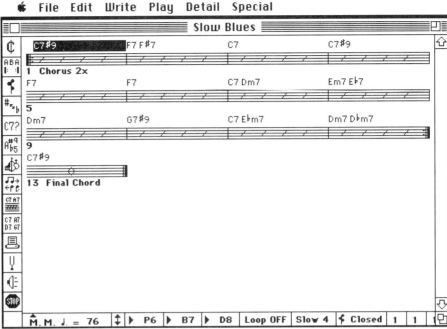

MiBAC Jazz main window with a full lead sheet

The student indicates the structural elements of the lead sheet—such as repeating bars, choruses, codas, and tempo—then selects a key, as well as style and performance options for each ensemble instrument. This illustration (also from Jazz) shows one way that the software can present the possible choices.

MiBAC Jazz selection window

Once the performance is planned, the computer uses the defined parameters to create an actual performance. Commonly, each time the computer performs, the results are different to a greater or lesser degree. The student can evaluate each realization, and change aspects of the instructions if something isn't working exactly right. For example, this window from Jazz allows the student to determine what kind of chord voicings will be used in the piano part.

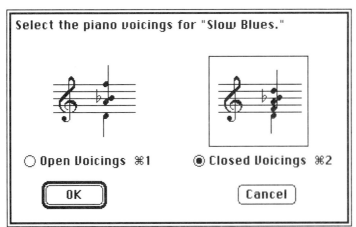

Piano Voicings dialog box in MiBAC Jazz

If a student loses his or her place during a particular performance, the piece can be stopped immediately. In order to master difficult passages, the student can slow down the performance—or tell the software to repeat a passage over and over for rehearsal purposes. Over time, the student can also work on more abstract issues—the kind of harmonic ideas to use over a given set of changes, the efficacy of certain scales, how to find a melodic "skeleton" in a tune—in short, much of the knowledge and many of the skills an improvising musician needs. Some of these programs let the student save both the accompaniment and the solo performance (assuming it's performed on a MIDI instrument) as a MIDI file. This file can be used in a sequencer later.

Smart Sequencers

In contrast to dynamic lead sheet software, smart sequencer software is stylistically nonspecific—and places more emphasis on the student's activities in creating an ensemble performance. The application provides little or no musical data. Instead, the student enters the raw musical material for each instrument. This music can consist of a wide range of musical styles for a much more varied set of instruments. The primary contrast between conventional sequencers and smart sequencers lies in the way they interpret the data entered into them. A conventional sequencer plays back the music exactly as recorded and edited by the user; a smart sequencer plays back its own interpretation of what the user enters and edits.

Smart sequencers share a number of features in common with conventional sequencers. They typically have a set of tape-recorder-type controls that allow the user to record and play multiple tracks on different MIDI channels. Smart sequencers also use Program Changes and MIDI Volume, allow for tempo changes, and display a counter. Once the student enters some music, he or she can edit its pitch and rhythm, create subsequences, and perform many other functions commonly provided in quality sequencers.

In contrast to conventional sequencers, smart sequencers provide sets of filters that the user can apply to individual instruments, or to the ensemble as a whole. The effect of these filters can vary widely. They can interpret the original music quite abstractly, or impart relatively few or subtle changes to the original music. The user can specify a percentage or weight by which various filters affect specific musical elements such as pitch, note duration, or articulation.

The illustration below shows the main screen from Jam Factory, a program developed by Intelligent Music, and now available from Dr. T's. It is divided into four quadrants, labeled *P1, P2, P3,* and *P4,* which correspond to four "players." Each player produces notes and/or chords independently on its own MIDI channel (or channels). Among Jam Factory's many features is the ability to randomize to a user-specified degree music recorded by the user into each player. Pitch and duration information can be treated separately. For example, the rhythm of a passage can remain the same while the notes are played in a different order—or conversely, the notes' order can stay the same while the rhythm changes.

The top right corner of each player's box contains a set of bar graphs that can be modified with the mouse. Darker bars represent pitch playback, and lighter ones, duration. High values entered into boxes farther to the right cause the original pitch or duration order for that player to be more randomly scrambled on playback. Higher values in the left-hand boxes increase the playback's resemblance to the original performance. In the middle of each player's box is a set of four "ring-toss" type controls. These controls weight the articulation and velocity of the notes as they are played. The settings in the P1 box divide all the articulations for the performance into four types, placing a minimum articulation (in this case, controlled by MIDI Velocity) on half the notes, a maximum Velocity on one-fourth, and a median Velocity on one-fourth. The broad gray bar just below and to the left of the pole indicators determines the range from which the minimum and maximum Velocities are set.

Jam Factory allows recording on multiple tracks and uses tape-deck-type controls.

The music that emerges from a smart sequencer can be much more complex and harder to control than that which results from a dynamic lead sheet program. Therefore, performances that come from the software not only have a much broader range of possible ensembles and styles, but a broad range of possible successes and failures as well. Consequently, the main educational value of this software most often comes from the student's efforts to create an ensemble that sounds good. It leads the student to analyze just what it is that makes for a pleasing (or not so pleasing) composition and performance.

Practice Software

At present, most practice software is aimed at piano (or perhaps more accurately, keyboard) practice, performance, and instruction. A good example of this is Ibis Software's NotePlay for Windows, which displays notes on a grand staff and offers thirty-six levels of one- and two-handed melodic and harmonic drills for developing sightreading speed and accuracy.

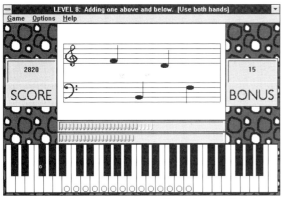

a simple two-handed exercise in NotePlay for Windows

A very exciting type of practice software that is beginning to emerge is *intelligent accompaniment* programs. This software can analyze a student's performance dynamically, providing an interactive accompaniment that follows the soloist. An example is Concerto Accompanist, currently under development at the Conservatory at the University of Cincinnati. It tracks pitch, tempo, and dynamic changes in the piano part being played by the student. Pitches are used to help the accompaniment locate where it's supposed to be. Tempo is translated into playback speed of the accompaniment (and the sensitivity with which the program responds to tempo changes is user-definable). Volume sensitivity allows the MIDI orchestra to play louder or softer according to how hard the student is playing. The operating screen has transport controls like a sequencer, along with a preview button that plays a few bars at the current location. It also features individual volume sliders for each instrumental voice in the orchestra, so the student can change the orchestral balance if he or she so chooses.

⌘ File   Edit   View   Label   Special   DD

Concerto Accompanist		
Location ◁▭▭▭▭▭▭▭▭▭▭▭▭▭▭▭▭▭▭▭▭▭▷ Bar		1; Beat 1
Master volume ◁▭▭▭▭▭▭▭▭▭▭▭▭▭▭▭▭▷ Tempo 144		

| ⟨ ··· ⟨ ···· | → | → → | ◆ | |→| | ‖⟨ ··· | →‖ |

Mozart K. 466 (I)		

Piano/0	M-1	◁▭▭▭▭▭▷	Flute/64	M-7	◁▭▭▭▭▭▷
Violin I/48	M-2	◁▭▭▭▭▭▷	2 Oboes/66	M-8	◁▭▭▭▭▭▷
Violin II/48	M-3	◁▭▭▭▭▭▷	2 Bassoons/67	M-9	◁▭▭▭▭▭▷
Viola/48	M-4	◁▭▭▭▭▭▷	2 Horns/55	M-10	◁▭▭▭▭▭▷
Cello/48	M-5	◁▭▭▭▭▭▷	2 Trumpets/53	M-11	◁▭▭▭▭▭▷
Bass/48	M-6	◁▭▭▭▭▭▷	Timpani/77 (-12)	M-12	◁▭▭▭▭▭▷

the main screen from Concerto Accompanist, an interactive practice application, set up for a performance of a Mozart piano concerto

The Miracle Keyboard system takes a comprehensive approach to practice software, and includes some drill exercises as well. It is a hardware and software package that provides an interactive learning environment for beginning students on a wide range of computer platforms, from Macintosh to Nintendo. The package provides all the software and hardware necessary (apart from the computer), including a forty-nine-note MIDI keyboard.

The Miracle Keyboard system's metaphor is that of a conservatory, where the student moves among different rooms for different activities: administration, classroom, studio, practice room, arcade, and performance hall. After registering in the administration room, the student is free to wander to different rooms as he or she wishes. Lessons happen in the classroom, typically followed by practice sessions in a practice room. The program monitors the student during each lesson. The program praises the student if the task is accomplished satisfactorily. If the student is having some difficulty with the lesson, the program restructures or breaks down the task (e.g., telling the student to practice each hand separately). If the task seems insurmountable, the student can then go to a more suitable lesson, or something more fun, like the video arcade.

the arcade from the Miracle Keyboard system

The program contains a rudimentary sequencer in the form of the studio room. Here, students can make up their own music or have the program arrange a piece used in the preceding lesson for ensemble accompaniment. The video arcade room contains drill exercises, but dresses them up in the form of video games that let the student shoot down arcade-style ducks by playing the right notes—or save parachute jumpers by playing the right chord.

Exploration Software

Exploration software is not based on any standardized musical or educational concepts, but uses computers and synthesizers to create unique educational tools and environments. For example, the computer itself may become a musical instrument, with the keyboard and mouse controlling the sound like the buttons and valves on a conventional instrument. Or, the computer may be used to write music by itself, once it is given the parameters for composition by the user.

Some exploration programs use the native sound-generating capabilities of the computer, and don't actually require any MIDI equipment to function. This approach does appeal to those on a tight budget (although connecting such a program to one or more MIDI instruments will improve the quality of the sounds it generates).

Computer composition software usually comes in the form of a music programming language, which can be text oriented or graphically based. As with any language, these programs demand time and study to use and master. The natural home of such software is a music composition program in a university or conservatory.

Computer instrument software turns the computer into a new kind of MIDI instrument, providing a graphic interface that is by definition unique. These applications can appeal to students as young as age five, and can also be great fun for adults.

Music Mouse

Laurie Spiegel's Music Mouse turns the mouse of a Macintosh or Amiga into an intelligent MIDI controller (and it can use internal sounds as well). Moving the mouse across a grid on the main screen, bounded on all sides by a reference keyboard, plays up to four notes in a variety of patterns. Fast mouse movement results in a rapid succession of pitches. Slow movement results in slower music with longer durations.

the playing grid in Music Mouse

Pitch information is created by the position of the mouse on the grid, and can be interpreted in several simple ways. The user chooses from a variety of pitch sets, including diatonic, chromatic, Middle Eastern, and pentatonic. This lets the student explore the sound and effect of various common tonal materials. Parallel or contrary motion between the voices can be specified. Turning on the *patterns* option causes notes to sound automatically—and mouse movements simply serve to change the relative pitch of the voices as they follow the pattern. Options also exist for playing chords, arpeggios, and single lines. Assigning the output of Music Mouse to different synthesizers can serve as a great tool for exploring the resources of the synthesizers and testing combinations of various programs and tone colors.

Ovaltune

Like Music Mouse, Ovaltune, by David Zicarelli (author of M), turns the Macintosh mouse into a MIDI controller. However, instead of being restricted to a keyboard grid, the mouse draws a variety of colored graphics on the screen that relate to MIDI data. Ovaltune provides various tonal pitch sets from which to choose. It also allows the user to create pitch patterns and trigger rhythms by the relative direction and speed of the mouse.

Ovaltune is unique in its association of interesting graphics and mouse movement. Large mouse motions result in louder and faster music, and create larger shapes across a bigger portion of the screen. Small motions draw little shapes and produce softer, slower sounds.

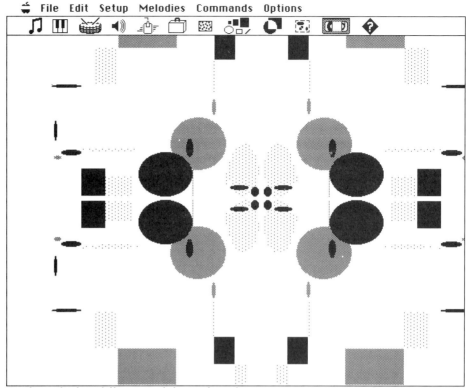

Ovaltune displays different sized shapes that relate to mouse movement and MIDI output.

Harmony Grid

Harmony Grid, by Hip Software, offers yet another twist to the mouse-as-instrument model. As in Music Mouse and Ovaltune, the user selects certain pitch sets (such as scales or modes). The user then moves the mouse across a grid to play pitches—and the speed of the mouse controls note duration. Like Ovaltune, Harmony Grid connects the music to a graphic display—a "harmonic grid" that offers an alternative to the normal keyboard or staff representation of pitch structure. The harmonic grid limits the notes that the mouse will play, so that the student always creates music within the bounds of a specific scale or mode.

In the illustration below, you can see Harmony Grid's scale selection options in the upper left-hand portion of the screen. Its performance options for various single-note and multiple-note triggerings appear along the top of the screen. In the grid that represents the mouse's playing field, whole-step relations go from left to right, and half-step relations go up and down. The notes of the scale in use are circled on the grid. A keyboard at the bottom of the screen provides a more common pitch reference and gives the mouse an additional playing interface.

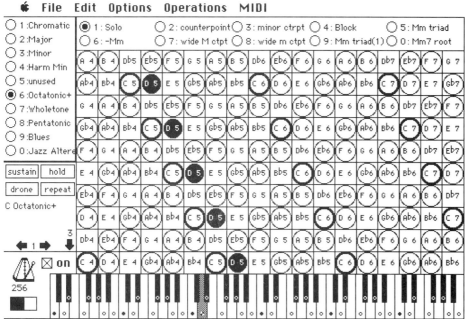

the Harmony Grid main window with a major key selected as a scale

The grid's pitch layout encourages the student to explore the whole-step/half-step underpinnings of scales. The pitch layout can be altered to explore different types of interval relationships—and how they serve to structure scales and pitch materials. The illustration that follows shows how the program can be set up to explore octatonic scales. Minor seconds result from moving the mouse from left to right on the grid—and minor thirds result from up and down movements.

Harmony Grid with octatonic scale selected, and 1 and 3 designated as vertical and horizontal coordinates

Max

Composition programming languages can be categorized as *real-time* and *non-real-time*. Non-real-time languages allow the composer to specify sounds, pitches, and so on, as numerical lists. These are then compiled like any other high-level computer program, and the result is a performance of a piece of music. Real-time music language environments can handle input and output simultaneously while they execute a performance. Most modern real-time languages use MIDI as at least one input or output element. These languages can be used to create a compositional environment that resembles an instrument or an entire composition—or even more likely, something in between.

Max, written by Miller Puckette and David Zicarelli and distributed by Opcode Systems, is an excellent example of a real-time composition program. Max provides the user with a graphic/object programming environment. The user places objects on the screen, arranges them in certain orders, draws connections between them, and enters data into them. The results of programs written in Max (known as *patches*) are as diverse as the user's imagination allows. Max patches may be used as MIDI performance filters, debugging tools, software instruments, and software compositions.

The illustration below shows two input and output devices, with boxes displaying the MIDI input/output results. Clicking on the on-screen keyboard triggers a synthesizer and displays the MIDI data played in the boxes below it. Notes played on a MIDI controller cause the appropriate MIDI information to be displayed in the boxes on the left-hand side of the window. The educational value for advanced students is obvious. Any kind of MIDI-based tool can be created with Max—and exploring the vast capabilities of the language can be an investigation of the nature and structure of music itself.

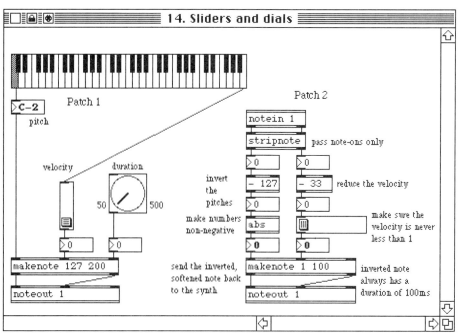

Max uses sliders and dials as input and output devices. Boxes list the MIDI input/output.

Compose

Compose, by Charles Ames of Buffalo, New York, is a non-real-time music composition programming language. It accepts no direct MIDI input; rather, compositions created in Compose are typed in, compiled, then run or performed. Compose was written as a vehicle for teaching advanced concepts in serial and algorithmic composition as practiced by Boulez, Stockhausen, and Xenakis. The illustration below shows a Compose program designed to write a simple motet.

File   Edit   Unit   Action   Score

```
THE SEQUENCE
    PITCH SEQUENCE
    PITCH: Sequence

        MAIN PHRASE
        SCORE: Phrase
    Assigns:
    Items:      LCM
    Sections:   THE EVENT

        TALEA VALUE
    REAL            COLOR
            INT ITEM 2
In          INT ITEM 1
            INTEGER: Items
So
    Source: TALEA
```

```
THE EVENT
    SCORE: Event

Assigns:
Period:     THE SEQUENCE
Duration:   PERIOD
Channel:    1
Program:    -1
Velocity:   96
Pitch:      PITCH SEQUENCE
```

a program in Compose, designed to write an isorhythmic motet passage

Programs such as Compose are very involved and require a great deal of time and effort to master. They represent the evolution of previous music programming languages like Music V and C-Sound into the current consumer market of personal computers and MIDI equipment.

Applied MIDI Software in Education

While applied MIDI programs such as sequencers and notation generators are not specifically designed as educational tools, they do have broad educational functions. In a sense, any use of MIDI equipment is, by definition, educational. You have to learn how to use it first, and that effort teaches you something about music and logic at the very least, and often much more. Every time you compose a sequence or copy a score, you are involved in musical activities that foster exploration and learning. However, there are also specific educational goals that applied MIDI programs can be used to achieve. Similarly, generalized hypertext development systems, while not specifically geared towards education, can be combined with MIDI hardware and software to make powerful educational tools.

Sequencers

Sequencers do not have to be complex to serve educational goals. As long as a sequencer allows multitrack recording and playback, basic editing capabilities, and some way of displaying the recorded data, it can be a powerful educational tool. Sequencers are excellent vehicles for dictation exercises, in which a student is asked to listen to a musical passage and notate or play back what he or she hears. Sequencer files can be created and used for this practice exactly like dictation tapes. The student can write out the examples on manuscript paper or using a notation program—or play them back into the same sequencer. If he or she uses the last approach, or if the notation program has MIDI playback, both audible and visual feedback are available to the student.

206 • Midi for the Professional

Sequencers are also excellent tools for analysis of music. Several companies, including Romeo Music and MidiSoft, sell Standard Midi Files of classical repertoire on disk. Many companies sell sequenced versions of pop tunes. The latter are primarily geared for solo nightclub performers. However, the best of them can be educational as well (inasmuch as well-crafted jazz or pop arrangements arc well worth studying by those who would be jazz or pop composers).

All of the features of sequencers can come into play when dealing with prerecorded compositions.

- The tape transport and counter give the student instant access to any part of the music.

- Tempos can be changed without affecting pitch.

- Mute and solo controls can isolate or eliminate individual instruments.

- Piano-roll or notation display allows the student to analyze elements visually.

Sequencers make good tools for analyzing a student's performance as well. The many ways sequencers let you see and hear a composition allow teachers and students to examine playing styles, mistakes, timing issues, differences in hand strength, and many other aspects of performance technique.

The most obvious application of sequencers, however, is in performance itself. A great variety of educational performance activities can be designed around a simple sequencer. In addition to the performance and practice applications we talked about earlier, sequencers work well in other areas of traditional music. One area is that of performing and exploring classical chorales, string quartets, orchestral music, and other forms. In studying chorales, a track can be muted, and the student asked to sing or play the missing line—providing performance options for keyboard harmony, instrumental study, and solfège. In chamber music, a sequenced piece can serve as a dynamic score that can be examined for thematic material, formal divisions, harmonic progressions, and the like. The absence of notation will demand that the student hear a theme to identify it, rather than deduce it from the score. The instant random access also allows more associative exploration of the sound of a given work.

Sequenced orchestral works can serve as a basis for orchestration projects and exploration. For example, a student might experiment with reassigning string sounds to wind sounds, or expand a piano sonata or a string quartet into a piece for full orchestra. Teachers of conducting can create for students an ideal performance that pays special attention to nuances of phrasing, note lengths, attacks, subtle tempo changes, and other appropriate elements. Similarly, conducting students can be given raw Midi sequences and asked to make the changes in tempo, articulation, and dynamics in preparation for dealing with a real orchestra. Their teachers can then evaluate these artistic decisions and help them make the best aesthetic choices without the need to have an entire orchestra present during the process. Only when the student is fully comfortable with his or her interpretation do the human instrumentalists need to be called in. Of course, a sequencer is invaluable for students who want to learn how to simulate the sound of a real orchestra with synthesizers—using such mixing techniques as panning, reverb, equalization, and delay.

Transcribing an orchestral score into a sequencer—either using a notation front end or by playing each part in on a keyboard—is a fine way to get a student to know the inner workings of a complex classical piece. The same is true of jazz and pop composition. Using a sequencer to create an entire ensemble gives the student intimate knowledge of the role each instrument plays—and provides an exceptionally flexible palette for composing. The process of composition can begin away from the computer, where the student writes a song or arrangement on paper, and then enters it into the sequencer. At that point, audible feedback allows the student to feel his way through each track, looking for complementary music and adjusting previous tracks.

Notation Software

The principal features that make notation software useful in education are similar to those of sequencers.

- MIDI playback

- solo/mute and locate functions that can isolate passages and staves of music

- on-screen editing

While full-featured notation programs are good for generating publishable output, a simple point-and-click program is perfectly suitable for a wide range of educational applications. Notation software is especially effective for sight singing, solfège, or any kind of interpretation of notated music. Files can be set up with ear training materials like scales, intervals, and chords in various arrangements. This enables the teacher to structure material to complement a student's particular needs or course of study. As with sequencers, notation programs provide the advantages of isolating voices, changing tempos, and having a large palette of tone colors.

Performance and practice exercises can also be created in notation programs, though the size of the computer screen may limit the length of the music to be read. However, very fast computers with quick screen redraws can often overcome this limitation. Typical music theory and composition disciplines, such as counterpoint, harmony, and orchestration, have a natural compatibility with notation software. This is an option in any situation where the student is writing on manuscript paper and handing in assignments to a teacher. Assignments such as composing a counterpoint to a cantus, realizing a figured bass, or orchestrating a piano reduction can easily be created and completed in computer format. In fact, research shows that when a counterpoint assignment is realized on a computer, the average student will play the example back more than twenty times in the course of creating it. In this way, the student places far more emphasis on the sound and aesthetics of the result than on simple rule-checking.

Hypertext Software

Hypertext software—such as SuperCard and HyperCard for the Macintosh and the Asymetrix's ToolBook for the PC—provides great flexibility in educational contexts. This format allows learning materials to be created by a software company, teacher, or the student.

Music Mentor, from MIDISoft, is a hypertext document that incorporates MIDI into a music education and entertainment environment. It divides music history into five periods, with each section further divided into melody, rhythm, harmony, timbre, texture, and form. All the program's music is stored as MIDI files, accessible by a sequencer—or by Music Mentor as it discusses passages and works. A simple MIDI sequencer is designed into the program so the MIDI files can be explored in various ways.

A HyperCard stack created at New England Conservatory for teaching eighteenth- and nineteenth-century harmonic practice is an example of a custom program prepared by a teacher. The stack is a complete harmony textbook, including explanations of voice leading concepts with notated and MIDI musical examples. The stack plays MIDI files to illustrate voice leading concepts as they are discussed in text windows and displayed in notation.

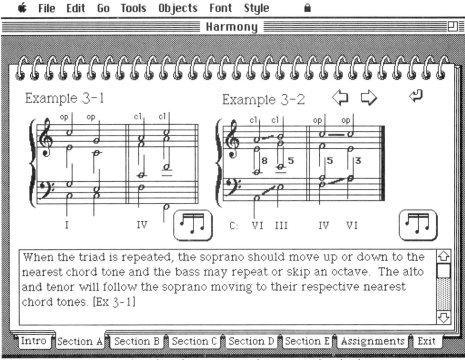

a custom-made HyperCard stack with notation, explanation, and a play button

Students can create their own hypertext documents as a type of musical journal or notebook. For example, students of music history can create an organized theme library with excerpts from listening lists, notes, and documentation.

Hypertext and other customizable development systems represent the future of computers and MIDI in music education. Just as the best music teacher is one who adapts his or her techniques to each individual student, the best educational software is that which can be altered to suit each particular environment. Commercial sequencers and other programs will continue to be highly useful in educational contexts. However, as the tools evolve and become more universally available and easier to use, the most effective results will come from the creative application of programs like HyperCard and Max to educational problems.

Chapter 12
Programming With MIDI

When you look at the wealth of commercial MIDI software available, you'll see that an amazing amount of musical and extra-musical tasks can be accomplished with a computer and MIDI devices. Some musicians, researchers, and educators want to "roll their own"—and create new applications not available from a commercial source. You may need a custom program for a unique task. Although others might be able to use it too, their numbers aren't large enough to justify commercial development. Perhaps you have a fabulous idea for a product that you wish to develop yourself, then have someone else market it. All of these situations happen constantly in the world of MIDI, and it's one of the things that makes working with MIDI an intensely rewarding (and sometimes frustrating) experience.

Using High-Level Languages

MIDI applications can be written in many ways. Commercial programs, created by professional programmers, are written in a general-purpose high-level language. This language is usually some variant of C, or occasionally, Forth or Pascal. Any popular general-purpose language is supported with a large amount of documentation, a large user base, compilers, debuggers, and other helpful development tools that can be used by any programmer. To get programs written in general-purpose languages to speak MIDI, programmers need special *drivers*: small programs, often written in assembly language, that give larger programs access to the hardware that connects the computer to the MIDI cable. Programmers may write their own drivers or take advantage of pre-written drivers (sometimes called *libraries* or *toolboxes*) for specific computers and MIDI interfaces.

Another advantage of writing in a high-level language is that the resulting programs can often be ported from one platform to another. For example, a programmer writing in C on the Mac can use much of the same code when creating an IBM version of the program (although the drivers, and the commands used to access them, will be different). This allows software sellers to address far larger markets than if they were to limit themselves to a single platform.

Programs Within Programs

Custom MIDI programs may also be written within existing MIDI programs. The "hacker" sensibility of the 1970s and early 1980s is still very much alive in the MIDI world. As a result, some MIDI developers are eager to give users the ability to customize their products, and include hooks for doing so. For example, the late Jim Miller's sequencer and notation software for the IBM, Personal Composer, included a module that allowed adventurous users to write their own applications using a dialect of the LISP language. A new version of the program is scheduled to be released for Windows—and it will continue to offer user programmability. Similarly, Dr. T's Music Software offers T-BASIC, a module for modifying files and creating new functions within their Keyboard Controlled Sequencer (or any other application that runs under their MPE operating system).

User-Friendly Languages

A third method of creating custom MIDI programs is to use libraries created for simpler programming languages. This approach allows nonprofessional programmers to join in the fun of creating custom applications. These simpler programming languages present a more user-friendly interface and are easier to learn than professional high-level languages. However, they also tend to be more limited in their capabilities and are often much slower. The slowness is at least partially attributable to the fact that user-friendly languages are *interpreted,* rather than *compiled.*

In a compiled language (a category to which most professional high-level languages belong), the code written by the programmer is converted into assembly or machine language before it actually runs. This makes maximum use of the computer's power, but also makes it difficult to trace errors while the program is running. Programs written in an interpreted language are converted into machine language at the same time their instructions are being executed. This means that the computer can report back any programming mistakes while the program is running. It also means the machine is doing double duty, so the instructions are executed more slowly. BASIC (especially early versions) and Apple's HyperCard are both examples of interpreted languages. We'll examine both of these later in this chapter. Dr. T's T-BASIC tries to speed things up by using a fast interpreter that compiles each instruction as it is entered.

Dedicated Languages

Yet another approach to creating music on computers is to use a dedicated language. In the days before MIDI, the computers used to create music were either custom-built research machines—or hulking mainframes and mini-computers from IBM and Digital Equipment Corporation at university computer centers. Designed mostly to keep track of student schedules and overdue library books, these academic computers needed their own special languages to coax them into making music. These languages included Music V (the fifth descendant of Music I), Music 11 (for the DEC PDP-11), and Music 360 (for the IBM 360). Even with such languages, the computers couldn't make sound on their own. They would print the results of their compositional computations onto digital tape, which then had to be converted into analog audio by a separate device. Composing in this environment was not exactly a real-time phenomenon—and was not for the impatient or faint of heart.

There are still composers who like to work this way, writing music directly on a computer, working with non-real-time languages to specify vast arrays of musical parameters, and then sitting back and listening to the results. Fortunately, the computers they are working on are smaller, and are directly connected to sound-producing circuitry. This might be on a separate chassis, on a card inside the computer, or may even be built right into the computer (like the 56001 digital signal processing chip found in the NeXT machine and the Atari Falcon030).

Most of these languages have also recognized the power of MIDI, and have utilities built in that allow data to be input or output via MIDI. The data is used to produce sound through MIDI sound modules, or it is used to control various parameters of the sound-producing hardware in real time. Some examples of these are the Kyma system from Symbolic Sound Corporation for the Macintosh; CSound, written by Barry Vercoe of MIT, which runs on Mac, NeXT, IBM, and UNIX machines; HMSL, an extension of the Forth programming language developed at Mills College (and available for the Mac and Amiga from Frog Peak Music); and Charles Ames's Compose for the Macintosh.

Finally, there are dedicated high-level languages expressly for MIDI applications. These recently developed languages are graphic-oriented, rather than text-oriented, making them potentially much easier for non-programmers to use. Since they are optimized for MIDI manipulation, they can be very fast (even though they may not be fully compiled). Two examples of these are HookUp from Hip Software and Max.

Platforms

Before we get to specific products, let's take a brief look at the general considerations involved in writing software for the various personal computers found in MIDI studios. A typical computer program, like a spreadsheet or database, doesn't give a fig about how fast data comes in or goes out. It runs at whatever speed it feels comfortable. In a MIDI program however, timing is everything. Getting the bits in and out at precisely the right times is a tricky task—and each platform has its own requirements for making this happen.

Apple Macintosh

Almost all Macintoshes have two serial ports—known as the modem and printer ports. Either or both of these can be used for MIDI if they're connected to an appropriate MIDI interface. Getting MIDI to go out the serial ports requires assembly-language drivers that broadcast the appropriate bits at the appropriate times. This is accomplished using operating system interrupts whose timing is based on the computer's internal timers. The MIDI interface translates the serial output into MIDI with a UART (Universal Asynchronous Receiver/Transmitter). MIDI input is handled the same way: the MIDI data comes into the UART and is translated into serial data, which is then read by interrupt-driven software drivers. The Macintosh serial port operates at 1MHz, so dividing and multiplying the clock rate to read and write MIDI (which runs at 1MHz/32) is a simple operation.

Originally, every Macintosh software developer had to write his or her own MIDI drivers. Some drivers were developed and placed into the public domain for intrepid developers. Since none of these had the formal approval of Apple, they tended to become obsolete as Apple changed and upgraded its system software. These drivers all worked on the same principle (and almost all MIDI interfaces were compatible with almost all software). In the very early days, there were three types of Macintosh MIDI interfaces, which were differentiated by the clock speed of their UARTs: 500kHz, 1MHz, and 2MHz. However, putting a software switch into a program to make sure it could run with all available interfaces was a trivial task. Although all standard interfaces operate at 1MHz today, such switches remain in most programs as a relic of those times. (Special devices that use faster speeds, such as the MIDI Time Piece and Studio 5, are discussed later.)

software port and speed switch from Sound Designer

However, even if the different programs used identical drivers, they were incompatible. Although the Macintosh's multitasking System 7 allows several MIDI applications to be in memory at once, it was impossible to get two or more applications to address a port at the same time. One driver would simply prevent any other from working. Solving that problem became the job of MIDI Manager, an addition to Apple's system software that first appeared in 1989.

MIDI Manager provides a standard driver and set of toolbox "calls" that any developer can use. It allows a large number of applications not only to address the serial ports, but also to address each other. In this way, a Patch Editor, for example, could dump its contents into a sequencer without the data ever leaving the computer. MIDI Manager comes from Apple with documentation that, for historical reasons, is written for Pascal programmers. However, most C compilers for the Mac have the ability to read Pascal externals, so this is not a major problem for seasoned programmers.

MIDI Manager had a rocky start. Since it used up a lot of CPU overhead, it slowed the performance of the software (although not the MIDI stream itself) in less powerful Macintoshes. It also dealt with external synchronization in an unclear way. Subsequent releases of the software have cleared up some of the problems, and almost all Macintosh software authoring programs now support MIDI Manager. Many commercial software products still include their own drivers to give users the option of not using MIDI Manager.

IBM-PC and Clones

The IBM-PC and its many clones present a problem for MIDI programmers. Its serial ports are designed to operate at modem speeds (2,400, 9,600, and 19,200 bits per second), which don't divide or multiply evenly into MIDI speed. On the other hand, IBMs have slots for peripheral cards, which early Macs (and today's compact models) lack. Therefore, most IBM MIDI interfaces are on cards.

The first, and for a long time, the predominant way of getting an IBM to speak MIDI was through a system made by Roland, consisting of an external MIDI processor box connected to an internal card, known as the MPU-401. (Cards were also available for the Apple II and Commodore 64, but they didn't catch on.) The cable connecting the components actually became a limiting factor as machines got faster, and Roland eventually came out with a version that brought all of the electronics inside.

The MPU-401 could run in two modes: *Smart* and UART (or "dumb"). In UART mode, it acted like a simple serial interface, dependent on the host machine for all processing and timing—and requiring each program to provide its own output and input drivers.

In Smart mode, it offered eight buffers for MIDI data, each of which could handle sixteen tracks. It could process MIDI data itself and keep track of its own timing, without making the host computer work hard at all. This meant that a slow machine, like the original 8088-based IBM-PC, would have no trouble handling complex MIDI streams. The MPU-401's Smart mode had two problems. Programming it was very difficult. Also, any MIDI commands defined subsequent to the original MIDI spec (such as MIDI Time Code) were not recognized by the card as legitimate MIDI commands.

Another problem arose when multitasking environments became available for the IBM. If two MIDI programs were running, one in Smart mode and the other in UART mode, you could switch from the Smart to the UART program, and the MPU-401 would change modes just fine. However, when you went back to the first program, the MPU's Smart mode would have been lost, and the typical result was a total crash. Programmers who wanted their software to work in all possible environments found they had to work in UART mode, which negated a majority of the advantages that the MPU-401 offered in the first place.

Several manufacturers came out with MPU-compatible cards, using Roland's own chipsets or equivalents of their own design. Many of these cards offered variations: some allowed MIDI Time Code to pass through in Smart mode, while others provided multiple MIDI Outs, and thus extra channels. Some software could take advantage of these extra features, while other programs could not (but at least they were all more or less compatible within the limits of the MPU-401 protocols).

There have been other forms of interfaces, however, which have made life interesting for IBM software writers. Laptop computers don't have room for slots, so some companies make interfaces that really do hang off the serial port. These devices only work with software that can handle the complex mathematics of turning serial port bit rates into MIDI. Still other manufacturers make interfaces that connect to the parallel port. Yamaha was responsible for a couple of unusual implementations. One was a card marketed under the IBM name called Music Feature, which was actually an FB01 eight-voice, four-operator FM synthesizer with MIDI inputs and outputs. This device required a whole new set of tools for its access. Another implementation was an IBM-style computer marketed under Yamaha's own name called the C1. This system had multiple built-in MIDI ports, and required yet another set of programming tools.

With the growth of multimedia, new internal sound-generating cards for the IBM have appeared, many of which have MIDI input and output capability. Some of these are compatible with existing protocols, and some are not. Most recently, the situation has shown signs of calming down a bit, with the introduction of Microsoft's Windows and IBM's OS/2 operating systems. Programming for recent versions of Windows is not unlike using Apple's MIDI Manager. The Media Control Interface introduced with Windows 3.1 allows software and hardware designers to write drivers that talk to the operating system. The operating system itself handles the internal communication, and makes sure that the hardware and software interact properly. The result is that software writers no longer have to write six different versions of every program. And yes, there is an MPU-401 driver for Windows, so no manufacturer's hardware need be obsolete. The Multimedia Presentations Manager/2 under OS/2 has similar potential. In fact, Roland has a version of the MPU-401 for OS/2 (although it's unclear if other MIDI designers will be developing software or hardware for the system).

Commodore Amiga

The Amiga has a single serial port whose rate can easily be changed in software to the MIDI baud rate, so getting it to generate MIDI is actually quite straightforward. An Amiga MIDI interface merely brings the output voltage of the serial port in line with the MIDI specification and provides the required optoisolator. Commodore provides its developers with software tools necessary for addressing the serial port.

The Amiga presented developers with some serious problems when it came to running MIDI in its early incarnations. Although most of those challenges have since been met, the machine remains something of an orphan in the MIDI world. The early problems were due largely to the fact that the Amiga was designed as a true multitasking computer, so providing an accurate, steady timing reference for a single application was difficult. Interrupts generated by the operating system for tasks that had nothing to do with MIDI (like redrawing the screen) could occur at any time—and this would cause timing problems in the MIDI stream.

Successful Amiga MIDI developers use a timer for the serial port other than the normal operating system. For example, The Blue Ribbon SoundWorks (whose Bars and Pipes is probably the leading Amiga sequencer) uses timing information from one of the computer's four audio channels. This channel is set up at a carefully controlled sample rate to act as a master clock for the application. Another trick that Bars and Pipes recommends to developers is to limit the number of screen colors to eight, so that screen redrawing doesn't occupy too much of the computer's time.

Since the one serial port can run at any of a variety of speeds, it would be possible to have it generate several MIDI streams, multiplexed together. These could then be broken up into individual MIDI cables. In fact, Blue Ribbon manufactures such a device, which has three separate MIDI lines. Alternatively, expansion boards for the serial port are available. These can potentially be used for multiple MIDI interfaces, or to run MIDI and another application in the port at the same time.

Atari ST

The Atari ST was considered a major player in the MIDI world right from the beginning because it has built-in MIDI In and Out jacks, as well as a non-standard Thru function. Introduced soon after the Apple Macintosh, the ST was far more popular among MIDI users in Europe than in North America. This was partially due to the fact that the price differentials between the two machines, while significant in America, were astronomical in most of Europe.

The native Atari operating system, GEM, comes with its own MIDI drivers and makes it comparatively easy to write simple MIDI programs for the Atari. Advanced programmers may find GEM a bit slow and cumbersome, or that mouse movements or clicks can induce timing errors. Some programmers have hacked their way through the operating system—rewriting the screen display code or throwing out menus and desk accessories in order to maximize the timing accuracy. This, as you might expect, requires some fairly hefty assembly-language chops.

The single Midi In jack means that, if you want to use Midi Sync or MTC with a program and input other midi data at the same time, you need an external hardware merger. The single Midi Out jack precludes multiple-cable systems, but various manufacturers have developed multiple-cable boxes that hook onto the computer's serial port. These devices are all based on similar designs, so the major software suppliers have found it relatively simple to accommodate all the different hardware boxes.

The latest Atari, the Falcon030, uses a standard midi jack configuration. It also features an on-board S6001 DSP chip for relatively simple integration of high-quality digital audio with other applications.

Other Platforms

The personal-computer market does not stand still, and attention must be paid to new companies entering the field. The NeXT computer showed great potential for the musician, but the promised commercial midi software for the platform has yet to materialize. The machine remains popular for research and development, especially in applications that include digital audio.

Silicon Graphics may be the next major player in the field with their introduction of the relatively low-cost Iris Indigo. The company has put together an impressive team of music and audio professionals, headed by former Todd Rundgren keyboardist Roger Powell. (Powell was the author of one of the first midi sequencing programs for the PC.) Although no midi products for the Iris Indigo have yet appeared, a good deal of development seems to be underway at several software companies.

Midi Programming Tools

Now we're going to take a look at three commercial products for the Apple Macintosh that are designed to allow midi users to create their own custom applications. There are similar development systems for other computers, but the platform that currently supports the most diverse collection of midi tools is the Macintosh.

MidiBasic

Basic is one of the easiest programming languages to learn. In fact, early personal computers (like the Apple II and Commodore 64) used it as their native programming dialect. With the advent of high-powered user-configurable information handling programs like Excel, 4th Dimension, Omnis, and Lotus 1-2-3, the need for a simple programming language has diminished. Thus, basic is not nearly as popular as it used to be. It's still worthwhile for doing small chores, however, and basic programmers can do some very neat things with midi via MidiBasic. This program is made by Altech Systems (not the speaker manufacturer) of Shreveport, Louisiana. It is technically a library of machine-level routines that can be accessed with special commands from a program running in a popular dialect of basic on the Macintosh, Microsoft's QuickBasic. The commands can be loaded into a basic program with ResEdit, Apple's software for moving *resources,* or special chunks of code, from one place to another. Alternatively, commands can be loaded by including the command *LIBRARY MIDIBASIC* at the beginning of the program, which finds the routines and loads them into memory.

The MidiBasic command set is fairly simple. It includes instructions for setting up input and output buffers, counting how much data is in them, getting and sending strings of data to and from the buffers, filtering data, time-stamping data as it comes in, echoing data, rechannelizing data, setting tempos for outgoing data, and sending and receiving Timing Clocks. Armed with these, and the extensive commands available in QuickBasic, you can create an enormous variety of MIDI programs, both simple and complex. One drawback of MIDIBASIC is that it's not compatible with MIDI Manager, so any programs created with it cannot be used simultaneously with any other MIDI programs.

Here is a simple example of a MIDIBASIC program. We'll leave out the commands that deal with housekeeping and setting up buffers, interfaces, arrays, and so on—and just show you the kernel of the program.

This routine (written by Allen Marsalis) lets you create ten chords of up to ten notes each and store them in memory, and then recall them by playing a single note.

```
MidiThru                                                          Turn on MIDI Thru so you can hear the
                                                                  notes you are playing.
NextChord:
      ChordCount=ChordCount+1 : PRINT
      PRINT "Hit note in chord";ChordCount;"which you'll use to play back chord"
      Status = 0
      Data2 = 0
      WHILE (Status < 144 ) OR (Status > 159) OR (Data2 < 1)     Read incoming MIDI data. Unless the
            MEvtIn Status, Data1, Data2, Time&                    Status byte is between 144 and 159—a
      WEND                                                        Note On—and the second data byte—
      BaseNotes(ChordCount) = Data1                               velocity—is not zero, ignore it.
      PRINT "Hit mouse button to finish building chord";ChordCount
            NoteNumber=0

NextNote:
      NoteNumber=NoteNumber+1
      PRINT "Hit note";NoteNumber;"in chord";ChordCount;"or mouse to quit"
      Status = 0
      Data2 = 0
      WHILE (Status < 144 ) OR (Status > 159) OR (Data2 < 1)
            MEvtIn Status, Data1, Data2, Time&
            IF MOUSE(0) < 0 THEN EndNote                          Click the mouse if you want to stop
      WEND                                                        building the chord.
      ChordNotes(ChordCount,NoteNumber) = Data1
      IF NoteNumber < 10 THEN NextNote                            If you've recorded ten notes, go on to the
                                                                  next chord.
EndNote:
      NoteCount(ChordCount) = NoteNumber-1
      IF ChordCount = 10 THEN Play
      INPUT "Build another chord (Y) or (N) ";answer$
      IF answer$<>"N" AND answer$<>"n" THEN NextChord             Whenever you want to stop, or when
                                                                  you've built ten chords, you can play them
Play:                                                             back.
      CLS : PRINT "Now ready to play....Hit mouse to Quit"
      MidiThru 0                                                  Turn off MIDI Thru.

Note:
      WHILE MOUSE(0) > -1                                         Click the mouse to stop.
            MEvtIn Status, Data1, Data2, Time&                    Get a note.
            Flag = 0
            FOR ChordPlay=1 TO ChordCount
                  IF BaseNotes(ChordPlay) = Data1 THEN            If the incoming note matches one we have
                        GOSUB PlayChord                           in memory, play the chord associated with
                        Flag = -1                                 it.
                        ChordPlay = ChordCount + 1
                  END IF
            NEXT ChordPlay
      END

PlayChord:
      FOR i=1 TO NoteCount(ChordPlay)
            Result = 0
            WHILE Result = 0
                  MidiNow Status, ChordNotes(ChordPlay,i), Data2,  Play the notes in the chord.
                        Result
            WEND
      NEXT i
RETURN
```

Strictly speaking, all the variable names in this program should be followed with percent signs (%), which is Microsoft's way of letting you specify that you want them to be integer variables. These variables are a lot faster and easier for the computer to handle than floating-point variables. This program (with a lot more bells and whistles for dealing with non-note data) took the original programmer about an hour to construct. Once you get used to BASIC, MIDIBASIC requires very little additional understanding—and if you're clever, you can do some very interesting things with it.

Unlike some earlier versions of BASIC, QuickBASIC lets you save your finished program as either a run-time or standalone application. A *run-time* application needs a special, *play-only* version of BASIC to operate, which interprets the program as it goes along. If you give the program to someone else, you also have to give him or her the run-time version of BASIC. A program compiled as a standalone application is "double-clickable" in Mac terms. This means that the program needs no companion software, and so can run quite fast. A compiled MIDIBASIC application can be fast enough to do real-time sequencing. In fact, a simple sixteen-track sequencer comes with the MIDIBASIC software when you buy it, along with the original source code so you can analyze the programming techniques.

HyperMIDI

As mentioned earlier, HyperCard is a highly user-friendly development system that Apple started giving away with all Macintoshes in 1987. It can be used to create databases, make interactive presentations, crunch numbers, or do any of a huge number of tasks. It is graphically oriented, and uses HyperTalk, a programming language that was designed to be as close to plain English as any computer language yet developed. (In 1992, Apple stopped giving away HyperCard. A run-time version is still included with all Macs, but the full development system has to be purchased from the company's Claris division.)

One of HyperCard's most important features is that it is extendible. By the addition of external commands and functions (XCMDs and XFCNs), it can be taught to do tasks it was not originally designed to do. These commands and functions are small programs written in C or assembly language, and put inside HyperCard with a resource editor. Several sets of externals are available for doing MIDI chores with HyperCard. Opcode's MIDIPlay, and a few others, are designed for editing and playing back MIDI files or specific MIDI commands. A more extensive set of tools, which accommodate both MIDI input and output, is contained in EarLevel Engineering's HyperMIDI.

The original HyperMIDI was shareware, but when developer Nigel Redmon came out with the 2.0 version, he decided to make it into a commercial product. The shareware version is still available, but it lacks many of the more advanced features of the commercial version. Also, the shareware version is not compatible with MIDI Manager, while the 2.0 version is not only compatible with MIDI Manager, it requires it.

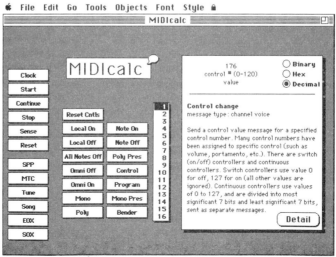

a HyperMIDI card

The command set for HyperMidi is extensive, and quite powerful. Through Midi Manager, it can address up to six different input ports and six output ports. It can synchronize either to Midi Clocks or Midi Time Code, and it can keep track of time-stamped events with a resolution of one millisecond. It has special commands for transposing, filtering, echoing, delaying, channelizing, and velocity-mapping Midi data. In addition, it has utilities for converting between various types of data (numeric or alphabetic)—and for reading and writing both Midi files and unformatted binary data files (for patch dumps).

One of the most powerful tools in HyperMidi is a *slider maker*. This lets you create a movable on-screen slider of any size that can generate any kind of data you want. You can set upper and lower limits for the output data. You can also specify a delay between subsequent bytes to prevent overloading Midi buffers in receiving devices. Sliders are especially useful in patch-editing programs, where each parameter can have its own slider. HyperMidi's slider maker even has provisions for calculating and sending checksums on the fly for those synthesizers that demand a checksum with every received SysEx command. Sliders are also useful in algorithmic composing or file playback programs, where they can be used to scale Velocity or Volume, make Controller changes, or set up real-time transpositions.

Here's a HyperMidi card in which the sliders all send out Controller 07 on the various Midi channels—in other words, it's a cheap mixing console.

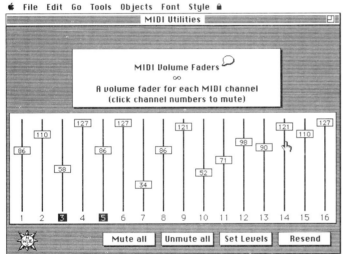

HyperMidi slider fun

Here are a couple of examples of HyperMidi *scripts*. A script is the set of HyperTalk commands associated with a HyperCard object (or *handler*), which might be a button, a card, a field containing text or numbers, or an idle state. These examples do not contain all the setup and housekeeping commands, but simply provide the scripts for the individual handlers. When a single button is pressed, this routine plays an arpeggiated C major triad, with each note one-half second after the previous one.

```
on mousedown
    hmWritemidi "144 60 64 500:144 60 0"
    && "144 64 64 1000:144 64 0"
    && "144 67 64 1500:144 67 0"
    && "144 72 64 2000:144 72 0"
end mousedown
```

The && concatenates each line with the one before it, inserting a space (so this is actually all one command). HyperMidi assumes decimal numbers (you can use hex if you precede the numbers with an *hmConvert* command), so the *144* is a Note On on Channel 1, the *60* is Middle C, and *64* is the velocity. The *500:* is a timing mark, in milliseconds. It says that 500 milliseconds after the command starts to execute, send a Note On, number 60, with velocity 0—in other words, a Note Off. Then immediately send a Note On, number 64 (E), and at the 1000-millisecond mark, send the appropriate Note Off, and so forth.

Now here's a script that takes incoming MIDI notes, transposes them an octave up, inverts their velocity (high velocities become low and vice versa), and sends them out on a MIDI channel three higher than the one it came in on. (The line with the number string maps each channel so that the output is three higher than the input—and wraps around channels above 13.)

```
on opencard
  hmSetEcho 1,1                route incoming MIDI directly to output
  hmSetTranspose 1,"+12"       transpose notes up one octave
  hmSetVelocity 1, "!"         invert the velocity response
  hmSetChannel 1,"4 5 6 7 8 9 10 11 12 13 14 15 16 1 2 3"
end opencard
```

Finally, let's create a slider that can adjust the LFO speed of a patch on a DX7 tuned to receive Channel 1. HyperMIDI includes a stack called *Slider Edit* that does most of the work for you. Open that stack, and enter the following values:

min: 0
max: 99
slider message: 240 67 16 1 8 x 247

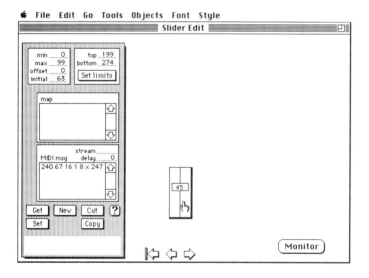

Now every time you move the slider, it sends out this complete message, which is a System Exclusive message that addresses that particular parameter of that particular synthesizer. The position of the slider (a number from 0 to 99) is substituted for the "x." You can now use the Slider Edit stack to copy this slider in its entirety into a custom stack of your own.

Max

Max is a graphical programming language developed by Miller Puckette (at IRCAM), and David Zicarelli (author of M, Opcode's first DX7 editor, and many other significant MIDI programs). It was named in honor of Max Mathews, who was the founder of the computer music laboratory at Bell Labs and is considered to be the father of computer music. Max was introduced in 1990, and is available commercially on the Macintosh from Opcode Systems. Another version of it is distributed by IRCAM, as part of a complete workstation based around the NeXT computer. We've talked a little bit about Max in previous chapters, but here we'll discuss it in more detail.

Max consists of a library of *objects* that the user puts on a screen and connects with *patch cords*. Objects, which are actually little modules of code written in C, can have inlets and outlets for receiving and sending data. For example, a simple button with one outlet that triggers an action is called a *bang*. A clock module, which sends out a bang at regular intervals, is called a *metro*. It has two inlets, one for turning it on and off, and the other for setting its speed. A *number box* displays data going through it. A *toggle* acts as an alternating on/off switch. There are also a full set of arithmetic, logical, and relational objects, as well as delay lines, switches, and gates.

More specific to MIDI applications are *notein* and *noteout* objects for inputting and outputting MIDI bytes. *Makenote* creates a Note On followed, after a specified time, by a Note Off. Sliders, rotary dials, and on-screen keyboards provide graphic displays of settings. *Bendin, pgmin, ctlin, polyin,* and their complementary output objects respectively control Pitch Bend, Program Change, Controller, and Key Pressure messages. All told, there are about 150 objects in Max's vocabulary.

A complete program in Max is called a *patch*, which is very true to the original meaning of the word (which described the interconnection of modules in an analog synthesizer). Here is an example of a simple Max patch.

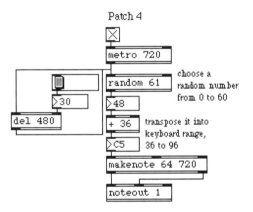

At the top of the patch is a toggle, which turns the metro module on and off. When metro is on, it outputs a bang every 720 milliseconds. These bangs go to a random number generator, which chooses a number from 0 to 60. They also go to a delay line, whose delay time is adjusted using the slider (the "480" in the delay object is just an initial value). The delay line generates a second bang, which also triggers the random number generator. In this way, the random number generator puts out two numbers every 720 milliseconds. The difference in time between these two numbers (and therefore, the rhythm) is specified by the delay slider.

The random number generator's output is increased by 36, so that it is in the normal MIDI note range. (You don't want to listen to too many MIDI notes lower than 36.) This goes to a makenote module, which plays the note with a velocity of 64 and a duration of 720 milliseconds, and sends it out the MIDI port.

Once you create a patch, you can turn it into a *subpatch* and use it just like an object to simplify and save space on the screen display. Other tools for making patches easier to look at are a *Segmented Patch Cords* option, which lets you make patch cords out of right-angled segments, as well as a *Hide On Lock* command. This command hides any selected objects and/or patch cords when you've finished working with a patch, and "locks" it to prevent anything from happening to it.

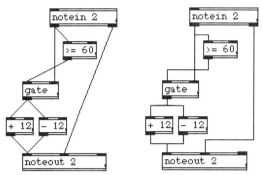

normal and segmented patch cords

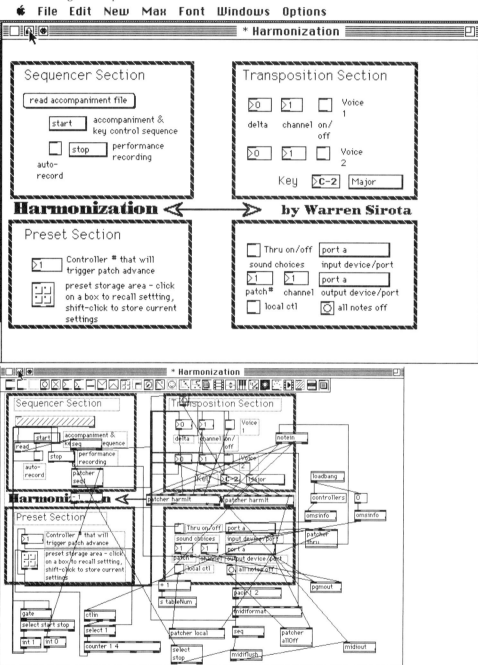

a complex patch, locked and unlocked

This brief description merely scratches the surface of the power of Max. In just the first couple of years since its release, dozens of developers have created complex custom patches for many functions. These include editors and librarians for General MIDI sound modules and reverb and effects units, MIDI analysis tools, algorithmic composition programs, and even complete console automation systems. Any Max patch can be analyzed by anyone who owns the program, and so the community of developers who share knowledge and techniques has grown quickly.

Max is programmed like an interpreted language, but runs more like a compiled one. That's because most of the work is done by the object boxes themselves, which are small C programs. When you connect boxes with patch cords, the language also immediately makes sure those connections are coded as efficiently as possible. For particularly complicated patches, an *Overdrive* mode is available, which ensures that the data I/O gets the highest priority—and that screen redrawings and other nonessential functions are allowed to slow down to get out of the way.

Like HyperCard, Max is extensible, and many Max developers are constantly creating new objects to tackle new tasks. Some of these are distributed to other Max users by their creators, while others are supported by Opcode and included in the company's periodic upgrades to Max. Symantec's Think C is used to create new objects—and Opcode supplies developers with the necessary hooks and tools, along with extensive documentation.

The extensions for accessing digital audio files were created at CNMAT in Berkeley, California. These are now part of the Max package. There are also extensions that allow the system to accept data from Bio Control Systems' Biomuse and the Mattel Power Glove through a GoldBrick interface. Max has a number of multimedia-oriented extensions, including commands for playing QuickTime movies, as well as controlling CD audio, CD-ROM, and video laser disc players. Max also has an extension for displaying PICT files, which can be treated as "sprites" and/or strung together in a sequence to make animations. Here is an example of a patch that accesses a CD-ROM player from a MIDI keyboard. The on-screen *comment boxes* explain how it works (thanks to David Roach).

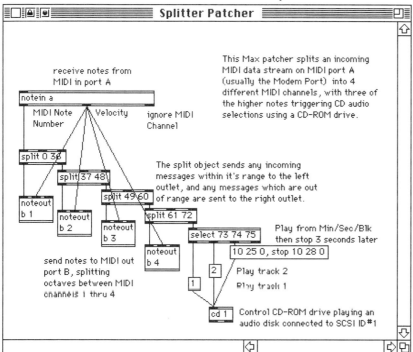

David Roach's CD-ROM splitter

Writers of Max patches are encouraged to distribute their products independently of Opcode, but at present, patches require an accompanying run-time version of the language in order to work. Opcode makes this available as Maxplay, which sells for about $100. Patch creators can buy multiple copies of Maxplay from Opcode at half price, and pass it along with their patches to customers who don't have either the full system or the run-time version. This situation may be only temporary: an "installer" program has been written for Max that can turn patches into standalone double-clickable applications which won't need Maxplay. Opcode is now considering making this program available to developers.

Although Max was created for music applications, some users apply the program to non-musical tasks. Bio Control Systems uses Max to monitor physiological data. Some programmers are creating complicated business projections with Max instead of using conventional spreadsheet programs. Codeveloper Zicarelli certainly considers Max to be far more than just a music program when he calls it "the most flexible and powerful environment for writing C code." He points out that "unlike writing an entire application from scratch, you can write a little fragment and interconnect this fragment with other possibilities to make the most out of it."

As powerful and fast a language as Max is, it presents a very intuitive interface, making it an attractive tool for programmers at all levels and from many different disciplines. It may not replace Excel in the boardrooms of corporate America, but it promises to be a major player in the development of music and multimedia software in the next few years.

Chapter 13

MIDI Into the Future

MIDI has survived and thrived because it can expand and evolve without changing its basic nature. The hardware hasn't changed much, nor is it likely to. MIDI jacks and cables will probably always remain the same. However, at the software level, the creators of MIDI deliberately left many doors open for adding new commands to the MIDI language. In fact, as MIDI has evolved, the number of doors has even increased, along with the numerous additions to MIDI 1.0—some small and some larger than the original spec itself.

What's important about all these changes is that they are retroactively compatible, which means that they do not make any existing MIDI equipment obsolete. If you send a MIDI device a command that was added to the MIDI spec after the device was made, the device simply ignores the command. For example, if you send a MIDI Machine Control Locate command to a Roland MSQ-700 (which is an older hardware sequencer), nothing happens. However, more recent devices can be designed to respond to the new parts of the MIDI language, so a new version of a software sequencer that understands MMC will locate itself correctly when it receives such a command.

Most changes in MIDI are new commands: additions to the spec. Occasionally an existing command will be redefined, but only if the MIDI community agrees that such a redefinition will not cause problems in any current equipment. Before we talk about some of the recent changes to the MIDI language, let's look at the mechanism by which these changes are made.

Who's in Charge Here?

Nobody owns MIDI. MIDI is in the public domain—and anyone is welcome to implement it in their hardware or software without asking permission or seeking a license. (As you will see, the one thing you can't do is publish the MIDI specification.) Two nonprofit, volunteer organizations oversee the specification: the MIDI Manufacturers Association and the Japan MIDI Standards Committee. The MIDI Manufacturers Association (MMA) is made up of companies in America and Europe. Most of the major producers of MIDI hardware and software in the U.S., Canada, and Europe are members of the MMA. Along with them are pro-audio companies who may or may not currently include MIDI in their products but have potential interest in it. The membership also includes publishers of both magazines and music, computer companies (including Apple, IBM, Atari, and Microsoft), and a few independent consultants (including the authors of this book). Membership in the MMA is not cheap, but it is open to all who are actively involved in the design or manufacture of MIDI products. Each member, regardless of size, gets one vote. The Japan MIDI Standards Committee (JMSC) has traditionally consisted mostly of the major music hardware companies in Japan: Yamaha, Roland, Korg, Casio, Kawai, and so on. Recently, the membership has expanded to include software makers and other smaller manufacturers.

These organizations, contrary to some people's perception, do not act as "The MIDI Police," telling manufacturers when they are doing something wrong. The MIDI community itself does that. Suppose a piece of equipment comes out that does something horrible in response to perfectly respectable MIDI commands—or periodically sends a load of digital junk down the MIDI line that causes other equipment to lock up or scramble itself. The manufacturer will hear about the problems from users, distributors, and magazine reviewers long before any official organization could act on them. In almost all cases, the manufacturer can correct the problems, although sometimes a manufacturer may be forced to pull the offending product from the market. Needless to say, this costs a lot of money, so manufacturers are generally careful to get their MIDI implementations right the first time.

The primary roles of the MMA and JMSC are to propose and approve changes to the MIDI specification. Each organization can independently propose a change, but both have to agree to it before it becomes part of the spec.

How Does MIDI Get Changed?

In the MMA, the mechanism for making a change in the spec is fairly straightforward. The first step is for a member to propose it. (Someone outside the organization can actually make the proposal, but a member has to be the official sponsor of it.) A working group of several members is then set up. This group includes a chairman (usually the person making the proposal) and anyone else interested in contributing to the proposal. Each working group also has a technical representative, who is a member of the MMA's Technical Standards Board (elected each year by the membership). The proposal is then debated, with most of the debate taking place electronically. All MMA members are currently offered memberships on PAN, an international computer communications network set up to serve the music industry. A private, members-only forum is set up to discuss MMA issues. The pros and cons of the issue are debated, and changes in the proposal are often made as the debate goes on. (Some proposals don't get past this stage, if the opposition is too great, or if there isn't enough interest.) When the debate is over, and the proposal has been molded into its most acceptable form, the Technical Standards Board decides that it is ready for a vote. Proposals are also published in a document called the *Technical Standards Board Bulletin* (*TSBB*), which comes out a couple of times a year, and is distributed to all members. The TSBB contains the text of all current proposals (although sometimes a particularly large proposal will get published separately), as well as texts or summaries of the discussion surrounding each proposal. If there are proposals that are ready to be voted on, a ballot is sent out. Members are asked to vote by mail or electronically within a specified period of time. A majority of voting members is enough to pass a proposal. If a member votes against a proposal, he or she is encouraged to state the reasons why. This way, if the proposal is defeated, discussion can continue on it until it becomes something acceptable to a sufficient number of members.

After the MMA approves a proposal, it is then sent to the JMSC. If the JMSC rejects it, it tells the MMA why. In most cases, changes can be made in the proposal to satisfy the JMSC. The MMA votes again on the altered proposal, and it is resubmitted to the JMSC. The process can work the other way around, with the JMSC proposing a change to the spec, and the MMA accepting or rejecting it. The two organizations have worked extremely well together over the years. Although there have been differences of opinion, and a few proposals sent back by one or the other for revisions, this cooperation has allowed MIDI to mature and progress quite smoothly. Only when the MMA and JMSC have passed a proposal are manufacturers allowed to use it in their products. A manufacturer who implements an unapproved version of a new addition to the spec runs the risk that the addition will be changed during the debate process. In fact, this has occurred on a couple of occasions, and the manufacturers were forced to upgrade products that were already in customers' hands in order to make them conform with the final version of the addition.

Another responsibility of MMA members is to keep discussions of new proposals confidential within the organization. The purpose of this is not to exclude the organization's workings from outside influence or scrutiny, but to prevent proposals being released to non-members prematurely. If an early version of a proposal shows up in a magazine article (and this has happened), there is the possibility that readers might think they were seeing an official change in the MIDI spec. This might cause readers to start to develop software around the published information. However, the approved proposal might be quite different from what was published, and they would have to do everything all over again when the change in the spec was officially released.

Confirmation/Approvals and Recommended Practices

There are two types of additions that can be made to MIDI: a *Confirmation/ Approval* and a *Recommended Practice*. A Confirmation/Approval is needed when a new command is created, or an existing command is redefined. A Recommended Practice usually concerns a new application of existing commands—or may be a formalization of a function or application that some manufacturers are already implementing. An exception to this division is that a new Universal System Exclusive command is considered a Confirmation/ Approval if the first sub-ID (which creates a new family of commands) is newly defined. If it is the second sub-ID (a new command within an existing family that is newly defined), the addition is considered a Recommended Practice.

Thus, MIDI Time Code is a Confirmation/Approval. Standard MIDI Files and General MIDI are Recommended Practices (except for General MIDI On/Off commands, which are Universal System Exclusive commands with unique first sub-IDs). Confirmation/Approvals are considered part of the MIDI specification, while Recommended Practices are considered as separate documents.

Recommended Practices are not completely binding. For example, if a new synthesizer comes out, it does not have to have a General MIDI mode (a Recommended Practice). However, if it does have a General MIDI mode, it must respond to the General MIDI On and Off commands (a Confirmation/Approval). If a sequencer manufacturer wants to use a format other than Standard MIDI Files (a Recommended Practice) for storage, it may (and in fact, most do).

System Exclusive Numbers

The other function of the MMA and JMSC is to assign System Exclusive ID numbers to manufacturers. Many members don't need SysEx IDs. However, if a manufacturer wants to have its devices talk to each other using SysEx commands, it must apply for an ID and pay a fee. The appropriate governing group issues the manufacturer a unique ID. If the manufacturer later decides it doesn't want the ID (or goes out of business) and has produced no products that use it, the ID number can be reassigned. When SysEx IDs were single bytes, they were considered prime commodities, and so making sure that all IDs were actually in use was important. Now that the three-byte convention has been adopted, there's more room for flexibility. However, it's still crucial that manufacturers do not simply appropriate SysEx ID numbers, but get them through legitimate channels from the governing body in order to avoid potentially serious conflicts.

The International MIDI Association

The other organization closely involved with MIDI is the International MIDI Association (IMA). The IMA offers memberships to anyone interested in MIDI, and periodically publishes a bulletin discussing changes in the MIDI spec, new applications, and significant new products. While MIDI itself is in the public domain, the right to publish the MIDI specification is assigned exclusively to the IMA. The IMA sells copies of the basic spec, and copies of large additions to the spec (such as MIDI Machine Control and MIDI Show Control). You don't have to be an IMA member to buy these documents, but members do get discounts.

The New Additions

Since the MIDI spec was first adopted, many new commands have been added to it that have had a profound effect on the way people use MIDI. Two of the most significant additions have been MIDI Sample Dump Standard and MIDI Time Code, discussed earlier. There have also been small changes, such as the assignation of MIDI General Purpose Controllers and Registered and Non-Registered Parameters. Except for MIDI Time Code's Quarter-Frame messages, all the changes in the specification have been in two areas. The first is definitions of various Continuous Controllers. The second is new Universal System Exclusive commands (which make it possible to create a nearly limitless number of new commands). Since the MMA and JMSC were formed, there have been over a hundred proposals to add to or modify the MIDI language in these areas. Most of these proposals have passed. Here are some examples of items recently approved by the governing bodies, which indicate some of the directions MIDI is taking in its second decade.

Bank Select

The Bank Select message was added to the MIDI specification in 1990 as a newly defined Continuous Controller. In the first years of MIDI, 128 programs per device was considered sufficient, even extravagant. Newer devices, however, have program memory that can hold hundreds of different sounds—and some can also access external memory such as cartridges, RAM or ROM cards, and disks. Many of these devices have program maps that let you assign MIDI Program Change numbers to any of their 128 programs. However, there needed to be a way to access these programs without that kind of user preparation. The Bank Select message was the answer.

Probably to avoid numerical confusion, Controller 00 was not assigned to anything during MIDI's first years. Modulation Wheel, the first controller, is number 01. So Controller 00 was an obvious choice for Bank Select. Bank Select is a two-byte (14-bit) command, with its Least Significant Byte expressed as Controller 20H (32 decimal) and the Most Significant Byte as Controller 00. A Bank Select message has no immediate effect on a sound—it simply selects the memory bank from which subsequent Program Change messages will get their sounds. It sets the number of programs now accessible via MIDI at: 128 (MSB) × 128 (LSB) × 128 (Program Changes), or just over two million.

There is an unfortunate problem with the Bank Select message. Most 14-bit Controllers can be sent without their LSB. In fact, the majority of sequencers and synthesizers only recognize the MSBs (Controllers 0 through 31)—and for all intents and purposes, the LSBs (Controllers 32 through 63) don't exist. The Bank Select definition, however, departs from this convention and specifically states that you must always send both bytes. Unfortunately, quite a few manufacturers have been careless in their implementation of Bank Select. Some devices transmit only one byte—either the LSB or the MSB. Others, when receiving Bank Select, treat it the way they do every other 14-bit Controller. They ignore Controller 32 (the LSB) and look for Controller 0 (the MSB). If the transmitter sending the Bank Select command is sending an LSB (either by itself or in combination with the MSB), a receiver that ignores the LSB will not switch banks. The result is that until every manufacturer gets its act together, whenever you use Bank Select, you need to know how the receiving device implements the command.

Portamento Control and Legato Footswitch

Portamento (41H, 65 decimal) is one of the original MIDI Continuous Controllers. It switches the glide function of a synthesizer on and off. The time it takes for such a glide to occur is Controller 05 (although how the values of 0 through 127 translate to milliseconds or seconds has been left up to each manufacturer). Portamento Control and the Legato Footswitch are newly defined Controllers, designed to provide more control over these functions. Portamento Control is effective in Poly mode, and Legato Footswitch when moving between modes.

Traditionally, when a polyphonic synth is sent a Portamento On command, it glides to any notes subsequently played. How these glides are handled is dependent on the individual synth's design. Especially when moving from one chord to another, voices may cross, some glides may take longer than others, and changing just one note may cause glides to occur on several notes. Glides might occur only between held notes, or from the last notes played, even if they are not being held when the new notes are played. Portamento Control straightens out these ambiguities.

Chapter 13 **MIDI Into the Future** • 227

Portamento Control is Controller number 54H (84 decimal), and was adopted in 1992. Its third byte is the note number of the source of the glide, that is, the note being glided from. When a Portamento Control message is sent followed by a Note On, the Note On will start at the pitch specified in the Portamento Control message, and then glide to the pitch specified in the Note On. By itself, the Portamento Control message does nothing. It only affects the next note played. This allows individual control over the source and destination of notes within a glided chord. By sticking a Portamento Control command in between the notes of a chord, an individual note within that chord can be glided to without affecting the others. By interspersing Portamento commands and notes, different notes can be glided in opposite directions. The time of the glide is still controlled by Controller 05. By and large, this command is designed to be used in sequencers, where commands can be timed with precision. It's doubtful that this feature will be of much practical use in live performance.

Legato Footswitch (44H, 68 decimal), adopted late in 1991, addresses a different aspect of this function. This Controller is highly useful in live performance. Like most Controllers in its numerical range, it is a switch—so that values below 64 (decimal) are considered Off while values 64 and above are considered On. When a synthesizer receives a Legato Footswitch On command it goes into Mono mode, so it can only sound one note at a time. Legato style involves playing a new note before the previous note is released. This styling changes the pitch, but does not retrigger the envelope. (Whether the notes glide or not is controlled by Controllers 41H or 54H.) When Legato Footswitch is off, the synth reverts to whatever mode it was in previously, whether polyphonic or monophonic.

While Legato Footswitch already exists on many synthesizers, until 1991, there was no standard way to access it. Some synths do it automatically when they receive a Mono On command (Controller 7EH), while others need an extra System Exclusive command (or a Portamento On) to keep the new notes from re-attacking. This Controller provides a simple, universally acceptable method for putting synths into Legato mode—and separates the legato function from the Portamento function. Obviously, existing synths will not respond to Legato Footswitch, but new synths (or upgrades of older models) will be able to take advantage of it. The designers of the command pointed out in their presentation to the MMA that the command was not only applicable to keyboard-based synthesizers. MIDI guitar players could use it to switch between solo and rhythm (chordal) modes. Wind-controller players could use it to switch between a true wind-style, single-note playing mode, and a polyphonic mode that lets them "paint" chords with arpeggios and sustain pedal.

File Dump

One of the things left out of the original Standard MIDI File Recommended Practice was a way to communicate files over a MIDI line. Standard MIDI Files are great as a medium of exchange between different sequencers and other programs on disk. It is also possible to send MIDI files over a telephone line using modems, and in some cases, through the "clipboard" memory of a multitasking computer. However, the only way to get a file to transfer from one device to another over a MIDI line was to play it. This means that file names, tempo information, markers, and other nonperformance data get lost in the transfer. Since one of the major uses of Standard MIDI Files in post-production situations has been to exchange tempo maps for synchronization purposes, this is a serious limitation. It also means that timings are not preserved perfectly. Simultaneous events can exist in a MIDI file, but not on a single MIDI line—and the errors introduced could be quite detrimental to the music, particularly after multiple transfers.

File Dump is a Recommended Practice. Its set of commands falls under the category of Non-Real-Time Universal System Exclusive, and the F0 7EH header is followed by a sub-ID of 07. It is made up of several different messages. The Dump Header includes a parameter that can identify the file as a MIDI file, a Macintosh file, an MS-DOS (IBM) file, or one of several other formats. It also can contain a file name, and the number of *Data Packets* that are to be sent subsequently. The Data Packets follow, each containing up to 128 bytes of file data. An unlimited number of Packets can be sent, each identified by a unique number, and each with a checksum byte to ensure correct transmission. An End of File message then follows (which is particularly important if the length of the file was not specified in the header). There are also some optional commands, which can be used in a closed-loop system, like handshaking flags, including *ACK* (acknowledgment of the last Packet sent), *NAK* (non-acknowledgment and retry request), *Cancel*, and *Wait*. All of these are sent back from the receiving device to the transmitting device. There is also a Dump Request message, which enables a receiver to initiate a File Dump.

MIDI Show Control

MIDI Show Control, adopted in 1991, is among the larger additions to the MIDI spec, and potentially, the most revolutionary. It is a set of new Universal Real-Time System Exclusive commands, with a sub-ID of 02.

Live shows—including rock concerts, Broadway musicals, and museum exhibits—have become more and more reliant on high technology in recent years. A large number of computerized systems for executing lighting cues, moving curtains and backdrops, activating robots, shooting off fireworks, and many other aspects of live performance have appeared on the market to meet that need. As you might expect, few of these systems are able to communicate with others, a situation analogous to the state of electronic musical instruments before MIDI.

MIDI Show Control (MSC) is an attempt to standardize the command language of live performance. The original proposal came from outside the MIDI world. It was conceived by the United States Institute for Theatre Technology, and brought to the MMA by Richmond Sound Design, a Canadian company specializing in theater sound and automation. It doesn't necessarily replace the communications protocols that exist between controllers and devices within certain systems: for example, remote light dimmer boxes still have to be connected to the lights they control with a dedicated cable. However, MSC provides a way for the various systems to communicate with each other so they can be controlled from one central computerized station, much like a MIDI studio is controlled from a sequencer. As MIDI does with musical instruments, MIDI Show Control allows for manual operation of performance events, as well as automatic control (sequenced and/or timecode-based).

STAGE MANAGER® 3000 by Richmond Sound Design. EM Demo Show		
LIGHTS	2.	House Lights Up
SOUND	2.	Walk-in Music
MECHANICS	2.	Curtain In
PROJECTION	2.	Pre-show slides
PYRO	10.	Opening Spectacular-Explosions

LIGHTS Cue List 1		
00:00:13		
PRESS F10	2.	House Lights Up
00:29:30:00.0	6.5.	House Lights Out
PRESS F10	10.	Opening Spectacular-Lightning
00:00:02:15.0	11.	X-Fade to Red – Auto Follow

SOUND Cue List 2		
00:00:13		
PRESS F10	2.	Walk-in Music
00:15:00:00.0	4.	Slow fade up – Walk-in Music
PRESS F10	10.	Opening Spectacular-Thunder
PRESS F10	20.	Attack Noises

SFX Cue List 3		
00:00:13		
00:30:00:00.0	7.	Gentle Earthquake
PRESS F10	10.	Opening Spectacular-Earthquake

MECHANICS Cue List 5		
00:00:13		
PRESS F10	2.	Curtain In
00:30:10:00.0	9.	Curtain Up
PRESS F10	10.	Opening Spectacular-Collapse

LASERS Cue List 37		
00:00:13		
00:26:00:00.0	5.	Lissajous Chase
00:26:00:00.0	5.	Lissajous Chase
00:26:00:00.0	5.	Lissajous Chase

PROJECTION Cue List 92		
00:00:13		
PRESS F10	2.	Pre-show slides
00:25:00:00.0	3.	Pre-show slides – Slow Dim
PRESS F10	10.	Opening Spectacular-Montage

VIDEO Cue List 128		
00:00:13		
00:30:05:00.0	8.	MC Announce
PRESS F10	10.	Opening Spectacular-Attack

Richmond's Amiga software

An MSC command consists of a Device ID (which can be specified as "all devices"), a Command Format (what category of device is being addressed), a Command, and data relating to the command. Using both Device IDs and Command Formats gives the system enormous scope: within each of 51 categories of equipment, 112 devices and/or 15 groups of devices can be specified.

The Command format categories are broken down into seven groups:

- **Lighting:** including strobes, lasers, and chasers

- **Sound:** including sequencers, CD players, tape machines, and effects devices

- **Machinery:** including flys, lifts, turntables, robots, floats, and barges

- **Video:** including tape and disc players, switchers, effects, and character generators

- **Projectors:** such as film, slide, and video, as well as dissolve units

- **Process control:** which refers to things like compressed air and CO_2, water, smoke, fog, and natural gas

- **Pyrotechnics:** such as fireworks, flames, explosions, and smoke pots

There are many undefined categories within each of these groups for future expansion, as well as a "reserved" category for extensions and an "every device" command for things like system-wide resets.

The command set is equally comprehensive. Most of the commands have a variable number of data bytes associated with them, to accommodate a cue list of any complexity. A complex cue reference might read "cue 235.6, list 36.6, path 59," referring to a specific subsection of a cue, on a particular version of a cue list stored in a specific directory on a particular storage medium. This means decimal points and delimiters must be communicated. Multiple lists from multiple sources mean that cues for lighting, curtains, and effects can be maintained completely independent of each other—and still be controlled from a single station.

Time Code numbers following standard Midi Time Code formats can be sent within a command, or separately. Most commands are designed so that they can pay attention to MTC or not, as the situation requires. Multiple cues can go on at the same time, some of which follow Time Code and some of which follow their own clocks.

Some of the main MSC commands include:

Go. Start a transition.
Go Off. Start a transition to the "off" state.
Stop. Discontinue a transition.
Resume. Continue a transition.
Timed Go. Execute a transition over a specified period of time.
Load. Pre-load a cue that might not be instantly executable.
Fire. Execute a preprogrammed macro.
All Off. Turn off everything without disturbing control settings.
Restore. Turn everything back on to where it was.
Reset. Stop all running cues and go to the top of every cue list.

A set of commands expressly for sound cues includes:

Sequence Increment and **Decrement.** These commands follow a predetermined cue list.
Go/Jam Clock. Set a device's internal clock to a specified time, lock to Time Code, and execute the transition.
Start Clock, Stop Clock, Set Clock, and **Zero Clock.** Instructions to an internal timer.
MTC Chase On and **Off.** Set the internal clock to follow MTC, or to stop following it.

In its current incarnation, Midi Show Control is designed for one-way (or open-loop) operation, with a controller sending messages to receivers which act without communicating anything back. Work is being done to add provisions for closed-loop operation, which would allow receivers to tell controllers whether they were ready or not, and generally improve the sophistication and reliability of MSC systems. Contact the IMA for more details if this is an area of particular interest to you.

Tuning

One of the first criticisms of MIDI was that, by assuming a finite number of pitches (128), it locked users into strictly Western, equal-tempered, twelve-notes-per-octave musical scales. Music based on the scales of non-Western countries or European music before the Baroque era was not considered in the design of the spec. Like many criticisms, this was valid, but hardly fatal. Many synthesizers, and especially samplers, allowed their pitch scales to be adjusted to microtonal tunings (such as seventeen notes per octave). The scales were still equally tempered, however, so historical tunings such as *just intonation* and *mean-tone* were still impossible. Some intrepid programmers worked out ways to play specific Pitch Bend commands with specific notes to achieve nontempered tunings, but this limited them to one note per synth. It also required extensive hand-coding of the MIDI data, which was not for the faint of heart.

Before long, synthesizer manufacturers recognized that nontempered scales were something their customers wanted, and tuning tables were introduced. Some of these let the user individually tune each note in the synthesizer's range. Other synths were tuned globally: All the C notes would be a certain distance flat or sharp from equal temperament; all C♯ notes would be a different distance; all the D notes, another; and so on. The tuning tables could be accessed using System Exclusive messages, so computer-based editors could be used to construct them. Some designers came up with clever ways of switching tuning tables in the middle of a performance with standard (non-SysEx) MIDI commands. While this solved the problem for users of those individual synths, it was felt that a universal way of addressing alternative tunings was desirable. Hence, the MIDI Tuning Recommended Practice was adopted in late 1991.

Among the features that the Practice includes is instant access to as many as 128 different tuning memory locations (just like Program Changes). It also allows the user to change the tuning of a note while it is sounding without glitching or other audible artifacts. Other features include the ability to change all 128 MIDI notes independently in either a single command or multiple commands, as well as an extremely high resolution for setting pitches.

The Tuning Change command is sent in real time, and can change one or several notes. It is a Universal Real Time SysEx message, so it starts with the bytes F0 7FH (followed by the Device ID of the unit to be tuned). This is followed by the Tuning standard sub-ID (not yet assigned) and a "note change" (as opposed to a bulk dump) sub-ID, which is 02. Then follows a program number, which allows the tuning changes to be made in the current program (or in the background in a different program in RAM, which can be called up later). Then follows a byte expressing the number of changes that are going to be in the rest of the message, which can be anywhere from 1 to 128. Finally, the tuning data is sent in four bytes. The first is the MIDI key number of the note that is going to be changed. The second is another MIDI key number (which may be the same as the first) designating a base frequency for the note to be tuned. For example, if this number is 43H (A above Middle C), the base frequency is 440Hz. Then there are two more data bytes, which specify the distance in fractions above the base frequency of the semitone that the note is to play. Since there are fourteen data bits in the two bytes, the resolution is equal to 1/16,384 of a semitone, or .0061 cents (a *cent* is 1/100 of a semitone, or 1/1,200 of an octave).

Here's a simple example. If the data bytes of a Tuning message are 3C 43 00 00H, it means that when you play note 3CH (Middle C), note 43H (A above Middle C) will sound (440Hz). A more complex example is. 43 42 7F 7FH. When A above Middle C is played, the note that sounds is the G♯ just below it, raised 16,383/16,384 of a semitone, which calculates out to 439.9984Hz—a minutely flat A note.

Take another example: 54 54 40 00H. When the C note two octaves above Middle C is played, the note that sounds is a quarter-tone (half of a semitone) sharp—1077.1649Hz, as opposed to the standard, equal-tempered pitch of 1046.5024Hz. Do you think there's enough resolution here?

If multiple notes are to be retuned within this message, additional sets of four bytes are sent. If no change is desired for a note (which is not necessarily the same as setting to its normal pitch), data bytes of 7F 7F 7FH are sent. At the end of the message, of course, is an F7H (end of SysEx) byte.

The changing of Tuning programs is handled with Registered Parameters. The Registered Parameter number for this function has yet to be assigned, but it will function the same as all Registered Parameters: Controller 64H and 65H messages with values designating the Tuning Program Change message, followed by one of three Controllers. If it is a Controller 6 message, it is followed by the value of the desired program. If it is a Controller 60H message, this is followed by a value of 7F to increment the program number. A Controller 61H message is followed by a value of 7F to decrement the program number. A second Registered Parameter, also awaiting assignment, will specify a Tuning Program Bank, which allows users to potentially have access to 16,384 different Tuning programs.

The MIDI Tuning Recommended Practice also describes Bulk Dump and Dump Request commands which transmit entire tuning tables from one instrument to another instrument or computer. The Bulk Dump command uses the second sub-ID 01, followed by the program number, the program name (which is sixteen ASCII characters), and the 128 tuning definitions. Since the notes are defined in order from 00 to 7FH, the destination key does not need to be specified in each group of bytes, so only three bytes are necessary per note instead of four. The data is followed by a checksum byte, and then an EOX. The Dump Request uses the second sub-ID 00, and follows it with the number of the program it wants, and then an EOX.

Beyond MIDI: Local Area Networks

Multiple cables, balanced-line converters, SMDI, and operational workarounds provide solutions to many of the problems that MIDI users face today. However, as MIDI becomes more integrated with other types of data, like video and digital audio, more comprehensive solutions are already being sought by high-end users. These solutions are taking the form of *Local Area Networks,* or *LANs*. LANs are very common in computerized offices where data on multiple machines needs to be shared. Although there are many different kinds of LANs, they all use high-speed protocols to transfer data among multiple destinations. MIDI itself can be thought of as a LAN that runs at a medium speed. It is faster than most modem-based networks, but slower than many dedicated network lines. Making MIDI faster involves designing a fast LAN that carries MIDI as a subsidiary.

The MIDI Time Piece

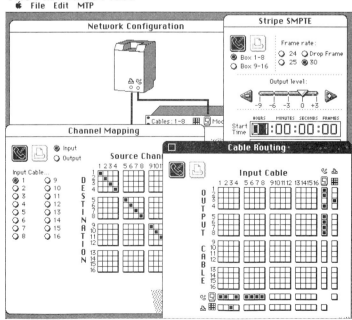

routing software for MIDI Time Piece

The first successful Midi lan was the Midi Time Piece from Mark of the Unicorn. The original Midi Time Piece (MTP) was a midi interface for the Macintosh. However, the newer Midi Time Piece II works with both the Mac and IBM-PC and also includes front-panel controls and internal memory for 128 setups. It connects to the computer with one or two serial cables, and has eight Midi Ins and eight Outs. Each of the eight inputs and outputs are completely independent, sixteen-channel ports, that can be addressed individually using special driver software. This gives the user 128 midi channels to play with. To allow this multiplexing of the multiple midi lines, the serial cables connecting the computer and the MTP operate at speeds faster than midi. (The exact speed is determined by the software using the device, and the processor speed of the Macintosh it is running on.) Not surprisingly, the first software product to take advantage of the device was Mark of the Unicorn's sequencer, Performer. Other manufacturers soon included Midi Time Piece drivers in their software as well.

In addition to its multiple-cable handling, the Midi Time Piece converts smpte to Midi Time Code (or Mark of the Unicorn's proprietary Direct Time Lock). The Midi Time Piece can also act as a smpte generator. It also has cable routing facilities, so that it can send midi data from any input cable to any output cable without going through the computer. There are filters available on each cable for removing specific unwanted midi commands—including Active Sensing, Channel or Key Pressure, or System Exclusive messages—or all data on specific channels. These filters can be enabled between the input devices and the computer, so that the computer never has to deal with the unwanted data. Alternatively, the filter can be used between the computer and the output devices, so that they can receive filtered data. Two Midi Time Pieces can be connected to a serial cable, and each one addressed independently, providing the user with sixteen midi cables. Since the Midi Time Piece can handle incoming and outgoing midi and Midi Time Code on a single serial cable, two Midi Time Pieces can be connected to each of the Mac's two serial ports. This allows for a total of thirty-two cables, or 512 midi channels.

The Studio 5

Taking the lan idea a step further is Studio 5 by Opcode Systems, a Macintosh midi interface/timecode handler with fifteen independent Midi Ins and Outs. This device is connected to the Mac with one or two serial cables. The Studio 5 software includes many real-time functions. It can create *Virtual Controllers* that can process real-time data you send from a physical Controller. It will remap, scale, transpose, and filter Note, Velocity, and Controller data. Virtual Instruments allow a single sequencer track to address any number of devices on multiple midi channels, and each device can be fed the data differently. Individual Program Changes, transposition, filters, and Velocity and Controller scaling are available for each device. When the sequencer sends out a Program Change, individual packets of System Exclusive data can also be sent to each device. Like the Midi Time Piece, multiple Studio 5 units can be linked.

Opcode MIDI System

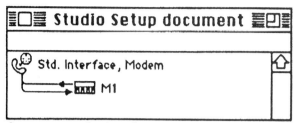

the setup screen for Opcode's OMS

To accommodate the complexity of the Studio 5, Opcode created a software driver that is actually a major addition to the Macintosh operating system. It is called Opcode MIDI System, or OMS, and its job is to intercede between the software and the Mac's serial outputs. Here, it massages and manages the data so that it can be used to its best advantage by the Studio 5. OMS is now required by all Opcode sequencing and patch editing software. It comes in the form of an INIT, or startup document, and an application. OMS also lets the user permanently wire a large number of MIDI devices into a system, and change their configurations in the software without recabling. Complex system configurations can then be stored on disk and recalled instantly.

OMS can be complex for the first-time user to install, but once it's in, it is essentially invisible. Reconfiguring devices and adding new ones to the setup is a fairly straightforward procedure. To make sure OMS was accepted by the larger Macintosh/MIDI community, Opcode includes drivers not just for its own Studio 5, but for the MIDI Time Piece, and for standard one- or two-port MIDI interfaces. It also includes a provision for allowing applications that do not recognize OMS to bypass it automatically.

Initially, Opcode kept a tight rein on OMS, allowing access to other developers only if they were willing to sign complex and fairly expensive licensing agreements. In 1993, in the face of a proposed competitive system from Mark of the Unicorn called Free MIDI, Opcode radically eased the restrictions on OMS. Several other Macintosh MIDI developers immediately announced their support for it, and it appears likely that OMS will become a *de facto* standard on the platform.

MIDI Manager

Apple's MIDI Manager doesn't strictly qualify as a LAN because it resides and operates in just one piece of hardware. MIDI Manager is a subset of Apple's Sound Manager. Its primary goals are to get different MIDI programs to work simultaneously and to be able to communicate with each other, without running MIDI cables out of the Mac and back in again. Specifically, working simultaneously means allowing multiple programs to address the serial ports at the same time without interfering with each other. Getting programs to talk to each other is known as *Inter-Application Communication*, or *IAC*.

MIDI Manager is compatible with the MIDI Time Piece and OMS devices. When these applications are in use, they have their own icons which show up in PatchBay—and can be interconnected according to the user's needs. The networking aspect of MIDI Manager allows several interesting possibilities. Since two programs can run simultaneously, one feeding the other, an algorithmic composer can dump its output directly into a sequencer. This means that there's no need to save the output as a MIDI file from one program and then import it into the other. Similarly, a patch librarian can do a bulk dump of the current set of sounds in a synthesizer directly into a sequencer. The next time that sequence plays, the first thing it does is load the synth with the appropriate patches.

MIDI Manager has another important function, and that is to allow the Mac to address internal sound-producing devices over MIDI, without using any MIDI interfaces or cables. Some of the internal devices are Digidesign's SampleCell, a RAM-based sample-playback unit on a NuBus card; MacProteus, also from Digidesign, which is a ROM-based sample player equivalent to E-Mu's Proteus/1 sound module; and the Macintosh's own internal sound chip, which is accessible through applications such as Passport Designs' Sound Exciter (unfortunately no longer in production). MIDI Manager provides access to them from any application, again through icons that appear in the PatchBay window and wires connecting them to the appropriate programs. OMS can also handle communication with some internal sound devices. Future versions will also allow for Inter-Application Communication.

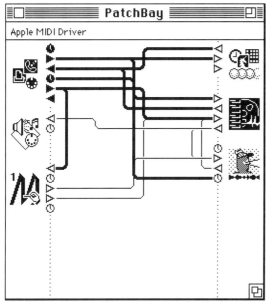

PatchBay is a part of MIDI *Manager that lets you connect many applications in a Macintosh.*

SMDI

SMDI, the SCSI Musical Digital Interface, was discussed in previous chapters. While it is a wonderful way to exchange sample data between devices quickly in an "off-line" mode, it's not suitable for real-time MIDI applications. The reason for this is that SCSI, unlike serial protocols, is data-packet oriented, and was not designed for real-time control of remote devices. Therefore, it is subject to interruptions as various devices on the network vie for time on the cable. This would interfere with the timing on a MIDI stream to the extent that the results would be unusable.

MediaLink

The most advanced MIDI-oriented LAN to date is the MediaLink system, from a Southern California company called Lone Wolf. Introduced in 1989, MediaLink supports large amounts of MIDI data, as well as timecode, a variety of serial protocols, digital audio, video, PA-422 (a protocol for remote control of large sound systems), SCSI, and direct bus links with Intel (as in IBM computers) and Motorola (as in Macintosh, Atari, and Amiga) CPUs. All this communication can fit, much of it simultaneously, on a single fiber-optic cable, which can be up to a mile and a half long.

The cable handles data bidirectionally, and is *frequency agile,* which means it can handle different data protocols running at different speeds simultaneously (from a minimum of 110 to a maximum of 20 million bits per second). This maximum rate is 640 times MIDI speed, or about 24 times the rate of professional digital audio signals. The guts of the system are incorporated into a single VLSI chip, the ML2001A. This is supplied on a three-inch square board known as the MicroTap. Other small (5 1/2 square inch) circuit cards that snap together are known as *Media Interface Modules,* and serve to connect the fiber optic cables with conventional MIDI data streams or the other data formats. The MIDI module contains In, Out, and Thru jacks—and several hundred jacks can be hooked to nodes anywhere on a MediaLink system.

Software for controlling the flow of data is in the form of three programs known collectively as *V-NOS,* for *Virtual Network Operating System,* available for Macintosh, IBM, and Atari computers. The programs use graphics to build and interconnect networks of different kinds. The Virtual Studio program hooks together audio, video, MIDI, and other devices, creating what the company calls *LanScapes.* Virtual Venue is used to design performance-space networks, and Virtual Control is used to design control panels for sending and displaying information in a network. The software even includes a "Chat" channel so that different operators at different nodes on a network can communicate with each other.

So far, Lone Wolf's system is finding homes in two types of settings. The first is multi-room MIDI studio complexes, where communicating data between rooms is necessary, and cable lengths would run longer than fifty feet. The second setting is large live performance venues, such as stadiums and opera houses which need MIDI control over equalizers, mixers, and other devices far removed from the central control station. Not only can these devices be controlled from a central location, but they can report back over the same cable their current operating conditions, including such problems as clipping or thermal overload. A number of professional audio companies, such as QSC, Rane, Carver, TOA, Fender, and Peavey, are providing slots in their equalizers, power amplifiers, and mixing boards for the MicroTap board. This allows the devices to be easily connected to a MediaLink network. The company is also making a push in the home-entertainment market to provide interconnect and remote control capability for large domestic audio/video installations.

MediaLink is far more than simply a faster way to get MIDI data from one place to another. The company is hoping that it becomes a *de facto* standard in the audio world for transferring all kinds of data over long distances and through complex networks. Like MIDI itself, its strength is that it is retroactively compatible with existing standards.

The Evolution of MIDI: A Forum

To close this chapter, the authors are privileged to give readers a rare glimpse into the mechanics of the evolution of MIDI. The following pages contain a verbatim transcript of an actual, on-line discussion. It began innocently enough with a rhetorical question, and ended up as a major debate concerning a highly significant, but ultimately flawed, proposed addition to the MIDI Specification. We are printing this "insiders" debate here, with the permission of the participants, because we think it provides a fascinating insight into the minds of those who care deeply about MIDI and its future.

Topic 276:	MIDI message specifications and deficiencies
# 66: JHHL	Tue, Jul 14, '92 (16:57)

Here's a rhetorical question: is there any machine out now that responds to every defined MIDI message? In theory this could be done on the Peavey, or on computer based platforms. I'm sure you can pick any message up in Max or HMSL, but has anyone written anything which actually responds to EVERY MIDI message defined? What a selling point that would be...

Then the parser could be separated from the tone generators and sequence synchronizers and the like.

67: CYBPUNK   Wed, Jul 15, '92   (10:07)

Lord knows the line "complete MIDI implementation" or somesuch used to be a standard line of many products a few years ago...
Hmmm...what sort of instrument would deal in not just the normal MIDI messages, but also MIDI Machine Control, MIDI Show Control, sample dump, file dump, and retuning messages? I guess it's theoretically possible that an exceptionally well-endowed sampler/digital audio player with apps on the pro etc. side could...

68: JOHNW   Wed, Jul 15, '92   (19:01)

With the complicated home theaters that some people are doing these days, maybe it would be some sort of integrated synth, sample, light show, with machine control for the stereo and tv. The really complete home entertainment center!
P.S. Don't forget to wire the toaster.

69: ZICARELL   Thu, Jul 16, '92   (09:39)
Hmmn...
Proposal for MIDI Toast Control (MTC) specification. Preliminary draft.
TOAST DOWN (0x9N)
                        N = slot number (0 - 15)
                        d1 = toast color (0-127)
                        d2 = downward velocity (0 = TOAST UP, 1 = slowest, 127 = fastest)
TOAST UP (0x8N)
                        N = slot number (0 - 15)
                        d1 = toast color (0-127)
                        d2 = upward velocity (0 = slowest, 127 = pops out of toaster and on to plate)
DARKNESS (0xBN)
                        n = slot number to change (0-15)
                        d1 = knob number
                        d2 = knob value (0 = lightest, 127 = darkest)
The darkness change message allows real-time control over the toast color, however, delays between receipt of the toast down message and the darkness change message may result in lower toast color values being unavailable.

71: CBM   Thu, Jul 16, '92   (23:31)
I feel very strongly that the curve of the darkness control should be spelled out in this proposal. Let's calibrate this thing.
Darkest = Pantone Process Black.
We should only specify this in a bread-independent color space, like CIE-Loaf.

72: JOHNW   Fri, Jul 17, '92   (00:00)
I also believe that 7 bits of resolution is insufficient for darkness and toast color. Also, the spec needs work if it should apply to toaster ovens as well.

73: CYRUS   Fri, Jul 17, '92   (02:05)
This whole discussion is pointless. My calculations show the bandwidth requirements for continuous real-time control over toast is roughly 500 megabits per second. I'd recommend a HIPPI port that runs at 800 Mbps instead of a relatively slower MIDI port.

74: CYBPUNK   Fri, Jul 17, '92   (10:50)
CBM, now let's think about this calibration bit. Do you want to stunt the creativity of future toasters (people and objects) by hard-defining the allowable range? What if a person wanted to go outside of this range? Shouldn't the range be a user-programmable limit saved in flash ROM in the toaster per patch (pastry, white bread, etc.)? Is standardization more important than creativity?

However, I can imagine how useful it would be for someone like Negativland to be able to go on the road to any city, borrow any MIDI-compatible toaster, and make sure the correct amount of burn took place during their concert. Should we have compliance tests to make sure all MIDI toasters indeed perform properly?

And how should running status and active sensing be treated?

75: JOHNW   Fri, Jul 17, '92   (12:28)

What about having several standard browning curves with room for extra custom curves?

76: CYBPUNK   Fri, Jul 17, '92   (16:04)   3 lines
I could go for that...maybe even a Toast Browning Curve Dump Standard so people could edit and load their own over MIDI...

77: RIK   Fri, Jul 17, '92   (19:37)
Cyrus is right again.

78: CONIGLIO   Fri, Jul 17, '92   (23:33)
All this discussion has left out an important point. You should be able to specify when the browning is to be completed (i.e., the toast is ready for consumption).

I think we need timing information-MIDI Toast Time Code (MTTC)-so that the user can schedule the toast to be ready up to a week in advance. Unlike the browning factor, resolution is not as critical.

79: JOHNW   Sun, Jul 19, '92   (12:26)
Would this standard be applicable to other devices? I could imagine having my coffee grinder be interfaced to the coffee machine and the bread maker. This would let me sequence fresh coffee and toast to be done by the time my alarm goes off in the morning.
MIDI sequencing at its finest.

80: CYBPUNK   Sun, Jul 19, '92   (13:59)
Well, we should then use the same family of messages, and then have one sub-ID to specify device and an open-ended parameter field. As far as sequencing goes, again, the underused Cueing portion of the MTC spec would be fine-tell a device when it is supposed to execute, and it can backtime itself by the appropriate amount without the user having to slide events in the sequencer. Send MTC throughout the house via TRON or CEBus or whatever and mornings might be a bit easier to deal with... Multimedia (controlled by MIDI) at its finest.

81: ZICARELL   Tue, Jul 21, '92   (09:50)
This morning I burned my croissants heating them up in the oven. I think all the suggestions are good, but we need to find a way for the toast itself to be a source of sync. This way, the gradually browning croissant could trigger a note-on letting me know that I damn well better get back in the kitchen.

82: CYBPUNK   Tue, Jul 21, '92   (10:41)
Error reporting, like in MMC or the proposed closed-loop version of MIDI
Show Control.

83: TOYS   Thu, Jul 23, '92   (00:44)
You are all forgetting that, MIDI-controlled or not, the toaster is ultimately
an analog device. Thus, there will be a need for a Decrumb command to
correct for the Crumb Accumulation errors that are inherent in toasters.
Now that I think about it, well need to accommodate the multislice toasters
(>2 slices) as well as standard. Perhaps a Mono Decrumb and a Poly
Decrumb command?

84: LHOGAN   Sat, Jul 25, '92   (01:04)
Of course, if the toast were prepared in pixel fashion (I'm thinking ahead to
the ultra compact toasters of the future), it would be possible to have a
scanning toaster that would brown each area of the toast according to the
color feedback from the carriage that carried the laser toaster. Although this
is a hardware problem and so not directly related to the business of MIDI
spec, the MIDI spec should be open ended enough to account for future
improvements in toasters such as this.
A three dimensional robot armed pixel laser toaster could do a lovely job
on a handmade croissant of any description, even preparing half of said
croissant to the taste of the user, and half to the desires of the user's
significant other. Of course, scoring such preparation requires a totally new
music notation as well, as auto clef division at C4, for example, would not
be sufficient to assure proper division of an imperfectly formed, though
delightfully irregular, handmade croissant.
I'm sorry about this excursion into the realm of hardware in this forum, but
somehow I get the feeling that if you told Mozart what you put into an
Ensoniq EPS16+ to get out music, he would have a cow, or at least a steak.
Perhaps with toast.

85: MOCHA   Wed, Aug 5, '92   (13:24)
The toast up message needs to have velocity values capable of launching the
slice to any destination. So naturally, there needs to be a direction vector,
not simply a scalar value.

86: CYBPUNK   Fri, Aug 7, '92   (11:54)
Should we support Polyphonic AfterToast, to launch each slice in a multi-
toastal toaster with independent velocities and trajectories?

The discussion ended at this point, as the participants were apparently
running out of bad puns, and a Working Group was never formed, so MIDI
Toast Control was never included in the MIDI 1.0 Specification.
      We didn't make this up: this discussion actually did take place. To set the
record straight, it did not take place on the official MMA Forum in PAN.
Rather, the discussion happened on The Well, a public network based in
California and created by Stewart Brand (of *Whole Earth Catalog* fame) where
a lot of high-tech types hang out and occasionally let their hair down. Many of
the participants are actually former or current members of the MMA, and they
include some major figures in MIDI development; veterans of debates just like
this, but dealing with real issues. Our thanks for permission to use this material
go to Cyrus Azar, Michael Coffey; Mark Coniglio; Rik Elswit; Louis Hogan;
Henry Lowengard; Chris Muir; Larry Oppenheimer; John Worthington; David
Zicarelli; and a fellow who, for various reasons of his own, wishes simply to be
known as Cyberpunk.

Index